Belgrade
Among the Serbs

BELGRADE
Among the Serbs

Florence Hamlish Levinsohn

Ivan R. Dee
Chicago 1994

Maps by Victor Thompson

Library of Congress Cataloging-in-Publication Data:
Levinsohn, Florence Hamlish, 1926–
    Belgrade : among the Serbs / Florence Hamlish Levinsohn.
      p.   cm.
    Includes index.
    ISBN 1-56663-061-4
    1. Yugoslav War, 1991– —Yugoslavia—Belgrade (Serbia).
2. Belgrade (Serbia)—Description and travel. 3. Levinsohn,
Florence Hamlish, 1926– —Journeys Yugoslavia—Belgrade
(Serbia). 4. National characteristics, Serbian. I. Title.
DR1313.52.B45L48   1994
949.7'1024—dc20   94-29375

To Adam, Isaac, and Emma

Contents

Acknowledgments

I want to thank all those in Belgrade who made this book possible, who so warmly welcomed me and talked so openly with me, but especially Mira Blagojevic, Predrag Dordevic, and Ljiljana Dimitrijevic, who made my visit not only enlightening and profitable but also a great enjoyment in the midst of great sadness. I hope they will all feel that this book serves them well. Those American Serbs who were so helpful, especially Betsy Lalich, Mirko Popadic, and George Bogdanich, also receive my gratitude, as does David Moss, great jazz drummer and writer, who urged me onto this project and helped sustain me through it, and whose love for Yugoslavia affected me so deeply. I want to thank David for all his generous friendship, help, and instruction, and for the good times he gave me in Belgrade. My dear family and friends also deserve my thanks for indulging my obsession and encouraging me through this past year.

No acknowledgments for this book could stand without a word about my kind friend Philip Krone, who first suggested this project and was as always helpful and supportive, both intellectually and personally. Nor without a humble tribute to Rebecca West, whose book about Yugoslavia inspired me almost daily in this effort, and to the many scholars and writers who educated me about various aspects of Yugoslav life and history, even those with whom I disagreed. Anthony Di Iorio read the manuscript and made valuable suggestions from his perspective as a historian specializing in Yugoslavia, for which he has my gratitude. As does Christine Newman, who so generously read proof.

I thank Ivan Dee for his willingness to take on this venture, for his enthusiastic support, and for his graceful editing. Most of all, I thank John Keefe, without whose financial help I could not even have begun, and who has selflessly supported, listened, counseled, and, above all, encouraged me throughout, even though he knew only what an ordinary well-read person would know of Yugoslavia and in fact at first thought the whole project a little crackpot, but came to support it wholeheartedly. Without all these people, those I knew well or came to know well, and those I came to know only through their books, I could not have written these words. For the record, this book is my sole responsibility. I owe no allegiances to anyone except my informants and mentors.

F. H. L.

A Note on the Text

The transliteration of the Serbian language from the Cyrillic alphabet into the Roman is heavily studded with diacritical marks. Without a guide, these are beyond understanding for the general English-language reader. I have therefore chosen to print names and words from the Serbian without these marks.

We human beings ought to stand before one another as reverently, as reflectively, as lovingly, as we would before the entrance to hell.

Franz Kafka
A Letter to Friends, Family, and Editors

I see that though Yugoslavia is a necessity, it is not a predestined harmony.

Rebecca West
Black Lamb and Grey Falcon

Belgrade
Among the Serbs

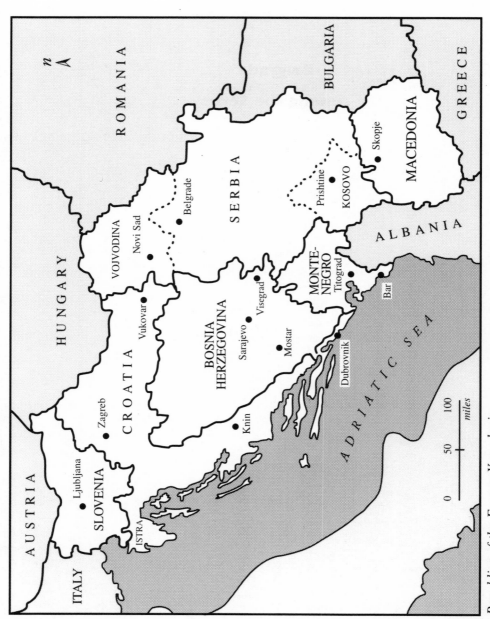

Republics of the Former Yugoslavia

Prologue

On my very long trip in the fall of 1993 from Chicago to Belgrade, the capital of Yugoslavia, which now comprises Serbia and Montenegro, I talked with a young man who had emigrated to the United States from Serbia in 1990 about the tragic breakup of his native land and the terrible wars that followed. I was dismayed by a feeling that I was flying blind, that for every idea I had about the Yugoslavs, another contradicted it. Would I be able to find some truths, untangle my own confusion in order to explain the roots of the wars that had torn Yugoslavia apart, the worst conflict created by the end of the cold war? I would have to resolve my own ambivalence if I was to get beyond the continuing simplistic description of the Bosnian Muslims and Croatians as mere victims of the bloodthirsty Serbs. From all I had read and from my conversations with American Serbs and others, I knew that the story was not so simple. Are wars ever so simple? The Serbs had been crucial actors in two world wars and could once again be at the heart of grave disturbances in European relations. As Slavenka Drakulic, a Croatian writer, says in *The Balkan Express*, "This war . . . is a dangerous civil war that threatens to change the face of Europe." I was setting out to try to set the record straight about the Serbs. But here I was going to Belgrade figuratively as well as literally in the clouds, with few earthbound ideas to guide me.

My trip home was more comfortable. I had found some of the

answers I sought. And I had been profoundly moved by my experiences in Belgrade. This book is the product of that trip.

My first impressions of Belgrade had been gathered in an earlier two-day visit there in 1990. Those two days left me with strong impressions: a city of mixed influences—Eastern and Western, a busy commercial city that was also the capital, with a variety of government buildings mixed with four- and five-story residential buildings, wide boulevards, hotels, museums, myriad little shops, theatres, restaurants, cafés, women in mink coats, and the other amenities of an open Western city. But also an Eastern city. I had Turkish coffee in little cafés run by Muslims in which I was the only woman—and clearly a surprise visitor. While most buildings I observed in the city were Western influenced, the structures in a major outdoor market as well as the still unfinished, largest-in-the-world Saint Sava's Serbian Orthodox Church were of Byzantine design. The only churches I saw in the city were Serbian Orthodox. The National Museum abounded in ancient religious frescoes. The written language, including street signs, was Cyrillic. A people looking both to the West and the East, two such disparate cultures—how did they meld the two?

There were plenty of signs of the kind of state management we associate with communism: my hotel was state property in shabby condition—nothing worked, though the service and the meals in the restaurant were quite decent. In the restaurant one morning I met a CBS engineer who told me he was installing satellite transmission lines because the phone service in Yugoslavia was so bad and the network was anticipating that the Yugoslavs would be the next—the last—to rebel against their Communist leaders.

CBS and the rest of the media and the U.S. government did not anticipate that the rebellion in Yugoslavia would take the form of a devastating civil war. It was not a rebellion against communism; it was a rebellion by the nationalist Catholic Croatians and Slovenes and the Bosnian Muslims against the nationalist aspirations of the Eastern Orthodox Serb leaders. The wars in Bosnia Herzegovina and Croatia were religious-ethnic civil wars over disputed lands and control.

The Serbs of Yugoslavia did not rebel. The Communist leaders simply changed the name of their party, and the Serbs continued to support them. But the rebellion by the Slovenes, Croatians, and Bosnian Muslims was not against communism, though they paid lip service to that popular idea in their part of the world, the Croatians especially claiming that their war was with the Communist regime of Yugoslavian President Slobodan Milosevic, as if there had not been a history of events between the Serbs and the Croats that made this war all but inevitable.

Yugoslavia had not been since the 1950s a traditional Communist state. In fact, when the savage war in Croatia broke out, Serbia had moved further toward privatization than Croatia had. In 1990, while there were plenty of signs of economic problems—pockets of poverty, rising inflation and unemployment—the Yugoslavs were still largely content with the mixed economy that included what Tito had called self-management. It had made the Yugoslavs a prosperous people in a relatively open society, though political control was pretty tight. Drakulic says Yugoslavia traded its comfort and freedom to travel for its political freedom. But it was not economic conditions but the threat of Eastern Orthodox Serb dominance, combined with their own religious and nationalist strivings, that triggered the rebellions of the various states of Yugoslavia.

While the state-run media had carried out a small purge of journalists not favorable to the government, the media in Yugoslavia were still reasonably open in 1990, providing informative news and entertainment. In that earlier visit the only other sign I had of a repressive regime was a soldier racing across the street to threaten to confiscate my camera for photographing a lovely old building that turned out to be army headquarters. The soldier thought I was a spy; I finally convinced him that I was only an innocent tourist.

After this earlier visit I had read a good deal, yet I still felt that I had no real sense of the people of Belgrade and could not sort out a great profusion of contradictory information. When I told American Serbs and others that I was making another trip, in 1993, I was warned by some that conditions in Yugoslavia under the draconian United Nations economic embargo were like post–World War I Berlin, that crime was rampant, that everything was terribly scarce. There would be no heat or hot water. My visit would be hell.

Others reassured me that, while economic conditions were certainly harsh, most goods were still available, if in much smaller quantities and very expensive, because the black market was highly efficient. Hotels still had toilet paper, heat, and hot water, if not in the same volume one would have found before the embargo. The crime rate was high only relative to the years before the embargo, when there was practically no crime.

Some people warned me that the society was a dictatorship and that people would be afraid to talk with me. Dr. Mary Coleman, writing in the fall 1993 issue of *Psychohistory*, said, "It is horrifying to note that the Balkans . . . bear an increasingly grim resemblance to the Nazi Germany of fifty years ago."

Others reassured me that Yugoslavia was still an open, civilized society where people, even those in the government, would be warm and friendly.

There is a widespread attitude in the West that Serbs are a primitive people. Having been in Belgrade, I knew that at least in that big urban center this was not true. But regularly flitting through my mind was a sentence in Rebecca West's monumental 1941 book, *Black Lamb and Grey Falcon*, in which she quoted her Serb guide as saying, "We have no art, we have no literature, we have something else. We have war." Would I find, indeed, that the Serbs, below that citified exterior, had no culture except war?

Rebecca West also implied strongly that among the Serbs is a great sense of victimhood based on centuries of being wronged—first by the Ottoman Empire, then by the Austro-Hungarian Empire, then by the Nazis, then by the Russians. Anthony Di Iorio, an American historian specializing in Yugoslavia, called it paranoia, but added, "They always have enough evidence for their grievances." I had read enough history of the Serbs to be prepared to see among them the same kind of paranoid thinking I'd seen among Jews, American blacks, and other minorities who have been the world's victims and have developed a victim mentality. On the other hand, another American, David Moss, a musician who had had a fifteen-year love affair with Yugoslavia, insisted I would find no such thing, that the Serbs were the most open, cheerful, earthy people he had ever encountered. Rebecca West had said the same thing even while suggesting their victimhood. Could these people see themselves as victims and still be the open people West and Moss described? Are paranoids ever open, friendly people?

So I was going into a land about which I had many impressions and questions but no firm ideas. I would talk to a variety of intellectuals whom I believed could give me an articulate description of their culture and the roots of the terrible wars that had torn their country apart, wars that would most likely make very difficult any cooperation among Serbs, Croatians, and Bosnians in the future, cooperation that was indispensable. Until the Slovenians, Bosnians,

Croatians, and Macedonians seceded from Yugoslavia in 1991 and 1992, the various states had been an economically interdependent nation, sharing communications, raw materials, foodstuffs, and manufactured objects, as well as an army. Now the army had split into four different armies, each national group withdrawing from the Yugoslav army to form its own. Splitting up the economy would not be so simple; they would need to trade with one another.

What had led to the terrible rupture of Yugoslavia, I wanted to know. Were the Serbs actually the murderous warriors described in the U.S.? Were they latter-day Nazis, as some in the U.S. asserted— like the Germans in World War II, revenging themselves on those whom they believed had earlier vitally damaged them? Was their society a closed dictatorship, as some said, or an open democracy?

I wanted to know what the Serbs in Belgrade had to say about the wartime atrocities attributed to them by the U.S. media. It didn't seem reasonable that the atrocities had all been on one side. That isn't normally in the nature of war. More important, I had read widely about the atrocities against the Serbs committed by the Croatian Nazi puppet state in World War II. While the numbers vary greatly, it is probably safe to say that the Croatians slaughtered as many as 600,000 Serbs by outrageous methods; in Bosnia the formerly majority Serbs were reduced to a minority of the population by the Muslims. Were these people suddenly merely the victims of the Serbs?

I had learned from an unimpeachable source that the Bosnian Muslims and the Croatians were each paying thirty thousand dollars a month in fees to an American public relations firm, Ruder Finn, to tell their story to the world. Ruder Finn was accused by some of a massive disinformation campaign that attributed to the Serbs atrocities actually committed by Muslims and Croatians. A representative of the agency had told an American Serb filmmaker, "It's not our job to investigate the facts given us by our employers." James Harff, comanager of the Washington Ruder Finn office, who worked on the Bosnian and Croatian accounts, accused me of working for the Serbian government when I inquired about such a campaign. Harff launched into a fierce defense of the Bosnians and Croatians and an attack on the Serbians. He ridiculed my trip to Belgrade because "it's a totally closed, dictatorial society with no free press."

But in the spring of 1994 a UN investigation gave some weight to the claims of the Serbs that a number of attacks on Muslims had been staged by Bosnian government troops in order to stimulate Western military intervention. For instance, on April 15 the *Chicago Tribune* ran a dispatch from Zagreb reporting renewed and extended attacks by the Serbs against their most recent target, Gorazde, in retaliation for NATO bombing raids of Serb positions. This time the Serbs had taken UN personnel hostage. In the second half of this story there appeared these lines: "Serbs denied the shelling, saying that it was a Muslim ploy to encourage further NATO raids. *After this week's raids, the UN suggested that Muslim-led Bosnian government forces were responsible for the shelling in Gorazde after the Serbs had stopped—possibly an attempt to provoke more [NATO] raids* [my italics]." This discovery by the UN, like an earlier report that an alleged Serbian shelling of a Sarajevo marketplace—that led to NATO bombing of Serbs—had turned out to be the work of Muslims, didn't seem to alter the UN's course in holding the Serbs responsible for the destruction. It was as if these reports that the Muslims had bombed their own people had not been made. In fact, the UN immediately denied the report on the Sarajevo marketplace by its own agency, UNPROFOR (United Nations Protection Force).

On the other hand, Dr. Mary Coleman told me that Serbs were using World War II photos of Croatian and Muslim atrocities against the Serbs and claiming them as current.

Could I find some truth in all this? Could the Serbs document Croatian or Muslim atrocities? And how did the Serbian intellectuals feel about their brethren fighting in Bosnia and Croatia?

I was swept into Belgrade's culture and its misery on my first day when David Moss and a friend of his took me to Skadarlija, the Montmartre of the city, a charming, colorful section that was being restored before the wars started and where some work was still going on. Skadarlija had always been jammed with people, David said. It was empty now. People could no longer afford the luxury of eating out and were not in a mood to stroll. The economic consequences of the UN embargo had made Skadarlija almost a ghost town.

My modest hotel was also quite empty. The management was thrilled to have an American guest who would pay in dollars. Inflation, raging when I left there in November 1993 at about 5,000 percent, had made their dinars worthless. Each time I exchanged money I got more dinars than the time before—billions, which lasted only a few days. Everything cost a fortune by Yugoslav standards. Nevertheless, people who were very hospitable to me would not permit me to reciprocate. That I was a journalist getting a story made no difference; I was their guest.

I talked to a great mélange of people—journalists, novelists, government officials, lawyers, doctors, judges, painters, literary critics, economists, philosophers, members of Parliament, and others with whom I drank the ubiquitous Turkish coffee or plum brandy of the Serbs in their offices or homes or at the International Press Club or the Independent Press Club. Some of them took me to lunch or dinner; all of them gave me at least a couple of hours of their time, and some of them gave me much more.

Some readers may ask why I chose to talk only to intellectuals, why I limited myself to Belgrade, and why I chose to write this book largely as a series of conversations with these intellectuals. First— and I am not alone in thinking this—historically the ideas promulgated in any society begin with the intellectuals, whether at the right, left, or center of the political spectrum. If one wants to know how a given society is thinking and will be thinking about an issue, one must go to the thinkers. The ideas of nationalism that engulfed Yugoslavia in the last ten years began in the Academy of Science in Belgrade. I limited myself to Belgrade because it is there that the intellectual life of Serbia is to be found.

As for the form of this book, I have great faith in the direct words of the people involved, the trees in the forest. This may be a feminine trait, as Virgilia Peterson wrote in her 1961 book, *A Matter of Life and Death*—"If men must forever be forgetting the bloom and blight of individual trees in the frenzy of their quarrels over the forests, is it not all the more imperative for women to keep vigil around the felled trunks and the seedlings? The singular is lost in plurality. Yet it is the singular within the plural that gives the plural significance. The plural is no more than the sum of the singulars that go into it. So in the end it is the singular that counts."

Wandering the narrow, badly neglected streets and the wide boulevards of Belgrade, I observed the shops and houses of ordinary people. Hundreds of people, many of them among the 700,000 refugees from Bosnia and Croatia, stood behind piled-up cardboard boxes selling anything they could find to earn a few dinars to supplement their meager government stipends. Miles-long lines of well-dressed people waited patiently for their "Bush packages"—so-called because they were a product of the embargo—cooking oil, flour, and salt that the government was handing out along with bread.

I found no fascism in Belgrade. While there was control of the state-run media, there was also a strong independent press and electronic media. Most of the 100 political parties were totally ineffectual but free to voice their opinions. There was no military presence in the city and very few police. The government was stalemated because it had no majority in Parliament. It insisted it held no political prisoners, and had in fact very few criminal prisoners by American standards. In place of a populace afraid to talk, the Serbs turned out to be the most voluble people I'd ever met, clearly unafraid to say anything they wanted.

Instead of fascists I found a greatly saddened, bewildered group of strong democrats, though I found it hard to describe as democrats the free-market economist whose attitude was "let them eat cake," or the antiwar activist who said she hoped Serbia would lose the war. All the people I met were over forty; the young people I had hoped to talk with had fled. It was estimated in late 1993 that 300,000 had emigrated, some fleeing conscription into the army early on, most of them young intellectuals who saw no future for themselves in the besieged Belgrade. A number of people thought it would take fifty years for Belgrade to recover from the effects of the UN embargo.

I found a highly intelligent, highly educated group of intellectuals in Belgrade, most of whom could nevertheless make no sense of what had happened to them in the last few years. Until the mid-1980s they were a prosperous nation with a reasonably open society and a relatively free press, though there were already signs that the economy—a mixed economy designed to resemble the worker-controlled economy envisioned by early Social Democrats—was beginning to come apart. Somehow, despite rising inflation and the emigration of many young people for lack of job opportunities, the Serbian intellectuals, enjoying privileged positions, failed to see the handwriting on the wall. They were living well, traveling widely, reading the world press along with their own. Most of them didn't make the connection between the rising nationalism in Serbia and the crumbling of the economy, though the same phenomenon was occurring throughout Eastern Europe and the Soviet Union. They couldn't relate to the problems of those countries, for theirs had been a relatively free society.

Most of them saw the rise of nationalism that began in the early eighties and reached its peak in 1989 rather as a natural development in a country that had been plagued by nationalism, albeit a suppressed nationalism, throughout its history. After all, it had been put together artificially as the kingdom of the Serbs, Croats, and Slovenes in 1918 after the World War I defeat of the Austro-Hungarian Empire and the Ottoman Empire, both of which had occupied parts of what was to become Yugoslavia (literally land of the South Slavs). It had been the Western allies' gift to the Serbs for the indignities they suffered in the war with Austria-Hungary, but it was at best a pyrrhic victory for the Serbs. The Slovenes and the Croatians were not happy with the dominance accorded the Serbs. Continuing nationalist outbreaks in that new kingdom, which had been constructed on democratic principles, and unrest caused by the onset of the Great Depression, forced Yugoslav King Aleksander to restructure the country's administrative boundaries and in effect declare a Serbian dictatorship. This supplied more ammunition for the Croatian nationalists especially, who conducted a worldwide campaign of disinformation to discredit King Aleksander and the Serbs, and waged sabotage at home, bombing railroads that caused the deaths of many foreigners and were attributed to the king's tyranny and Serb barbarity.

From the start the kingdom was an irreconcilable combination of Roman Catholics, Muslims, and Eastern Orthodox peoples. Hitler easily tore it apart in 1941 when Croatia and Bosnia became the Nazi puppet Independent State of Croatia, after the Serbs refused to accede to Hitler's demands and were heavily bombed and invaded by the Nazis.

With the peace came a civil war between Communist Partisans and former German allies joined by the Cetniks, followers of the royal government-in-exile, a war won by the Partisans. Marshal Josip Broz Tito, a brilliant despot who knew when to grant freedom and when to withdraw it in order to maintain stability in a highly unstable environment, again put the country together. He kept a tight rein on nationalist sentiments, though these sentiments never disappeared and began to swell in the early 1970s, leading to a new constitution that granted more national sovereignty to the states.

After Tito's death in 1980, without a strong leader to succeed him, the government became a hydra-headed, revolving, multirepublic ruling clique. The rise of nationalism was inevitable, as it was with the relative democratization under Mikhail Gorbachev in the Soviet Union and in other parts of Eastern Europe. Almost from the day of

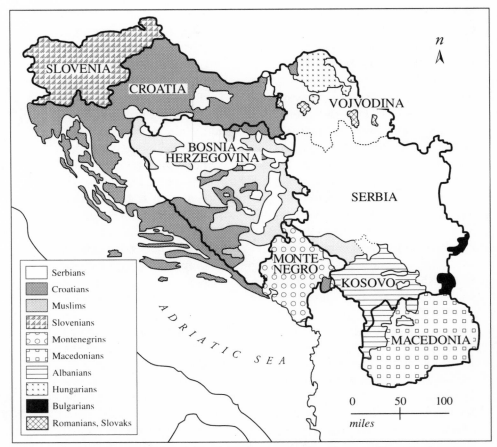

Approximate Major Nationalities Distribution in the Former Yugoslavia

Tito's death, Yugoslavia's various ethnic groups were at one another's throats. The last federal prime minister, Ante Markovic, attempted to convince Parliament to accept his plan for a new free-market economic system, free multiparty elections, and a union of the country's republics, but he was literally shouted down by nationalist leaders in the republics, each of which held its own elections instead in 1990. The most extreme nationalist parties, those who branded democratic elements as treasonous, were elected.

Most of the Belgrade intelligentsia didn't share the aggressive "Greater Serbia" sentiments of President Slobodan Milosevic, but most failed to see his propaganda as the cynical move it was—covering his government's inability to halt the breakdown of the economy, a not unfamiliar move by political leaders. Milosevic was a Communist turned Socialist who probably never had a serious nationalist thought in his head until the mid-1980s when he saw nationalist sentiments arising so clearly, and exploited them. That his campaign drove the Slovenians, Bosnians, Croatians, and Macedonians to secede, and led to wars in Bosnia and Croatia, was still little understood by most of my Serbian friends. They did not attend the massive gathering in Kosovo in 1989 that Milosevic called to celebrate the six hundredth anniversary of the legendary defeat of the Serbs by the Turks. A million Serbs came from all over the country. Most Serbs didn't hear or didn't take seriously his warlike speech calling for a greater Serbia, in which he asserted, "If we must fight, then by God we will fight." They only dimly realized the terrible effects of Milosevic's nationalist campaign and remained bewildered by the resulting wars and the subsequent Western attitudes toward them that led to the embargo in April 1992.

The UN embargo was a singularly strange development in the events of the war. To protect themselves from Serbian domination and to further their own nationalist aims, and with the strong encouragement of Germany, first Slovenia, then Croatia, then Bosnia Herzegovina, and later Macedonia and Kosova declared their independence from Yugoslavia. Immediately Milosevic sent the army into Slovenia. It scarcely fired a shot but very quickly gave up and retreated. Slovenia had always been almost a stranger in Yugoslavia, with its own language and customs. Croatia's secession was a different matter. More than 600,000 Serbs lived in Croatia. Following the election of Franjo Tudjman as president there in April 1991, a declaration of independence in June 1991, and the announcement of a new constitution that outlawed the Serbs' Cyrillic language—a purely provocative act because only a tiny number of Serbs still wrote the Cyrillic script—a wave of anti-Serb sentiment erupted, particularly on state television, and some of the Ustase, the fascist government of World War II, were slowly restored to power. Serbs were fired from their jobs, including the police, and were taunted and even threatened with death. Fear grew among Serbs, for whom the memories of the Croatian slaughter of Serbs in World War II were poignant. At the same time Tudjman had recently published his *Wastelands of Historical Reality*, in which he wrote, "Genocide is a natural phenomenon, in harmony with the societal and mythologically divine nature . . . recommended . . . whenever it is useful for the survival or the restoration of the kingdom of the chosen nation, or for the preservation and the spreading of its one and only correct faith."

Serb apprehensions stoked an anti-Croatian campaign led by Milosevic, particularly vehement on state television. In his book *The Fall of Yugoslavia*, Misha Glenny notes that "a surprisingly broad spectrum of people in both Croatia and Serbia singled out Croatian Television (HTV) and Yugoslav RTV as two of the most culpable war criminals of the Yugoslav tragedy."

Exactly who started the war in Croatia and how it started depends on who is telling the story. The Croatians insist the Serbs started shooting first. The story most often told by the Serbs is that the Croatian police fired into a gathering of Serb men. Most of the fighting took place in the Serb-dominated Krajina region that had declared its independence from Croatia. What followed was a terrible struggle with atrocities on both sides and the destruction and near destruction of several towns and cities. The worst fighting ended only in December 1991 when the UN sent in a peacekeeping force, though sporadic skirmishes continued. The fight was bitterly nationalist, with Serbs and Croatians killing each other, but it was also a fight conducted by the Yugoslav Federal Army to deny the Croatians their independence, to preserve Yugoslavia.

Meanwhile, earlier in September, after Germany had recognized the independence of Slovenia and Croatia in December 1991, Bosnia petitioned the UN for recognition of its independence. Germany acceded almost immediately and led the rest of the UN to follow. But Bosnia was an ungovernable state. Its Muslim president had been jailed in the 1970s when he circulated a tract announcing his intention to convert Bosnia into a Muslim state; and a series of nationalist-oriented parties, representing Muslims, Croatians, and Serbs, all at one another's throats, were unable to agree on anything. Bosnia was also a state that provided what have been called "the best executioners in the concentration camps" of Croatia in World War II. Here also the Serbs feared the impact of a Muslim state, though President Alija Izetbegovic talked of a democratic pluralist state without ever detaching himself from the dominant Muslim political party.

Meanwhile, Milosevic and Tudjman were trying to bring off a deal that would split Bosnia between Serbia and Croatia, a deal doomed to failure and then to war. The spark came on March 1, 1992, with the

Muslim killing of the father of the bridegroom and the wounding of a priest at a Serbian wedding in a suburb of Sarajevo. A few weeks later, in the town of Siekovas near Sarajevo, Muslims invaded the town, killed all the men and children, and burned down eighty homes. War then started in earnest with the Serb shelling of Sarajevo. The Muslims seemed hopelessly outnumbered and outgunned, and it appeared that the worst offenders were the Serbs, with the help of the Yugoslav army. Reports coming out of Bosnia portrayed the Serbs as bloodthirsty savages, raping, murdering, and plundering, though some independent observers insisted that the accounts of Serb atrocities were greatly exaggerated. Nevertheless, in April 1992 the UN imposed draconian economic sanctions on Yugoslavia. Milosevic's reaction was swift. He withdrew the Yugoslav army from Bosnia, leaving the Bosnian Serbs to fight their own battle, supported by irregular paramilitaries from Serbia, Montenegro, and the army of the Krajina Republic. The sanctions, however, were not lifted.

The Serbian intelligentsia in Belgrade had many ideas about the sources of their troubles. Like many of the intellectuals of prewar Nazi Germany, most were overwhelmed by the events of the last few years. There was a large antigovernment demonstration in March 1991, and a few dissidents took action against Milosevic either in the media or in protest groups or politics. A few others saw themselves as the victims of an international conspiracy. Most refused facile explanations and argued the issues passionately. But by the time I talked with them in late 1993, their lives under the sanctions had become so arduous and painful that they had little time for more than mere survival and little interest in talking about anything but the effects of the sanctions. People were dying daily, though I witnessed some humorous efforts to get on with a normal life.

Rebecca West, in her wisdom, was right about the Serbs. They are open, warm, loving, and spontaneous; but with the exception of the dissidents who dismiss such ideas as bunk, they also see themselves as victims of history. They are not paranoid; this victimhood they nourish in their souls is confined to their view of themselves in history. I was more than a little startled the first time I heard a Serb say that his people are like the Jews. "Serbs are like the Jews," Aleksander "Fredi" Mosic, a retired civil engineer, told me, "though they, of course, have suffered longer than the Serbs have.

But like them, we have suffered long years of persecution and murder. We have been overrun, tortured, killed, and been stolen from by the Turks, the Austrians, the Bulgarians, the Germans, Tito, and now once again it is happening, this time by our longtime friends, the Americans. [In the 1950s and early 1960s the U.S. supplied Yugoslavia with money and materials to launch its economy as a buffer against the Soviet Union when Tito withdrew from the Cominform, and in later years encouraged the International Monetary Fund and the World Bank to grant large loans to Tito. The Serbs, perhaps rightly so, saw the U.S. as the great power behind the embargo.] But we will survive, as the Jews have. The difference is that most of the civilized world recognizes now the infamies against the Jews, and the U.S. arms the Jewish state against their current enemy, but we're now seen by that so-called civilized world the way the world saw the Jews until the death camps were opened, as villains to be ostracized at the least, to be murdered at the most.''

These sentiments were repeated to me many times over. The Serbs mourn the deaths of the Jews in their country as much as they mourn the deaths of their own thousands—of the eighty thousand Jews in Yugoslavia at the start of World War II, sixty thousand were murdered by the Nazis and their allies. Many of the rest were saved by Serbs, not least because they so fervently identified with the Jews as martyrs—victims—to the rapacity of so many destroying peoples. The great legend of the Serbs—the historic battle to save their extensive and highly developed kingdom from the Turks in 1389—corresponds directly to the Jews' legend of the Masada, where some thousand Jews committed mass suicide rather than surrender to the Romans in the first century A.D.

In the Serbian legend, the Tsar Lazar appealed to God for guidance in a crucial battle against the Turks. One famous epic poem describes Elijah telling Lazar:

Tsar Lazar, of honorable stock,
Of what kind will you have your kingdom?
Do you want a heavenly kingdom?
Do you want an earthly kingdom?
Saddle your horses, tighten your horses' girths,
Gird on your swords,
Then put an end to the Turkish attacks!
But if you want a heavenly kingdom

Build you a church on Kosovo:
Build it not with a floor of marble
But lay down silk and scarlet on the ground,
Give the Eucharist and battle orders to your soldiers,
For all your soldiers shall be destroyed,
And you, prince, you shall be destroyed with them.

The tsar chose the heavenly kingdom and, just as he was building his church, the Turks attacked. He and his army "of seven and seventy thousand soldiers" were destroyed in June 1389, and "All was holy, all was honorable / And the goodness of God was fulfilled."

This is the legend that has stirred the hearts of Serbs for hundreds of years. The Turks ruled them with infamous cruelty and barbarity for five hundred years. Little wonder the Serbs identify with the Jews.

For the Serbs as well as the Jews, it appeared that, at the end of World War II, at long last, they were free to determine their own future. It didn't quite work out that way. First the Serbs fought a civil war, then they found themselves under the iron fist of Stalin through his henchman Tito. Free of that weight, when Tito rejected Stalin, they continued to suffer Tito's indignities, though these paled by comparison with Stalin's. In Tito's last years and after his death Yugoslavia enjoyed relative peace and tranquility. When the great nationalist cry brought war in 1991, it renewed what literary critic Vladimir Dzadzic calls "the Kosovo determination"—the life mission of the Serbs to redeem themselves from that early bloody defeat. It makes them fierce warriors and at the same time gives them a sense of themselves as victims of outside forces, much like the Jews who became fierce warriors in defense of Israel and who have at the same time a sense of themselves as the world's victims.

Interestingly, the Serbs have the support of many Jews, though it is mainly Israeli rather than American Jews who speak up for them. Most American Jews, including the leadership of the U.S. Holocaust Museum, support their government's position and have publicly condemned the Serbs. In Israel, however, one regularly finds public support. In a February 1994 op-ed piece in the *Jerusalem Post*, Israel's English-language paper, Joseph Lapid, a columnist for *Ma'ariv*, after condemning the Nazification of Croatia and Bosnian president Alija Izetbegovic's tract on Bosnia's conversion to a Muslim state, wrote, "We Jews identify with people who have shared our fate. We understand them when they say 'never again,' and act accordingly. We appreciate their motivations and identify with their fears, without condoning their misdeeds."

The feeling that they were once again victims of the world under the UN sanctions prevailed among most of the Serbs I met. When these people told me that conditions in Belgrade were now worse than they had been under the Nazi occupation, and as I wandered about the city observing some of the effects of the sanctions, including empty store shelves and long breadlines, I wondered whether they might be right. The sanctions were imposed on Yugoslavia while that nation's army was still fighting in Bosnia. When the army was withdrawn and Yugoslavia was supplying only medicine and food to the Bosnian Serbs, the sanctions remained intact, were in fact broadened, creating the impression that Yugoslavia was the most aggressive warrior in the field. The distinction between Bosnian Serbs who were fighting and Yugoslav Serbs who were not was rarely made. Why was Yugoslavia's withdrawal from the fighting never recognized by the UN? Was it because of a disinformation campaign conducted by the Bosnians and the Croatians via their American public relations agents? Could that alone account for the harsh punitive measures the West had taken against Yugoslavia, one of the severest economic embargoes in history? And did it account for the fact that when the Serbs denied a given battlefield action against the Bosnians, insisting that the Bosnians had instead fired on their own people in order to gain more sympathy for their cause, and these actions were recorded by independent photographers, these charges were ignored? It defies logic that the Muslims and the Croatians, having slaughtered hundreds of thousands of Serbs in World War II, were suddenly mere victims in this war.

Europe and England have an old enmity against the Serbs that the U.S. seems to have adopted willy-nilly. Rebecca West refers over and over again to the prejudice among Europeans toward the Serbs. She quotes her husband as saying, when he arrived in Belgrade where she was lying ill, "I thought of Belgrade . . . as the Viennese talk of it, as the end of the earth, a barbarian village."

In a speech to the House of Commons on March 27, 1941, Winston Churchill said, "Early this morning the Yugoslav nation found its soul. A revolution has taken place in Belgrade, and the ministers who but yesterday signed away the honor and freedom of the country are reported to be under arrest. This patriotic movement arises from the wrath of *a valiant and warlike race* [my italics]." Churchill used the name Yugoslavia instead of Serbia, despite the fact that Croatia was about to make its devil's pact with Hitler. One has to wonder why he used the expression "valiant and warlike race" for the Serbs. Were they more warlike than the Austrians, French, Spanish, Dutch, Belgians, Germans, Turks, and his own people who had been waging bloody imperalist, nationalist wars for hundreds of years against all kinds of people all over the world, while the Serbs were in captivity under the Turks and their only warlike behavior was an occasional uprising?

In his 1950 memoir *A Long Row of Candles*, C. L. Sulzberger, chief foreign correspondent for the *New York Times*, described the people of the Balkans as having, along with a variety of primitive traits, a "splendid talent for starting wars," though he also admitted he "adored them."

Churchill also promised "all possible aid and succor [to the Serbs]" and to "make common cause with the Yugoslav nation and we shall continue to march and strive together until complete victory is won." As an expression of that "common cause," the Allies bombed Belgrade and other Serbian towns, with no satisfactory explanation ever offered. By contrast, Croatia and Bosnia, German allies, were never bombed by the Allies.

The historian Anthony Di Iorio told me, "The notion of the Serbs as a barbaric race has been widespread, especially in the German-speaking world." One of the sources of this myth was the Roman Catholic church, reaching back to the schism between the two churches in 1054. The Roman church was deeply involved with the slaughter of Serbs in World War II. The church sees the simple, fundamentalist structure and ritual of the Serbian Orthodox church as competition and as a degradation of the Christian church. Thousands of Serbs in Croatia, in World War II, were forced to convert to Catholicism under the threat of death.

While there is nothing in their nine-hundred-year history to indicate that the Serbs were ever barbarians, they were, with the other peoples of the Balkans, quite primitive. Under the oppressive rule of the Turks they were denied education, industry, commerce, and self-government. The Serbs' culture consisted of their religious art, some epic poetry, and folk music and dancing. The industrial revolution and the Enlightment did not touch them. It was only when they were finally free of the Turks in the late nineteenth century that they began to acquire some of the aspects of what we call modern civilization. The West, rather than offering help or sympathy, offered them its disdain, as so often happens between the weak and the strong. But in my travels I have never met a better-educated, more cultured, or more intelligent group of people than I met in Belgrade.

There was also some of what Rebecca West had seen fifty years ago: these people were close to their roots. I came to understand patriotism from them, not flag-waving jingoism but a deep love for and pride in one's country and culture, a willingness to recognize its defects and to laugh at its foolishness.

"You Have Some Cigarettes, Please?"

A trip from Chicago to Belgrade that would normally take no more than ten hours began at 6 p.m. Friday and ended at one o'clock Sunday morning, Yugoslav time—twenty-four hours in all as a result of the UN sanctions prohibiting planes from flying in or out of Yugoslavia. One had to fly into a bordering country, usually into Budapest, Hungary, and then ride the bus for six hours to Belgrade. My Serbian travel agent in Chicago suggested I take a Romanian flight to Timisoara, just over the border, followed by only a two-hour bus trip. The idea of a Romanian airline was not a reassuring one, but I had so dreaded the long bus trip after arriving in Budapest already jet-lagged that I quickly agreed.

The Romanian line had promised a modern jet, but we traveled in an old Russian plane in which the narrow seats did not recline and there was six inches between rows. I felt sorry for my six-foot-plus seatmate as he struggled to find a place for his legs. I was glad I had gotten my papers in order before I left. The Chicago departure was delayed about two and a half hours, and then the stopover in Amsterdam was delayed another couple of hours. The trip was made bearable—enjoyable—by my seatmate, Mile Manic, a handsome thirty-something man with heavy eyebrows over aviator-style glasses, thick dark brown hair, eyes that seemed to grin, a strong chin—a gentle-looking man despite his height and big, well-built frame. He

was a Serbian traffic engineer who had emigrated to the States in
1990 because he could see nothing but a bleak future for his country.
He was returning now to visit his family and friends. When he left
the economy had been faltering badly, and chances for advancement
in his field looked hopeless. The Yugoslav government had never
paid much attention to its infrastructure, and he had been overruled
time and again in his efforts to bring some order to traffic planning.
"It was all just nuts," he told me. "The whole economy was based
on an idea that was good in theory, but nothing worked right. I
worked in it for ten years and I know."

I told Mile I had read that Tito had destroyed his own good idea of
"self-management"—an old Social Democratic idea of worker-op-
erated companies that had transformed Yugoslavia from a Communist
economy to a semimarket one—by insisting that all hiring and firing
be controlled by the Communist party. Jobs were allocated not by
competence but by party loyalties, as happened all over the Communist world. This was certainly true, Mile said. "You could never
say to a worker, 'You aren't a good worker. You make too many
errors. You are too slow, or whatever.' It was just so awful to see so
much incompetence. Even though I was a manager, I couldn't do
anything about it." Mile was not a Communist. Most people in
Yugoslavia weren't, he said, so in his position as manager he was
forced to hire and fire by party orders. Eventually incompetence ruled.

We talked most of the time we were en route about the history of
the conflicts in Yugoslavia, the wars, the sanctions, his family, his
education, and the friends he missed. He spoke an almost perfect
English that he learned in school in Belgrade. He wouldn't let me
tape his words; he was one of those convinced that the Yugoslav
government had become a harsh dictatorship, and he feared he might
endanger his family in Belgrade.

"This war is not for normal people," Mile said, "it's for the
brainless. But it has to end. It's a disease that will be cured. People
will finally start thinking, 'That's not the way to solve the problem.'
But capitalism won't solve the problem. No way. You can see that in
Eastern Europe. They have to find a third way. People who have lived
under socialism just don't understand capitalism, and you can't just
impose it on them the way they imposed communism. Communism
was dictatorial, and you could try to force people to do things, but
you see the results in Eastern Europe and Russia. Capitalism is
democratic. You can't force it on people. But the different countries

that used to be Yugoslavia are going to have to learn to trade with one another. They are too interdependent. They are used to being one big economic unit. They can't make it alone."

Could the self-management system of the former Yugoslavia be the third way? "Possible," Mile said, "if it is done in more democratic ways, more rationally, but I'm not sure. Too many people associate that system with Tito, and he was hated. But who knows? Right now there is no economy except the black market.

"I hope to God Clinton doesn't decide to send troops in there. They will fight to the death. They are defending their land and their history and they are fierce fighters, always have been. This nationalism they have now is madness. I was never taught to hate anyone, not at home or school or anywhere. I always knew there were differences between my Catholic and Muslim friends and me. But hate them? Never! We were all Yugoslavs. On the other hand, Tito always stressed the difference between us as if he wanted to divide and conquer. Serbs never liked Tito much. He was a Croat and a dictator!"

Tito does seem to have ruled by division, having created in the 1970s a group of new autonomous republics within the current Yugoslavia. Serbia was divided into three separate entities, Serbia, Vojvodina, and Kosovo. Autonomy was given to Bosnia as a Muslim state despite the fact that three religions had lived side by side there for hundreds of years with Serbs in the majority until World War II when the Croatians, in collaboration with the Nazis, slaughtered or drove out great numbers of them. Tito's moves were interpreted by Serbs as efforts to reduce their influence as the most numerous people in the country.

Finally our plane reached the nightmarish one-runway airport in Timisoara, the site of the first uprising against Nicolae Ceausescu, the Stalinist-style dictator of Romania. The airport, a relatively modern building, looked like a war zone with soldiers everywhere. Later, on the bus, I asked the Romanian bus owner why all the soldiers. He replied, "All airports have soldiers." No, I said, all airports are not filled with the military. "There's a lot of terrorism out there. We have to be careful," he warned. Terrorism? Well, Romania is surrounded by countries in various states of war—in the former Yugoslavia and the former Soviet Union that Romania lies between. But they are local wars, not likely to spread into Romania. So much for the new democratic Romania.

After about two hours, during which I was severely reprimanded for not having a visa for this brief stop in Romania, charged twenty-three dollars for a transit visa, grabbed by the sleeve and yelled at by soldiers when I mistakenly walked into a forbidden area, put through a slow, primitive, laborious customs inspection, and reluctantly permitted to use a filthy unlit toilet, we boarded the bus to Belgrade. Driving through the decaying, picturesque, ancient city of Timisoara, we saw occasional five- and six-story post–World War II apartment houses, each apartment with its own balcony, typical of so much Eastern European housing built after the war. The builders knew that many of the residents would be former peasants who would need a spot of fresh air and a place to garden and hang the wash. At the edge of town were some of the uglier housing developments; no balconies there, only high blank walls pierced by windows. Then we were out in the equally picturesque and decaying countryside of tiny stucco houses with thatched or tile roofs, where farmers were driving their horses and wagons back to their barns at day's end, where haystacks were clearly piled by hand, and where cattle, sheep, goats, horses, and chickens roamed freely and elderly women in black stood at the roadside watching—what? We passed an old horse-drawn hearse with hand-painted decorations, glass-sided so that we could clearly see the plain wooden coffin within, preceded and followed by what looked like a whole town on foot of men and babushka'd women in black.

After a couple of hours of driving we reached the border and I had my first grim look at Belgrade. Along the road to the border crossing was a mile-long line of cars and buses loaded with all manner of goods. Mile explained to me that people from Belgrade had gone to Timisoara to buy because there was nothing to buy in Belgrade—a consequence of the sanctions. I watched a woman rearrange her parcels, presumably more easily to get by the border guards. She had toilet paper, cans of oil, cans of what Mile guessed was gasoline, sacks of what was either flour or sugar, cans of what I thought was baby formula, and a variety of other items I couldn't identify. Some people were buying for their families and friends; others were buying goods they would sell on the black market, Mile said.

The bus driver drove to the head of the line but was waved back. He backed up the mile to the end of the line. I remembered the travel agent telling me there had been some trouble at the border the week before, when these trips were initiated, but it had been cleared up.

Obviously the trouble hadn't been cleared up. The line was hardly moving, and there was a mile of cars before us. We would be there all night.

Two more times the bus driver went to the head of the line only to be sent back, further each time, having lost his place in the line that kept getting longer. It was six o'clock on Saturday evening, prime shopping time. I asked the owner of the bus why we hadn't been able to go to the head of the line as he had promised when we arrived. He told me we had to wait for the shift change of border guards. Obviously he had bribed guards whose shift had been changed. The shift change would occur about eight o'clock, he said. At about nine we did indeed drive to the head of the line and successfully cross the Romanian border. The bus owner had taken all our passports to show the Romanian guards and had encountered no difficulties.

Fifty feet beyond was the Yugoslav border. A half-dozen cars and buses were ahead of us. Mile told me to let him speak for me if the border guards questioned me. He worried they might be hostile to an American. The guards microscopically examined the goods in the cars and buses ahead of us. I wondered why they forced everyone to take everything from their cars for inspection. Mile had told me that the border guards often confiscated goods to sell on the black market. Or perhaps, Mile suggested, the guards were actually doing their job and investigating for smuggling, which he said was rampant in Belgrade. In fact this endless, arduous routine investigation seemed to be pretty wasteful. Everything taken out of the cars and buses was returned. Perhaps the system wasn't so wasteful to the border guards, though. Perhaps it was used to extract bribes from these shoppers. "The whole system operates on bribery," Mile said.

Finally it was our turn. The guard looked at our passports without comment and then, with the exception of one woman who had five huge suitcases loaded to the breaking point, surely suspicious to guards on the lookout for smuggling, our luggage was given only a brief look. The woman who was so loaded with luggage was indignant: she was simply bringing back things for herself. It looked like she had bought out Chicago.

Just beyond the border we stopped at an old restaurant-saloon. The toilet was an ancient hole in the floor in an unlit cubicle with a wastebasket for whatever one had in hand in the way of toilet paper. Some of the passengers bought what looked like fried bread. I bought two shots of vodka in a paper cup to take along on the rest of the trip.

I wanted to buy a bottle, but Mile stopped me. "They want too much money," he insisted. The bottle of Baltic vodka was ten dollars. Later, in my hotel room, I sent the bellboy out for a bottle. He brought me a Stolichnaya for ten dollars. Obviously, for English-speaking people, the going rate for a bottle of vodka in Yugoslavia was ten dollars.

Watching the Serbian men—the travelers (most of my fellow travelers were Serbs) and the guards—I realized how easy it might be to look at them and see warriors. Taller than average, well-built, handsome men with sharp, hard features, one might easily envision them as mighty soldiers. They are, except for the Swedes, the tallest, biggest men in Europe. I felt sorry for the occasional short man, though Yugoslavs may not suffer the short-man complex that Americans endure. Interestingly, a closer look at these men revealed intelligent and sensitive expressions, even a little like they might be slightly mad, what Mile and what Pulitzer Prize–winning author Charles Simic, in the *New Republic*, called "Serbian madness." Mile went further than Simic. He said, laughing, "The Serbs are all mad." He pointed to the woman whose baggage had been inspected. The Serbian border guards had been generous to us, not tearing our luggage apart. Perhaps the bus owner bribed them. But this woman had aroused the curiosity of all of us. One of her packages was a cardboard box tied with string that she said held electronic equipment.

"Who brings electronic equipment from overseas?" the guards wanted to know. "Serbs," Mile answered, laughing. "She couldn't figure out that bringing such equipment from overseas, with all you have to go through to get home, when you can buy good equipment in Europe doesn't make sense. We just don't have very good mathematical skills." But she would have had to go through border guards wherever she shopped outside Yugoslavia, I said to Mile. "You're right. So I'm a little mad myself. I think all this stuff makes us a little crazy, but then we wouldn't be in all this stuff if we weren't a little crazy. Even me. Though I got out of it, my family is still there and I worry about them all the time. That can make you crazy."

But now that he had lived in the States for three years, did he think Serbs were crazier than other people?

"Well, the Serbs have a terrible history, and they make a lot of it. That maybe explains it. But yes, altogether, there is something a little crazy about the Serbs. I can't explain it better. I'm no psychologist." I hoped that in the weeks ahead I would find out whether Mile was right, and if he was, why Serbs are crazier than other people. I suspected that, though we had come to know each other quite well in these hours together, Mile might have felt forced to say something of this sort to help explain to an American the events in his native land, what he viewed as collective madness that he had trouble understanding.

We arrived at the Hotel Slavija in Belgrade at 1 a.m. Mile got a taxi and dropped me off at my hotel, the Hotel Park, a few blocks away. I had been warned that the streets of the city were dangerous, but they looked safe enough to me as we drove through little narrow streets filled with people so late at night. Perhaps there were lots of pickpockets among them, but bodily harm was unlikely to occur in those crowded streets.

At the hotel the clerk called a man to help me with my luggage, telling me I could go straight to my room, which was small but clean and pleasant for this inexpensive hotel.

When I awoke the next morning, not much refreshed, I went into the bathroom hoping to get a shower. There was no hot water. I wasn't surprised. I'd been surprised the night before when I found hot water for a bath when I arrived. There was a great shortage of oil and gas. I had expected to have little hot water or heat in the hotel. Fortunately the weather was still mild.

Back in my room after a Serbian-style breakfast of eggs fried on a slice of ham in the hotel dining room, I called my friend from Chicago, David Moss, who'd made Belgrade his second home. He invited me for drinks that evening. I then went to the reception desk to get a phone book to look up the numbers of some of the people I wanted to contact. The phone book was a mystery. It was in alphabetical order only from letter to letter, not within the letter—for two million people—though it was printed in Roman rather than the Cyrillic most commonly used in Belgrade. I asked help from the clerk. I gave him the first name on my list, Vlada Andjelkovic, a documentary film promoter, a cousin of a man in Chicago who had left town before he could give me Vlada's number. "Oh yes, Vladimir," he said. My friend in Chicago had given me his cousin's nickname. The clerk asked for an address. I didn't have one. "But look," the clerk said, "there are eleven Vladimir Andjelkovics in the book." How he found this was a mystery. And there were equal or greater numbers of duplicates for all the names in the book. And most, I noticed, ended with *ic*, pronounced *ich*.

Belgrade seemed to be one homogeneous city. The rest of Serbia is much more heterogeneous, with Hungarians, Albanians, Russians, Romanians, Germans, Gypsies, and others living together. But unlike other countries where the capital attracts many different nationalities, the capital city of Serbia seemed to be inhabited mostly by Serbs, though of course the telephone book did reveal other nationalities. But Muslims living in Belgrade, for instance, unless they had Muslim first names, wouldn't be distinguishable from Serbs in the phone book. As Serbs or Croatians who had converted to Islam under the Turkish occupation, their surnames would still be Serbian (or Croatian, which is the same language).

Without addresses for all the names on my list, I was lost. I couldn't figure out the phone book system, and the clerk didn't speak enough English to explain it to me. I cheered up realizing that most of these people were sufficiently well known that I would probably be able to find them through one of the journalists for whom I did have numbers. The clerk didn't give up, though. He started calling down the list. Number four was my Vlada. Jubilantly the clerk called me to the phone, and I made my first contact in Belgrade. Vlada's mother told me he was out of town, but she would tell him to call me when he returned.

When I finished my call the clerk asked, "You have cigarettes, please?" I thought it a little improper for a room clerk in a hotel to be begging cigarettes in return for his help, but I knew that everyone in Belgrade was broke and that, like everything else, there was probably a shortage of cigarettes. I went to my room and brought down a pack of my precious Carlton low-tar cigarettes. Soon I was going to have to smoke Yugoslav cigarettes, probably as strong as most other European cigarettes. If anything could end my habit, Yugoslav cigarettes might do it. I had brought enough Carltons to last only a week.

The Hotel Park was a modest nine-story post–World War II accommodation with a tiny no-frills lobby—a few uncomfortable couches and nondescript end tables with paper flowers as decoration. It had one small guest elevator and another for the help that seemed to be in better working order than the one for the guests, and a huge, pleasant dining room with good service on the second floor and a big coffee shop on the ground floor. My fourth-floor room was sparsely furnished with two comfortable twin beds, built-in bedside shelves, one cupboard, a desk, a closet, and a small bathroom. I had trouble imagining living and working there. It was obviously a businessman's room, not one designed for someone who would spend hours there every evening reading and writing. The size and sparseness of the room was partly compensated for by the large wall-wide window that overlooked an old building with gargoyles grinning from the cornices and a large parklike area beside it, a government building perhaps, or a school. Beyond were attractive mid-rise apartment buildings with balconies filled with plants and flowers. This altogether pleasant view would help me overcome some of the claustrophobia that the room engendered.

With his friend Karl Haupt, an American filmmaker, David picked me up in Karl's Mercedes at eight. We drove through the dimly lit streets of Belgrade, along several wide boulevards, through a tunnel, then through some narrow streets to Skadarlija, an old, wide cobblestone street four blocks long, closed to cars and lined with galleries, studios, offices, apartments, outdoor cafés, and fancy restaurants. The sounds of Gypsy violins broke the near silence in the streets. As we wandered on this balmy October evening, I was feeling grateful that Belgrade's weather was much milder than Chicago's. People here were still wearing summer clothes.

Skadarlija was once the most popular street in Belgrade, jammed with tourists and local people. There were no tourists now. No one any longer came to Belgrade, the seat of iniquity, and the locals could no longer afford to eat out and were not in the mood just to wander and chat and stop for a drink. The effects of the embargo had made a ghost town of Skadarlija. Still, the waiters stood about chatting among themselves, and the musicians played for a handful of customers.

We settled down in David's favorite outdoor café to order drinks and an array of Serbian treats. I was still too exhausted from the arduous trip to retain much of our intense four-hour conversation about Yugoslavia's problems, though I recall asking a lot of questions. I wished I had brought along my tape recorder. Both men were intense and outraged by the embargo. They had elaborate conspiracy theories about the causes of the war and the imposition of the UN sanctions. I thought they were both quite mad, zealots the like of which I hadn't seen since my days in the antiwar movement in the 1960s. But I had to consider what they were saying. Both of them had been in and out of Yugoslavia for years and had done a good deal of research. Could it be that Germany was once again entertaining expansionist ideas, Machiavellian in its encouragement of the secessions first of Slovenia and then Croatia and finally Bosnia in order to create small weakened nations that it could control? It was certainly true that Germany had led the West to recognize these states, despite highly placed warnings that this would lead to civil war. The meager media coverage of anything but the battlefields in the last year seemed to indicate that Germany was not actively involved in the UN and the European Union's (formerly the European Community) negotiations over the war; but perhaps it was no longer necessary for Germany to take such an active role now that its purpose was achieved—these countries were at war with one another and could only emerge from the wars in a weakened position.

On the other hand, Germany was so beset with its own problems after unification with East Germany. Was it logical for Germany to pursue expansionist plans? Or were such plans an effort to overcome its internal problems?

In mid-1993 Germany had asked that the UN sanctions on Yugoslavia be lifted, no doubt in pure self-interest because it could no longer tolerate the masses of immigrants flowing across its borders. Germany's free immigration policies were under siege by its right wing that was becoming strong enough to threaten the government's position. Yet it was true that Germany had long sought a direct opening to the Adriatic Sea, whose coastline borders Croatia and Montenegro, and ports on the Danube that has its longest coastline in Serbia.

David and Karl spoke of worldwide conspiracies by the West finally to destroy Yugoslavia. I couldn't dismiss all this conspiracy talk entirely. Europe had changed mightily since the end of World War II, but that change had resulted in large part as a consequence of the united Western front, under the leadership of the U.S. against the Soviet Union. Now there was no more Soviet Union, and its separate states were fighting one another much like the Yugoslavs and were suffering terrible economic disarray. Was it possible that the cooperation among the Europeans would fall apart now that they didn't have a common enemy, that the old nationalist enmities would reappear with the plots that had plagued Europe for so many years? Certainly the Europeans had not been able to project united action on the Yugoslav front. Were these Yugoslav wars really not purely local but rather a product of the age-old battle over the gateway from East to West that Yugoslavia is, as David and Karl tried for several hours to convince me? Much as I was ready to listen to such theories, I remained pretty convinced that they were mad, that certainly Germany played a terrible role, but that the source of the troubles was in Yugoslavia itself. I wondered, as David and Karl talked, is this what I would be hearing as I spoke with Serbs?

That morning, Karl told us, he had joined a group of elderly men who had been taking a little rowboat equipped with an outboard motor out into the Danube River to intercept foreign barges en route to Hungary, Germany, and other destinations. Because of the sanctions, barges were required to have UN permits to traverse Yugoslav waters. Most didn't. This little citizen-action group, Karl told me, sent up flares, stopped barges, demanded to see their permits, and, when they weren't produced, offered to negotiate. They would ignore the absence of the papers in exchange for cash or shipments of food or medicine. For instance, they would arrange for a shipment of five thousand dollars' worth of penicillin, one of the crucial drugs that Yugoslavs couldn't buy because the UN sanctions committee was refusing import permissions for food and medicine, despite the fact that they were explicitly exempt from the embargo. Shipping companies complied because getting the UN permits was a terrible hassle, often taking months. These three elderly men in a rowboat arranged shipments of fuel oil and food in addition to medicines from the shipping companies. They were, Karl said, one of the few groups in Belgrade who were able to respond to the embargo with rebellious, constructive spirit—unless you included all the black marketers who were getting rich on Belgrade's shortages. "Most people just seem resigned to seeing their society fall apart. They just sit around and wring their hands—the ones who don't commit suicide or die from starvation or illness."

2 True to David's prediction, everyone I phoned this morning was happy to talk with me. No one expressed hesitation. It seems that talking to an American journalist was such a novelty and represented such a unique opportunity to tell their story that they were eager to talk. They all seemed to assume that I was on their side, whatever side that happened to be—and there were a variety of sides represented, as I learned later. I got names from a variety of sources and didn't know, in most cases, where they stood on issues. The dozen names I got from Article 19, the anticensorship group based in London, I knew to be opponents of the government, but I didn't know the positions of most of the others to whom I'd been referred by American Serb friends and acquaintances.

My first interview was with Mirjana Kameretzy, who volunteered to come to the hotel because she would be in the neighborhood. She was a Serb who was married to a Russian who had died many years ago. At first her face looked almost deformed, her mouth twisting to the left as she spoke in a grainy, deep, smoky voice. As we sat talking over Turkish coffee in the hotel dining room, she in the impeccable English of those who learned it at school, with a dry sense of humor, her face gradually changed, became vibrantly lovely, her dark eyes shining, her mouth no longer squirming. She was short and thin, intense, wearing worn blue jeans, a bulky yellow cable-knit sweater, and sneakers, no jewelry, no makeup, her greying black hair cut off bluntly just below the ears and hanging straight. She had been the Belgrade correspondent for the *New York Times* since 1952. Just out of art school, planning to be an artist but needing to earn some money, she had accidentally fallen into this job. But she had soon proved her worth. The *Times* had been getting her some money from time to time as other correspondents came to Belgrade and brought her dollars; she could no longer receive checks by mail since, under the embargo, U.S. banks no longer did business with Yugoslavia.

Since the wars began, Mirjana had not filed any stories for the *Times* because she didn't want it said that "I am saying this because I am a Serb." She knew her viewpoint might often be at odds with her editors'. Instead she helped other *Times* writers with background, leaving them to handle the stories however they chose. And what did she think about the stories they were writing? She shrugged and smiled. "I sometimes tell the correspondents their stories are not fair. I think they pay much more attention to the other side. But I also think the government here is not always taking the right stance with the press. I'm not talking about propaganda, but I think that, probably because of fifty years of a Communist regime, they don't know how to do it properly. The other sides have been much more able in their efforts to tell their story the way they want to. Every single day I get releases from this Ruder Finn in Washington. First it was for Slovenia, then for Croatia, then it was Bosnia. And then it was Kosovo. They call it the Kosovo Republic even though they are still officially part of Serbia." Kosovo, for centuries Serb land, was now more than 90 percent Albanian and had declared its independence though no one had yet recognized it.

Serbia could not get such outside help because of the embargo?

"Not only that, but they don't have the money as well," Mirjana said.

Did Bosnia have more money than Serbia?

"They get the money from Pakistan or Saudi Arabia, from the Muslim countries. And Serbia can count on Russia for help, but Russia has no money for itself. And Croatia gets money from its emigrés abroad. A few months ago I was visiting my daughter in Canada and heard Tudjman [Croatia's president] on the radio asking for help. An awful lot of money is coming to him from the Canadian emigrés and Americans and Australians." A massive emigration from Croatia had occurred with the civil war in Yugoslavia that followed the end of World War II, when Tito's Partisans took over the country. Many of the emigrés had been implicated in the slaughter of Serbs, Jews, and Gypsies while Croatia was a Nazi puppet state.

My interview with Mirjana was exhausting. It was as if she had been waiting for more than two years to tell her version of the Serb story, feeling stifled by her self-imposed ban. She scarcely hesitated between sentences. I called her first because I expected, as a correspondent for the *Times*, that she would be more objective than others. I expected her to be expert and articulate. I wasn't disappointed. She had been following the media, talking with all kinds of people, keeping abreast as if she were still a working journalist.

Mirjana told me she thought the world's media were not fully telling the Serb side of the story. "I think the Serb side has been ignored. I think this has happened because it's hard for people to change their focus. The story began in Slovenia when the Yugoslav army *was* the aggressor, and then in Croatia too at first. But when the story began to change, people had a hard time changing with it. People tend to get stuck with an idea. I also think Germany was pushing very hard that Yugoslavia should not continue in one piece, and its attitudes influenced the world and the press. For a long time before the war, Germany was supporting this idea and encouraging the Croatians and the Slovenians to separate. It was a terrible mistake for everyone to recognize Slovenia and Croatia, but it was what the Germans wanted. Then the same thing happened with Bosnia. People on the outside would not understand what that meant to the Serbs.

The day Bosnia was recognized, the 6th of April, was the date people here remember so well. It was the Nazi bombing of Belgrade in 1941. The recognition on that day was unbelievable to the people here. For the Serbs, that day brought back all those terrible memories of World War II under the Germans."

Why was Germany pushing for the breakup of Yugoslavia?

"I don't know. It is very difficult to understand. But it is clear that in the very near future Germany is going to be so strong they will be able to do anything they want." It was the same theory I'd heard the night before from what I'd considered two mad zealots. This woman was clearly not a zealot.

Did she think the Germans wanted to rebuild their empire?

"Well, not the way it was, but . . . you know, the Germans feel a natural affinity to the Slovenians and the Croatians. They were under the German [Austro-Hungarian] empire for so long [before World War I]. They didn't have their own country like Serbia did. They are more Germanic peoples, more industrious—you know, forget about the past, think about the future. The main character of the Serbs is to be much more involved with tradition, with their history. During the Communist regime it was not proper to think about such things, and the Serbs felt as if they had lost their identity. This is why Milosevic became so popular, because he was always speaking about the Serbs as a third nation, how they had to get their identity back."

"When I was here in 1990," I said, "just before the election, I was reading the English-language paper and found it very hard to fathom Milosevic. On one hand he was talking about maintaining Yugoslavia at all costs. And on the other he was making strong nationalist speeches filled with hate for the Croatians. But he got away with it. And people obviously loved it."

"They did. The people felt that during the Tito regime they were somehow suppressed by that regime. It was always favoring other parts of the country and not Serbia. And Serbia was the biggest republic, of course, the most numerous. Serbs felt a great deal of injustice was done to them. For instance, a great many factories were moved out of Serbia to Bosnia, Croatia, and Slovenia. Not a lot of people knew about that. I knew certain economists and so I knew about it. The explanation given, curiously, was that the parts of the country that were not devastated in the war should receive the same help as Serbia which was badly devastated and getting supposedly disproportionate assistance. So factories that had been in Serbia were just moved to other parts of the country. The explanation does not make sense. Why take factories away when you are trying to rebuild an economy? The Serbs felt it was to strip them of their power.

"It was always a mystery. You know, Croatia was not bombed by the Allies, but Belgrade and other towns in Serbia were. On Easter Day in 1944. I recall that day very well. I was a child. We were used to seeing the Allied planes flying over because they would bomb Romania which, of course, was a Nazi puppet. But that day—it was a lovely sunny day and the children were running into the streets to watch the Flying Fortresses. And it was the typical sound, which I can still hear in my memory. And then there was another sound, the sound of the Deutsche Luftwaffe shooting at the Americans. And one plane was shot and we saw the two pilots jumping out of the ship. And the children were saying, 'Those two pilots are going to land in our garden.' So we were running to save the American pilots. And my mother was absolutely frightened and told us to come in the house because in each house lived a German soldier. We had an officer. But we wanted to stay with the pilots.

"After that the bombs began. It was carpet bombing, and certain parts of Belgrade were completely wiped out. This was, after all, after the Nazis had already bombed us. All the smaller one-story houses in Belgrade, they don't exist anymore. And then there were several more bombings of Belgrade and then other towns in Serbia. And we were fighting on the side of the Allies! At this same time Croatia, a Nazi puppet, was never bombed. It was crazy. And no one knows why."

Though Mirjana was disturbed that the Serbian side of the war story had not been told in the world press, she said she did not defend what she described as "the crimes that were committed in this war. I cannot defend some of the killing in Bosnia. But you have to remember that the bloodshed against the Serbs and the concentration camps for them in World War II were far worse than anything we have seen in this war. In the parts of Croatia where Serbs lived then, entire villages were destroyed. As bad as it was in Croatia, it was worse in the western part of Bosnia. The Croats called the Muslims the 'flowers of Croatia.' There were Catholics, even priests, involved, but the Muslims were the worst executioners in the concentration camps. They even had one military unit that fought with the Nazis in Stalingrad."

I was reminded of a passage in *Genocide in Satellite Croatia*

1941–1945 by a French historian, Edmond Paris. He wrote: "Hatred and sadism in the form of various tortures were prevalent and cannot be compared with atrocities committed even in the darkest medieval times. The means of torture were the following: red hot needles forced under the finger nails; red hot irons placed between the fingers and the toes; whipping by chains; plucking out eyes; mutilating various parts of the body; placing salt in open wounds; tightening chains around the forehead until the eyes popped out and the skull was fractured; placing a person into a wire enclosure, called a hedgehog; confinement to a room filled with blood to the ankles. . . ."

"Once Bosnia declared itself a separate republic," Mirjana went on, "we all knew what would happen. There would be blood up to the knees, as we would say. And if this would come to Serbia, the blood would come up to the ears. So we knew. We knew exactly what would happen in Bosnia. We were warning the other countries about this.

"We have not understood the Allies, Europe and America. How come they are willing for the outside borders of Yugoslavia to be changed but not the inside borders, when those borders were drawn artificially?" The Yugoslav wars have been essentially about its internal borders, about the demands of the Croatians and Bosnians that they maintain the borders drawn up by Tito. These borders removed land from Serbia and followed no ethnic lines; in fact they mixed ethnic groups with the hope of making a united Yugoslavia of highly disparate peoples. The Serbs fighting in Croatia and then in Bosnia were fighting to regain old Serb lands for Serbia or to establish separate republics on land traditionally held by Serbs, such as the Krajina in Croatia.

Mirjana told me, "Actually, the Croatian policy was a shortsighted one. They could have had all the Serbs of Krajina on their plate and in twenty or thirty years they would all have been Croatians. With no war. Instead, when Tudjman came to power the Cyrillic alphabet of the Serbs was not allowed. Serb newspapers and magazines could not be published. People were thrown out of their jobs. This is why they rebelled.

"As for Bosnia, I don't agree with what they are calling concentration camps, I would call them prisoner-of-war camps. But there are endless stories in Belgrade of people who escaped from Bosnia and the suffering they went through. There are between 700,000 and 800,000 refugees in Yugoslavia from Bosnia and Croatia. And some of them are Muslims and those who are mixed Bosnian and Serb or Croatian and Serb. It is all unbelievable. When I went to inquire about some of these people, I was given only initials. I was told I could not use their names because they still had relatives back in Bosnia. But to present this information to the UN or any of the other countries, you had to give the full names."

Had Mirjana seen the "prisoner-of-war" camps? She had not. Did she believe they were as described in the West, with people starving to death? "I can believe that," she said. "You see, Bosnia is a very mountainous country. They don't have very much food. Yugoslavia is actually shipping food to the Bosnian Serbs and to the Krajina because those people are starving. Regardless of whether they are Muslims or Serbs in Bosnia, they are really starving. What you've seen in the camps is that the Serbs are just not sharing their little bit of food with their prisoners, but they too would be starving if it weren't for the Yugoslav shipments."

What did she think about the rapes of which the Serbs were accused? "If the numbers of Serbs in Croatia and Bosnia by comparison with the Croatians and the Muslims are correct—and I have no reason to doubt the census—then the Serbs must be supermen. [Serbs are a minority in Bosnia and Croatia.] And the rapes of Serbs by the Muslims and Croatians are not even mentioned. There are some terrible stories, including some babies that have been born here in Belgrade after the women had been raped. There was a case of a mother who gave birth to a girl and refused to see the child. There are many of these stories." Mirjana told me that these stories had all been documented by the Serbian Council for Information, along with other atrocities committed against the Serbs.

"One story they're telling in the States is that Serbs are using rape to populate Bosnia with Serbs," I said.

"That's utter nonsense. Rape is terrible, and I don't say that the Serbs didn't do it and many other things just as terrible. But their side should be published. That story is just utter nonsense invented by the Muslims."

"I have heard in the States that 97 or so percent of the Yugoslav budget goes to the army," I told Mirjana.

"It is 75 percent. That is to maintain the army in Yugoslavia, not to fight in Bosnia, though."

"I've also heard that 70 percent of the army is Serbian."

"You have to understand, when Yugoslavia was one nation the

army consisted of people from all the republics, but the Serbs are the most numerous people, so naturally the army was mostly Serbian. [The Yugoslav army was the fourth largest in Europe, maintained because of the continuing fear of an invasion by the Soviets.] After the recognition of independence and the start of the war—I would call it a civil war really—the Serbians in the army came to Serbia, the Slovenians remained in Slovenia, the Croats in Croatia, and the Bosnians the same. Now the Yugoslav army has other nationalities as well—Russians, Hungarians, Albanians, though the Albanians are refusing to be drafted, and, of course, the Montenegrins, though there are very few of them. Their population is less than 600,000.

"But who is fighting in Bosnia is the Bosnian Serbs, supported largely by the Serb army from the Krajina, the Krajina Republican Army, because they have proclaimed their own republic, which of course has not been recognized by anyone. And then you have irregular paramilitary troops who go to fight under the Krajina army. But the regular Yugoslav army is not fighting in Bosnia."

"If the regular army is not fighting in Bosnia, why is the budget for it so massive?" I asked.

"Because it is felt that the army must be maintained at full strength in case of attack."

"I am assuming that the army can't buy any equipment or arms now, under the embargo. I know that the Yugoslav munitions plants are in Bosnia. Are they accessible to the Serbs there so that they can get arms?"

"Well, a few are on Serb territory and a few on Croatian territory, but the majority of the munitions plants are under the control of the Muslims now."

"So the Muslims can get munitions there?"

"Well, if the plants are still operating. Nothing is really operating in Bosnia now. No, they are getting arms from the Muslim world."

Was Yugoslavia supplying arms to the Bosnian Serbs? "I would imagine some, but I don't know. But since the borders have been so dramatically closed, it may be hard. Most of what Serbia is helping the Bosnians with is food. That's why we have such a shortage of food here. I couldn't buy bread for two days now."

I described to Mirjana the breadline I had watched outside the hotel dining room that morning, where the well-dressed mixed with those not so well attired and the ages ranged from twenty to seventy or so. They had received, along with large loaves of bread, other commodities I couldn't identify.

"Flour, sugar, cooking oil—because it's rationed now," Mirjana explained. "Washing powder too is rationed. Half a kilo [a pound] of sugar a month per person, six kilos of flour a month, about half a kilo of washing powder."

"In the States very few people still bake their own bread. Do women still bake bread here?"

"Not generally, not under normal circumstances. But now, unless you get up in the wee hours of the morning, you can't buy any bread, so people use this flour that the government gives out to make their own bread."

"When I first saw this line I assumed the food was being given away, but then I saw people with money in their hands. They pay for these handouts, I take it."

"Yes, but only a pittance. All the food that is rationed is very cheap, almost nothing. But, of course, you have to realize that in such conditions of shortage there is always a black market. Anything you want to buy, you can get on the black market if you have the money. And remember to calculate not in dollars but in deutsche marks. Inflation has made the dinar worthless. The black marketers will not take dinars most of the time. We pay, for instance, for fifty kilos of sugar, about seventy deutsche marks [about forty-two dollars]. You can buy anything on the black market if you have the money, but of course now no one has any money because there is so much unemployment, because the embargo has wrecked the economy. If you want to get things cheap, you have to queue, and I refuse to queue. I would rather not eat."

David and Karl had told me that in Belgrade there were now wars between black marketers. Was that true?

"Well, I wouldn't say it was that bad, but Belgrade is no longer the safe town it was. I used to take my dog for a walk late at night, and one time, when I mentioned it casually to a friend, he was shocked. 'You are taking your dog for a walk at midnight?' I said, 'Of course.' But now it's not so safe. There's every day some shooting with some killings of people. The last three days there were three people involved in some black market, maybe some arms or drugs, who were killed."

"And I heard that two elderly people a month are committing suicide."

"That is true. There is a big increase of suicide because on the pension the elderly get, they cannot live. They only get seven deutsche marks a month to buy everything. And they can't get any medicine. They don't let us import drugs and medicine and spare parts for medical equipment. It takes months to get anything if we can get anything at all.

"Refugees from Bosnia and Croatia are also in a bad way. We don't have enough for ourselves, let alone the refugees. We are sacrificing for those refugees, but they are not getting enough."

I told Mirjana that one of my Serbian-American contacts had suggested I take some medicine to give to people I met in Belgrade. I had brought with me half a dozen very large bottles of aspirin that I would give to one of the doctors I would meet, so she could give them to patients. "That's good," she said. "We have no aspirin, and when we can buy it at the pharmacy it is very expensive."

Another story we heard in the States, I told Mirjana, was that the president, Slobodan Milosevic, was a dictator. "He's a strong man, yes," Mirjana said. "Is he a dictator?" I asked.

"Well, I wouldn't quite call him a dictator. I don't agree with his policies, and I don't like his way of moving people. But I have a feeling that morale does not exist in this country any more. The way I was taught people should behave is just not being done anymore. There is a lot of corruption. But I do not believe, as Milosevic claims, that those who are leaving the country were involved in the corruption. You know, it is estimated that about 300,000 have already left. He doesn't want to admit that people are fleeing the country because they have no future here. And I do not believe in elections that were not quite fair, I would say. On the other hand, on state television they showed the publisher of the *New York Times*, and he was very outspoken. You wouldn't have that in a dictatorship. It is hard for me to call it a democracy. But what is democracy, after all? I cannot call it democracy when they use the tanks to defend it. [The government sent tanks into the streets in 1991 to crush large demonstrations aimed chiefly at state control of television.] To defend whom? To defend the people? To defend the power? I was disgusted when I saw tanks on the street in 1991. But there is still much freedom."

"I was told that 65 percent of the Yugoslavs still support Milosevic. Is that true?"

"I would say yes, but for a reason. The two main TV channels that the government controls can be seen throughout Yugoslavia, whereas the other channels that broadcast a different kind of information, different views from the government's, do not reach outside Belgrade. So if people read the press, which is not run by the government, or can get the independent TV channels, they will have a different view. But they don't read the papers, many of them because they can't afford to buy them anymore. The prices have gone up, and people just don't have any money. So they watch television, which is free. And what they get on the major channels is Milosevic's message about how good his government is. For instance, a few weeks ago he declared that inflation would be curbed soon to only 50 percent, and now I see that it has gone not down but up—to over 2,000 percent. And it rises every day, practically every hour. We are very close to what it was in Germany after World War I, and if this goes on... I don't know.

"People talk about the lifting of the sanctions as if it will happen tomorrow and things will be all right again, but the sanctions are not going to be lifted. When the UN started talking about sanctions two years ago, for days I could not sleep because I knew what was going to happen. People didn't realize. I tried to tell them what was going to happen, but they didn't believe me. And now they talk about when the sanctions will be lifted. But even if they lift them now, the country is completely ruined. Nothing is working."

But, I countered, "it isn't only the sanctions, is it? Inflation started in the country in the 1970s, didn't it?"

"Well, yes," Mirjana said. "And I remember when Tito died, there were big shortages of many things. And my friends, the journalists, would come, and they wouldn't even have to ask me if I knew about the shortages. There was also a shortage of electric power. But this now is much worse. Now again we're going to have electricity shortages this winter. They are still selling it to Slovenia and even Croatia in order to get some money. And this winter, when there will be shortages of heating oil and wood..."

"Wood?" I asked. "Are some people heating with wood stoves?"

"Oh yes. I still have tile stoves. In certain parts of old Belgrade and in the villages people still heat with wood or coal. So if they can't get that, they'll use electric heaters, which will place a huge burden on the supplies. They are already warning of brownouts."

"Mirjana, to change the subject some," I said, "everywhere there is a big difference between urban and rural populations. I assume that Belgrade is very different in some respects from the countryside. Is there less nationalism in Belgrade than in the countryside?"

"Yes. But Belgrade is not the same anymore. You see, when the war started, many young people left the country because they could see no future here. Already for a number of years there had been no future, no employment, nothing. So all kinds of educated people, highly qualified people, went to the United States in order to survive. Meanwhile, since the war, in Belgrade we were getting a lot of young people from the Krajina and from Bosnia. They refuse to go back now because they simply do not want to go and fight and be killed, and so they are staying here. So the face of Belgrade has changed. You find a lot of newcomers, not urban people, a lot of people who came with nothing."

"Many of them," I said, "were ignorant peasants and more nationalistic? Those two things go together, would you say?"

"I would say so. And also, those people who were fighting, I think they have changed. I think their psyche has been changed after all they've seen. They are rougher, more cynical. That's why we see shooting. The population is now armed. Almost everyone carries a gun."

"How much do you think Milosevic's intense nationalist campaign has encouraged that? That is, the urban population can listen, think it through, and maybe reject it. But the more ignorant sections of the population tend to be more easily sucked in, would you say?" Mirjana thought for a moment and then said, "Well, yes, but I would also say that Milosevic's campaign gave them some kind of security." In *Yugoslavia: Collapse, War, Crimes*, published by the Center for Anti-War Action in Belgrade, Julie Mostov writes, "In an environment of radical social transition and rapidly deteriorating economic conditions, people need to find some bearing and support. The vacuum left by the breakdown of old institutions and identities was quickly filled by 'recovered' networks of community and by historical collective identities. The idea of facing a new set of political and social institutions was daunting to people, and nationally defined communities presented a positive vehicle through which to meet this challenge. . . . People had had little experience with political associations that normally provide important linkages or mediating networks for individuals in liberal democratic societies. . . ."

Where efforts were made to introduce the mediating networks Mostov refers to, Mirjana said, they were often not understood. While there were about a hundred political parties in Yugoslavia, most of them opposed to Milosevic, many of them were frivolous, and most had been unable to attract much more than a handful of followers. "In a way," she said, "those kind of people coming from a small village to something that is completely unknown to them couldn't understand the talk of the opposition, which was too intellectual for them. I would say that the radicals opposing Milosevic are even more extreme nationalists than Milosevic, but theirs is cast in a more intellectual way." Here Mirjana was referring mostly to the best known of the oppositionists, Vuk Draskovic, a writer who had a small following in Belgrade but whose reputation was based on a highly nationalist book and who rose to prominence as a nationalist but later dropped that emphasis to oppose Milosevic.

"When Milosevic rose to power in 1987, he was playing on that nationalist theme, and he did not know when to stop. I recall at that time that most of the shops in Belgrade had his picture in their windows. A number of bus drivers had his picture up. Even some of my friends had his picture in their cars. I was shocked. I was a Yugoslav, but all of a sudden I didn't know who I was. Those things were all sad.

"At the same time nationalism was also building in Croatia and Slovenia. Even before that I recall attending a government press conference in Slovenia, and I observed the nationalism going on there and I was shocked.

"But I have the feeling that this was all being prepared many years ago, by the regime and by Germany. Speaking to the refugees from Croatia about what happened five and six years ago, it was clear what was going to happen."

"I have the impression from reading," I said, "that Tito encouraged national identities by granting special republic status to the various ethnic groups, religious groups like the Muslims, while at the same time putting the lid on nationalist aspirations—that it was a divide-and-conquer process."

"When Tito was forming those republics," Mirjana said, "the explanation was that he didn't want to make the same mistake as was made after the First World War when Serbia was actually dominating the country. The other republics, especially Croatia, resented that. But I find that the division of the country in royal times [under King Aleksander after World War I] was a fair one. You see, they divided it into the *banovina*, which meant regions under civilian authority, not into separate republics as Tito did. There were no official borders, not these strict borders that Tito erected. That system was far more fair than Tito's divisions. He made Bosnia a republic when Bosnia never before existed as a country. He made Muslim a nationality. Muslim is a religion, not a nationality. When Tito first created Yugoslavia it was a centralized state, which might have worked. But then, under pressure to democratize, he decentralized it, and the state was like a cart with each wheel pulling in a different direction. It cannot work. There are railroads with different engines in each republic."

"So the breakup of the country was inevitable?" I asked.

"Well, it was. But it took a long time."

"What held it together—Tito?"

"Yes. He was a master at giving lessons to one and then changing them for someone else. Many people under him were very dissatisfied, but they kept quiet to protect their jobs."

"He was a genius, wasn't he?"

"Yes, he was. Somehow he kept it all going. But he loved the good life, the love affairs." We laughed together about Tito's women, his private zoo on an island in the Adriatic, and another smaller zoo at one of his houses in Belgrade where he confiscated people's houses in order to build his mansions and his gardens.

"But it's all sad, very sad, because our country was really beautiful, a rich country that was badly managed. Our economy was never in really good shape. [It was largely propped up by foreign loans that began to be called in in the late 1980s when the cold war ended and Yugoslavia lost its strategic position as a buffer state.] But there was much that was good. In Bosnian villages they built modern houses with running water and all that sort of thing for the first time, and now there's not a single village left. I was in Bosnia and it was a horrifying scene. You see village after village that does not exist any more. Not a single living soul there. Not a cat or a dog. [About 60 percent of rural Bosnia is Serbian.] Before World War II there were no roads, and then after the war there were good asphalt roads. There is no asphalt any more. There was electricity in even the most remote villages. No more. And Sarajevo and Mostar, beautiful old cities, they do not exist any more. The mosques and the Orthodox churches and Catholic churches have all been blown up."

So it is clear, I said, that the destruction is on all sides, almost willy-nilly. "Yes," Mirjana said, showing the first emotion of the afternoon. "But what happened to the Serbs has not been published."

I took Mirjana back to her remark that there were certain things she wouldn't defend. "If the Serbs say they were never aggressors in their history, that they didn't start the fighting, then that is not strictly true," she said. "But it doesn't make any difference anymore. I did not lose any of my family in this war, but I lost a lot of my family in the last war. Still, I may understand what is going on now, but I can't justify it. But if I had seen my daughter being raped or my son being killed, I don't know how I would react. I also think that people who claim to be educated and civilized—it's all phony. Beneath the surface there is an animal. I wish I could have an answer, but I really don't have it. I only can say one should remember and forgive."

That should have been the end of the interview, but I could not let Mirjana go quite yet. I had one more big question that I wanted her to answer for me. "Can it be possible for a people to celebrate the legend of the great defeat of Tsar Lazar at Kosovo six hundred years ago?" This was the legendary crucial battle against the Turks in which Lazar chose an eternal heavenly kingdom over the worldly defeat of the Turks, who then ruled Serbia with great violence for five hundred years.

Mirjana was clearly tired. She said, limply, "Yes, we are a strange people. Any other nation would not celebrate defeat. But you have read Rebecca West." I had indeed read West. After discussing the suicide of Lazar that only a few years later led to the enslavement of his people as a symbol of those who would rather "be right than do right," West wrote, "This is the Slav mystery; that the Slav, who seems wholly a man of action, is aware of the interior life, of the springs of action, as only the intellectuals of other races are. . . . Yugoslavia is always telling me about one death or another. . . . Yet this country is full of life. I feel that we Westerners should come here to learn to live. . . . Perhaps we are ignorant about life in the West because we avoid thinking about death. One could not study geography if one concentrated on the land and turned one's attention away from the sea." A romantic view, as much as West's discussion of the Yugoslavs is; nevertheless it is probably a fair characterization that helps explain the Serb mentality.

"You have to understand," Mirjana said, "that Serbia in that time was a great empire, and we are very proud of that. [The last king of old Serbia, Stepan Dusan, has been compared with England's great Queen Elizabeth two centuries later.] But so was Greece a great empire, but they're gone. We're still living that legend. For myself, I say, 'I shall go to heaven some day, but while I'm here I would like to live with my two feet on the ground. I would like to know my history, but that is not all my life. I like to think of the future.' It was clever of Milosevic to gather the people like that for the celebration at Kosovo, because during the Tito regime you could not celebrate your Serbian heritage, you could not celebrate your Christmas or many other things. A number of children were not baptized, not Christians. So suddenly someone comes and speaks about your identity, not only to the Serbs in Serbia but also to the Serbs in Croatia and Bosnia and Macedonia, and suddenly you find a renewer, a leader. I don't think he is as popular as he used to be, but he still has a lot of power."

We were both tired. It had been a long, intense afternoon. As I walked Mirjana out to the hotel lobby, I promised a call in a couple of days to talk again. Still exhausted from the trip, I went up to my room, poured myself a drink of vodka, renewed my makeup, and got ready to go at five o'clock to meet Snezana Popadic, the half-sister of a contact I had made in Chicago. She was meeting me at the Hotel Slavija, a few blocks from my hotel and near her house, which she said would be difficult for me, a foreigner, to find alone.

I hoped the walk to the Slavija and then to Snezana's apartment would refresh me and enable me to do another interview. Instead I found myself apologizing to Snezana for my fatigue and pleading that we simply have a little conversation together. She brought out some Turkish coffee, and we settled into her cozy but spacious apartment decorated with modern furnishings, a lot of lovely objets d'art, the latest electronic equipment, and lace doilies. She told me about her family history, about her father who had served in the royal Yugoslav army in World War II, had been captured by the Germans, and had disappeared after the war, only to turn up many years later in Chicago with a new family. She went to Chicago in 1975 to meet him for the first time since she was two years old. The pride she expressed in her father who had been a Cetnik—one of those who, in World War II, fought the Partisans harder than they did the Germans—warned me that Snezana was probably one of the nationalists who had urged on the war against the other Yugoslav republics. Many Cetniks emigrated after the war for fear of reprisals against them for not having fought the Nazis harder and for opposing the Partisans.

Never married, Snezana had lived with her now deceased mother and aunt who had scratched out a living as seamstresses. She had finally been able to buy her apartment after years of paying into a fund. While the apartment was comfortable, the mid-size building in which she lived was like my hotel—shoddily built, poorly maintained.

Snezana had been a translator for the Yugoslav airlines for nearly twenty-five years and spoke English like a native, but since the embargo that prevented the airline from doing business with foreign nations, there had been little work for her. She explained that her company was still paying its employees, but the wages were not even a quarter of her former salary. Employees were working alternate months so that no one had to be laid off. The company's only revenues were from a few intrastate flights and bus lines. Now fifty-five, Snezana was eligible for a pension, but at the time that amounted to about eleven dollars a month, not enough to buy bread for a month. Pensions were not paid by individual companies but by the government; they didn't depend on what you had earned but were uniform for all retired people. Snezana had been teaching English to supplement her reduced salary and was managing to live reasonably comfortably, though she dreaded the winter when there might be no heat in her building.

"But I feel much worse for all those babies and old people who don't have enough to eat. It is so terrible. I am young and can take care of myself. They are so helpless." The brightness of Snezana's shining blue eyes faded in a film of tears as she talked. "It is all so sad. We were such a happy people. We had everything. With my mother and aunt and I all working, I always had plenty of money. I traveled all around the world. I got some discounts for working for the airline, but only a little. We all traveled. Yugoslavians were the second most traveled people in the world after Canadians. I went to Italy to buy my clothes, and so did many others. We had a good life. Now it is all destroyed, and I don't know how we will recover." Snezana was now having her clothes tailored in Belgrade because ready-made clothes were much more expensive. "Labor is cheaper," she explained.

Serbs were masochists, Snezana told me. "They are always trying to help people at their own expense." Was this part of the victim mentality I had heard about, in part the feeling that the other Yugoslav republics never appreciated the Serbs' efforts on their behalf in fighting off the various conquerors that had overrun the Balkans since the fourteenth century? "You might say that. Certainly we are a strange people, always feeling that we must help others. We are known for our generosity and hospitality, as if, if we were not kind to people, they would harm us. For instance, you'll never find a Serb treating you the way the French treat visitors.

"We are a strange, slightly crazy people," she told me. "We are always trying to please. We'll do anything to please. We let people do their will with us." But, I countered, "you have certainly fought back over the centuries—against the Turks, the Austrians, the Nazis. And you have been aggressors at times in history, and certainly in the current war you started out as the aggressors." She seemed uneasy with my comment and replied, "Well, yes, but our thinking, our way of dealing every day in the world with people is as I've described, which in a way is more important. We always think we must be humble, as if we were slaves, as if we shouldn't assert ourselves or we'll be punished. I don't know if that's what you mean by a victim mentality, but it seems to me it could be described that way."

Snezana is a plump, greying, tired-looking woman except that her blue eyes glisten in her round face. She has a quick, eager smile, a high-pitched birdlike voice, and a nervous laugh that seems to say she is eager to please. In the break in our conversation she went to the kitchen to prepare a bit of supper for me, what she called mincemeat pie, a delicious flaky meat pastry followed by a piece of heavenly flourless nutty chocolate cake. She had bought the ingredients for the cake with her most recent fee for English classes. These treats were left over from a party she had given the night before for a young cousin who was emigrating to Canada, over which she expressed great sadness. "But there is nothing else for the young people to do," she said.

At 7:45 Snezana walked me to the corner where Dr. Ljiljana Dimitrijevic, a friend of David's, was to pick me up to take me to a performance of the Belgrade Philharmonic. We said goodbye with promises to talk again soon.

Ljiljana whizzed me across the city in her little Yugo, pulling up in front of the rather pedestrian-looking hall and parking on the sidewalk right at the entrance with many other cars parked there. The hall was good-sized, with 875 seats on the main floor and in the balcony, with wood-paneled walls, a spacious, unadorned lobby with a large cloakroom, and clean, ample washrooms. The lobby was filled with well-dressed middle-aged people, as one sees at symphony concerts everywhere. They all seemed to know one another. The chatter filled the high-ceilinged room. Once again I was struck with how tall and attractive were the Serbian men. One doesn't see a great many tall men in American concert halls. And the women, handsomely, stylishly dressed, were also very attractive and on the whole taller than

Western women, though Ljiljana was not among these tall women. A striking woman with a great mop of tightly curled midnight black hair, very dark, luminous eyes, sharp features, and very little makeup, she stood out even in this good-looking crowd, not the least for her elegant, understated clothes. No doubt she had bought them in Italy on one of her trips to visit her sister who lived in Rome.

The audience filled every seat. Obviously the embargo had not ended the cultural life of Belgrade. While most people in the city were living on the barest rations, there were still people who could afford to buy symphony tickets, which were expensive in Belgrade though much cheaper than in the U.S. While the audience seated in the hall was mostly middle-aged or older, after intermission the aisles lining the walls were filled with mostly young people. Ljiljana explained that at intermission the doors were opened free to everyone without a ticket, for standing room. "Most concerts are also broadcast on television, and they have a big audience," she added.

As undistinguished as the building was, so was the orchestra, though the audience didn't seem to mind. It was about half women—the first violinist was a woman—and most of the players were young. Under the guest baton of a young Russian conductor-cellist, Alexander Rubin, the orchestra performed creditably a fiercely modern but quite accessible composition, clearly influenced by Western modernism but more melodic, by a young Belgrade woman, Isadora Zhebeljan. The piece received no more than a polite reception, just as such compositions receive in the U.S. Rubin then played the Haydn Concerto for Viola, Cello, and Orchestra No. 2, which overjoyed the audience. Rachmaninoff was also a happy choice.

At intermission Ljiljana introduced me to Cedomir Mirkovic, an imposing man who was president of the Social Democratic party, of which Ljiljana and her husband were members. Mirkovic gave me his card, and I promised to call for an appointment. He was eager to talk with me, he said. This was the beginning, I realized, of that process which would enable me to meet far more people than I would have time to talk with. Those I would meet would introduce me to others whom they were sure could tell me more about the Serbian side of the story of the war and events in Belgrade. Snezana had mentioned a couple of people she hoped I would talk with. Now Ljiljana was bringing me people. David had told me she knew the entire intelligentsia in Belgrade and would be a valuable resource.

I invited Ljiljana to join me for coffee after the concert, but she begged off. She was too tired. So was I. We would talk again the next day, and I would see her the next evening at the Serbian-Jewish Friendship Society executive committee meeting to which she had invited me. I gave her a twenty-dollar bill which she promised to exchange for dinars for me. She had offered to do my money changing with her street vendor because she could get better rates for me than in a bank or other legal exchange center. As with all other commodities, the black market money economy was the most flourishing.

Back in my hotel room I poured myself a drink, undressed, and sat down to write this day's journal. Already I felt as if I'd been in Belgrade a week instead of only two days. So far I had talked only with women. David told me that he'd found the women in Belgrade "rather fierce, dominant and aggressive, but very feminine." The role of women here was certainly an interesting sidelight.

Ljiljana told me she wanted to take me to the symphony so that I could see that Belgrade was not the barbaric place it was described as in the Western press. Snezana proudly showed me around her apartment and fed me delicious food as if to say, You see how well we live here. None of this felt "crazy" to me, despite the talk of Serbian craziness.

3 The Yugoslavs are the poorest billionaires on earth. Ljiljana brought me an envelope full of dinars that she got from her street money changer, Draga, in exchange for the twenty dollars I had given her last night. The package contained 390 billion dinars in 50-billion dinar notes printed on thin paper, as most European notes are, in two colors with a historical figure—pretty, and almost worthless. How does one face up to going to the market for a loaf of bread with billions of dinars? The thought was stupefying.

Ljiljana laughed as I opened the envelope and stared at the money, astonished. "This is what has become of us," she said. "We laugh through our tears. What else can we do? This is what the embargo has done to us."

She brought the envelope to me at the headquarters of the Serbian-Jewish Friendship Society on the ground floor of a modern high-rise building on a largely residential street in central Belgrade, where I would attend her 5 p.m. executive committee meeting. The Society had three large rooms, attractively decorated—a central room where classes were taught, an office, and a meeting room with couches and chairs that held about a dozen people, the room where the executive committee met every Tuesday. The secretary brought in a tray of coffee and tea, and everyone settled back for the meeting, for these people obviously a comfortable routine enhanced by the presence of an American journalist who would listen to them.

The Serbian-Jewish Friendship Society, with branches in the U.S. that call themselves the Jewish-Serbian Friendship Society, was founded in 1988 by a group of eminent elderly Serbian intellectuals—including Dobrica Cosic, the former president of Yugoslavia, a famous novelist—to stimulate friendlier relations between Israel and Yugoslavia. Tito, in a rare tribute to the Soviet Union, had always refused to recognize Israel, but after his death that breach was repaired, and now Israel had twenty-two sister cities in Yugoslavia, the most important of which was Belgrade–Tel Aviv. The exchanges with Israel, however, had been temporarily shelved. Though there was much support for Serbia in Israel, the country had officially supported the UN position in Yugoslavia's war, so diplomatic relations were all but severed. "They have to," one committee member said, "because they are part of America's military-industrial complex. They are entirely dependent on that complex for survival. Whatever they may believe as individuals, the state must follow the U.S."

Within several months of its founding, the Society had recruited some ten thousand members, about half of them Jews. The Belgrade group had lost touch with the Society's Croatian members since the war began. There were no phone lines between the two countries. Borders were closed. To travel to Zagreb from Belgrade, one had to take a six-hour bus ride to Budapest, then another six-hour ride to Zagreb, a trip that once could be made in less than six hours. And taking the bus was necessary because there was such a shortage of gasoline in Belgrade that no one could drive that distance. The committee members said they had no hope of countering the anti-Semitism that has arisen in Croatia as a consequence of the Nazification of that country, and they had no idea what their colleagues there were doing about it or how they were faring. I received one report from a Jewish leader in Zagreb that Jews were not yet in danger, but he didn't know what the future would bring.

While the Society offered classes in Hebrew and other subjects, it seemed to function mainly as a debating forum for the charming, aging intellectuals who formed its executive committee. Ljiljana was the exception, the youngest of the members by about fifteen years, and the only woman on the executive committee. She said little and took her cues from her elders, but as a gentile she seemed strangely committed to this mission. She was taking Hebrew lessons, was strongly identified with the purposes of the group, and planned to go to Israel when the sanctions were lifted and she could again get a visa.

For now the Society's mission was twofold: counter any anti-Semitism that might arise in Yugoslavia as a consequence of American Jewish support for the embargo and for military attacks against the Serbs, and muster support for Serbia among world Jewry. It was unlikely that local Serbs would turn on the Jews in Yugoslavia; they were viewed by many Jews worldwide as the least anti-Semitic people. A writer in the *Jerusalem Post* wrote in February 1994, "The Serbs are one of the very few philosemitic people in Europe; . . . a great majority of them tried to help 'their' Jews during the Nazi occupation." But the peculiarly close relations between Serbs and Jews might turn ugly, like family members in a fractious disagreement, though at the time there was no evidence for such a development.

The committee members were outraged that the Holocaust Memorial Museum in Washington had invited to its opening ceremonies the president of Croatia, Franjo Tudjman, who had written a book denying the reality of and at the same time justifying the Holocaust, but had not invited Dobrica Cosic or any other Serbian representative.

Cosic was not present at the meeting I attended, but eight members of the executive committee were there, hearty and strong-looking though all but Ljiljana were over seventy, some white-haired, others balding, some in suits and ties, others more casually dressed in sweaters and slacks. Their main purpose that evening was to discuss a letter they would send to Jewish organizations around the world that supported the embargo and the use of military power against their fellow Serbs in Bosnia. The committee was appalled by American Jewish support for the Bosnian Muslims who had slaughtered so many Jews in World War II. They were convinced that Jewish support "for aggression against Serbia is an extraordinarily cynical policy that results from Israel's dependence on the U.S.," one member said. Another added, "It is a terrible violation of the Jewish ethic to support this policy. They have forgotten how Serbs tried to save Jews from the Nazis and how Serbs and Jews were slaughtered together and how there never was here, like in Central Europe, anti-Semitism before the war."

Of the eighty thousand Jews in Yugoslavia before World War II, twenty thousand survived—a large proportion compared with other Eastern European countries. Most of the survivors emigrated to Israel after the war. Only six thousand were left in Serbia, with fifteen hundred in Belgrade. Every Serbian city had a synagogue led by a lay leader because there was only one rabbi serving them all. The practice of Judaism had been discouraged under Tito, like all other religions, but after his death in 1980 there was a rebirth of religious practice.

Serbs' intense identification with Jews as fellow victims of the criminality of nations leads them to a series of comparisons between the Jews and themselves. "What is happening to us now," one committee member said, "is *cold* genocide, not hot genocide as happened in the war, with death by gas and gun, but by deprivation and starvation and perhaps, at some point, by guns as well."

One of the members pointed out to me a strong parallel between Nazi propaganda against the Jews and the current propaganda against the Serbs. For example, the accusation of mass rape by the Serbs, he said, was comparable to the accusation of ritual child killing leveled for many years against the Jews. The accusation against the Serbs of wanting to control all of Yugoslavia was comparable to age-old accusations against the Jews of wanting to take over the world, of controlling various industries, and so on. All his fellow members strongly agreed. Another said, "These accusations are pure propaganda. Rape is a traditional part of war, but there have been no more rapes by Serbs than by Muslims or Croatians. As for wanting to control all of Yugoslavia, all we wanted was equality."

"Yes, indeed," another member said. "Tito's policy was to undercut Serbia in order to control its influence and the Serbs who live widely through all the republics. We wanted to regain influence that Serbia legitimately deserved."

I felt as if I were in a small ivory tower cut off from the rest of Serbia as I listened to these garrulous men talk heatedly and often obscurely, as intellectuals sometimes do, about the economics and politics of Yugoslavia and the failure of Leninism. Where had they been when Milosevic was proclaiming loud and long his dream for a greater Serbia? How did they miss the process by which Milosevic's nationalism contributed so greatly to the secession of the other republics and then to the wars? How did they manage to overlook the mess the Yugoslav economy had been in when they talked about how, had it not been for the sanctions, Yugoslavia would have created a new economic system, different from the free-market economies that were having so much trouble getting started in the rest of Eastern Europe? Instead they all agreed that Yugoslavia had had "an incremental plan for denationalization in which appropriate steps would gradually be taken toward capitalism, but the sanctions destroyed all that."

As state control was reduced and more capitalism was introduced in the late 1980s, high inflation and joblessness arose, just as happened throughout Eastern Europe and the Soviet Union whenever privatization was taking place. Certainly Serbia was further along toward privatization than most of the rest of Eastern Europe, but I had gathered from my reading that no hard planning was being done, that instead the economy was simply floundering under Milosevic's leadership. He seemed to be more interested in whipping up nationalist hysteria than putting the economy together. In fact his nationalist campaign was merely a cover for his not having a clue about what to do about the economy. How had this little band of Serbian intellectuals missed all that? I decided to hold my questions for another visit, or perhaps forever. Most of these men had been cloistered in the academy or had comfortable jobs that no doubt protected them from reality. Now they were retired, trying to live on pensions that had been reduced to almost nothing, their savings frozen or stolen by the bankrupt government. Suddenly they were confronting what must have been a terrible reality. Why disturb their fantasies?

At eight o'clock, when the meeting ended and I had promised to return the following Tuesday, I went with my friend David Moss, who had served as my interpreter, to find a taxi to take us to the Saint's Day party of Milic od Macva, Yugoslavia's most famous, richest painter. David said he had another appointment. Would I mind if we stayed only an hour or so? I was grateful; I was still jet-lagging. We drove through the city to a hilly, wooded section that looked like wild countryside with only an occasional house but was in fact within the city limits, along with several other such sections.

The huge house, almost mansionlike, in a bowdlerized Serbian Byzantine style, had been built by Milic and his friends. It stood on a large plot of land where he grew apples, grapes, and a variety of vegetables.

As we entered the house we were greeted by men who looked like bodyguards. They escorted us to a table that held a large bowl of a delicious concoction of ground wheat, sugar, vanilla, and crushed walnuts, surrounded by hunks of bread and bottles of wine, a religious tradition for this *slava*, a personal Orthodox holiday, the birthday of one's patron saint that all Serbs celebrate. We made our way into the huge party rooms, four of them, overflowing with people sitting down to dinner on metal plates. I estimated 150 people, arty or professional, rough-hewn or very smooth—a great array of men in business suits and others in blue jeans, women in prim suits and dresses, smartly coiffed, others in great finery, and others in elaborate arty costumes—artists, writers, musicians, business people who were Milic's patrons, a few priests, relatives, and some political cronies. At our table sat a filmmaker and his girl friend, a cabaret singer, a painter, and a Yuppie-style businessman who had done postgraduate work in mechanical engineering at the University of California at Berkeley, returned home to work, and, at forty, decided he "needed to make some money." Two years ago he had gone to Moscow to open an engineering company. He was getting rich, he said, but might not live to enjoy it. "The Mafia kills foreign businessmen in Moscow who don't pay up," he explained. He and his attractive wife had obviously bought their clothes in Italy or France and were in sharp contrast to the artists at the table who wore blue jeans and sweaters or simple, slightly arty dresses. He was one of Milic's patrons.

After the soup, David went to find Milic to introduce him. He had warned me that the artist was eccentric. Wearing a light blue military-style suit with brass buttons zigzagging down the front, sporting a greying beard and a great head of grey hair, Milic was a small, slightly rotund man with a broad smile and bright blue eyes. Shaking my hand happily, he talked away at me in Serbian. I nodded with what I hoped was a small bit of graciousness. It was clear that he didn't know or care that I didn't speak his language. Then I made a fatal mistake: I mispronounced his name. I had neglected to ask David to spell it out for me so that I would get it right. Milic was incensed. He gave me a look of pure contempt, muttered what David said was an obscenity, and marched off in a huff. We stayed at the party until 3 a.m., but Milic never gave me another look.

The second course was a veal stew, followed by roast pig done over an outdoor open fire, Serbian-style dolma, roast lamb, and an assortment of tiny, very rich cakes, plum brandy (slivovitz), the traditional drink of the Serbs, coffee, and French brandy. All the while the Yugoslav white wine flowed freely. The lavish meal, I learned, was commonplace among the Serbs, as was the absence of vegetables and the abundance of meat. In the market that afternoon I'd seen tomatoes, cabbages, potatoes, and scraggly carrots for sale—no other vegetables, just as in Hungary and Czechoslovakia, where I'd also missed vegetables. Others reported the same scarcity in the Soviet Union.

The meal had been prepared by Milic's friends and supervised by his sister, a plain-looking woman who seemed put upon and who also did a great deal of the serving and clearing. Milic had obviously bought all this meat on the black market; no such plenty was available in ordinary stores, as I had learned earlier in the day on a visit to a couple of markets to see for myself the empty shelves I'd heard about. The shelves, the meat counters, the fruit and vegetable bins were indeed empty. A few rotten-looking pears were on sale. Some potatoes. Cheese was in relative abundance. There was a little meat, too—ham and veal, at about fifteen dollars a pound. The wine shelves held a few bottles, as did the soda shelves. A box or two of cereal. Some milk. Plenty of mineral water. Everything was very expensive. The overall impression was barrenness, with people hunting for something, anything to feed their families, anything they could find and afford to buy. I had found a little independent food shop down the street from my hotel that was more abundantly stocked, obviously bought from the black market. I bought a few pears that looked much healthier than those in the supermarkets.

After the meal I took a walk through Milic's house, up the stairs to his studio and private living space. All the rooms were filled with a grand mélange of antique furniture, and every inch of the walls was covered with his paintings—dark, grim-looking, semisurrealist landscapes and portraits, realistic portraits and religious art that had me wondering what the other art in Belgrade was like if this artist was the most famous. I'd been told that his best market was in Belgium, where there was more money to spend on art. These paintings were not even masterfully rendered—quite amateurish, in fact, and quite oppressive in their dark, somber tones and heavy-handed symbolism. I was glad Milic wasn't speaking to me; I find it difficult to speak well of work I don't like.

Back at the dinner table I asked David what had happened to his resolve to leave in an hour. It was now 10:30. "I didn't want to drag you away," he said, "you seemed to be having such a good time." A few minutes later Milic began the speechmaking for which he apparently was also famous. This painter sounded like a mighty prophet as he began denouncing the West. "The West is evil. I want nothing more to do with it. Once, as a painter, my identity was linked with the West. No more. Serbia is all." For the next five hours Milic ranted this line, then read his poetry, introduced others who joined him in his nationalist ravings or read their poetry, then took the floor again to continue his own harangue. Some applauded him loudly, others applauded politely, others sat on their hands. Had I left Belgrade the next day, I would have gone away believing that Mile Manic was right, that the Serbs were mad with their newfound nationalism. David told me that Milic was widely approved as a painter but dismissed or despised for his politics by most of the intelligentsia. Clearly, however, he had company in his madness. Though some obviously disagreed with what he said, I sensed overall a great fondness for this highly eccentric artist.

Sometime around 2 a.m. David rose angrily to defend the American people. "Their government is wrong in its policies," he said in his perfect Serbian, "but the American people are good people, just as the Serbs are good people." In this setting, knowing Milic, he didn't dare add that he thought that the Serb government was also wrong in its policies. He would no doubt have been thrown out. The crowd applauded loudly, almost as if they were relieved to praise the Americans they had always admired. Milic stood by stoically, as if understanding that an American would have to say these things. When David finished, Milic put his arm around David and gave him a bear hug as if to say, "All is forgiven."

At about 3 a.m. Milic called on everyone to join him in song to end the party. A man with a lovely tenor voice rose to lead the singing, which many people stood to join. They began with an 1806 song, "Stand Up, Serbia," which says, "Wake up, Serbia, you have slept too long. There is an avalanche. Wake up." Then they worked their way through a variety of other nationalist tunes, ending with "Boze Pravde" (God Is Justice), the Serbian national anthem, with music by a Slovenian musician who threw in his lot with the Serbs and with lyrics by a famous Serbian poet, Jovan Jjordjevic (1826–1900), that say,

God of Justice, thou who hath saved us
from destruction 'til now,
Hear again our voices
and from now on be our salvation.
With thy mighty hand lead, defend
the future of our Serbian heritage.

I took away from that party the memories of a great variety of people, a broader mix than at any party I could remember.

I wondered how many other gatherings in Belgrade resembled this one. "Too many, I suspect," Karl Haupt, a friend of David's, said somberly. David disagreed. "Milic is the most militant nationalist in the city." But he didn't sound much different from some of Milosevic's speeches I had read, I told David. "Yes, but most people just don't carry on that way. Many of them may be moved by what Milosevic says, but they don't have Milic's wild personality. And most people don't get caught up in politics that way."

"Probably not, but many of them may carry the same sentiments around inside them. Those sentiments have led some men to take up arms and join the Serbs in Bosnia in a holy war," I said.

"True, but the opposite sentiments have kept many men at home, have led some to desert the army, and have led many Bosnian and Croatian Serbs to come to Yugoslavia to escape the fighting," Karl said.

David and Karl had laughingly told me that such late-night parties on weekdays were common in Belgrade. "The Serbs never sleep," they said. Back in my hotel room, I wondered how I was going to survive this sort of routine. I half hoped I would get no more such invitations, and at the same time I looked forward to them. People more easily say what's on their mind in the middle of the night, half drunk.

4 I had met Mira Blagojevic, who owned Super Travel in Belgrade, on the phone from Chicago. My Serbian travel agent had put me in touch with her. She would get me a modestly priced hotel with a decent restaurant and adequate room service, and she would handle my hotel bills so I could get the full advantage of the black market exchange rate. We talked a couple of times. She was friendly and helpful, and I expected her to be a pleasant, rather bland young woman, based on my experiences with travel agents in the U.S.

I began to wonder whether I might be wrong in my expectations when I approached her office in an old building across from an art gallery in Skadarlija. A small, attractive metal sign with her agency's name on it was attached to the front of the crumbling building. As I walked up three flights of dimly lit stairs amidst falling plaster, I was nervous about what I might find. But Super Travel's offices were light and airy, freshly painted, and handsomely furnished with simple modern furniture and gauze curtains at the huge windows. Interiors in Belgrade rarely matched exteriors; I hadn't yet met enough people to determine whether the same was true for them.

Mira Blagojevic was in her fifties, a tall, large-boned, slightly heavy-set woman with a little pot belly. She was a handsome woman with great, round grey eyes and soft greying blond hair, a slightly smoky, sweet voice, elegantly dressed in a grey plaid suit and silk blouse, diamond studs in her ears, and a charming seductive manner. As I opened the door she called out, "That must be our American guest. Welcome!"

Mira invited me into her office and asked her pretty, shy young assistant, Ljubica, to get us some coffee. She lit a cigarette, leaned forward on her desk, and asked, "So what do you think of Belgrade?" I told her about Milic's party, leaving out the political part, not knowing yet what her sentiments were. She laughed and said, in softly accented English, "We all used to eat like that all the time. We had a very good life, but now Belgrade is a very sad city. But I hope you will like it and enjoy your visit. Milic is a very funny man, very famous."

I told her about my trip. "I was afraid something like that might happen. I'm sorry you had to have such a bad time of it," she said. It was over, I assured her, and I was considering going back on another airline. Could she handle that for me? "Of course," she said, "I'm here to do anything I can to help you."

Mira had been in the travel business for thirty-five years, the first thirty working for the Yugoslav airlines, part of that time in New York and Chicago. A few years ago she had opened Super Travel and had done well with it. Now she was specializing in trips to foreign-language schools, especially in the U.S., for people who expected to work or study abroad. But her business, like most other businesses in Belgrade, had declined badly, and she was anxious about it. People no longer had money to travel. Most of her customers were emigrés— one-way tickets with no hope of more business.

Mira's only son, Andreas, who was twenty-three, was at the University of Illinois at Chicago studying for his doctorate in pharmacology. She hadn't seen him for nearly a year and missed him, but she was glad he was away from Belgrade, safe from the army. "I couldn't stand it if he went into the army. You never know what can happen now, any time. We may get attacked. They may send the army back into Bosnia. It is too terrible. I can't think of it. I don't watch television any more. I don't read the papers. I don't want to know. I can't stand it anymore."

Not being able to stand it didn't stop Mira from explaining to me the start of the Yugoslav wars. "When Tudjman came to power," she told me, "and declared that Croatia was a country for the Croats, the Serbs got scared that what happened in the war would happen again. So they said they wanted the Krajina, where most of the Serbs in Croatia lived, for themselves as an independent state. Tudjman said no, but the Serbs were convinced that was the thing they had to do. I don't know, no one seems to know, how the fighting actually started, but considering what was happening, it seems logical that the Croats fired first to stop the Serbs from getting their independence. But maybe the Serbs started it. No one knows for sure. Anyhow, it started in just one village and then spread, and then the Yugoslav army went in because the government wanted to keep Yugoslavia as a whole country. The Croats pulled out of the army and made their own army. And then came all the hell."

I asked Mira about the terrible destruction wrought by the Yugoslav army, for instance, the shelling of the beautiful old city of Dubrovnik on the Adriatic Sea. "That was propaganda," she said strongly. "You have to go and see. The old city was hardly touched. We have pictures. What the Croats did was to pile up tires behind the old city and set them on fire to make it look as if the city had been bombed, but we have pictures—and CNN had them too—that show that the old city is hardly touched. There was so much propaganda going on. The worst damage in the city was done to the Orthodox Church. That was not done by Serbs."

Of all the damage done by Serb and Croatians in Croatia, perhaps the alleged damage to Dubrovnik had struck me most. The Yugoslav army had shelled the town, provoked by Croats firing from historic monuments. I had read of its destruction with a sad heart. Here was Mira insisting that the news of Dubrovnik's destruction was greatly exaggerated propaganda.

"A lot of us have lost our property on the seacoast," Mira said, making very personal the fighting along the Adriatic. "I myself had a flat there. Everything was confiscated.

"The atmosphere is now so terrible. It is so unbelievable that it should happen there. I never thought of anyone as Serb or Croatian, each person was an individual. And now everyone is first asking what you are.

"You know, when Tito made the borders of the republics he ignored ethnic considerations. If you look at the map you'll see that Croatia is mostly a long, thin section along the Adriatic, where all the tourists come. The rest of the area, not so profitable, he gave to Bosnia. And a lot of Montenegro, also on the Adriatic, he gave to Croatia, even though the Montenegrins are mostly Serbs. And in Kosovo he encouraged the Albanians to come there to dilute the Serbian population. The border was open and he did nothing to prevent the mass migration. And they drove the Serbs out."

Mira described the process of blockbusting that was used to drive Serbs out of Kosovo. "They threatened them—if they didn't leave they would be killed. One man I knew was working in his fields, and they came and tied him up and blindfolded him as if they were going to kill him, and then threatened to kill him if he didn't leave. Thousands left. And now we could have a war there because the Serbs will not let the Albanians have their independence because we have all the great early monasteries there. It is the cradle of Serbia, so called. Serbs will not let Kosovo become an Albanian state."

I asked Mira how Tito drew the borders. "Well, under King Aleksander, there were no separate countries. He wanted to unify all the South Slavs, he said, but he certainly wanted to be the big Serbian king to rule over all Yugoslavia. Then, after the war, when Tito came to power, he also wanted to be the big ruler, but he was not a Serb but a Croatian. He carved up the country so the Serbs could no longer be the main power. In 1974 he divided Serbia into three parts, giving Vojvodina and Kosovo autonomy with a bigger vote in the Parliament than Serbia. Then, when Milosevic came to power, he said no to that division. He said we want Serbia to be whole again, and he removed the autonomy of Vojvodina and Kosovo. Now the Albanians in Kosovo have declared their independence."

Mira left out of her story the fact that when Milosevic came to power he not only revoked the autonomy granted Kosovo by Tito, he also stripped the Albanians of government jobs, including the police, and sent Serbs in to fill those jobs.

"As bad as those artificial borders were," Mira continued, "it was worse what Tito did about the ethnic languages. In America everybody can speak his own language at home and have his own customs, but English is the official language and everyone must learn to speak it. [In fact the U.S. does not have an "official" language, which has upset some people who fear Spanish is overtaking English and who object to "English as a Second Language" classes in schools.] Under Tito every group could speak its own language. The Albanians had their own language, their own schools. Slovenians have their own language. There was no official language in Yugoslavia, and that caused great damage, if you ask me."

Tito's encouragement of peoples to speak their own language was part of his overall plan to diminish the influence of the Serbs, whose language was dominant in Yugoslavia (until the war the language was called Serbo-Croatian), and to enhance his own power. While Tito cut across natural ethnic boundaries to create artificial republics, mixing all ethnic groups with the ostensible purpose of unifying the country, at the same time he heightened ethnic divisions by encouraging the use of separate ethnic languages and schools, two of the most crucial influences on the affairs of people.

"But no one complained," Mira said, "because Yugoslavia was united, and that was good for us. You know, I lived in Chicago for two years, and there are many Serbs there. In the Yugoslav Club we would celebrate Slovenian Night, Croatian Night, Macedonian Night—but we never had a Serbian night because the Serbs were afraid of antagonizing the others."

There seemed to be a lot of hostility to Tito among the Serbs, I remarked to Mira. "Yes, but on the other hand, the Serbs are the ones who kept him in power, and others resented that. Serbs were in the police and in the government and didn't complain about anything. It's very funny about Serbs. When we like somebody, you can be my equal and I'll do everything you say, not thinking with my brain. Even though Tito was bad in some ways for the Serbs, he was good in other ways. We had such a good life. Foolish, but that's our mentality. Emotional, not rational. Now I think we are trying, but of course it's very late. Now we are under this embargo, and our economy is ruined."

Mira's description of the Serbs as trying now to be rational seemed a little out of joint with the raw emotionalism I had observed at Milic's party. The rise of nationalism among the Serbs and their support of Milosevic over the past several years seemed to have little to do with rationality. Extreme nationalism is hardly a well-considered, rational policy. It creates the bitterest of hatreds of "outsiders" and has often led to disastrous wars. Tito understood this and used his knowledge to consolidate his power.

We talked about how, when the sanctions were lifted, the economy could be restored. I said the only path I could see was through the massive investment of foreign capital, but that didn't seem to be forthcoming in the Soviet Union and Eastern Europe. Yugoslavia had once been able to inspire loans and aid from the U.S. and the International Monetary Fund, but that was in the context of the cold war when Yugoslavia served as a buffer to the Soviet Union.

"I think we could rebuild by ourselves," Mira said. "If you know the Serbs in America, they are very hard-working people, very honest. They know how to save, how to build a business. I think we can do that here too, without communism always holding us back. I think we are very similar to the Jews. We're a very honest people. I'm talking globally, of course. You can always find the bad."

In fact I knew Serbs in Chicago who were quite successful in business and the professions. Mira thought that under Tito's rule there had been few incentives to work hard and save. The League of Communists, which Tito's party was called, controlled jobs, and even with self-management there was little incentive. But she was sitting before me as an example of the private enterprise that had slowly been developing in Yugoslavia among people of ambition. In the streets of Belgrade I had seen all kinds of small private businesses that had opened in recent years. Most of the retail shops were now privately owned. But the question of where the capital would come from to rebuild the economy in this bankrupt nation was not clear. "We will have to borrow," Mira said, "but we are safe borrowers."

Mira paused a moment, lit another cigarette, and said, "I don't think we deserved these sanctions. If the West knew the history of what went before, they wouldn't have been so quick to accept Croatia, Slovenia, Bosnia as independent, and our position would be understood better. But it was all under the influence of Germany."

Here was the German issue again. In the March 24, 1994, issue of the *New York Review of Books*, the German philosopher Jurgen

Habermas said in an interview, "If you look at the German elites it is possible to discern a powerful desire to turn Germany into an independent great power in the center of Europe, with its gaze fixed on the East." He referred to remarks made by Edmund Stoiber, the conservative minister of the interior in Bavaria, who said that "the Federal Republic should go its own way and have its own foreign policy, particularly with regard to Eastern Europe." Habermas commented, "This trend is gaining in strength and it can be summed up as the view that Germany must become a Central European great power again." A weakened Yugoslavia, with independent nations that feel strong ties with Germany, makes the Serbs' view of German mischief in Yugoslavia not quite so outlandish.

"It is so convenient for the West," Mira said, "to have this terrible situation in Yugoslavia, to have us so divided, fighting with each other. When I was in Chicago last December the propaganda against the Serbs was very high—all the terrible things the Serbs were doing to the young people in Bosnia. So many things. But now, if you look at the war between the Croatians and the Muslims, it is just as bad. You know, the Muslims are really Serbs or Croatians. This is a part of the world where people are like that [Churchill's "warlike race"?]. It's so terrible. I can hardly cut up a chicken, but they are killing like that.

"I don't think we had to have war. If only they had sat down to talk first. I think it was the influence of the Germans on the Slovenians first and then the Croats that led to the war. You see, the Germans have always wanted a path to the Adriatic through Croatia. And the Slovenians and Croats have always been close to the Germans. When the Croatians were celebrating their independence, they were singing German songs, thanking the Germans for their independence. And they are like the neo-Nazis in Germany. They have even taken up the old Nazi uniform again.

"You see, we Serbs are such a strange people. We will suffer so much just to show the world that they are wrong for thinking badly of us. When they said the embargo was coming, we said, 'Okay, let it come. It will do nothing to us. The world will see we can take it and survive.' "

Someone else had told me that Serbs are masochists. "We are, in the sense that we feel it is better to suffer than to try to explain that you are wrong. 'You will see one day' is our attitude. Absolutely crazy."

At that moment a friend of Mira's walked in, a tall, striking woman with long, blown-about dark hair, wearing a cotton jumper. Sloboda turned out to be the Muslim to whom Mira had referred earlier. She invited her to sit down and join our conversation and asked Ljubica to bring us all fresh coffee. She looked at my tape recorder and asked that I not use her real name. "My family is still in Dubrovnik, and they might be endangered. It is not good there," she said. Was the city destroyed? "No, of course not," she replied. "There was fighting there and things were hard, but the old city was not destroyed like Vukovar or Mostar. Nothing in Yugoslavia is any good these days, but things are all right in Dubrovnik."

I wondered how she saw Milosevic's nationalist campaign from her Muslim point of view. "It was not only Milosevic. It was all the Yugoslavs. It was the long suppression of people's identity—and then suddenly it can be expressed and it all boils out. The war is like a bad divorce. You have one TV set and I say, 'The TV set is mine,' and he says, 'No, it is mine.' And there is a fight, and he takes an axe and breaks it in two and says, 'Take your part.' It is something we all have in us. The Balkans were colonized by all kinds of barbarians—the Mongols, the Turks—and every one of them has left a little of their meanness in our blood. That's how we all reacted, and it's all very suicidal and stupid.

"Everything is now broken down and you're looking at the pieces. I want you to know that one year I went both to the Bahamas and Hawaii. The average American can't afford that, nor can Eastern Europeans. But we could. They hated us really, for what we had."

Mira added, "We had everything—lovely mountains, lakes, our beautiful rivers, everything, just everything in such a small country. And everybody liked it until the politicians—the Germans . . ."

"Yes, the Germans," Sloboda said. "You know, Yugoslavia is sort of the crossroads, and we always pay for that, for somebody else's interests."

Sloboda had some private business to talk over with Mira, which she did in Serbian. After she left, Mira and I took care of our business, arranging for me to come to her office once a week. I would give her dollars, and she would pay the hotel for me. Saying goodbye, she asked Ljubica to walk with me to Srpskih Vladara (the Avenue of the Rulers)—renamed from Marshal Tito Boulevard—and send me on my way back to the hotel. The streets in Belgrade, like so many old cities in Europe, are a maze of twisting byways. It didn't help that I couldn't read the street signs written in Cyrillic and so had great trouble following the map.

As we rounded the corner away from Skadarlija, we came to Trg Republica (Republic Square), a large lovely square with statuary, trees, and shrubbery, fronting the National Museum and the National Theatre. These baroque-style buildings had been recently restored, in sharp contrast to most of the city's crumbling buildings. Off the square led Knez Mihailo (King Michael), the main shopping plaza in Belgrade, a wide cobblestone street closed to autos, where all the shops were now almost empty.

On the square was a small group of people holding a large banner that Ljubica told me said, "Women in Black for Peace." She hurried me past, trying not to notice the demonstration. Clearly she did not want me to think she had any sympathy for these mavericks. Nor did I wish to give her the impression I had any particular interest in them. I didn't think she would understand a journalist's interest. I wondered whether I would see some of these people the next day when I went to visit the Center for Anti-War Action.

5 In the busy, noisy offices of the Center for Anti-War Action I was transported back to the early 1960s and the American antiwar movement. People sat around then, as here, waiting for the action to start; others dashed about as if the action were about to start; in fact there was not much action at all. As in those days, these people now were frantically trying to gain support for opposition to a war they hated.

The people in Anti-War Action, Belgrade Circle (independent intellectuals, they called themselves), Autonomous Women's Groups, Women in Black for Peace, and the Humanitarian Law Fund all shared this large suite of offices in another crumbling building in downtown Belgrade. Their tactics were nonviolent direct action, following Gandhi—petitions, round table discussions, demonstrations (they called them public manifestations). They would have liked to bring down their popular president. Essentially they were Social Democrats who favored a strong government support system for the poor, for culture, and for industrial development, and they were strong civil libertarians. Interestingly, the new Yugoslav constitution of 1990, with some notable exceptions, reflected their views.

"The trouble with our law," said Sonja Biserko, unofficial head of the center, "is that we have all possible bills for all situations, but they are just not implemented. If you are talking about our laws, okay, some of them are very decent, but it doesn't matter. So when you go to the officials of some institution, they always produce some piece of paper that doesn't mean anything."

The Belgrade antiwar groups suffered a considerable isolation because their government and their army were not playing clear, unambiguous roles in the Yugoslav wars. The government was now assisting their fellow Serbs only with humanitarian aid, though the oppositionists were certain that the army was still providing military aid despite all kinds of denials. Sonja insisted that 30 percent of Yugoslavia's military budget went to the Serbs in the Krajina and Bosnia. In addition, many Serbian paramilitary irregulars were helping the Bosnians—with government approval and assistance, the antiwar activists claimed. But Milosevic had turned from a ferocious warmonger into a peacemaker, trying to convince the Bosnian Serbs to compromise, with little success. The Bosnian Serbs had their own agenda, and Milosevic had little influence despite the West's assumption that the call was his. Thus the dissidents confronted not a clear-cut outrage but one small nation embroiled in a religious-ethnic civil war with complex historical roots. It wasn't easy to assign blame, yet the antiwar movement in Belgrade seemed to have followed the West in failing to see the war's complexity. They too believed that Milosevic could end the war with the proper will, despite the evidence that the Muslims appeared to refuse any compromise offered by the Serbs and seemed to be making every effort to prolong the war in the hopes of gaining more territory.

So the antiwar groups were not having an easy time. They were tiny and isolated, scorned by their citizenry, ignored by the government and the media. At the Women in Black demonstration I had witnessed the day before, most people seemed to be treating them as Ljubica had, dismissively. I saw no one taking their leaflets. The people in the Center for Anti-War Action felt as if they were crying in the wilderness.

Not only were they facing a complex war, but their own city was under siege. The whole Western world was involved in this war and was subjecting the Serbians, as the so-called aggressors, to a massive campaign of economic destruction. In this atmosphere the antiwar movement didn't have much of a chance of influencing their fellow citizens or their government, especially because the activists were wholly funded from abroad, specifically the European Community (EC).

At the center I met a young American who was a full-time volunteer sponsored by the Brethren Volunteer Service, a religious service organization in the U.S. Michael Szporluk was twenty-five and received a stipend of four hundred dollars a month plus travel expenses. The rest of the small staff was local, and its salaries were paid by the EC. The rent on the center's offices, its state-of-the-art computers, copiers, faxes, and telephones, along with stipends for staff, were paid for by the EC, with additional help from individual European nations and the U.S. When I asked Sonja whether there were any local contributions, she scoffed. "All those who support us are really pauperized now," she said.

The center got its money by writing grants for projects and submitting them to the EC and various governments. "All our projects concern human rights protection, and I think this is an issue that is usually supported by governments and foundations abroad. Otherwise we wouldn't be able to organize anything. To have all this equipment in the office would be impossible." For Sonja it was a perfectly rational and natural thing that this local political organization was financed by other countries that had imposed sanctions on its homeland. The sympathies of those other governments were the same as the center's—distinctly anti-Serbian. If some people in Belgrade who knew the source of the center's funds believed they had a fifth column in their midst, it wasn't surprising.

Funds were granted not for operations but for specific projects—publications, including an English-language newsletter publicizing the work of the activists; an SOS hotline for refugees; and other plans, the biggest of which was the war crimes tribunal to prosecute Milosevic and others in his government and the army as war criminals. It seemed to me that these projects must be very well financed. A conference called by the center and the Belgrade Circle produced a scholarly book, *Yugoslavia: Collapse, War, Crimes*, edited by Sonja, in 1993, funded by the EC with additional funds from Sweden and Switzerland. In this volume a variety of papers analyzed the course of events in the former Yugoslavia, the nature of international law, and breaches of that law by the parties in the Yugoslav conflicts. While the book was apparently planned to set the stage for a tribunal, in fact it pointed out that massive violations of international law had been committed by all sides in the dispute—scarcely a likely circumstance in which to fashion a war crimes tribunal.

Nor does it seem likely, in light of EC, U.S., and UN reluctance to act in the former Yugoslavia, that any such powerful action might ever happen. Still, Milosevic's government had a committee preparing a defense in case a tribunal did eventuate. I was scheduled to talk with the head of that committee the next week.

In the dry tones I had come to expect, Sonja explained that the war crimes tribunal had always received the center's strong support. "It should involve Milosevic and the government, but not the ordinary people who are the executors of their policy. But I don't think the international community is very serious about it. They just bring it up as an issue and then drop it and then bring it up again, but unfortunately I don't think they are pushing it too hard because they are negotiating with war criminals, so how can it be? Someone has to be defeated here in order to be sent to a tribunal. So how do we achieve that? That's the problem."

Sonja held the Western nations heavily responsible for their failure to end the war. Had they acted more effectively and swiftly, she said, the war might have been brought to an end quickly. First, they should have immediately recognized the independence of all the republics of Yugoslavia instead of waiting until war had broken out. "It is nonsense that Germany was doing something terrible in recognizing Croatia and Bosnia first. It was French and English fear of German unification that held the whole thing up. But Germany is the leading power in Europe and should take its responsibility, which it isn't doing. What's wrong is ignorance and inefficiency in the European nations, and a lack of a political will to act. I think they should have intervened militarily in the early phase of the war. I think they didn't expect such wars, such force, to occur so quickly."

"Do you believe the sanctions are justified?" I asked her. "Well, yes," she said, a little more softly than usual, "because they had to show some will to punish the side which was most responsible, and there are no other mechanisms short of military intervention, so it was the right thing to do. But the sanctions have had no effect on the war in Bosnia, and even here our conditions are not a consequence of the sanctions but of the war itself and earlier economic policies. The sanctions actually help consolidate Milosevic's power. He blames the sanctions for everything. Meanwhile they rob the humanitarian aid that comes in, medicines and everything. A lot of people never see the medicines because they have to pay a lot of money for it. Yet we get it free from abroad. What comes in goes to the black market, and a few groups are getting rich on that. Humanitarian aid comes in not only from countries but from private firms, but the moment it crosses the border you can't trace it. The sanctions really help Milosevic because he gets sympathy for his cause by blaming the sanctions for the problems of the country."

I asked Sonja how many volunteers the center had. She told me, "We don't have any regular volunteers. We have people coming in to do special projects. We like to be very professional. We have people working on special projects, like conflict resolution work for violence against the radicals in Serbia, because the legal system is so bad, and the SOS Hotline for displaced people, though we cannot help very many."

Until very recently Yugoslavia had had no independent politics. There had been a small dissident movement among intellectuals in the 1960s, following such dissidence throughout the Western world, but it had been quickly and easily emasculated by Tito. So this antiwar movement had no sources to draw from. And for the last fifty years, politics had been considered the province of professional Communists. While a lot of independent politics in Belgrade now involved ordinary citizens, the attitude that political organizations should be run by professionals persisted, and amateurs were given little credence.

Sonja refused to call herself the director of the center, though she was one of a handful of founders and clearly seemed to be the leader. One of the few women I encountered in Belgrade wearing pants, she was a small, slender, rather severe-looking woman of forty-five with short cropped hair and no makeup, soft-spoken with a deep, somber voice and a rather shy demeanor. Her manner belied her twenty years' experience as a special adviser on European affairs in the Yugoslav foreign office, some of the time in London and Geneva. She had left in 1991 to start the center in opposition to the country's policies. She was a true professional.

Did she feel that the Yugoslav peace movement had a chance for success? "No," she said, laughing softly. "No, we have never been such a liberal society as you have been. I'm talking about the absence here of highly individualized personalities. This is a very collective society, very tribal in a way. It is not a modern society. Modernism came here with communism. You have crises in modernism all over the world, and the responses to the crises are different. Here in Serbia, Milosevic saw that there was enormous energy for change, and he began to mobilize the people around nationalist sentiments. The masses are not educated, not cultured, and they went to a very primitive kind of nationalism that he has abused. In the name of nationalism he is allowing all kinds of criminal acts—smuggling, everything—and he is giving people more and more space to act so."

One of Sonja's associates, Aleksandra Beric-Popovic, a darkly attractive young woman wearing the only arty silver earrings I'd seen in Belgrade, joined us to say, "Milosevic knows how to manipulate people. He started with the Academy of Science, the intellectuals and people like that, but that wasn't so easy. So he turned to the common people who feel very good being part of a crowd because that's what they have always been under communism, and they are willing to follow him."

Sonja added, "This is even before communism. It is just the pattern of this society. We don't have people thinking, Why is it happening, how is it happening? If they find they can't buy bread, they may begin to think, but as long as they have even their small rations they won't raise their voices. They believe what Milosevic tells them."

"But it will soon happen," I said, "that no one will be able to buy a piece of meat, which you people seem to live on." Sonja and Aleksandra laughed, and Aleksandra said dryly, "Welcome to the Balkans."

"But," Sonja said, "many people have relatives and friends in the villages and the countryside, and they can still get food. Agricultural production is down from last year, and now Milosevic has managed to rob farmers as well. He dropped the price of wheat very low so he can now buy it and distribute it to the workers, but he really robbed peasants, like he has robbed citizens by robbing their bank accounts. [In 1991 Milosevic was accused by the other republics of stealing 18.3 billion dinars from the National Bank of Yugoslavia, when this amount was still a lot of money.] But of course that can't go on, and the peasants are now saying they're not going to produce more than for themselves."

"Under present conditions," I said, "this society has to come apart. Don't you think people here will then react as they did against communism in the rest of Eastern Europe?"

Aleksandra said hotly, "There they acted against communism.

Here they would have to act against nationalism, and they are all nationalistic. Milosevic gets big majorities in elections." But Milosevic did not win a majority in the last election.

Sonja added, "It's a sort of trap. There is a minimum of social consensus, only about nationalism. They won't give that up perhaps ever, but not in this stage at least. Milosevic is still pretending to guarantee a minimum subsistence. Now he is raising pensions a little. People know things will get worse as soon as the elections are over, but they still think only in the framework of mere survival for two months.

"We have this war for which there is no rational explanation, and perhaps soon Serbia will be losing. I hope so. Greater Serbia is a disastrous idea. Such a state cannot be a democratic or a liberal society. But in order to avoid thinking about what is really happening, people use the mythology as an excuse for everything. People don't want to look at reality, war crimes, and all that. Watching TV, seeing the destruction of all those cities, like Dubrovnik, they need some explanation."

I told Sonja I had heard of and read conflicting reports from Dubrovnik. "Some said the old town has not been damaged, others insisted it has."

"I don't know what those people are talking about who say there was no damage in the old town." Sonja was clearly irritated. "Every cultural monument was damaged. I have friends who've been there and taken photos. And many people fled the town. And the surrounding town is completely destroyed. People returned to the farms and are living in stables because the houses are destroyed and robbed. That was the point. The Yugoslav army pillaged the towns in Croatia." I didn't bother to tell her that others pointed to different kinds of photos and to a propaganda campaign against the Serbs. She was adamant in her opinions, and I wasn't there to argue.

Wasn't it true that Serbia and Poland had been the only Eastern European countries to resist the Nazis? "That's nonsense," Sonja said. "All Yugoslavs fought Hitler. So this is also mythology. Really, we should hire someone who is not emotionally involved to write the modern history of the Balkans. It shouldn't be written by people who are from this region, because they have so many sentimental obstacles to objectivity. You will often hear Serbs say Slovenia and Croatia profited by exploiting them, and now the Slovenes are independent and not exploiting us anymore, but they are much better off than we are here. Or even Croatia, which is partly destroyed by the war, still has a better functioning economy than we do. And now they are trying to tell us that the economy is so bad because of the sanctions, but no, it is because before the war it was already collapsing. Nearby we have several factories that haven't been operating for years. The economy would be in the same shape without the sanctions. The only way it could have been saved was with foreign investment, and we are not a good risk for that."

That Serbia's economy was in bad shape before the sanctions was certainly true, and it seemed clear that the government had no solutions. But that the sanctions contributed greatly to its collapse was clear in even the simplest analysis. Without raw materials, factories cannot function, and Serbia imported much of its raw materials. Without products to sell, retail businesses can't function, and Serbia imported many of its manufactured items and wasn't getting any from its own factories. Without markets in other parts of Yugoslavia and abroad, manufacturing based on local products fails. Without gas and oil, which was imported, the economy falls apart. Farm equipment, factory equipment, public transportation, and so on can't function without energy. People can't drive their cars, heat their homes, cook. The list goes on.

Sonja's attitude toward Serbia's history reminded me of Henry Ford's "History is bunk." To dismiss history, or distort it with regard to World War II, when the record of Muslim and Croatian collaboration with the Nazis was quite clear, was to fail to understand the dynamics of the society she was trying to influence.

I was reminded of a passage in the 1945 historical novel *Bridge on the Drina*, the most celebrated work of the Nobel Prize–winning Yugoslav writer Ivo Andric. In it Andric tells the three-hundred-year history of his hometown, Visegrad, on the Bosnian-Serbian border, where Serbs and their brethren who had converted to Islam under the Turks lived—uneasily yet peacefully—side by side until the murder by a Serb of the Austrian archduke at Sarajevo that led to World War I. Though the Muslims bemoaned the passing of the Turkish occupation of Bosnia, they found a new loyalty to the Austrians who now occupied them, a loyalty not shared by the Serbs. Andric writes, "Only then began the real persecution of the Serbs and all those connected with them. The people were divided into the persecuted and those who persecuted them. That wild beast, which lives in man and does not dare to show itself until the barriers of law and custom have been removed, was now set free. The signal was given, the barriers were down. As has so often happened in the history of man, permission was tacitly granted for acts of violence and plunder, even for murder, if they were carried out in the name of higher interests, according to established rules, and against a limited number of men of a particular type and belief. A man who saw clearly and with open eyes and was then living could see how this miracle took place and how the whole of a society could, in a single day, be transformed. In a few minutes, the [Serb] business quarter, based on centuries of tradition, was wiped out. It is true there had always been concealed enmities and jealousies and religious intolerance, coarseness and cruelty, but there had also been courage and fellowship and a feeling for measure and order, which restrained all these instincts within the limits of the supportable and, in the end, calmed them down and submitted them to the general interest of life in common. Men who had been leaders in the commercial quarter for forty years vanished overnight as if they had all died suddenly, together with the habits, customs, and institutions they represented."

Andric's description of what happened in Visegrad in 1914 might as easily describe what happened in 1992 in Sarajevo, but this time it was the Serbs who prevailed over the Muslims, with the bitterness nurtured of historical memories of those earlier days and of World War II. To dismiss the history of these people is the product of a mind too highly rationalized and sanitized of any imagination.

I asked Sonja how she viewed the start of the war in Croatia, whether it began as a consequence of the new constitution that discriminated against the Serbs. "All the constitutions of the newly emerging nations are based on ethnicity. It is the problem. But that was not really the main reason for the war. It was prepared before the constitution came out, but that document played into the hands of those who wanted war. The cleavage started in the Assembly before the republics declared their independence. Milosevic and Tudjman wanted war to consolidate their power."

Sonja was suddenly interrupted by a heavy-set middle-aged man who burst into the office with news of events in Croatia. The center was involved in planning a meeting in Zagreb, and this man was bringing news of it to Sonja, she explained. The meeting was called by a group around a magazine called *Erasmus*, funded by the National Endowment for Democracy in the U.S., a government agency set up to fund democratic developments, especially in Eastern Europe, which had received heavy criticism in Congress for some of the projects it was supporting. The Zagreb meeting, which was being kept very low profile, was designed to confront "people from the cultural world who are nationalists but still rational," Sonja told me. A similar meeting would later be held in Belgrade.

I wondered whether the center had been harassed by the government. "No, we have not become a target yet. They have denounced us as traitors, paid by foreign countries, but so far we have no serious problems. Once we thought they had stolen our computers, but we weren't sure it was the government—it could have been just an ordinary theft. The police never produced any kind of report. But we are not in Milosevic's way; we are irrelevant. In a way, we lend a certain legitimacy to Milosevic just by being here. If he doesn't bother us, he must surely be a democrat, yes? If we should become relevant, I think they will behave differently. Just a few days ago the concept of the programs at the independent TV station, Studio B, was changed, and it's finished now. They have sold off to Milosevic."

It seems that Studio B was no longer able to support itself and was forced to begin selling air time to, among others, Milosevic's Socialist party, one of the few political organizations able to pay the rates. It didn't "sell off" to the government but simply sold it air time in the process of going commercial. "The station director argued that they were neutral and would retain an independent voice, but Studio B has already changed. Several people have resigned, so it's not what it used to be. The director said it was necessary to go commercial, which means they sell to anyone who can pay. But only the big parties can pay, so we see, for instance, Arkan for two hours on TV." Running for Parliament with Milosevic's support, Arkan was one of those cited by the center for war crimes in Bosnia. It seems that independent TV in Belgrade had gone the way of so many independent media after a few years of idealistic programming.

There was a weary despair in Sonja's voice as she told me this story, much like the weary despair we hear so much in the U.S. in discussions about television and radio broadcasting. Unfortunately, Sonja didn't seem to connect the onset of capitalism in Yugoslavia with the loss of independent television; instead she viewed the change as a political betrayal, and apparently so did some staff members of Studio B. She viewed it in the same way that she did the potential harassment by the government of her center. Studio B, basically antigovernment, was definitely a threat to Milosevic, but he did not take over the station, he merely bought air time.

Sonja was no less cynical about the intelligentsia of Belgrade than about the common folk. Milosevic had won the support of so many of them, she said, because they wanted to hold on to the privileges they had enjoyed under the Tito regime. "They followed his nationalism as a way of retaining their privileges. Some are honest about it, but most aren't. The people at the Academy complained for years about the exploitation of Serbs, but all their talk was along nationalist lines. They never addressed the transformation into modern society in an appropriate way. It was all channeled into traditional nationalism, comparing Serbia to other nationalities in Yugoslavia. It was all in the pipeline for a decade. They published a lot of books about nationalism, but not very constructive. I don't deny the necessity of having some traditional nationalism. It's normal. But somehow the Academy people didn't recognize that Serbia was the dominating state in Yugoslavia, and that the other smaller nations of the country resented it. The Serbs wanted a highly centralized state; the smaller states wanted a decentralized state. So you had this confrontation. It didn't have to end in war, but Milosevic manipulated the army and everything else. He was the first separatist and thought he could win a war in six days. He didn't count on the resistance in Croatia and Bosnia."

As I thanked Sonja and left the center, I felt an immense relief to be out of the harsh light of her brilliant but bitter analysis of her nation's problems. I had heard over the years, particularly in the 1960s and early 1970s, much harsh criticism of the U.S. and similarly harsh criticism of their countries by other nationals, especially in England. But I had never heard anything resembling Sonja's. I had never heard anything comparable to her belief that the draconian UN economic sanctions against her own country were justified. During the years of the Vietnam War, among its opponents, I couldn't remember anyone saying, "I hope we lose."

I stopped to have lunch in a small café down the street from the center, where the bill came to the equivalent of thirteen dollars— more dinars than I had, an expensive lunch in an out-of-the-way café. I protested that the bill should have been much less, but my translator, a fellow customer, explained that I had misunderstood the menu. What I took to be the price in dinars was actually points. The price was not printed on the menu, only a point system cued to inflation. The price went up almost every day, the man explained. I offered American dollars. The waiter took my twenty-dollar bill and disappeared. He came back ten minutes later with my change in deutsche marks. No one who could help it dealt in the near worthless dinars.

From the café I took a cab to Mirjana's house, a dreadfully decaying stucco building on one of the tiny streets in central Belgrade. The walls in the hall looked like those in Mira's building—falling plaster, dimly lit. An archaic bell system brought Mirjana to the door of her second-floor apartment. People are so wonderfully unpredictable. I had anticipated that Mirjana's apartment would be a spare modern space in an old building filled with modern furniture and paintings and lots of books. The books were there—in huge floor-to-ceiling bookcases—medical encyclopedias (her husband had been a psychiatrist) alongside art books, history, biography, fiction, most in Cyrillic, a few in French or English.

It was certainly an old building, looking like it was two hundred years old, in fact built in 1922. Owned by Jews before World War II, it had been confiscated by the Germans, taken over by the Yugoslav government, and neglected by all. No central heating or hot water. Mirjana had large wood or coal stoves and an automatic hot water heater hooked up in her bathroom. There was electricity and a reasonably modern tiled bath with a shower. But spare and modern? Mirjana had moved into this large two-bedroom apartment when she married thirty years earlier and begun collecting books, art objects, and antique furniture. She hadn't stopped. There was hardly room to sit down in this overcrowded ancient-looking apartment. Only her office, a former bedroom, had a modern look with its computer, fax machine, and a desk covered with paper and books.

Mirjana brought Turkish coffee and we settled down to talk, I in a distinctly uncomfortable antique chair, she on a couch bed that she shared with her huge dog. We chatted amiably for a few minutes about life in Belgrade when the phone rang and she excused herself to take the call in her office from the *Times* correspondent in Paris. While she was gone I scanned her books and objets d'art, awestruck by a stone sculpture of what I took to be Lenin. Could this be true? When she returned and I asked her, she gasped, "My God, no, that's my husband."

Would I like to take a walk with her a little later to find some flowers for a friend who had just had a baby, Mirjana wanted to know. She would give me a little tour. I was pleased to have a break in interviewing, especially after the intense morning with Sonja. I took out my tape recorder to talk for a bit and discovered it was on the fritz. I was panicked. Buying a tape recorder in Belgrade was probably impossible, and if I could find one it would cost a small fortune. Mirjana assured me that she knew a good repair shop that would not charge much. She had only to find the phone number to be sure it was still there and open. So many shops had closed or were keeping short hours since the embargo.

After hunting through piles of papers, she finally located the phone number and called the shop to find, happily, that it was open.

We set off to find the repair shop and the flower shop. It was a balmy fall day, perfect for a long walk. On the way I remarked that flowers seemed to be the one product still in abundance in Belgrade. There were lots of little shops, and every little café, most of them empty of customers, nevertheless had fresh flowers on the tables. "Oh no, many shops have closed," Mirjana said. "Most have converted to other businesses, mostly coffee shops." There were lots of coffee shops in Belgrade. People couldn't afford to eat in restaurants but could afford a coffee, which was obviously plentiful. Restaurants had to buy food on the black market, which made prices prohibitive.

I had seen a number of flower shops in my trips around the town. On our way we passed a couple that Mirjana said did not have what she wanted. "You can't just send asters or daisies or those silly little roses that all these shops have to a woman who's just had a baby," she exclaimed.

We walked about a mile through the tiny, twisting streets, past rows and rows of small, empty-looking shops in crumbling, smog-smudged buildings with an occasional official landmark in between. The new buildings in the midst of all these old ones indicated where bombs had hit in World War II. The postwar buildings, most of them well designed, were built of the same stucco as the old ones. While relatively fresh, they already had the look of a society concerned with good design but neglectful afterward.

Finally we came to the florist Mirjana was seeking, a large corner shop that spread out onto the sidewalks in two directions, filled with dozens of varieties of beautiful, some exotic, blooms. "You see the difference," she said. She was right. The little flower shop next door to my hotel, indeed, had only a few asters, daisies, and tea roses that were cheering up my barren hotel room.

When Mirjana had finished selecting her bouquet and arranging to have it delivered, we set out to find the repair shop. It was exactly where she remembered, a half-mile away, and busy, jammed with television sets, VCRs, typewriters, and all manner of electronic equipment. Apparently people were trying to repair all their old electronic equipment. Little new equipment could be had in the city, and no one had the money to buy what had been smuggled in on the black market. I left my machine with the repairman who promised to have it ready the next day.

Back at Mirjana's flat, over more coffee, I asked her what she knew of the destruction of Dubrovnik. The old town, she said, had not been badly damaged, but everything around it was destroyed, along with other old seaside resorts on the Adriatic. One of the loveliest of those old towns, she said, had somehow been spared, "by some arrangement, I don't know how or why." I decided that one of the questions I would put to people was their idea of what had happened in Dubrovnik. It would serve as a small litmus test, perhaps, of where their sympathies lay.

The war in Croatia had its roots in the period between the two world wars, Mirjana told me, when Serbia dominated Yugoslavia, and Croatian politicians nourished thoughts about expanding their territory to incorporate parts of Bosnia Herzegovina and Dalmatia. This greater Croatia would help them escape Serbian domination. Actually, she said, these dreams went farther back in history, as did all the nationalist dreams of the former republics of Yugoslavia; during World War II those dreams were nurtured by the Nazis when they moved into Yugoslavia in 1941 and declared Croatia an independent state, incorporating large parts of Bosnia. Following the civil war in 1945 when Croatia was again reduced to a small state, the resentment was intense.

At first, Mirjana said, following independence and a wave of anti-Serb feeling, there were small skirmishes in the villages of the Krajina where the Serbs lived and were filled with anxiety about their fate in what looked more and more like the fascist state of Croatia. The towns set up roadblocks to keep Croatians out. Then, in one of those small skirmishes, a Croatian policeman was killed. Croatian bullies broke windows and destroyed Serb businesses. Meanwhile, back in Serbia, Milosevic was raving about these attacks. They served his purposes very well. As he called for a Greater Serbia, the Croatians could do no less. Gradually the war heated up. The government sent in the Yugoslav army.

This was no ordinary war. There were horrible atrocities against civilians on both sides. Disappeared people. Horribly mutilated corpses in open graves. Shellings and bombings. Villages burned down. A savage war no longer simply protecting Serbian villages on one side and Croatian villages on the other, but fighting even in the beautiful Adriatic coastal towns far from the Krajina. The hatred of Serbs and Croatians for each other that had been suppressed under the Tito regime came boiling forth and gradually spread across the countryside to Bosnia, igniting the fires of hatred between Muslims and Serbs.

Mirjana pulled from her piles of papers reports from the Serbian Council of Information documenting Muslim and Croat atrocities against the Serbs. As I scanned them, I was overwhelmed with the contrast between Mirjana's and Sonja's stories. I remembered a line from Misha Glenny's *The Fall of Yugoslavia*, which he repeats several times: "The only truth is the lie." I felt at that moment as Glenny must have felt on his journey through Yugoslavia, that people's lies are their truths, and I felt I had to escape. I said goodbye to Mirjana, promising to call soon, and set out for my hotel, a long but pleasant walk in the descending dusk that masked some of the decrepit buildings. I lost my way several times in the twisting streets but finally arrived half an hour later to the quiet of my hotel room.

When I reflected later on my day, I realized that Glenny had it wrong. These were not lies people were telling—nothing so flagrant. This was rather the drama of how history is filtered through individual minds, depending on personal needs, family background, and education. Mirjana had said she lost no relatives in this war but many in World War II. She had been trained as an artist. She was married and had two children. Sonja did not mention her family, had been trained as a social scientist, and was unmarried with no children. Those facts alone could account for very different views of history and current events. Both women were highly principled and well informed. What they made of their principles and their wells of information, however, was as different as the rugged mountains and calm waters that provided the picturesque contrasts of the Yugoslavian landscape.

Looking at these opposing views of Yugoslavia's problems, both with a knowledgeable view of a society in crisis, there emerged a frightening question. What was the future for this country with an economy in complete collapse; with a small but strong proto-fascist group, and the possibility of attracting a larger following; with a popular president who clearly had a great lust for power and a masterful ability to manipulate public opinion; with a moral fabric in decay as people plundered others in a black market that replaced the legitimate one; with no significant organized opposition to the status quo, and a population nurturing its history of ethnic hatreds and persecution—having gone to war partly to avenge that persecution and act out its ethnic hatreds? Wasn't this the kind of atmosphere in which fascism grew and triumphed in Europe in the 1930s? To some extent the same conditions existed all over Eastern Europe since the fall of communism, with the exception of the Czech Republic which was flourishing. But Serbia was almost a prototype, a cause for the greatest alarm.

6 *Borba* means struggle in Serbian. For the third time in its seventy-year history, the newspaper *Borba* was struggling to exist as an independent daily. It began as the organ of the Communist party under the between-wars regime of King Aleksander, with its first article written by Josip Broz, later known as Tito. It was a progressive paper produced by the country's leading intellectuals, with a small but loyal following. In World War II it struggled under the Nazis to stay alive underground to tell the Partisans' story. When the Communists came to power, *Borba* became part of a huge publishing enterprise run by the state. For nearly twenty years it reigned supreme as the largest-circulation daily in Yugoslavia and was well respected though owned by the party. Then, as Yugoslavs became better educated and more sophisticated, as they began to travel abroad and read foreign publications, as bridges with the West opened and the government became less repressive, enthusiasm for Tito and communism began to wane and *Borba*'s prestige declined. By the late 1970s it was a shell of its former self, read only by the hard-liners, the most loyal Communists.

In the late 1980s, as Yugoslavia's economic problems grew and as Milosevic pursued his ferocious nationalist campaign leading to deep fissures in the society, most of the newspapers aligned themselves with Milosevic. *Borba* took on a new life with a group of highly educated, dissident journalists who fled the other papers to recreate it as an independent paper opposed to the government. While the other papers and state-run television helped Milosevic wage his attacks on Croatia and the other republics, preparing for war, *Borba* conducted its own campaign against Milosevic. It printed all sides of that story because, as one of its editors told me, "That's what journalism is all about." But it maintained a steady barrage of criticism of Milosevic.

In 1989 Ante Markovic, then prime minister of the former Yugoslavia, pushed a law through Parliament enabling *Borba* to become a private enterprise. Shares were sold, and the connection with the state was severed. The idea threatened to backfire when moneyed interests close to Milosevic tried to buy the paper. To ward off this possibility, the paper offered its shares at low prices to its readers, and the response was overwhelming. People lined up outside *Borba*'s offices to buy just one share for a few dollars. Every day the paper published the names of the people who bought shares. It became socially correct among the intelligentsia to own part of *Borba*. In addition, a variety of artists' auctions were held to raise money. The federal government was able to buy only 17 percent.

Among those who purchased shares, however, was a business manager at the paper with ties to the government. He had been able to buy 34 percent of the shares and, with the 17 percent owned by the government, could influence decisions. The result was a new editor-in-chief. The staff felt its independence threatened and conducted a worldwide press campaign that effectively inhibited the government's pressure on the staff. As one editor described it, "The man who owned all those shares learned that he cannot just play games with the journalists." Since then the paper had remained independent. In one issue in October 1993 it published a piece charging that the federal government was attempting to destroy the paper by economic pressure.

The new *Borba* was not well received in the countryside. Of the forty distribution boxes in Yugoslavia, only a few were not destroyed. With the advent of the wars, it was no longer welcome in Croatia and Bosnia. By the fall of 1993 the paper's circulation was down to thirty thousand, sold only in Serbia, Montenegro, and Macedonia, with the Sunday edition of fifty thousand also going to Slovenia.

When I spoke with her, Gordana Logar was the foreign editor, a political columnist, and member of the board of directors of *Borba*. She was later elevated to editor-in-chief. I got her name, along with those of several other dissidents, from Article 19, an international anticensorship group based in London. A small, sandy-haired, stylish-looking woman in her fifties, with a warm, quick smile and an air of self-possession and busyness, Gordana was happy to talk with me but harassed by the pressure of putting out a daily paper with not enough resources. She called to postpone our first meeting and was a half-hour late for the second.

Gordana had been a journalist in Belgrade for thirty years, most of the time taking an independent stance at several magazines and newspapers. She started at Borba Publishing's *Evening News*, left to join a more independent weekly magazine, and went to *Borba* in the 1980s when the independents took it over. I met her in the grimy, no-nonsense lobby of the *Borba* building in which three people sat in a glass-enclosed cubicle screening visitors. When she was finally able to get away to meet me, she took me to the Independent Press Club a couple of blocks away because there was no place to sit quietly and undisturbed in her office. The Press Club was located in a noisy group of open spaces on the second floor of an office building in what appeared to have been a convention center or meeting place. One could always get a cup of coffee there and talk with journalists who were asserting their independence at their own publications—some of them under pressure. We sat over coffee at a long conference table in the main meeting room, with heavy traffic noises roaring from the busy street below.

"It is very tricky to stay independent," Gordana told me in her heavily accented English. (As she grew more comfortable, her English improved.) "We have very great economic pressure. In Croatia they stopped all the independent newspapers, but here they leave us alone, but they put great economic pressures on us. Most of the other papers are good professional papers, more independent than the state-run television, but not like *Borba*. For instance, I don't think Milosevic would have gained his power at all without *Politika*, the biggest paper now. But even *Politika* is changing, trying to be more independent. And we were the only one to report accurately the demonstrations [against state-run television] in 1991."

While everything in Yugoslavia was expensive, newspapers still cost only a few pennies. Prices were controlled by the government, which had steadily refused to let the papers raise their prices. As Gordana described it, "One egg is ten times the price of a daily *Borba*, so you see we are losing money every day." Selling advertising space was virtually impossible in the impoverished economy. The paper relied on subscriptions and newsstand sales for most of its revenues. Unofficially the government helped those papers that remained loyal to it by giving them tax exemptions; but these were withheld from *Borba*. Federal taxes were very high.

"I should say the ruling party has us tied up. We had to print in the newspaper recently that we can't afford to print all the news because we don't have money. We can only publish twenty-four or so pages, which is enough to tell what we absolutely need to, but the other papers have much more.

"Our readers are the liberals and young people who don't have any money. For instance, we had a letter from some students who said, 'We are twelve students who were buying twelve *Borba*, then we were buying seven, then three, and now we are buying one and fighting over it.' "

"Are you getting paid?" I asked Gordana.

"Yes, not regularly but sometimes. I am one of the well paid, getting about forty deutsche marks a month or so [twenty-four dollars]. It is crazy. Two years ago my salary was two thousand deutsche marks.

"What is very bad for us is that our young leaders are leaving the country and we are losing our readers. For instance, my daughter— she is a student at the Electrical Technical College here. More than half the people who were in her telephone book are not here anymore. She has lost most of her friends. They are writing from Canada, Australia, Great Britain, the United States, trying to do something for themselves. She wants to leave too, but I don't have money to send her abroad to school and I want her to finish school. She went for a while to the City College in New York, and she got a letter from her professor saying she could return, but it is $2,800 a semester and you have to pay for room and board and transportation, and I don't have that. Two of her friends just finished their college degrees, but they didn't want to have a celebration because they don't know what they will do. One of them wants to go to Germany, but he doesn't know whether he can get a visa. It is an absolutely desperate situation."

I told Gordana that I was amazed to see the crowds of people in the streets of Belgrade during the day. "I assume these people had government jobs and are now out of work," I said.

"Not only that. I think that 60 percent or more of those people are newcomers."

"Refugees, you mean?"

"We used to call them refugees. But the real refugees are in bad shape somewhere in the camps in Serbia or Montenegro. These people are mostly the people who are working at something—the black market. It is just the same as it was in 1945 after the war, the same situation. Chaotic! People are coming from nowhere. The middle class, intellectuals, liberals, independent journalists, physicians are the poorest class now, and these newcomers—you don't know who they are or where they're coming from. They are full of money because of this underground economy. It is not just operating on its own. It is very well organized, I'm sure, by the state, by the state-owned factories, by the banks. If they have products, they sell them to these people underground for more money than they could get in the regular market. All these fancy foreign cars you see, they have been bought somewhere in the black market by these newcomers."

"These newcomers are Serbs?"

"Most of them, yes, but when you are talking about the underground, ethnic origin doesn't make any difference. But there are others coming from everywhere, from Eastern Europe and other places, because this is a good place to earn money fast on the black market."

"Are some of these people Gypsies?"

"Yes, but you see, during Tito's time, those fifty years, the Gypsies were recognized as a minority and had a decent place in this society, with many very well-educated people. They still preserve their tradition; they want to live together. But now there are many who don't have jobs because their factories closed, and you can see them on the streets selling cigarettes or something. I met, for instance, a lady my age. She had on a Burberry skirt and a nice sweater, and she was selling cigarettes. She told me, 'I have no job and two children.' They queue in the morning in some stores where they sell cigarettes for low prices, and then they resell them for more, and that's the way they survive."

Borba had about 150 staff, 100 of them journalists, with correspondents in the other republics of the former Yugoslavia and in Washington, Brussels, Rome, and, until recently, Moscow. It retained the staff it needed to publish a much bigger paper while it was going broke, unlike American papers that operate with much smaller staffs. In Yugoslavia, as in most former communist countries, businesses were always overstaffed, making sure everyone had a job. Even with massive layoffs everywhere in post-Communist Eastern Europe, some companies with strong loyalties to their staffs retained them while cutting salaries, as happened at *Borba*.

The Moscow correspondent was fired because he was "too partial," Gordana said. "He was a very good journalist, one of those who changed *Borba* to an independent paper. But after the war started in Bosnia he had problems. His mother lives in a little Serbian village in Bosnia where all the young people were killed in the first attack by the Muslims. His mother and other old women stayed, and he then became highly nationalistic. It happens very often, you know. Sometimes you can't maintain your distance. For instance, I'm 100 percent Serb, but for the people in the ruling party, I'm a Serbian traitor. I was married to a Slovenian who is a great admirer of Milosevic, and he is a better citizen than I. And my daughter, who is half Slovenian, told me that she loves her country, but she doesn't know what she is. She had to fill out some forms for her college that asked her nationality. She asked me, 'What am I?' And I told her, 'You can be a Serb or a Slovenian or a Yugoslav.' She said, 'No, I can't be a Yugoslav. I don't recognize this Yugoslavia any more. I can write here South Slovenian, or I can write apartheid—without a country. I will leave it blank, I am nothing.' You see, it's very difficult to make these decisions, these alliances. And then, for a journalist it is hard to maintain the proper distance in all this turmoil."

I told Gordana about my foray into nationalism at Milic's party. "I am so ashamed of him," she said. I assured her that every country had such people, but she said heatedly, "It doesn't make any difference if such people exist in democracies, but here it is different. They have a great impact on the ruling party. Their word is something and mine is nothing. They are the patriots—the real decent people—and I am a traitor."

"What proportion of the people are 'traitors?' "

"I would say, as you say, *peanuts*. People who will say in public, 'I am against the war. I am against the nationalism,' maybe 10 percent. But many more people who are against the nationalism are silent. I would even say a silent majority. Some people say to me, 'You are so brave,' but I tell them, 'I have the facts, nothing else.' But people have to preserve their jobs, their families. I have an aged father and my daughter, but they are supporting me. Once, when I told my daughter I had a great offer with a paper that is not independent, she told me, 'If you are looking for a well-paid job, then be a professional clerk, they earn the most. So stay where you are.' And I said, 'And when you need something I can't get?' She said, 'We are going to survive, don't worry.' "

I asked Gordana to give me *Borba*'s view on the start of the wars. "Well, you know that Mr. Milosevic didn't want Yugoslavia to come apart. He wanted to be a new Tito. While he was pushing so hard for a centralized government with himself at the head, there was a lot of momentum in Croatia to have their own nation. And they really did a great deal of harm and violence to the Serbs in Croatia. But they got encouragement here to be nationalist from Milosevic's own power building and nationalism. I think both Mr. Milosevic and Mr. Tudjman and Mr. Izetbegovic too are aware that nationalism is a great tool. They all wanted to build up their power. Some people say Mr. Milosevic would be the pope if he could.

"After all the changes in Eastern Europe, after the end of the cold war, Yugoslavia was no longer important to the West. These leaders had to find something else besides communism to keep themselves in power. Nationalism was that tool. It started here, and then the others were afraid because there are so many Serbs. They remember their bad experiences of being controlled by the Serbs between the wars. You have to keep in mind the numbers: there are four million Croats and nine million Serbs. I'm not going to talk about all that past history. It is all bullshit. But you have to keep in mind that the Serbs, because of their numbers, really controlled the country, and the Croats didn't want that anymore. And you had many who were involved in World War II in the Krajina against the Serbs. Some of those people who had been involved in Hitler's crimes, and who escaped to other countries after the war and were forbidden to return during Tito's reign, were encouraged by Tudjman to return. Many of them came back and acted violently against the Serbs.

"Our thought at *Borba* was that we had already written about the nationalist movement in Serbia and why it was so dangerous. When it started in Croatia, when they brought back to life all those World War II symbols—the Iron Cross and all that stuff—the Serbs in the Krajina were frightened and were coming across the Danube into Serbia and Vojvodina. We wrote that Milosevic should go to the United Nations and everywhere else to tell the world what was going on with the Serbs in Croatia. But he didn't even turn his head. Every day the papers published the numbers of Serbs who had to leave Croatia because of the atrocities. Milosevic was making speeches about how the fascistic government had come alive—it was alive, by all means, but there were many tools to stop it, and he didn't use any. It was as if he wanted war.

"The greatest harm done was by Milosevic, not Tudjman. My late mother used to say, 'Please don't tell me about Mr. Tudjman. If he's killing somebody, he's killing Serbs. But Milosevic is killing Serbs too.' I think if Yugoslavia had stayed in the United Nations and had maintained communications with other nations, he could have saved the Serbs. If he wanted to. But he didn't want to. He just wanted to be a dictator, that's all. A couple of weeks ago I did a broadcast on Studio B, our independent TV, in which I said, 'I don't like to believe that anyone's need for power is more important than people. But I shall never understand why nobody here in Belgrade stood up when there was the first wave of refugees.' When the first boat came over with Serbs from the Krajina, the man in charge, the president, should have gone everywhere and said, 'Look what is happening to these people.' I think Milosevic was afraid that people would ask, 'What are you doing to the Albanians in Kosovo?'

"His theory was that the Serbs are part of Croatia, but the Albanians are a minority. In some ways that is true. You have to think about what minority is all about. Is it only numbers? Or is it important that a people have been there for more than twelve hundred years? Is that a minority or not? For instance, here in Belgrade, the Radical party, Mr. Seselj's party, which was very close to Mr. Milosevic until ten days ago—they went to Vojvodina in northern Serbia in the middle of the night to tell the Croats they had to leave. But these Croats had been in Serbia for four or five hundred years. They don't feel that Croatia is their home. Mr. Milosevic and Mr. Tudjman are changing people to think that way.

"Our position in *Borba* was that the Serbs were being oppressed in Croatia, that was obvious, but you shouldn't go digging out everything that happened in World War II. Just be honest and ask, 'Are they a legitimate minority in Croatia now, with legitimate human rights?' We have to abide by human rights and defend the rights of Serbs in Croatia and the rights of Croats, Slovenians, and others in Serbia. So it should be resolved in a civilized way. But I don't think Milosevic cared about that at all."

"Do you think he wanted war?"

"Yes. The war wasn't his first idea—that was to expand the power of the Serbs. He didn't want a confederation with the other republics, he wanted a dictatorship of Serbs. When he saw it was impossible to get it without a war, he wanted war. He started in Croatia, but it was perfectly obvious to some people that it would spread to Bosnia.

Some crazy people like me were certain it wouldn't spread to Bosnia because the society there is so mixed. They had a choice there. But after all the events in Croatia and Serbia, nationalism was awakened in Bosnia too, among each of the groups living there. The Muslims saw the Croats claiming a Greater Croatia and the Serbs claiming a Greater Serbia, so the Muslims decided they must do the same thing."

Was the violence in Bosnia worse than in Croatia? "Well, it was a short war in Croatia," she said.

Had the Serb atrocities there been worse?

"No, of course not, you have terrible atrocities on all sides, but you always have to look at the numbers. If you have a certain percent of Serbs—after all, the Bosnian Serbs have the help of irregulars from Serbia and Montenegro and the Krajina, and before the army withdrew you had a large Serb contingent in the army—then you will have more Serb atrocities. I can remember, before the war, we had an article by a lecturer from Harvard University who said, 'Because the Serbs are the majority in the army, everybody will blame the Serbs even if they don't start the war.' But the top generals were not necessarily Serbs. Many were Croatians, and they were the first to leave and create the army for Croatia."

I started to ask Gordana about the sanctions when a group of people began filing into the adjoining space for a meeting. Gordana suggested that we move to another place. There we met a *Politika* reporter, Kasimir Chaurs, who told Gordana that a high-level meeting of Serbs and Muslims was scheduled for later that day in Belgrade. Gordana and Kasimir laughed and agreed that nothing would come of it. Gordana said, "There is no point in trying to find anybody sane here now. We are all a little crazy." Kasimir added, "How else should it be?"

"My editor," Gordana said, still laughing a bit, "called me in to ask for more local news in my section. Local news in the foreign section? I told him I write about international things because I am the foreign editor, and I'm not going to change this. He said, 'Okay, but you should be writing more about the elections,' and I said, 'Fine, I always like to attack Milosevic.' They call me a traitor, but I don't mind, I've been doing it all these years. We had an editorial meeting and it was decided we had to attack Milosevic for something, and the editor-in-chief said, 'Gordana will write it because she's the most cynical of all of us.' I get picked to write all the anti-Milosevic stuff.

But I just try to have the facts. I get so mad. And then maybe I think I should be sorry I was so hard. But afterward I am never sorry.

"You asked me about the sanctions," Gordana said. "When they were imposed, our newspaper was not against them. Some of us, before the sanctions came, had written that if Mr. Milosevic persisted in his policies, we would get sanctions. Now, in the last four or five months, we are sure that the sanctions are the greatest thing that has happened for him. With the war he destroyed the economy and everything that was healthy and productive in this society. He created this underground economy. And now he has the greatest excuse. 'We are hungry because of the sanctions. That's why we are suffering, why we don't have medicine or anything.' And this stupid international community, especially the United Nations committee for the sanctions—they make it so that we must get permission to import medicine, and then they don't give permission, even though it's exempt from the sanctions. So all these sanctions are in place just for the sake of Mr. Milosevic. After all this time, some people in the international community who know what's going on should see how it is possible to make distinctions and allow us at least to import raw materials to make drugs if we can't buy the drugs directly. Or make a distinction for the universities so they can buy computers and other technical equipment. The universities have fallen apart; they can't teach any more." She paused, then angrily added, "The only distinction they make is for athletes. They allow them to compete in world sports events. And the athletes never protested against the government as the young people in the universities did. They were thinking only about themselves.

"People in the international community tell me they can't lift the sanctions because that would help Milosevic. They don't understand how he benefits from them."

Kasimir added, "They should be supporting the organizations that oppose the government. They should be saying, 'We are against this regime, but we are not against the Serbian people.' I don't believe in collective guilt. That's the same story we hear from Milosevic and Seselj about the collective guilt of the Croats and the Muslins in the last war. I think the governments of the world must understand our situation and support not only opposition parties but organizations like a media center and Soros [an opposition group in Belgrade, a branch of the worldwide Soros Foundation]."

"Some people are trying, but they really can't help anymore,"

Gordana replied. "Everything is now destroyed. The regime is destroying it deliberately because they have the excuse of the sanctions. And the ordinary people, standing in all those huge lines waiting for food, are talking about Mr. Clinton and what he has done. Don't tell me that most Americans aren't well aware of what's going on. It's absolutely stupid to say that the Serbs support Mr. Milosevic."

"They elected him," I said.

"It wasn't such a great margin, first of all. And second, everybody was aware that he stole the election. But the international community doesn't know what it's doing. When they want to justify the sanctions, they say the people elected Milosevic. And when they want to talk against him, they say he stole the votes. So the sanctions are absolutely counterproductive. I don't think it is possible to end them in one day, or altogether, but to keep them the way they are is pure nonsense, especially for the United States. We hear some congressman get up and say, 'We're going to support a free press' and such things. Our people see that on TV. We don't need that kind of help because people here think we are traitors if the U.S. supports us. It is absolutely impossible for us to work because of the threats. Every day I get calls saying, 'Be careful what you are writing about because you have a daughter.' We don't need that kind of U.S. help," Gordana said again angrily. "We could use money, but they only talk words that damage us with our own people. We need the sanctions selectively removed so that our life can return to some kind of normality and so that our young people will not leave. And let us have permission to import raw materials to make drugs. And say, 'We are doing that for the Serbian children, for the Serbian people.' We have experienced an increase in seven severe diseases that we haven't seen for ages here, like tuberculosis and vitamin deficiencies among the children and old people. And Mr. Milosevic tells the people, 'This is what the international community is doing to us. We have to stick together and try to survive. The long history of the Serbian people is the story of survival. We can do it.' And so on and on. And the ordinary people say, 'Yes, he's right.' "

"Do you think Milosevic is crazy?"

"I wouldn't say he is crazy, but he has some very strange ideas of how to get power and keep it."

"The economy is truly destroyed?"

"Yes, absolutely, and if that is what the international community wanted, the sanctions worked. It was bad before; Milosevic would have had to propose new economic programs, but he was saved from that. Now he can just blame the sanctions. I interviewed an American official who said, 'The sanctions work,' and I said, 'If you mean they work against the Serbian people and the economy, you're right, but if you mean against Milosevic, they don't work at all.' "

Gordana had to leave me then to attend the meeting in the next room. We agreed to meet again and said goodbye. As I strolled slowly back to my hotel along the Avenue of the Rulers, past the beautiful old gaily painted Moskva Hotel and the street sellers, I thought of the difference between Gordana and Sonja, with similar basic views, both of them despising their president and all that he stands for, but one so human and vulnerable, the other so icy and detached, the first so concerned for her fellow Serbs, the second so disdainful and contemptuous of them. Sonja was a loyal Communist for most of her life, a member of the ruling clique. Gordana spent most of her life as a "traitorous" independent journalist. Gordana was threatened and harassed, her job was made difficult by the government, while Sonja went about her work undisturbed. Gordana influenced thousands of people with her words every day; Sonja was ignored. It was tempting to draw a lesson about the fate of Communists and dissidents in post-Communist countries here, but given Yugoslavia's peculiar history in the Communist world, it was probably too facile to draw many conclusions and safer rather to attribute most of the differences to the very disparate personalities of the two women. But I couldn't rid myself of the stereotyped image of the cold, hard Communist, indifferent to the fate of her people, compared to the image of the dissident, in a continual state of despair for the lives of people and for her society threatened with death and destruction.

Most interesting in this comparison was that Sonja's disdain and contempt—near hatred—for the Serbs and support for the sanctions was a mirror of the same feelings expressed by the international community, a community that Gordana described as "stupid" and inhumane in its failure to understand the effects of the UN sanctions.

"Let Them Bomb Us"

7 At about 10:30 this morning, a little late, Ljiljana picked me up to take me to the International Press Club on Knez Mihailo, where I was to interview Cedomir Mirkovic, the president of the Social Democratic party. Just as she had on the way to the symphony on Monday night, Ljiljana drove like a cowboy, taking turns on what felt like two wheels, and racing up to traffic lights as if she might beat them if only she went fast enough. Then, at the light, she turned off the engine, explaining that this saved petrol. Sort of like turning off the lights when you leave a room for a few minutes to save electricity—which in fact has the opposite effect. Perhaps it made her feel better that she was beating the system.

The Press Club, on the third floor of a large modern office building, came as a surprise after stepping off the rickety elevator that was a feature of even the most modern Belgrade buildings and walking through a short, desolate-looking corridor. The club had a large, pleasant formal dining room with white tablecloths and flowers and two window walls overlooking the plaza, a square bar and comfortable lounge with leather couches, several conference rooms, one large room obviously designed for press conferences, and a room equipped with desks, phones, and a computer for the press. It looked like an organization befitting the needs of the press in the capital city of a small but confident nation that the former Yugoslavia had been. Now it was probably far too big for current needs.

We met Cedomir Mirkovic, who was called Ceda, in the lounge and proceeded to the dining room, where we took a large table and ordered coffee. The party included Ceda, Ljiljana and her husband, Branka, who was vice-president of the party, and David Moss, who would translate for me. I had requested an interview with Ceda, but the Dimitrijevics had obviously decided to "help" without consulting me, without knowing that I found group interviews less satisfactory than one-on-ones. Throughout the interview Branka sat silently while Ljiljana occasionally interjected something softly, almost as if she were commenting to herself, and nodded wisely.

The American musician, David, stood out in strong contrast to the Serbs. In his blue jeans, old shirt, and suede jacket, he looked like he had just rolled out of bed, which indeed he had, he said. The Serbian men, on the other hand, were carefully dressed in suits, white shirts, and silk ties, with Ljiljana in a smart navy blue suit, red silk blouse, and blue pumps. Ceda, looking like so many other well-dressed affluent Serbian men, wore an expensive hound's tooth check suit. Saturday morning, for these Serbs, was just as formal as any other day in the week. Or was this meeting with an American journalist an occasion to dress formally on the weekend?

Ceda, in his fifties, was a free-lance writer, a columnist for the newspaper *Politika,* and a literary critic with a number of books to his credit. Ljiljana added, "One of the best." For the last twenty years he had been cultural director of the major state-run television station, with complete freedom to program as he chose. Then for two months he was managing director until he was forced to resign. He had introduced too much controversial material, including news of the opposition. The government suggested that he return to his former noncontroversial post. He resigned instead and began devoting much of his time to politics, hoping to reform the government. Before founding the Social Democratic party he—and the Dimitrijevics— took no part in politics, like most Yugoslavs, though he was a nominal member of "a liberal wing" of the League of Communists, largely composed of the literati. He had been able to work quite contentedly and lucratively all those years because he had held a Communist party card. "As long as you didn't mention Tito's name, you could write anything you wanted," he explained. "It wasn't ideal, but what is? You could live with it." He was a very tall, big-boned, grey-thatched man with a long, strong but gentle face and demeanor, a deep, soft voice, and, like so many Serbs, a wry humor.

The Social Democratic party, a year old now, was the newest political party on the scene. "Former Communists made a number of attempts to camouflage themselves as Social Democrats, but our party was the first to actually model itself on the traditional Social Democratic parties of Europe," Ceda explained. "Actually, what we have here is probably closer to the center of the American Democratic party or maybe more like the Labor party in England." Until recently the party had had no rules for membership, but under new rules it now had a few thousand paid-up members.

Most of the hundred or so dissident political parties were refusing to participate in the forthcoming elections in December. (Only about ten of these parties had anything more than a handful of people, but they were nevertheless registered with the government. Most other post-Communist countries also had a great proliferation of tiny fringe political parties that clogged election ballots.) Many of the other parties complained that Milosevic's sudden call for elections would not provide enough time to conduct serious campaigns. "But Milosevic didn't act unconstitutionally, and it's perfectly natural for him to take advantage of the situation for his own party," Ceda said, "so we're talking about a democratic game, and we have to play."

Milosevic had at least one important reason for calling the election: to rid himself of the attachment to Vojeslav Seselj's Radical party that represented the ultra right. Milosevic had made a coalition with Seselj supposedly based on "patriotic sentiments," according to Ceda. "But it's clear that Seselj's ambitions have grown tremendously, and Milosevic has a lot of trouble on the international scene justifying his ultranationalism. It is doing Milosevic a lot of harm to continue his association with Seselj. We have said all along that if he renounces Seselj, we will support him. We discreetly offered our support of the dismantlement of that coalition when problems began to develop between them in the last couple of months, when Seselj tried to seize control of the government. But the fundamental problems go much deeper. Without Seselj, Milosevic can come out more clearly for peace and work more quickly and effectively to end the war."

The Social Democratic party supported an autonomous state for Krajina within Serbia, but, Ceda added, "We know that depends on the international community. Our party believes that the situation in Yugoslavia would be much better if relations between Belgrade and Zagreb were improved and if the former Yugoslavia could be made a free trading zone."

"A confederation?" I asked.

"In the beginning that's not really possible anymore. But perhaps for the future."

"Just partners, like Germany and France?"

"Something firmer than that. It's quite clear that the countries cannot exist economically independent. Especially for Bosnia, economic independence isn't possible. Bosnia came into existence only as part of the larger framework of Austria-Hungary. Later it became the nucleus of Yugoslavia—Yugoslavia in miniature. When Slovenia and Croatia became independent, it became clear to us that war in Bosnia was inevitable. Our party felt there were two extreme solutions for Bosnia. One would be the rehabilitation of the former Yugoslavia, an economic federation. The other solution is painful but realistic. It has to be divided into two parts, one Croatian, the other Serbian. We encourage that because we don't believe there are realistic conditions for the survival of a Muslim state. If a Muslim state were established it would force an incredible rearranging of borders in Yugoslavia and in Europe as well, because a series of countries have their own interests in the Balkans and in Europe. We feel it is dangerous to start shifting these borders around because there'll be no end to it. Personally, I would not shift any internal borders one yard."

"There are reports that Tudjman approached Milosevic about dividing Bosnia between them. Do you know anything of that?" I asked Ceda.

"Yes, we heard that, but neither of them has ever admitted such a meeting, and personally I don't believe it ever happened. At that time there was such a vicious war going on between Serbia and Croatia that it isn't possible that such a secret meeting could take place."

"But there were meetings among the presidents of the republics."

"Yes, but they didn't succeed in ending that war. There were objective reasons for that war."

"Yes?"

"It goes back to the fact that Yugoslavia was never democratized. And that was a real shame, because we genuinely had a liberal form of communism here. We were much, much closer to democracy than the other former Communist countries. But the international community took a destructive role. Some countries, especially America in the first phase, supported the retention of Yugoslavia. Mr. Baker, the Secretary of State, came and clearly stated he would support the survival of Yugoslavia at any price. At the same time others, primarily Germany, let Slovenia and Croatia know that they would support the dismantlement of the nation along the republic borders. That was already more than enough to create tension and start a war."

"What do you think was the motive of those who supported the breakup?"

"We believe there are a number of motives. Germany, of course, has always had interests in the Balkans. At the beginning of the century Germany was instrumental in the creation of the new state of Albania, for instance. [In fact, Albania was supported by Austria-Hungary and Italy.] We believe that one of the greatest mistakes of the Serbian leadership was believing that America, England, France would support the survival of Yugoslavia in opposition to Germany."

In fact, the international community all but incited the Yugoslav wars. In July 1991, following Croatia's declaration of independence, and after a trip to Germany, Tudjman boasted on Croatian television that he had spent more than two and a half hours in secret talks with President Helmut Kohl and then Foreign Minister Hans-Dietrich Genscher. "The talks were fruitful, and we were all satisfied," he said.

Having had a taste of what resulted from German meddling in Slovenia and Croatia, and emboldened by the cease-fire in Croatia it had accomplished, the European Community convened a meeting in February 1992 in Lisbon to solve the Bosnian problem. A cantonal solution was proposed, dividing Bosnia into units primarily Serbian, Croatian, and Muslim. All the Bosnian parties agreed the next month to the partition. Shortly after, the Muslim president reneged on the advice of then U.S. Ambassador Warren Zimmerman. Instead the U.S. urged the EC to recognize Bosnia Herzegovina as a unitary state. U.S. recognition, with that of the EC, followed the next month, despite all the signs that war would ensue. The Serbs, who are only about a third of the population of Bosnia but who occupy about 60 percent of the land, being mostly agrarian as opposed to the more urban Muslims, had boycotted the Muslim government's referendum on independence held earlier. They had threatened that if the republic declared its independence, they would form their own Serbian republic, an ominous threat of war.

The Serbs refused to live under a Muslim-dominated government, especially one led by a president who was vowing to create a Muslim state. The "Islamic Declaration" by Alija Izetbegovic, which had been secretly circulated and had led to Izetbegovic's imprisonment by

Tito in 1970, was published for all Bosnians to read in 1990. It called for a "renewal of Islamic religious thought and the creation of a united Islamic community from Morocco to Indonesia. . . . There can be neither peace nor coexistence between the Islamic religion and non-Islamic social and political institutions." It specified that "the upbringing of the people, and particularly means of mass influence—the press, radio, television and film—should be in the hands of people whose Islamic moral and intellectual authority is indisputable. The media should not be allowed—as so often happens—to fall into the hands of perverted and degenerate people who then transmit the aimlessness and emptiness of their own lives to others." Reading this document, which was widely circulated, might have given the Orthodox Serbs, and the Catholic Croats as well, more than a little pause about living in a state led by Izetbegovic.

It is difficult to believe that the U.S., in urging independence on Bosnia, was unaware of Izetbegovic's plans. Writing in the fall 1993 issue of *World Affairs*, Alex N. Dragnich, professor emeritus of political science at Vanderbilt University, wrote, "While it cannot be confirmed, there are strong reasons to believe that the president [of the U.S.] and his secretary of state, determined to achieve peace in the Middle East, were being pressured by Saudi Arabia to recognize Bosnia-Herzegovina. The Saudis, so the story goes, stressed to the United States that the Muslim leaders in Sarajevo were moderates, the type of Muslims that America was relying upon in the Middle East."

"We believe," Ceda went on, "that in the international community the U.S. is most important. But there is a general interest, it seems, in weakening the Serbian nation. Much like Tito did." David interjected, "It seems the Western world is continuing Titoism in Yugoslavia." The others shook their heads sadly in agreement. "Slovenia and Croatia," Ceda continued, "managed to convince the Western world that they wanted to run from communism. We think it was very important that Serbia didn't move more quickly to democratize. Instead the impression was created that Serbia was a new Moscow. It's not completely untrue. It's 5 or 10 percent true."

"I am having a great deal of trouble," I told Ceda, "deciphering the attitudes of the U.S. and the rest of the international community, but the hardest to understand are the Germans. Given all the trouble they're having since the Wall came down, what can they possibly gain from a tiny independent Slovenia, a slightly larger Croatia, and a Muslim Bosnia?"

"First is a port on the Adriatic. That has always been on their agenda. We also think they have wanted to demonstrate that their huge economic power could be expressed in political terms, and this was the perfect opportunity. And they have clearly succeeded. I was recently in Germany visiting the Social Democratic party there, and I was in the foreign office. A number of officials there admitted Germany's goals in Yugoslavia.

"But with all that, the real problem was the Serbian leadership's underestimating the separatist sentiments in the other parts of Yugoslavia. One of the mistakes was to have so many Serbs in the army, creating the impression that it was a Serbian army. In fact it was Yugoslavian, and it fell apart in those terms."

"Early on, before the wars broke out, what could Milosevic have done to appease the separatists in the rest of the country?" I asked.

"At the very earliest stages, at any price, he should have maintained the integrity of Yugoslavia. The central error was that first they should have held federal elections and then republic elections, instead of the other way around. Everything was upside down." The elections in the republics all produced highly nationalistic, jingoistic governments that created the secessionist movements. Had federal elections been held before the local ones, more authority could have accrued to the federal government, with a greater chance that some arrangement might have been worked out among the republics to maintain the integrity of the nation.

This may have been only a dream, though. Separatist aspirations in the various republics had been growing since Tito's death. And even before the elections in 1990, the Serbs and the other republics strongly disagreed on the kind of government they would create to replace the remnants of the Tito regime. The Serbs were bound to the idea of a strong federation while the other republics were equally bound to a weak confederation with a central government of very limited powers, less than those of the American federal government under the Articles of Confederation. The insistence on a weak federal government was a clear sign that the next step might be declarations of independence. The Yugoslavs had had quite enough of a strong federal state under Tito and were unwilling to continue that condition, unable to foresee that a truly democratic constitution might enable them to live freely in a strong federal state. Milosevic didn't help with his "Greater Serbia" calls. The combination of a fear of centralized government, Milosevic's nationalist campaign, and the mixed signals they were getting from the international community were enough to turn the other republics toward independence. On the other hand, the governments that emerged in the separate republics had hardly been models of democracy, and Slovenia and Croatia had elected as presidents former Communists. In Croatia especially, the Tudjman government was a harsh dictatorship that had sent many Serbs in Croatia fleeing to Serbia and Montenegro. There the Milosevic government was far more democratic, with a constitution that, if implemented, provided the form for a model democratic state, a far more democratic document than those of the other republics.

"To change the subject, I'd like to talk about the party's position on Kosovo," I told Ceda. As part of his effort to weaken Serbian influence in Yugoslavia and his ongoing flirtation with the Muslims—Egypt's Gamal Abdel Nasser was one of his closest friends—Tito had, in the late 1940s, opened Kosovo's borders to neighboring Albanians, offering all kinds of benefits to immigrants. The consequence was a flood of Muslim Albanian families with large broods of children. Slowly, over the years, Tito encouraged the Albanians to move into positions of power in Kosovo, asking of them only membership in the League of Communists. He also quietly encouraged a campaign, often violent, to drive out the Serbs and other non-Albanians. Over the years the highest birthrate in Europe and their control of the seats of power left the Albanians in full control of Kosovo. In the 1970s Tito conferred autonomy on them. But he never bothered to ensure that this largely uneducated, unskilled population would have jobs. And the systematic destruction of farmland in order to drive out the Serbs left the land lying fallow. In the 1980s Albanians, most of them poverty stricken, began rebelling against the government, demanding jobs and more benefits. The government responded with troops. Finally, in pursuit of a Greater Serbia, Milosevic rescinded Albanian autonomy, offered land and protection to Serbs willing to return to Kosovo, and removed Albanians from government jobs. Because the Albanians made up close to 90 percent of the population of Kosovo, the situation was explosive. The Albanians declared their independence and elected their own government, operating alongside the official Serbian government. As one of the mad moves by the so-called Albanian government, it was decreed that Serbian passports were no longer valid. But because the "Republic of Kosovo" had no official international recognition, Albanians had no effective passports. They also closed the Serb-run schools and the university, resorting to "home teaching" and issuing diplomas in the name of the Republic of Kosovo.

Even the most liberal Serbs insisted that Kosovo, the cradle of their civilization, must remain Serbian. "I know why Serbs feel Kosovo is Serb no matter what," I said. "But with nearly 90 percent of the population now Albanian, how do you realistically deal with that?"

"We have the same fears you do, that war will break out there. What we believe is that opening the borders even more would help solve the problem. But the Kosovo tradition for Serbs is hard to undo. And it is also formal law."

"But laws can be changed."

"Yes. We want the law to be changed. We don't want revolution. We are against the repression of the Albanians. But even we, who regard ourselves as the most liberal and democratic party, do not want to give up our historic lands."

"Isn't it possible that if Milosevic hadn't revoked Kosovo's autonomy, these problems might be less threatening?"

"We want Kosovo returned to its status as a state within Serbia, and we have criticized the government for not working more quickly and effectively to do that. But the truth is also that the Albanians have been encouraged in their revolt by Albania and the international community. The international community should encourage the Albanians to participate in the Yugoslavian nation. We understand the aspirations of the Albanians, but it is just unrealistic. Yugoslavia would certainly disintegrate if Kosovo were to be abandoned by the Serbs. It sounds crazy to put so much emphasis on history, but there is no reason to undermine the importance of history."

I wondered about the anti-Communist opposition in Belgrade. When Eastern Europe was having its revolutions, Belgrade did not produce an opposition—no Vaclav Havel or Lech Walesa. Was this because Yugoslavia already had a liberal communism?

"You're right, we had no underground political organizations. And the government was powerful enough, even after the collapse of communism, to eliminate any opposition. So we sat in our parlors having intellectual chats instead of having real political parties. Here I think nationalism took the place of democracy. That's a long story. Most of the criticism of the government was from nationalist complaints. For fifty years here, nationalism was the equivalent of anticommunism. So, when people in power became nationalists—like Milosevic—they were perceived as being good and democratic."

Suddenly it was time for David and me to go to another meeting. Ljiljana volunteered to drive us to the Serbian statehouse, where we were expected. Ceda agreed to meet with me again, and we said goodbye. As we were leaving the dining room, Ceda said, "I want to say that I think that ultimately the history of this country will be recognized, and millions of mixed marriages will make us one country. We will live together as the Europeans did after the world wars. I don't think it is constructive to change the borders to meet nationalist pretensions. Personally, I wouldn't permit anyone to move the borders by a single yard. But I know it will be done."

The legislative chamber of the Serbian Parliament was a lushly wood-paneled room, the only decoration being variegated inlays in the paneled walls and two huge crystal chandeliers. It was the site of a conference held by the Serbian Ministry of Information to honor foreign writers who "didn't sing the song that says that Serbia alone is responsible for all the horrors of this civil war." I had been invited, though I was the only writer there whose credentials for inclusion were still open to question. All the ministry knew about me was that I was an American journalist. All the other writers present, except for David who was writing a filmscript, had already published books— poetry, novels, nonfiction—in which their positions had been made clear. The minister, Milivoje Pavlovic, who chaired the meeting, had on the table before him sixteen books by authors present and absent who had somehow made the case for Serbia. Also present was a Serbian publisher living in Geneva, Mica Milosevic, who had published a number of these books. A couple of local writers and government officials rounded out the crowd of about twenty-five.

The occasion for the conference was the weekend-long International Writers Conference held each year by the Yugoslav Writers Union. In the years before the embargo, writers came from all over the world to participate. This year there were only a handful, and several of these now lived in Belgrade; there were two each from France, Germany, and Japan, and one each from Belgium, Greece, Taiwan, China, the Czech Republic, and Russia. David and I were the sole representatives of the United States. Two British journalists, Misha Glenny and Mark Thompson, who had written the only recent books on Yugoslavia in English but were not especially sympathetic to the Serbs, were notably absent. (Glenny revised his book in 1994 and displayed more sympathy.) I was the only journalist in the crowd; the others were novelists, poets, and academics.

We sat around a beautiful inlaid cherrywood circular table with our gifts from the ministry before us—a stunning book of the art and architecture of one of the earliest Orthodox monasteries—listening to long-winded, impassioned speeches by the writers proclaiming their faith in Serbia. Most of them said that the lack of justice shown the Serbs by the international community had impelled them to write. When it was my turn, I simply said I'd only been in Belgrade a short time, but I hoped to go back to America with some sense of the truth. I got the biggest round of applause for that short speech. Clearly, for this crowd of partisans one American journalist was worth ten Japanese poets.

The most impassioned of the speakers was Daniel Schiffer, a young French philosophy professor who earlier in the year had published, in French, *Requiem for Europe*. The Serbian translation had just been published. Schiffer was a tall, heavy-set, long-haired Gallic-looking man in his thirties who had a strong sense of himself. He told a story of how he had organized a three-day fact-finding mission on human rights in Bosnia for Elie Wiesel. Representatives of the world press accompanied the mission. They saw the biggest Serb detention camp and a Muslim camp. When Wiesel returned to the States, Schiffer said, he reported on the Serb camp but made no mention of the Muslim camp. On the basis of that three-day trip, Wiesel signed a letter by a group of intellectuals and writers urging President Clinton to bomb Serbian strategic points, bridges, and highways. "A Nobel Peace Prize winner urging war!" Schiffer exclaimed. "I wrote an open letter to Wiesel refuting him point by point. How could he urge bombing Serbia on the basis of three days in the country in which he admitted knowing nothing of the countries involved?" Schiffer said the letter was widely published in major papers in Europe and in the *New York Times*, and that *Times* columnist A. M. Rosenthal had criticized Wiesel on the basis of Schiffer's letter.

Schiffer also told us he had arranged and supervised the release of three thousand Muslims from the Serb camp he and Wiesel observed. I asked Minister Pavlovic if he could verify Schiffer's claim. "We know nothing of it," he told me. That seemed odd until I remembered how much chaos existed in this capital. Unless of course Schiffer was making a boastful claim, a possibility I couldn't overlook considering his general boastfulness.

Following what seemed like an endless round of speechmaking—made more endless by the need to translate into Serbian the speeches of non-Serb speakers—the state-run television and radio reporters crowded around me, eager to hear from an American. I told them I didn't have much to say yet, but they pressed me with questions, most of which I had to answer with "I just don't know yet."

From the meeting we were driven for lunch to the Representatives Club in a five-mile-square wooded area where Tito had his grandiose White Palace that included a private zoo. The club was a one-story flagstone and glass building with a bar and lounge, a huge dining room with lovely views of the woods, and meeting rooms. We had drinks in the lounge where I chatted with Schiffer, hoping to get more information about his rescue operation. He gave me details, which sounded reasonable, and the dates and names associated with his trip with Wiesel, then launched into an ardent speech about how only the Serbs were being demonized in this war. He seemed to see himself as the savior of the Serbs.

I also chatted with Fuitsu Hazumi, a Japanese poet who described himself as a goodwill ambassador of the World Congress of Poets. He now lived in Middlesex, England. Fuitsu told me that he had attended an international meeting of PEN, the writers' group, in the spring in Dubrovnik. Ah, an outsider's report on that fateful city. "I saw more damage by the IRA in London than there was in Dubrovnik," he told me. "There was only the most minor damage."

The Serbs eat their main meal at about three in the afternoon. This one was sumptuous, as I was learning most Serbian meals are—thick mushroom soup, lamb with carrots, spinach, potatoes, and moussaka, with white and red wines, both too sweet for my taste, followed by two kinds of rich pastries. The club obviously wasn't suffering the same shortages that other restaurants were.

Across the table from me was a sleepy-eyed, balding, slightly debauched-looking novelist and screenwriter, Branimir Scepanovic. He wore a dashing vintage rust-colored double-breasted jacket and brown trousers in contrast to all the dark suits in this crowd. One of his filmscripts had been bought by an American filmmaker, he told me through David's translation. A dry-witted, seductively smiling man, Branimir said he had read nothing of Saul Bellow's work since *Herzog* because he didn't believe he could ever do as well again. *Light in August* was his favorite of William Faulkner's novels, all of which he had read. Latin writers were very trendy in Belgrade these days, he said. "Everyone has read *One Hundred Years of Solitude.*" And what of Marquez's work since that one? Yes, them too, but not like the big one that changed literature around. Was James Joyce read here? "Of course!" he said with disdain, as if to say, "What kind of primitives do you think we are?" Kafka too was a favorite in Belgrade, a father to him.

When I asked Branimir about the work of the Czech writer Milan Kundera, whom I greatly admire, the Serbian-Swiss publisher down the table broke in. "He is irresponsible. A great stylist but an irresponsible writer," he exclaimed. Kundera ridicules some of the premises of the Czech dissidents, especially in his best-selling *The Unbearable Lightness of Being,* and is scorned by many in his native land. One Czech I talked to called him a traitor, though adding that he was of course a fine stylist. Branimir hadn't yet read his work.

Without knowing a word of English, Branimir had read in translation all the authors we talked about. Clearly Yugoslavia was in another league from those Communist countries where socialist realism prevailed, where modernist writers were not published, and where foreign modernist writers were not translated. When I was in Prague in 1990, Jack London had recently been translated and was a big seller.

The party was breaking up, with some people going home and others being shepherded to the Belgrade Book Fair. Branimir promised to arrange another meeting and to bring me a copy of his one novel that had been translated into English.

In normal times the annual book fair was an international gala, filling the huge domed circular convention center that was host to all the city's trade fairs. This year the fair was a shadow of its earlier self with representatives only from Russia, Greece, Macedonia, Switzerland, and Serbia. Serbia's publishing business has suffered greatly from the embargo, and publishers in Russia and Macedonia were not much better off. There was very little paper to be had. The publishers had plenty of room to spread out their wares.

I assumed we had been brought to the convention center to see the book fair, but it had been a long day and I could have done without it. I was wrong about the ministry's motive, however. In fact, we were taken to the fair to help publicize the Serbian translation of Schiffer's book, which was being introduced there. The ministry clearly had a close relationship with Schiffer's publisher and had made every effort to help him with sales of the book, a condemnation of the West in its relationship to Yugoslavia. We were taken directly to the publisher's booth and served coffee and juice. The conference participants were told to line up at a long table in the booth to give their endorsements to the media, who would be arriving at any minute.

I was the only one who demurred. I hadn't read the book. How could I comment on it? But I was trapped there. I'd been offered a ride back to the hotel by one of the assistants in the ministry, and she clearly wasn't leaving until this show was over. I took a walk around the fair, but reading none of the languages in which the books were printed left me at a certain disadvantage. I sat in the booth and chatted idly with the other writers as they waited for the media to arrive.

Not having read the book failed to deter any of the others. They all spoke warmly of it. The endorsements were long and windy. That gave a local journalist, obviously close to the government, plenty of time to work on me. Couldn't I just say something for the TV news? What could I say? I asked him. Surely I could find something to say, he urged. Finally, tired and unable to resist anymore, I agreed. When my turn came, I said I hadn't read the book, but it sounded like it might be worthwhile. I wouldn't have wanted that kind of endorsement of a book of mine, but Schiffer thanked me afterward.

When all the other writers had spoken, it was Schiffer's turn. He stood up, ran his hands through his hair, and began his long speech about his role in the *borba* of the Serbs. Most of his French was lost on me, but his tone and gestures weren't. He was a fervent defender of the faith, if not just a bit of a self-serving, publicity-seeking exploiter of the Serbs' misery. He had struck me as quite sincere, if overly dramatic, in our conversation at the club where he spoke English, but this inordinate display of chutzpah in the last two hours had raised the question. Perhaps he was both—a fervent defender of the Serbs and a great publicity seeker not averse to using the Serbs to advance his own cause.

As soon as Schiffer finished, the show was over and my driver came to get me. It was a long ride back from the outskirts of the city to the center, and my driver, her husband, and I talked about the cost of food and other effects of the embargo that everybody in Belgrade talked about all the time.

8 No appointments today until dinner at seven with Petar Lukovic, deputy editor of *Vreme*, Belgrade's most independent weekly magazine, modeled slightly after *Time* (which *vreme* means). After a leisurely late breakfast in my room, I sat down to my little desk for some light Sunday reading: "Rape and Sexual Abuse of Serb Women, Men and Children in Areas Controlled by Croatian and Moslem Armed Formations in Bosnia and Herzegovina and Croatia, 1991–1993," a report compiled by the Serbian Council Information Center and released in January 1993. The booklet consisted mainly of long, detailed depositions taken from victims of beatings, torture, rape, and sexual abuse in Muslim and Croatian camps, just the sort of thing one plans for a relaxed Sunday afternoon if one is in Belgrade in search of truth about the nature of the Yugoslav wars.

One story told was that of C.G., a Serbian male civilian, who was arrested in April 1992, a month after war had broken out, by a combined force of Muslims and Croatians. He was returning to his home in Prebilovci, Bosnia, after attempting to drive a friend, another civilian wounded by a sniper in the fighting in Prebilovci, to a hospital in Mostar, apparently some distance away. Prevented by Muslims and Croatians from reaching Mostar, he left his friend with a Yugoslav army encampment that had an ambulance. He recognized some of his captors who "cursed my Serb Cetnik mother and said that my father and six brothers were with 'Cetniks.' However, my father died nine years ago but they continued to curse him all the same." He was handcuffed and taken to "the camp at the tobacco station at Caplijina, a dry tobacco-processing plant. With me they arrested also D.B. and M.S., who were civilians. They put us in a cell, hermetically closed and full of tobacco dust. We spent a few hours in there, then Croatian and Muslim soldiers came over, blindfolded us with tablecloth rags and hit us with rifle butts. D. fell down on the floor collapsing from the pain, but they continued to hit him. How I remained on my feet, I know not myself. After the beatings, they bundled us in a car, blindfolded us and tied our hands." They were taken to another tobacco plant converted into a detention camp, where the beatings continued.

C.G. concluded his deposition by saying, "I was registered for the first time with the International Red Cross at Ljubuski, after being kept in the camps at Caplijina, Metkovic, 'Lora' in Split, Zadar and Duvno. Before that, they would hide us from representatives of international humanitarian organizations and the Croats used to threaten that they would kill us if we told anyone that we were tortured and starved. Once in Split, during a visit of ICRC representatives, I said what they were doing to me, so the next day I was severely beaten because of this. The camp commander was immediately informed of what I had said. They beat me so much that I hardly survived. P.P. called 'Panta,' who was arrested when his plane was shot down at Caplijina, was treated the same way because he also complained of the way the Croats had treated him in the camp. They kept telling us, 'What you see—you don't see, what you hear—you don't!' In all these camps, all of us Serbs were tortured bestially. I didn't tell you everything what I wanted, nor could I have done so. They took my life, what they have left is only my head."

The sentiments of the camp personnel are described by this victim in his story of how the prisoners were forced to sing anti-Serb songs with such lines as,

The Drina River is deep.
We shall ford the Drina
And burn Serbia.
When he forded the Drina
He was wounded in the leg.
Jure said not, "Woe to me!"
He said instead: "Chief Pavelic
We are ready to fight for the homeland."

Ante Pavelic was the "Führer" of the Ustase government in Croatia under the Nazis. The Drina forms a rough boundary between Bosnia and Serbia. C.G., along with several other prisoners, was exchanged for some Muslim prisoners after four months in camps. Among his other injuries were twenty broken ribs, a broken hand, and a broken leg, for which he received no treatment, though in one of the camps he was x-rayed to determine the extent of his injuries.

Another story was told by N.R., a twenty-year-old Serb woman who had spent seven months in a detention center where she was repeatedly raped by two men. She told the council, "I was first raped by a certain 'Pipica' and by Samir Malajhodzic of Sarajevo. . . .

Those two raped me all the time I was held in the camp. We were ill-treated by two dozen Muslim soldiers or so, but each of them would pick one girl for rape and didn't touch the others. The rapes took place in the room where we were all accomodated, so the other girls had to watch. The room next door was very small; they took us there for oral sex. I didn't get pregnant because a Muslim woman R.Z. provided me with contraceptives. [But] in early October [four months after she'd been taken] I got pregnant, too, because R.Z. was no longer able to supply me with contraceptives. The camp commander called 'Gravni,' I don't know his real name, asked me if I wanted to sign a deposition that I had been raped by Serbs. If I agreed, he said he would let me have an abortion. If not, I would have to keep the baby. I refused, although he tried to talk me into it for a long time. One girl, I don't remember her name, agreed in front of us her cell mates. The Muslims took her to the 'Jezero' gynaecological clinic, which is what they said, but she never came back. We found out from L. that the girl was killed. She saw her name on the list of killed Serbs offered for exchange by Muslims, in 'Gravni's' office."

N.R. was finally able to escape the camp with the help of the Muslim woman who had earlier supplied her with contraceptives. She ended her deposition by saying that in the seven months she had spent in the camp, "no humanitarian organization ever visited us, nor were we given any medical assistance."

The introduction to the council document said, "All the sides in the inter-ethnic and religious war in Bosnia-Herzegovina unnecessarily and excessively resorted to the practice of interning members of rival ethnic groups in camps and other places of forced detention. In doing so, they not only violated the provisions of the Geneva agreements but also made possible the massive maltreatment of the civilian population by their military formations even in cases when that population demonstrated readiness to be loyal to the lawfully or unlawfully established authorities. No side in the conflict can be exonerated from its share of responsibility for the practice of internment of civilians, especially women and children." Having said this, the introduction went on to criticize the International Red Cross for not extending its protection to Serb prisoners. "They were sorely remiss in their duty with respect to the protection of Serbs in Croat and Moslem controlled camps because they would procrastinate for months before eventually inspecting them and were not persistent enough in searching for hidden prisoners. In this way, many victims were deprived of the possibility of getting any protection whatsoever. Most ex-prisoners also have criticized their work, so that the Serb community in the former Yugoslav space will thoroughly have to examine the conduct of all international humanitarian organizations in the 1992–1993 war and assess whether it can have confidence in them and give them permission to operate in territories under its control in the future."

Coming from the U.S., where most opinions group near the center, listening to the extremes of opinion in Belgrade was a little shocking. Certainly among the leading intelligentsia in the U.S. one does not find such extremes of opinion; where there are extremes, they are held by people on the fringes of the society—the Revolutionary Communist party at one end, say, or the Ku Klux Klan at the other. In Belgrade, by contrast, opinions among leading figures ranged from those of Milic od Macva, who had pledged his soul to Greater Serbia and to a just war to win it, whose hatred of the West was maniacal, a position as extreme as the most right-wing attitudes in the U.S., to those who would have Slobodan Milosevic tried as a war criminal, not too distant from America's left-wing fringe. But in Belgrade highly respectable members of the intelligentsia were found at either extreme. Petar Lukovic of *Vreme* was among the antigovernment people. A former rock music critic for a popular state-run magazine, he began weaving political opinions into his columns when things began to go to hell in Yugoslavia. His opposition to the government was so intense that he was told to quit or be fired. He saved his job by going on sick leave for a year and a half, during which time he wrote a book on popular music.

Back to work for a few months, ever more adamantly political, he was finally forced to resign, but almost immediately *Vreme* was founded and he went to work for it. It was a natural home for him; the owner of the magazine and the other journalists he hired shared Lukovic's attitudes toward the government and planned to express them in the magazine. At first *Vreme* had a circulation of only about eight thousand. Three years later it had risen to about thirty thousand, mostly in Belgrade, and about 30 percent of its average seventy-five pages was advertising. While *Vreme* was mostly about politics, each week it contained a supplement featuring stories about computers or the economy, rock and roll, health, and so on. Petar told me, "You have to understand that those circulation figures are astounding, considering what we are. We are very extreme. About 70 percent of the magazine is about politics, attacking the regime. We do not put in our magazine people of all different opinions. People who read us are the people who agree with our political ideas." This sounded more like an expanded version of *The Nation* or *In These Times* than *Time*. Those two American magazines had about the same circulation nationally as *Vreme* did in Belgrade alone.

Vreme's staff of thirty journalists operated as a commune, sharing the magazine's revenues. Petar received about forty-five deutsche marks a month (twenty-seven dollars) as deputy editor, writing one of the only two columns in the weekly. He described his columns as satirical, his approach as that of "a satirist who mocks the members of the regime. My column is like Monty Python. It's a relief from the heavy politics of the rest of the magazine." As one of the leading dissidents in Serbia, Petar regularly traveled to the European capitals to talk about the politics of the wars in Yugoslavia.

Unfortunately, Petar said, *Vreme*'s future was not bright. Like *Borba*, it was losing its audience to emigration. Petar's claim that 30 percent of Serbia's population was illiterate and another 20 percent only functionally literate may have been high, but the numbers were growing as hordes of peasants came to Serbia—many to Belgrade—from Bosnia and Croatia. There was no audience for *Vreme* among Belgrade's newcomers. Still, *Vreme* was hawked on the streets of central Belgrade in search of new readers.

"But we are satisfied with our circulation, because a lot of other magazines are losing their readers. We have, I would say, a very strange audience. A very loyal audience. People who read *Vreme* are ready to give up milk, bread, sugar, luxuries, in order to have it. But we can't count on that money. Today it costs ten cents, tomorrow maybe only one cent, because of the inflation. Our aim is to sell more advertising."

One of *Vreme*'s big problems was getting paper. The one paper factory in Serbia was owned by the government and sold newsprint first to the state-run magazines. *Vreme* had some paper help from abroad, from the Soros Foundation. "But we can also buy on the black market," Petar said. "You can buy anything on the black market." It was manifestly silly to describe the secondary, or grey, market in Yugoslavia as a black market. Without it the economy would have collapsed. It was the only real market operating.

At the same time they feared the demise of *Vreme*, the staff was planning to publish another magazine titled *Vreme Entertainment*. "We are going to try to tell the young people here that we are going to beat the sanctions. We are not going to let them isolate us from the world. We are going to tell them what's going on in the world. What are the best movies, the best books, fashions, music, everything."

Petar and his tall, slender, pretty, blond wife, Vicna, who was dressed fashionably in black leggings and a long yellow tunic sweater, and looked younger than her thirty-eight years, took me to a busy, pleasant restaurant near their home in north Belgrade, a very old section of the city where there was a mixture of modern high-rise apartments and ancient houses. From the restaurant, where the veal steak tasted like shoe leather—the first poor meal I'd had in the city—we walked through barely lit, badly broken walkways to the high rise where the Lukovics had a modern five-room apartment on the eleventh floor, with a splendid view of the city. But a northwest exposure left them freezing in the winter because the inefficient central heating system barely reached them. They were thinking of selling or trading apartments, but conditions in Belgrade made that all but impossible.

Five-foot speakers on either side of the sofa and a wall of tapes attested to Petar's musical interests. The fashionable modern furnishings, electronic equipment, and household appliances that included, for instance, three different kinds of coffee makers, reflected his financial comfort. And scores of English-language books displayed his interest in world culture. A tall and fleshy man of forty-two, with piercing dark eyes and a mottled face, wearing a rumpled navy blue suit, Petar was a highly articulate and intense man of powerful convictions. He could talk steadily for hours, refusing to be interrupted, eager to convince, determined to control everything and everybody around him. I wondered what happened between him and his wife privately when publicly he cut her off almost as soon as she began to speak—while at the same time expressing love and affection for her.

Vicna made us a pot of powerful English coffee and brought out a bottle of Martell's and a plate of chocolates. We settled down to talk politics at about ten o'clock. "About my beliefs—I don't know whether they are right or wrong, but they are my beliefs," Petar said. "I think you have to start with the idea that all the evils in this country now—the millions of refugees, the millions getting killed, the catastrophic inflation, the nationalism, the fascism—all this evil started six years ago when Milosevic came to power. These evils started as a state project, as an ideological project. You should understand that everything we are witnessing today we have tested before in softer, smaller ways, through television, through media wars, political wars, all kinds of discussions and dialogues—simulations without arms—before these wars. So we were prepared for this kind of war. When Milosevic came to power he was ready to let Slovenia go, but he wanted all the power in the rest of Yugoslavia. People of Serbia, three years ago, had a choice between the war and Europe, between nationalism and democracy, between fascism and some very liberal ideas about harmony in Europe, between normal life and isolation and going to the garbage cans for food.

"This is a strange country because it is unbelievable the influence television has on the people. With the help of television, Milosevic made people think they made the right choice voting for his party. I should remind you that at the time Milosevic's slogans were 'peace, progress, harmony, unified Yugoslavia,' all that stuff. He was talking about everybody earning ten thousand dollars. Some slogans claimed we would be a new Sweden or a new Switzerland in a year or two. All this bullshit. It was obvious to myself and my friends that it was bullshit, but it wasn't obvious to most people. When those elections were finished in 1990, it was obvious we were going to have war.

"You must know that in 1989 we had a federal prime minister, Ante Markovic, who thought—and I thought so too—that if we had economic reform with free markets, free imports and exports, freedom of the press, and everything like a European country, the people would calm down with all this nationalistic stuff. But Milosevic used television, this evil tool, to explain to the people that what Markovic was doing was not for their own good. He told them that the money Markovic was distributing to people he was ripping off from Serbia. 'It's not good for Serbia,' he said, 'Serbia is threatened with these reforms.'

"If you think that a lot of people would see through Milosevic, you are wrong, because television was so powerful. There was no free television at that time, only the state's. And Milosevic repeated that message twenty-four hours a day, seven days a week, over a period of three years. So even intelligent people, even educated people, started to believe there was some kind of conspiracy among the other republics and then, in the second phase, that there was a world conspiracy against the Serbs, against the Orthodox. Everything, everybody, all the cars, all the animals, are hating Serbs. They believed that. There is almost a macro-conspiracy of hating Serbs. It's obvious we are talking about a propaganda plan that started in 1987 when Milosevic started his nationalist campaign here. He was always a Communist. In twenty-four hours he became an ardent nationalist. I don't believe in overnight changes in human beings. It isn't possible. The West didn't understand that Milosevic can be anything he wants to be. In order to protect his power, he can be a fascist, Communist, democrat, gay, whatever. Where the West is wrong is when they call him Communist. That's the foolishness of the West, that they portray him as a Communist dictator. For the West it's very simple, you know. They believe we have one bad guy in a country which is full of other bad guys, and in the other countries you have good guys. We don't have good guys in one place and bad guys in another here in the former Yugoslavia. Milosevic is just one very bad, very dangerous bad guy, not a Communist or a fascist or a nationalist, just a very bad guy who will do anything to hold on to his power."

Petar then drew an analogy. "What happened was as if in some small American town, a mayor turned out to be crazy, dangerous. Obviously, some people will rebel. But the rebels are not the pacifists. They are the guys like Dirty Harry who have guns but no ideas. Milosevic's anti-Croat campaign went on for two years. Obviously the Croats had to find somebody to stand up to Milosevic, so they found Tudjman. But he is stupid. He is everything that Milosevic is, but not as smart as Milosevic. So we have a bully against a bully. Milosevic is father to Tudjman. Without Milosevic, Tudjman could never be a leader or a president. And Izetbegovic the same way."

Vicna, obviously restless because she was effectively cut out of our conversation, turned on the television set beside her, playing it low, obviously intrigued by the highly explicit sex scenes. It was hard to concentrate on politics. Was this a locally produced film? No, Vicna explained, it was American. "But the embargo?" I asked, amazed. Vicna told me that the independent TV station and Politika TV regularly smuggled first-run movies and news clips from Europe and the U.S. and showed them late at night. "We get a good idea of what the rest of the world is saying about us from those smuggled news programs," she said.

With the television turned off, we returned to politics. I asked Petar to tell me about the history of the Politika publishing empire, most especially the newspaper *Politika*, which I knew to be the most popular paper in Belgrade. "When Milosevic came to power, *Politika* was the most powerful print media to support him. You found the most nationalistic articles there. That went on for about five years. Then Milosevic decided to take control of the publishing company. Suddenly there was a problem at *Politika*, which for eighty to ninety years was a great newspaper, always accurate and more or less independent. No one ever bothered them. You would have sworn, until they began to support Milosevic, that you read only the facts in *Politika*. Then Milosevic went too far and tried to take over. So they went on strike for two days and Milosevic backed off. Okay, he said, 'let them go their own way.' Then *Politika* and *Nin*, the magazine, and all the other company publications changed, quite a lot. Milosevic had betrayed them. Now I would say they are not opposition or even objective. I would say they are neutral, with a slight sympathy toward Milosevic. Which is much better than what we had. Because everybody read *Politika*. It was normal. You go to buy bread and you buy *Politika*. That was why the regime tried to get hold of it."

But Yugoslavia was quickly reaching a state similar to America's, where the print media were fast being replaced by television for the majority of people. "In this catastrophic situation, the first thing people are giving up are newspapers," Petar said. "People who are queueing for bread are not buying newspapers. That's why there's such a struggle for the control of television. Two years ago two people were killed in a huge demonstration organized by Vuk Draskovic to liberate television from state control. Even Seselj is today asking for 'normal' television."

"TV is pure propaganda?"

"It's *1984*," Vicna said.

"It's worse," Petar exclaimed. "I'm not saying ABC or CBS are ideal, but they are at least trying to reflect public opinion. Here television is not trying to reflect public opinion. It *is* public opinion. You can hear people repeating the exact same words they heard on television. It is shaping the minds of the people. Without television the people of Serbia wouldn't know how to think. The collective remembrance of the Serbian people is about ten seconds. You can see the population of Serbia as clay, and television as the sculptor. They make of this clay whatever they want. Tonight they say one thing, tomorrow something else." How many times have we heard such sentiments from critics of television in the U.S.?

"Belgrade is different. Here we can see Studio B and Politika TV. But the rest of Serbia watches only state-run television, which is telling them how to think, how to vote, whom to love this week, whom to hate. We are talking about a process that has been going on for six years, twenty-four hours a day, the heaviest propaganda the world has ever known." Heavier than that in the former Soviet Union or China? "Nowhere in Europe did television become the mightiest tool. Television-Serbia is Milosevic's private service. He doesn't hold news conferences. He doesn't talk to the other media. He just goes directly before the cameras on Television-Serbia. We cannot expect any changes around here unless television changes."

It seems not to have occurred to Petar that Serbians, like people all over the world, may spend more of their time watching the other two state television channels—culture and entertainment—than the news channels that Milosevic has preempted, that people might be as annoyed as Petar with the propaganda. Like his friend Sonja Besorski, he didn't have a high opinion of ordinary Serbs. It was also probably an exaggeration that the news station carried propaganda "twenty-four hours a day." Even Sonja didn't claim that. Which only slightly diminished the importance of the massive propaganda campaign conducted for the last six years by Milosevic.

"So would you say that Milosevic is a dictator?" I asked Petar.

"Ha! Of course! He's a modern dictator. He's a television dictator. He was the first to realize the strength of television and its influence. The first thing he did when he came to power in 1987 was to put his own man at the head of Television-Serbia." Some dictator who can be turned off by a flick of the switch and permits a fierce opponent to hawk on the streets a weekly magazine that gives 70 percent of its space to criticism of him. A testimony to the last twenty years of Tito's reign was that Serbs could use the word "dictator" so loosely. And testimony to the American shortage of information about Serbia was that U.S. officials referred to Milosevic as a Communist dictator.

"What I said before was that all the three wars we've had here were simulated first on television," Petar went on. "Milosevic was fighting but without arms, so the war was prepared. It was slowly building. Hysteria created on all sides—Milosevic here, Tudjman in Croatia, then Izetbegovic in Bosnia. All doing exactly the same thing. You already know in advance what your twin brother will do.

So I think that before the wars there were already secret agreements about the war in Croatia and in Bosnia Herzegovina."

"What sort of secret agreements?"

"Well, about Bosnia most certainly. I'm not sure about Croatia. It sounds crazy, but about Bosnia it is very rational. Both sides found the war useful for their own power. You know what I mean. I'll give you the example of Vukovar, which is very interesting. Before the war it was about 40 percent Serb. It is in the center of what Serbs claim to be their land, Eastern Krajina. The Serbs destroyed it completely. I said in an article, 'They liberated it to the ground.' But the fact is, when the fight for Vukovar started, Mr. Tudjman could have defended it. Lots of us think he deliberately wanted to make it happen the way it did. He wanted Vukovar to be destroyed because he wanted Croatia's independence to be recognized quickly. A week [more like a month] after the fall of Vukovar, Croatia was recognized as an independent country. Tudjman used Vukovar as a symbol for how Croatia was attacked and destroyed. For him it was great propaganda. That sort of thing has happened over and over again, on all sides. The powers have used it to further their political aims."

From his description of the fierce fighting in Vukovar that left the city in ruins, Petar left out the reputed roundup of five thousand Serbs who were put in camps, about a thousand of them killed, before the Yugoslav army entered the city. Those facts either supported his version of the events or contradicted them. If the Croatians were strong enough to round up, at gunpoint, five thousand local Serbs, why weren't they strong enough to defeat the Yugoslav army? Alternatively, perhaps the Yugoslav army, incensed by the massacre of the Serbs, fought so hard that they could not be defeated.

"Unfortunately for Milosevic, he couldn't hide one fact, that Serbs are always attacking somebody," Petar said.

"That's sort of in the nature of the beast, isn't it? There are more Serbs than others."

"That's exactly the reason they shouldn't have been fighting. This is too bad for Milosevic, what his Ministry of Information doesn't understand. Okay, they say, 'They provoked us.' Sure there were lots of provocations, but there were other ways to respond to them. Now there is a lot of talk about how the war in Croatia started, how *they* were so provocative. But the fact is that Milosevic used the stupidity of the Croatian government. The Croatians expelled the Serbs in their new constitution, which was very, very stupid. Nobody cared about the constitution, but it was a great excuse to arm the Serbs there, to give them orders to start the fight, and to get the Croatians to make more stupid moves. The point is, this war is very stupid, unbelievably stupid—but at the same time it is very clever. There were so many complicated plans. Like Seselj says, 'If the Croats do this, we will do this.' Anyone who thinks this war was spontaneous, a revolt of the people, is stupid."

I wondered whether Milosevic had underestimated his enemies. "Yes," Petar said, "he made one big mistake. He and everybody else thought this war would be very, very short. They thought they could crush the Muslims and Croatians very quickly and go ahead with the plan for a greater Serbia or a smaller Yugoslavia, which includes parts of Croatia, Bosnia, Macedonia. They have taken a lot—70 percent of Bosnia, 40 percent of Croatia. So the Serb side at this point is a winner, but the loss is terrible. We have lost 200,000 young people. A real brain drain. We will need five or six generations just to be on the same level of knowledge we had two years ago. And the isolation from the world, which despises us! Whatever happens in the future, even the Serbs who live in Serbia are not very happy to join their lands with some conglomerate called 'Big Serbia,' with Serbs who are outside of Serbia. I don't know who else is going to tell you this, but I'm going to say it: Serbs living in Serbia are completely different from those living outside Serbia. Those people are primitive. Usually 90 percent of them have been living in the woods and the mountains. We are talking about some wild, wild people—nationalistic, hating towns and anything that's urban."

Vicna interjected, "There are so many of them now in Belgrade—refugees, and the people hate them because the refugees are so sure that war was needed. The people here don't think like that. We blame those people because we now live so poorly. Especially the people who must support their relatives. They haven't enough for themselves."

"You should know about the Serbs in Croatia," Petar added. "One part of them live in Slavonia, which is the eastern part, near Serbia. These were the richest people in Yugoslavia. They had no reason to rebel against Croatia, but they were made to fight. They lost everything. Now they are here. And they are angry. They see the war now as the only way to get theirs back, by expelling Croats or Bosnians. They hate those of us who speak against the war. They don't realize they have been used. Milosevic didn't care about them or any other Serbs, as Tudjman doesn't care about the Croats, or Izetbegovic doesn't care about the Muslims. All they care about is their political interests. So when you read about the rights of Serbs, it's a lie. They don't care about anyone's human rights. But you can't control war. Only to a certain extent, then you lose control. It happened so terribly in Bosnia. All those leaders can't control their groups.

"So the people who came here, most tragically, were angry and became radicals, fascists, nationalists, because they found in these creeds the simple solutions to the most complicated problems. If you ask Seselj, for instance, what he would do if we had a nuclear accident like Three-Mile Island, he says, 'We'll destroy it.' Just simple answers to the most complicated problems. That's why this country has changed so much."

I asked Petar whether he thought many people in Belgrade were in a slight state of shock as a result of the emigration. "After so many years of hanging in there despite everything," I said, "people are now leaving in droves. I guess a lot of people also left after World War II, but that somehow was different, I sense. Some were fleeing communism and some were Cetniks fleeing the wrath of the Communists. But it probably wasn't as many and probably wasn't felt as strongly because the society was in such good shape for the first time in history."

"Yes," Petar said, "for the first time in our history we have cultural emigration. We have had emigration before, but it wasn't the elite of the nation. Now you can go to so many towns in Europe and find our cultural elites there—our writers, artists, journalists, academics. When I go to Paris or Zurich or Amsterdam, I find so many friends there. They are washing dishes and they are not happy, but for the moment it is better than here."

"Are you planning to leave?" I asked Petar.

"I would leave, but he won't," Vicna said. "He is too famous now to leave."

"What can I do if I go? Here I have a place. If I were twenty, yes, but now, at forty-two, it is already too late for me. But young people can find hope somewhere else. I don't want to sound tragic, but this is a country with no future. With the sanctions, without sanctions, with a new government, with an old government, with Milosevic, without Milosevic. This is a country without a future."

"Would you have said that in 1987?"

"No. I wouldn't even have said this three years ago. Then we were on the edge of being a full member of the European Community. But the extent of the damage that the Yugoslavs—I say that and I mean it: the Yugoslavs—did to themselves, not the Americans, not the Germans, the Yugoslavs themselves, is so great that we need at least thirty years with the most ideal international help, with an ideal population, with ideal liberal ideas to recapture what we had three years ago. It's impossible to think all that will happen, or that Serbs, Croats, and Muslims will be able to live together, that those people here will not be nationalists. So it will be more like fifty years before we can again be what we were before. The worst thing for me is how beautiful it was, how great it was, what we destroyed. If anyone had told me this could be done, I would have said it was impossible."

It was now about 2 a.m. and Vicna was offering still another pot of coffee. I asked this time for Turkish coffee; the English brew she'd been serving was so strong that I was sure there would be no sleep for me that night. For reasons beyond me, Turkish coffee didn't have the same insomniac effects of regular coffee. I did hear somewhere that the darker the blend, the less caffeine. Having solved the coffee problem, Petar returned to the problems of Yugoslavia.

"For almost two years we have not been able to phone between Croatia and Serbia. The problem is political, not technical. They could easily fix the connections in twenty-four hours."

"If they agreed."

"Of course. They don't want us to talk to each other to learn what is happening—that it is not so terrible in Belgrade as they hear on television in Zagreb, and not so terrible in Zagreb as we hear on television in Belgrade. Literally, everybody here has friends, family, lovers in Zagreb. Vicna's whole family is in Croatia. She hasn't heard from them in two years. I'm the only connection between them. When I go abroad, I call them.

"I have to tell you that what we have in the former Yugoslavia is not just nationalistic regimes but anarchy. You cannot call this society a Communist or a democratic or a fascist or a protestant or a sexual society, or what have you. None of those. It is an anarchist society. Mainly it is a criminal society. It is based on criminal activity from the bottom to the top. Not just because of the sanctions. They were actually beautiful for this regime. The regime made small people into criminals, to humiliate them, to make them fight for their survival."

I told Petar that when I had talked with Gordana Logar, she had objected to my suggestion that Milosevic had been provocative in his relations with Croatia and Bosnia. Perhaps she didn't understand the English word?

"Perhaps," he said. "In fact, there has been provocation on all sides. Milosevic was one provocation after another. Then, when Tudjman came to power, everything he did was provocation. One provocation brings another, and so on. It's a crazy game. And in the end there is just one big provocation, and that's called war. You don't have to be smart to figure this out. The same game started in Bosnia Herzogovina; the only difference now is that you have three sides. All three sides are responsible for terrible atrocities, terrible crimes, at different levels. There are more Serbs so they are doing more, but all three sides are guilty.

"If you understand politics it was really crazy when Milosevic called a press conference and said, 'What are we going to do about this? All three sides are shooting at one another. It's not just the Serbs.' What if you have a civil war in Chicago, where the blacks and whites are shooting each other, and the mayor says, 'What are we going to do? Blacks and whites are shooting each other. It's not my fault.' But people tend to forget who started it. These days only a few people will tell you the truth about how the war in Bosnia started. Everybody's going to tell you what's happened in the last five months, or the last five days, or the last five hours. But nobody talks about the most important thing: who started this madness? I would say the same thing about the war in Croatia.

"The war in Croatia started the moment Tudjman was in power. I'm not sure he was thinking about war, but deep down inside I think he wanted war. He was doing the same thing that Milosevic was doing in Serbia."

I said I understood that the war in Bosnia started after the EC recognized its independence. Petar said, "They hoped it would avoid a war."

"But in fact it led to the war. Is that correct?"

"I'm not one of those who believe that. With or without recognition, the war was inevitable. Serbians used the recognition as an excuse to start the war. And Muslims and Croats used the fact that the Serbs started it to make the war. But this war was planned long before. Karadzic and Milosevic wanted war in Bosnia."

"Would military intervention by the West have stopped the war immediately?"

"Yes, I think so. In 1991 military intervention in twenty-four hours would have scared the shit out of Milosevic's army or the Croatian army or anybody."

"And that would have been that?"

"Listen, the front lines then were fifty kilometers. Now the front lines in all Yugoslavia are about three thousand kilometers. And now the U.S. is talking about bombing. Where were they three years ago when it would have been a simple thing to stop the war?"

Vicna turned on the television set again, without the sound. She apologized; it was a film she really wanted to see.

I asked Petar if he would have become a political writer if things hadn't gone to hell in Yugoslavia. "No," he told me. "That was one of the beauties of the former regime. If you didn't want to get into politics, you could write about anything you wanted. Most people were bored with politics. Culture, everything was much more interesting. Unfortunately, the situation changed so much that we all had to change. You had to deal with politics or politics would deal with you." I thought that perhaps if more people had been involved earlier in the politics of the country, history might have taken a different turn. Most likely the complacency that prevailed throughout Yugoslavia for so many years led to the ease with which Milosevic came to power and built the base that enabled him to destroy his country. As we say in the U.S., it's best not to leave politics to the politicians.

"Have you been harassed?" I asked Petar.

"Once, when I was a rock critic, I was attacked physically. If you exclude threatening letters, phone calls . . ."

"That's what I mean."

"In Serbia I find that normal. I've had terrible phone calls, threatening letters. Almost every issue I get a letter that I'm a traitor, that I'm going to be killed, that I deserve to die. Before the war, during the war. It happens here. You have to be cautious. I am one of the most extreme critics of the Milosevic regime. You never know what's going to happen. I'm not foolish, but I'm not scared. I go out like always." I was amazed that Petar regarded the harassment he received as normal Serbian behavior. Did he think people like himself in other nations didn't get the same kind of treatment? "No," he said, "Not like the Serbs. We are a strange people."

I told Petar I had been to visit the Serbian-Jewish Friendship Society and about the Jewish letter advocating the bombing of the Serbs that was discussed so heatedly there. He told me that everybody in Serbia knew about that letter because Milosevic had discussed it on television. "But not the actual letter. He never read the actual letter. He just talked about it, about how it called for the bombing of Serbia. He even tried to start some anti-Semitism about it, because some of the names were Jewish. But it was not all Jewish, just some. But people were talking about how the Jews were always our friends and now they want to bomb us."

"I want to tell you that many, many Americans are in favor of bombing Belgrade," I told him.

"It's a little late now, but if it would bring an end to all this, I wouldn't mind," Petar said. "The more and more this catastrophic situation goes on, the more convinced I am that we have to destroy everything and build from the ashes. Not Yugoslavia. Yugoslavia is dead. This is Serbia-Montenegro. That's all. We have to start all over from the beginning."

It was now 3 a.m. We were still wide awake from all the caffeine we had imbibed. The chocolate helped too. The brandy had hardly dulled us at all. But I was beginning to get anxious. It was time to go. Still, I had one more question. Kosovo.

"Unfortunately, I am not an optimist about Kosovo. I think on both sides—the Serbs and the Albanians—there is so much extremism which has been building. On the Serbian side they say the Albanians want to take the holy lands and join Albania. On the Albanian side they don't trust any Serb. They cannot see the difference between Milosevic and me. And that's a big problem, because if you have two sides that cannot have a dialogue, the only dialogue will be war. Unfortunately, I think it will end in the bloodiest of wars.

"The Albanians have no democracy there. It's a democracy like here. But what the Albanians hope is that Milosevic stays in power and keeps doing what he's doing, refusing to talk to them, making all kinds of demands on them. They hope it gets so bad they can internationalize the situation, and then they will get Kosovo with the help of the international community. But it can't happen that way. The Serbs will not stand for it. There is a solution: if all the Serbs there who are against Milosevic—and there are a lot—get together with the Albanians and kick him out, and kick out the equally bad Albanian leadership, they can all sit down and talk together. They could find a good solution. I have many good friends there who want that and could make it happen. But it won't happen. Instead both sides feed each other crazy problems, and slowly it builds until some spark will ignite the bloodiest war. But not now. It's not the right time for either side. And the Albanians are under pressure from the Americans not to make any foolish moves. Milosevic knows the Albanians have the promise of the Americans to intervene on their side. So I think it will go on like this for a long, long time. Maybe it will be the same thing in ten years."

It was a terrible way to end the evening, but I realized that Petar's pessimism and cynicism made a brighter note impossible. There were, in fact, few bright notes in my conversations with Serbs. The one that prevailed throughout, however, was the impression of intelligence and compassion I heard in their voices. Even this forceful elitist, cynical and pessimistic about the majority of his countrymen, showed real compassion for their plight.

9 This was the day I was to go to Mira's office to pay for my week's lodgings and food at the hotel. She also offered to call Meme, her black market money changer, to exchange some dollars for me. Mira told me that Meme supported herself and her family by working part-time as international student exchange officer at the University of Belgrade. It used to be a full-time job for her, but now there were few international students at the university. So Meme also worked part-time for Mira and as a money changer. She was a small, stout, sad-looking woman, her hair pulled into a tight bun at her neck, with no makeup or jewelry and dark, shabby-looking clothes. She spoke perfect English but didn't speak often. She brought me fifteen dollars' worth of dinars that she said equaled twice her current month's pay from the university. Her salary had been cut by far more than half.

After I had given Mira an eagerly requested report of my visit so far, she asked, "But you aren't hating it here?" I reassured her that I felt quite the opposite. With all the problems, I was finding it both depressing and exhilarating. "You aren't sorry you came?" she pleaded. She wanted so much for me to love her city that I could not give her enough reassurance. It took a little while before I realized that she was acting as a voluntary public relations counsel for the city, hoping she could influence me to go home and paint a picture of a beautiful city under siege.

In fact Belgrade is not a beautiful city; it is too grimy, too decayed-looking, and lacks the beautiful eighteenth- and nineteenth-century architecture of a Paris, Budapest, or Prague, or the stunning twentieth-century architecture of Chicago. Yet with all its grime and decay, the lackluster old architecture of its housing stock and public buildings, and the absence of many historic buildings and monuments as a result of enormous damage in two world wars, it nevertheless has the charm of an old world city mixed with the new. There is still a sense of the small provincial city—with its narrow twisting streets, outdoor markets, parks, and old churches—that Belgrade was before World War I; but this is mixed with a modern, late-twentieth-century metropolis, the capital of a major nation, with large, handsome public squares, wide boulevards, huge neon signs, and a few modest knockoffs of the international-style buildings one sees in American and European capitals. Here most modern structures are stately buildings of moderate proportions. I took photographs of the view from my hotel room that offered a microcosm of the city—gargoyles on the school building across the street, greenery in the school yard, a mix of old and new mid-rise apartment houses, and in the background a couple of taller, more modern buildings.

But the physical quality of the city was almost overwhelmed by the sight of streets crowded with people standing around idly, or trying to sell something, anything, from the top of a pile of cardboard boxes, or walking to nonjobs, nonshopping, or nonlunch appointments. The unemployment rate was staggering, there was little to buy, prices were high, and people had no money to buy anything. Restaurants were empty. Nevertheless, the streets were crowded with people carrying bags, ready to buy a loaf of bread should they find one. One brought one's own bag. And there were breadlines. The people who weren't walking were gathered, as many as a hundred at a time, at tram stops in the middle of the street, waiting to crowd onto the few trams still running. The buses had been removed because of a lack of oil, making travel on the trams at midday worse than rush hour on the New York subway.

As I grew to know the city, I could distinguish the refugees from the natives; city people looked quite different from their country cousins. There were lots of refugees on the streets. I had learned that when I wanted to ask directions, I should try to find someone well dressed carrying a briefcase. Such a person would be a native and might speak English. But there weren't many such people on the streets. Instead there were a lot of poorly dressed people who looked like peasants.

Whatever charm this city had was considerably diminished by these depressing sights. And I was tired of eating veal. When I arrived and saw so much veal on the menu at the hotel, I was thrilled. But ten days later, having eaten veal nearly every evening, prepared in half a dozen different ways, I would have given almost anything for a piece of lowly chicken or beef or pork, none of which seemed to exist in Belgrade. Or pasta. And some green vegetables. I did have fish one night, at a fish restaurant near the hotel, but it was fried, which is not to my taste. But there was a war on in Belgrade, after all. Not a shooting war—an economic war that the West was waging against Serbia and winning easily.

The physical damage was in malnutrition, suicide, and death because of the lack of medicine and medical supplies. But the damage was also psychological. Belgrade faces were either sad or grim; I didn't see many smiles. On the other hand, I also saw very little rudeness. People on the trams were considerate in their crush, and in the streets there was none of the shoving and pushing that one gets on the streets of New York, for instance. People queued up patiently, and in shops clerks were patient while people struggled with their funny money, the value of which changed almost hourly.

When I told Mira I needed to buy cigarettes but hated dealing with the black market because the sellers didn't speak English and I felt I was being robbed, she offered to take me to a shop to buy them. She took me to a place that described itself as "duty free," a small version of American discount stores. It had a small stock of foreign goods and took my dollars. Previously operated by the state, it was now privately owned. Belgrade had quite a chain of state-run import emporiums that were apparently now operating with smuggled goods. At the "duty-free" shop, where I found a clerk who spoke English, I bought English Rothman's, described as a mild cigarette, for far less than the shops and the black marketers were charging, but passed up a sixteen-dollar bottle of Ballantine's scotch for a four-dollar bottle of vinjak, the national brandy, that Mira took me to buy in a little local food shop.

Back at the hotel, after sampling the vinjak, which was rough and ready for my nerves frayed from lack of sleep, I lay down for a short nap before my dinner later with Mile Manic. I reflected on my American annoyance that so few Serbs spoke English. What chance does a foreign visitor to the United States have of finding store clerks, taxi drivers, hotel maids, or any service personnel who speak their language? We arrogantly expect the whole world to speak our language. The wonder is that English has, indeed, become such a universal language that most educated people everywhere do speak it. Mile had told me that it was taught in the schools in Belgrade. But as several people explained, Belgrade had a considerable amount of illiteracy. It was likely that all those service personnel and black marketers had had little schooling.

Mile picked me up at seven and took me to a lovely old place on the outskirts of town that he said was one of Belgrade's best restaurants, expensive and good. The sure sign of luxury in the restaurant was the wood paneling—ceilings and walls done in lovely decorative woods. It was almost empty. We had a couple of cocktails, and I asked him to order a good Serbian meal for me. He ordered—what could I say—the ubiquitous veal steak, fried mushrooms and fried cheese, and two bottles of fine red wine.

In our mellow mood he told me stories of his family and friends, his favorite slightly mad uncle, his early life in Belgrade, his schooling, and his sadness at feeling he could never return for more than a brief visit. We chatted for three hours, scarcely mentioning politics, the war, or the embargo. We kissed fondly at my hotel door, and I promised to visit his family soon.

10

Today, for the first time, I got hopelessly lost in the maze of Belgrade streets. It took me more than an hour to find my way to the offices of the Soros Foundation. First I discovered they had moved since I obtained their address from Article 19. I had foolishly not checked the address against the one I'd been given two months earlier by the London organization. It took quite a while to find someone in the building who spoke enough English to explain that the foundation had moved; then came the always impossible task of getting through to telephone information service for the new address. Then the cab driver dropped me at the wrong address. My fault. I had given him the wrong number. I walked a mile in search of the right one.

Later I tried to walk back to the hotel, having been given directions and told it was only a few blocks away. I wandered through what felt like half the streets in central Belgrade, stopping in shops to browse. Numerous tiny shops on all the side streets still had a little something to sell—jewelry, women's clothes, books, furniture, art objects, whether handmade or smuggled in or taken from old stock that had been stored away. Most of what I saw was quite lovely, but with prices rising daily I didn't dare spend any of the dollars I'd brought. There was no way to get more money. I'd been nervous traveling with a few thousand dollars in small bills which I'd been advised to take. I had brought only what I had estimated I would need, with a small addition for emergencies that I now feared would be eaten up by inflation. Furthermore, none of the shopkeepers I encountered spoke English, and I expected, in this poverty-stricken land, that upon hearing a foreign tongue they would charge me outlandish prices, just as the café owners and taxi drivers were doing. I had more than once paid ten dollars for a one-mile taxi ride, cursing the situation in which I couldn't communicate with the cab drivers, couldn't figure out the funny money, couldn't walk because I couldn't find my way in the maze, couldn't read the street signs, and couldn't easily ask the way because so many people spoke no English and the Serb language is hard as hell to pronounce so that I couldn't make myself understood in my few words of Serbian.

Suddenly, a couple of hours after I'd started this short walk back to the hotel, I found myself on a street I recognized as being only a couple blocks from my destination. Sheer luck. It was five o'clock. I had another appointment at six.

The Soros Foundation was founded by George Soros, an American multimillionaire born and raised in Hungary. Soros fled communism after World War II and went to London, where he was graduated from the London School of Economics. He began playing the market with unusual success. In the 1970s he established his foundation to fund efforts to bring democracy to countries where there was none. He started in South Africa but soon gave up there. Shortly after, he opened an office in Hungary and followed that with other offices in Eastern Europe. In 1991, after making a deal with then Prime Minister Ante Markovic, he opened the office in Yugoslavia. The first joint project was to fund young intellectuals and scientists for work and study abroad.

Then the war started and Markovic was thrown out of office. The original plan had to be abandoned. What had been the executive board of the Yugoslav Soros Foundation, with members from the various republics, was broken up to form foundations in each of the former republics.

Slobodan Nakarada was managing director of the Yugoslav Foundation. Another tall, handsome, highly articulate, dramatic Serb, thirty-eight years old, an economist by training who previously was counsel for international affairs for the Yugoslav Parliament, Slobodan had a thatch of black hair, full black beard, horn-rimmed glasses, and was wearing an elegant fisherman's sweater and chinos. He had quit the Parliament in 1992 when Milosevic's undemocratic influences began to overwhelm him. Speaking English almost like a native, he took only a little more than an hour to spell out the role of his foundation and the difficulties of trying to function in Belgrade as an antiwar American organization whose founder had contributed heavily to the Bosnians.

"Very soon after the war broke out, we figured we had to do something about it, and we started organizing ourselves. Very rapidly after that the sanctions came, and we had to change our status. We couldn't do what we wanted to do. The agreement between Mr. Soros and the federal government was never implemented, so we decided, with Mr. Soros, that we would become an independent foundation outside the government. That's how we registered with the government, and that's the way we have functioned." The budget the first year was $620,000. Since then, "budget" was a meaningless word. Whatever money the foundation needed was brought in surreptitiously from Budapest—"a very complicated process," Slobodan said.

Most of the projects consisted of humanitarian help. "We just distributed a shipment of medicine and medical equipment worth five million dollars. We have a team of doctors that works with the foundation. We have a whole system to help hospitals throughout Serbia."

The Soros Foundation also provided help for children. More than 2,500 refugee and Serbian kids were taken to summer camps in 1993. Funds were also given to students, academics, and others who were invited abroad to attend meetings or give lectures, though the number of such people was small because of the sanctions. Slobodan corrected my impression that those invited abroad were dissidents.

"No," he said emphatically, "they are students, scholars of all kinds with a range of political attitudes." This prompted a mild outburst. "Unfortunately, I think the West still has not accepted that we have here people who believe they are Yugoslavs and not Serbs or Montenegrins or whatever. We're a minority, and unfortunately nobody accepts us as a minority. But there are people who consider themselves Yugoslavs. I don't consider myself anything else. Facing the nationalistic problem that exists in this country, we are completely independent. We do not cooperate with the existing government, especially because we are an American institution. And we've been hassled a lot about that, especially because Mr. Soros was one of the signatories of the famous letter in favor of bombing Serbian positions. The president of the Yugoslav Foundation is right now in New York discussing that letter. Mr. Soros can have his position, but that doesn't mean we have to agree with those sentiments.

"But we're branded as an American institution working to open up the country to an American takeover, or I'm called a CIA agent. A few weeks ago I had a radio interview, and they asked me if I was a CIA agent. I said, 'If someone can prove that, I'm going to write to Washington and tell them to pay me the wages that I haven't yet received.' But the minute you are branded as American, you are bad, you are trying to destroy this country."

Slobodan was concerned about the brain drain in Belgrade. "In the last three or four months, because of the sanctions, 17,000 young people have left because they can't find any kind of work. This foundation is bombarded with requests for help with projects. We have 150 people coming daily for scholarships or programs they need financed. We don't give any cash here. We give equipment, books, such things for research, or airplane tickets. If we give money for living expenses, it is paid from Budapest or New York."

I told Slobodan I had seen several young men in the lobby, as I waited to see him, who looked like they had come for humanitarian aid. "They looked very depressed to me."

"You won't find anyone in Belgrade who looks very happy," he said. "Your perception of someone being depressed may be different from ours. These people are not coming for humanitarian help. They want scholarships or help to work on a program, or want to work with us on some program of ours. Our general help is oriented toward hospitals and big institutions, such as the university, where we can help more people. One of our biggest efforts is for the refugees. We buy food, clothing, shoes, medicines, school equipment for refugees, of which there are now 800,000 in Yugoslavia."

Soros was the only foundation in Yugoslavia, compared with other countries where there are hundreds or thousands, as in the U.S. Until just a few years ago the government functioned as the "foundation" in Communist countries. Such private ventures didn't exist. Foundations are built on the profits from free enterprise and are designed to supplement government funding. Now the governments of these countries are poverty-stricken, and their role in funding science, technology, and the arts is severely limited. In Yugoslavia it scarcely existed. "So you can imagine the pressure on us," Slobodan said. And, as in the U.S. in the 1980s and 1990s, when government funds for social welfare were drastically cut, most of the foundation's funds were being used for such projects.

Soros also helped fund the independent media. "We help *Vreme* and *Borba* and *Republika* and Studio B TV and Radio B92 and a whole lot of radio stations throughout Yugoslavia. Of course the government is not keen on what we're doing here because they think we're undermining their policies. I have the opposite feeling. I think we're doing positive work. In some ways I think we're buying social peace for the government because we're helping so many people. Because we see the social structure of Yugoslavia going to pieces, we're planning programs that will help not only the refugees but everybody, because soon there will be little difference between the refugees and all the rest."

"The refugees serve a useful propaganda purpose for the government?"

"Yes, and a very big voting machine for the government. The government is using them." The refugee vote—one could vote in local elections if one lived in the city for two days—was strongly nationalistic, hence strongly supported Milosevic.

Like other dissidents, Slobodan believed that "the sanctions have not fulfilled their purpose, and they never will. Especially because people in the West don't understand our mentality here. They say, 'A good Serb is a dead Serb,' a phrase I have heard in the West. We are completely satanized. People don't want to believe that, yes, the Serbs have a lot to answer for in this war in Yugoslavia, but that it is a much more complicated story, and that all sides have much to answer for. What is not understood is that if the sanctions were removed, Mr. Milosevic's government would collapse.

"Unfortunately, he gets a lot of help from the opposition. It is not unified. All the groups are working for themselves. All think they're the smartest. They offer no alternative to Mr. Milosevic. In the opposition there is no one person who can rise, whom the people can relate to. All these opposition leaders are egocentric. They feel that what they represent is the only way for the people—and the people, seeing this, don't have a choice. These elections in December will not change the situation very much. I hope Mr. Milosevic wins completely because then, after the winter with the total collapse of the country, the whole blame will fall on his party, and then the people will realize that his party is not the right one."

I told Slobodan that when I had left Petar Lukovic a couple of nights before, at 3 a.m., slightly sloshed, I had had an image of Milosevic hanging by his feet, like Mussolini, after the bombing of Belgrade. "That is extreme," Slobodan said, "but understandable. But you have to understand first that Mr. Milosevic is a very smart politician who is making the right moves. The opposition are not making any right moves. They never have any alternative plans. Mr. Milosevic doesn't have to do much besides watch them do everything for him. Also, he is slowly realizing that if he is to be accepted in the West, he must make some concessions, which he is doing—concessions on free parliamentary elections, concessions on human rights questions, concessions on the Bosnian question. At the same time he is working hard to bring peace in Bosnia because he wants the sanctions lifted. He knows that the sanctions can bring social unrest to topple him, and he can't allow that. I don't like him, but I have to respect him. He has good moves. He's smart. No, I don't think he will be hanging from a tree. I think he is here to stay for a long time. It's going to be a show of democracy, but he will control everything."

"Like Tito?"

"Yes, like Tito in many ways. But Tito was smarter. He gave concessions to everyone who gave him problems. Milosevic is still learning. You know, he had a chance to become a great leader because he was offering the Serbs big ideas, among them that Serbia was sacrificed by Tito. But that's losing ground now. It is one thing to offer big ideas to a people who have never had anything, but we had a good life and now we're going back to the Stone Age. The people will reach a limit of tolerance, and then there will be great social unrest. I think Mr. Milosevic is aware of that."

"You don't think that point is very close with this terrible inflation, all this funny money that no one can figure out or buy anything with?"

"As long as the people still get some crumbs, still survive, Milosevic will still have leverage. A few days ago I was talking to a taxi driver who told me, 'I only had to wait six days for gasoline.' I said to him, 'You shouldn't have to wait six minutes. When you think like that, you are helping Milosevic survive.' And he told me, 'Ah, yes, but I'm functioning. That's all that counts.' Nobody understands this. Yugoslavia is very difficult to understand."

I told Slobodan that some of the people I'd talked to had said Yugoslavs were slightly crazy. "But no one can define it really. They just know in their hearts and their heads that they are crazy."

"'Craziness' is too harsh a word," Slobodan said. "It's a question of perspective. Here we have a very small country that has living in it I don't know how many nationalities and minorities. Each of them demands recognition now. Under Tito, everybody pointed to Yugo-slavia and said, 'Look at how they solve their national minority questions. They have their own language, their own schools.' Now the thing has turned over. You can't deny history forever. But when you look around the world at what's happening with this question, no one wants to look anywhere but at Yugoslavia. Everything here is bad, everywhere else is good. When they talk about secession, nationalistic movements, it's always Yugoslavia. What about Italy, Spain, the Soviet Union? I don't think Yeltsin will be able to solve the problems there. I talked to my counterpart in Russia and told him, 'Why don't you guys use us as an example? Fight against national-ism. It brings destruction, poverty, pain, and a lot of dead people. That's the basic thing. Fight against nationalistic movements.'

"The West made a huge mistake by not helping Yugoslavia financially when Mr. Markovic was in power. If they had given us economic aid, it would have made a great difference. As an econ-omist myself, I think Mr. Markovic had a fantastic plan that would have solved our problems. There would have been no need for nationalistic movements because the economy would have solved the problems. But without the aid, Mr. Markovic was powerless and finally was thrown out of office. The EC came here and looked things over and went back and said, 'We're not giving them any money because those six presidents of the republics will all use it for nationalistic purposes.' Now the tragedy is that those presidents are now presidents of independent states. Economic aid could have stopped that.

"The West is playing a very smart double game. On one side they say, 'We want to support the democratic powers, the opposition powers,' but on the other side nobody's helping. Nobody's coming. Nobody even wants to hear what is happening here. As I said before, Serbia has a lot to answer for in this tragedy, but there are many questions for which Croatia and the Muslims must answer. And nobody in the West wants to hear this. Any resolution passed in the UN will be to punish Serbia. And then you'll have a huge, huge reaction in Yugoslavia.

"You know, we have always traveled everywhere. Now, it's not written on my forehead that I'm opposed to Mr. Milosevic, but it's written in my passport that I am Serbian, and I get hassled wherever I go. Any border I cross I am branded as someone who has done something terrible. No! Not everyone in this country has done something terrible. But unfortunately we pay the price for a few. And the sanctions only help Milosevic. He can say, 'Hey, the whole world is against us. The U.S. is a huge country that wants to destroy us. Germany wants Yugoslavia to become a zone where they can dump their trash—they want a cheap market, cheap labor.'

"You know, we lived with the illusion that our people were highly educated and well informed. Now we conclude that our people don't know anything, that they are badly informed. Basically they no longer care who is in power. They simply want bread, a school for their children, peace, and an opportunity to get a job. We had all that. Soon you'll have this ridiculous situation in which people will say, 'Why don't we get the Communists to come back? When Tito was here we had forty years of peace. We could travel anywhere we wanted, we had prosperity. Oh, we didn't have all the human rights that we might, we didn't have the free press that we should have, but who cares? We lived a normal life. What is happening now? What kind of democracy is this if I can't travel anywhere, I don't have anything to eat, there are no jobs, people are dying?'

"Elections are scheduled for the 19th of December. It was a smart move of Milosevic's, instead of waiting until after the winter when people will be without heat." Our conversation was taking place in late October, two months before the scheduled parliamentary elections, but there was little electioneering except that on state-run television. The only organization with funds to campaign was Milosevic's Socialist Party, though the independent media were giving space to the few oppositionists who were participating in the election. The exception was the well-financed campaign of Arkan (Zeljko Raznatovic), the candidate of the Party of Serbian Unity, who was one of the most bestial of the paramilitary irregulars fighting in Bosnia and was a wanted criminal in Europe. Milosevic was allegedly backing Arkan to retain his Albanian seat in Parliament. The city was plastered with large posters of his smiling, darkly handsome face, dressed in a suit and tie. No military garb; his image was being cleaned up. All predictions indicated that Milosevic's candidates, including Arkan, would win by a landslide.

I asked Slobodan for his theory about the start of the war. He said, "You know that the Yugoslav army was the third or fourth largest in Europe. It is rumored that there was some apprehension about that in Europe. But that is aside, though it's important. When Slovenia announced its secession from the country, if the army had gone in and stopped it, there would have been a lot of people all over Europe complaining how terrible it was. But this was an internal matter for Yugoslavia, and there would have been no more secessions. They would have been stopped in their tracks. But it didn't happen that way. The army wasn't unified. Many army officers didn't want to do what they were supposed to do." The army had moved into Slovenia supposedly to take control of airports and other strategic points and gain control of the borders, but it hardly fired a shot, and fled after only a brief exchange. The Yugoslavian Red Cross reported that, in all, forty-nine people were killed in mild skirmishing.

"Do you think Milosevic deliberately let Slovenia go, as I've heard?" I asked. Slovenia had always been a somewhat anomalous appendage of Yugoslavia, closer to the Germanic people than the Balkans, with its own different language and with few Serbs living there.

"Milosevic didn't care about Slovenia. Everyone knows that. But Croatia and Bosnia Herzegovina should never have been recognized by the international community until certain guarantees were given to the Serb minority, to assure them equal rights, which Tudjman didn't want to talk about. Germany and Austria got involved and were pushing too fast. When Croatia got its independence and the war broke, we talked with people in Bosnia. We had a peace caravan going to Sarajevo. We talked to a lot of EC officials and we told them, 'Listen, don't allow Bosnia Herzegovina to be recognized as an independent country until a lot of these national questions are answered. The minute you give them the opportunity to become an independent country, we're going to have war.' The answer we received was, 'Don't worry, everything is under control.' They recognized Bosnia Herzegovina, and we got the war. The Serbs did not participate in the referendum on independence in Bosnia, and they thought they had a legitimate right to protect their own territories. I don't agree with that. I believe that the only way to settle a problem is to sit down and talk about it and not kill each other.

"Everybody everywhere used that war for their own purposes. But the Serbs had no allies. They relied too much on Russia, and that backfired on them. By contrast, Croatia had all the European countries behind them, especially Germany and Austria. Now the European countries admit, 'Yes, we got involved too fast.' But how do you expect a huge organization like the EC to confess a mistake? You're never going to hear that. And you have an administration in the United States that is playing games—one day Clinton says one thing and the next day something else. You can hear people in the street here say, 'If he's going to bomb us, let him bomb us and get it over with. Let's do something. I just want to live a normal life.' Milosevic used that. He knew the EC was not happy about this bombing. He asked, 'What will it solve? Will these bombs just kill Serbian children?'

"Milosevic is trying to get Izetbegovic to accept the 36 percent of the country that the Bosnian Serbs have conceded. He tells him, 'If you don't take that, you'll end up with 2 percent.' And he's right. But so far Izetbegovic is holding out for more.

"Journalists ask me, 'Will the sanctions fall if Milosevic falls?' No! Next will come Kosovo. The question is, what other concessions do we have to make before the sanctions are lifted?"

What was Slobodan's solution for Kosovo?

"Kosovo is a huge traditional problem. Unfortunately, this country lives on huge traditions."

"I find it so strange that the Serbs are still celebrating a battle they lost."

"Don't tell a Serb that. It's never been decided. Did they lose or did they win? They lost on the battlefield, but it was the beginning of the decline of the Turkish Empire. So it wasn't altogether a loss." It took only five hundred years for the Turks finally to be overthrown after that fateful battle that supposedly began their decline. I did wonder again if the Serbs weren't a little crazy.

"The Serbs will answer any Albanian claim for independence with emotion, with 'Never!' People in Europe and America don't understand that. Kosovo is a rich region—agriculturally, minerally—and is unexploited. The West knows that. At the same time the Albanians have been doing ethnic cleansing there for years. They have been pressuring Serbs to get out, kicking them out. When questions about this were raised with the international community, no one wanted to discuss it. Now, when the Albanians claim independence, they are encouraged by the Americans and the Europeans. I agree that Kosovo should have autonomy within Yugoslavia, but that can only be resolved by sitting down and talking. We have sponsored two meetings between Albanian and Serb intellectuals, and now we are planning a third. But the Albanian leadership is stupid, it doesn't want to sit down and talk. And Milosevic is the same way."

"So you think there will be war?" I asked.

"I don't think so. Mr. Milosevic can't allow himself that kind of pleasure. People here in Yugoslavia will not fight. They are up to their necks with losing family and friends and fighting this poverty. He had a lot of men refusing to fight in Croatia and Bosnia. There would be even more in Kosovo. He's going to have to sit down and negotiate. How he's going to do that, when he's going to do that, no one knows. It's a mess.

"The smartest thing Tito did," Slobodan continued, "was put an Albanian in the presidency there and tell him to control his people— and he did. But when Tito was gone, Hodak wanted more, and Milosevic said no. Then they went so far [in 1990] as to proclaim their independence. But the Albanians don't want war. They know the Yugoslav army is too strong for them, and they'd be wiped out. There is a huge concentration of military and police forces down there. It would be a massacre. And Serbia could always say it was an internal matter—they're not about to let the Albanians secede.

"But again the West is doing the wrong thing. We've had UN and other international officials tell us that the sanctions were brought on not because of Bosnia but because of Kosovo. That's very bad. If they want to help, they have to be much smarter. One would hope that an outsider would be more objective and see more clearly how to solve the problem, not just jump in and say, 'I'm a specialist on the

Yugoslav question, and it's very easy to solve.' I want to say to them, 'Listen, guys, come and talk to me. Let's go to the field together. Come and meet some of the intellectuals and you'll find there's a whole variety of questions you don't even know about, you don't have answers to, and we don't have answers to, either.' But it is crucial that we sit down and talk and stop killing each other."

I asked Slobodan to tell me more about the harassment the foundation had suffered. "Most of it is verbal, though the police have asked certain of our members to step in for 'informal talks' which turned out to be about the foundation. We are suspect because we are an American institution and because we are not ethnically cleansed: we have people from all over the former republics working here. Mostly we get crank calls and threats, and we don't get the media attention we think we deserve for our humanitarian efforts. But that doesn't stop us. They bug our telephone and sometimes they follow us, but we ignore that."

Slobodan was leaving town, and I didn't expect to see him again. I asked why he hadn't left the country. "Somebody has to try to do something in this country. If everyone leaves, we're just going to leave them an open plate to do whatever they want. As long as we can function the way we do, and as long as we have the support of Mr. Soros, we are going to do this."

Ivan Jankovic's legal offices were in yet another crumbling stucco house in central Belgrade, on a tiny street I almost missed. As the near universal surfacing material in Eastern Europe, stucco was obviously not the most durable. Newer buildings, apparently constructed within the last few years, were still white and whole, but given the economic conditions facing Belgrade in coming years, they too would likely join their brothers and sisters in the process of decay. Some few mid-rise office buildings were of poured concrete or steel, but they were a tiny minority in this stucco-happy city where contemporary builders and architects didn't look back to see what happened to these surfaces. On the other hand, some of the newer stucco buildings might remain clean a lot longer if the city was not able to get its industry up and running again. I was left gasping at the thought of restoring most of the buildings in Belgrade to avoid further decay. Given the probable future of this city, it was clearly not in the cards for many years to come, if ever.

But like all the other interiors of these old buildings I'd seen, Ivan's office was in sharp contrast with the exterior—clean white walls, antique furniture standing amidst computers, fax machines, file cabinets, and the other appurtenances of a lawyer's office in a lovely high-ceilinged space—three offices, a bathroom, and a kitchen in what had been an old European-style apartment. He shared the space with his two partners. Wearing a heavy yellow pullover and blue jeans, Ivan was equally elegant-looking, with a great shock of prematurely white hair—he was in his forties—and strong, somewhat stony features. He was the first small Serb I'd met, at about five feet, five inches. He had what I was beginning to see was a national trait—a wry, cynical wit interlaced with a deadly serious, in his case almost a scholarly, or lawyerly, approach to his work and to the problems of his country. This was reflected in his speech that was highly precise, English with a British accent, and slow, as if he were considering every word he said. This was quite different from the other Serbs to whom I'd been talking, whose speech was fast, rushing pell-mell as if they feared they wouldn't have time to say all they wanted. Certainly it was far different from his friend Petar Lukovic, who had recommended I talk with him. Though Ivan didn't exhibit the bearish napoleonic traits so common in short men in America, he was clearly a man who would not suffer fools gladly. He was quick and curt with me when I asked questions he considered foolish, and the tension, even hostility, under his words often left me silent, grasping for a reply. When we parted he said he had enjoyed talking with me. I felt compelled to say, "I hope so."

Ivan Jankovic specialized in intellectual properties—patents, trademarks, designs, and copyrights. After receiving his law degree at the University of Belgrade, he went to London for graduate studies and then spent the years 1970 to 1976 at the University of California at Santa Barbara, earning a Ph.D. in sociology and criminology. Since then, though he had not specialized in criminal law, he had done research in that field and did a little criminal work "for pleasure." Most recently he was defending draft refusers and army deserters.

As we sat across from each other at a small antique desk, drinking coffee served by his maid, Ivan explained to me how the sanctions had hurt his business. "Often our clients or potential clients in other countries, who seek to protect their intellectual properties in Yugoslavia, are specifically barred from making payments for our services. In most countries—yours is an example—regulations have been passed relating to the sanctions against Yugoslavia, specifically allowing payments for the maintenance of intellectual property rights. But while our clients can hire us to protect their rights, they cannot make payments because the banks do not do business with our country. You can see how that might affect our practice."

In addition, there had been a dramatic decline, Ivan told me, in the amount of work he had been asked to do by foreign businesses. "There's practically no technology transfer, practically no joint ventures that we would be doing as part of our practice. Most of our colleagues are affected the same way." As a consequence of this diminution of his regular practice, he had taken on more than his normal number of criminal cases, mainly those having to do with the military. "There have been a fair number of prosecutions, mostly of young people, for either nonreporting or desertion. I have tried to take on as many of those cases as I could, partly out of sympathy for these young people."

"If the situation is the same here as it was in the sixties in the U.S.," I noted, "probably those young people had no money to pay you."

"Yes," Ivan replied, "I didn't charge any of those people anything." Of the six thousand cases pending in the military court of Belgrade against deserters and draft refusers in 1992, Ivan was able to handle only about a dozen, most of whom reached him through the center for Anti-War Action. But only about one-third of the six-thousand were actually tried. The others, Ivan said, had been or were likely to be dropped.

I wondered whether the draft resisters and deserters opposed the war in principle. "I believe such individuals or groups have left the country. As you must have learned when you visited the Center for Anti-War Action, there are actually very few activists there. Some of the men I handled had simply tried to hide from the military without any very articulated feeling against the war."

"They were just saving their skin?"

"Yes, essentially. And among those who deserted, most were reacting to a chaotic state in the army, especially in November 1991, which seems to have been the most critical month for the Yugoslav army. I can't make any generalizations, but those individuals I handled seemed to think they were risking much more than they would otherwise by being in units that were obviously mishandled by incompetent commands and a lack of proper equipment. In some cases the degree of disorganization was so high that entire units refused to go to the front. Some of my clients were later prosecuted as instigators of such mutinies."

Of the dozen men Ivan defended, none went to jail, and only two or three were convicted and received suspended sentences. "Literally all of them have since returned to their units or gone into the army and served their military time."

"So their actions were clearly not political at all?"

"You be the judge."

I asked Ivan whether, in addition to the center, there were any organizations doing draft counseling. There was one each, he said, in Vojvodina and southern Serbia. "How about in Bosnia and Croatia?" I asked.

"Yes, I've heard of them, though I've had no personal contact with them. There may also be such groups abroad among refugees, exiles, asylum-seekers, or just people staying temporarily in foreign countries."

I wondered whether the government was prosecuting so few of the deserters and refusers because it was politically unwise or because it was simply too heavy a burden for the courts. "Both," Ivan said. "The military court has done hard work on a small number of cases where the officers were in the dock. That was the result of successive purges of the former Yugoslav army, which was schooled and socialized into a Yugoslav ideology." In the 1980s, while the various heads of the republics were fighting with one another for primacy, the army remained aloof from all such political infighting. But within the army there was a growing dispute about its loyalties. It was independent of the Milosevic government, though its goals and interests mostly coincided with Milosevic's at the time, namely the survival of the former Yugoslavia. Yet the army was not immune to the rising nationalism in the republics, and confusion was growing. The top brass of the army was mixed, with many of the officers from republics other than Serbia.

When skirmishing between Croatians and Serbs in the Krajina began in 1990, the army intervened to maintain stability. "Obviously it didn't succeed," Ivan said, "partly because it wasn't very efficient and partly because the political differences within the army led it to behave inconsistently. In many cases it acted impartially in Croatia, and in other cases it acted for the Serbian side, partly because of the commanding officers' choices and partly as a result of the dispute over the army's role. But you know the end of that story.

"Now clearly, with Yugoslavia disintegrated and the army split among the various former republics, the present Yugoslav and Serb governments saw a need to restructure the army and get rid of the Yugoslav ideology as well as non-Serb officers. In those purges, large numbers of high-ranking officers and some lower ranks as well were dismissed in one way or another, and some of the top generals were brought to trial. Some trials of traitors were concerned with the disintegration of Yugoslavia. Such trials never came to clear ends. The court either refused to convict or the Supreme Court of Appeals overturned the convictions."

"So the consequence of all these purges and trials is that the army was not functioning well, leading to all these desertions," I said.

"That seems to be the case," Ivan replied. It is worth remembering here that much of the fighting in Croatia and Bosnia was done by paramilitary irregulars and that in May 1992 the Yugoslav army was withdrawn from the field in Bosnia Herzegovina. Prosecutions of army officers and soldiers were mostly designed to keep the Yugoslav army ready for an attack.

When I told Ivan of my fantasy of seeing Milosevic hanging from a tree, he smiled and said, "I recommend one drink less. You are certainly right that there is strong emotion about Milosevic here, and there have been assassinations of kings in the nineteenth and early twentieth centuries, or elected officials who were prosecuted or assassinated. There may be some people harboring such feelings, but I doubt that it could happen."

What were his attitudes toward the president? "I think his politics have been shown to be extremely dangerous and extremely destructive. It is a commonplace, though true nonetheless, that he saw a road to power in the mid-1980s in a radical change from communism to nationalism. He saw that chance and used it. Clearly he couldn't have made such a success without support in the environment. He is fascinated by power as unrestricted and unfettered as can be."

"Would you call him a dictator?"

"Colloquially, yes. By political theory, however, I do not believe he qualifies as one. But in the commonsensical meaning, he is a dictator."

"The Parliament is a rubber stamp?"

"The Parliament has very little power, but that is traditional. You must remember that for fifty years this country was without a parliament in the usual sense of the word. Fifty years is a long time to overcome, to obliterate many traditions. This also affects the other former Yugoslav countries and the other former Soviet and satellite countries. They just don't know how to function effectively."

"Do you have any faith that things might be improved after the new elections in December?"

"I don't think they will be held. What may intervene is an escalation of the war between the Croats and the Serbs. I am convinced that the basic conflict there has not been resolved and that it will arise again now that most of the goals of the Serbs and Croatians in Bosnia have been achieved.

"In theory at least, there are options for a peaceful resolution of the conflict, but everything that has happened in the last few years seems to indicate that a violent solution is more likely." In 1993 there were about thirty-thousand UN peacekeeping forces still in Krajina, having been brought in early in 1992 after six months of massive destruction and brutality from both sides.

"They have been shown to be ineffective," Ivan said, "partly because of the mandate. They are barred from using force—mercifully, I would say. We have seen how the UN troops operated in Somalia. But that's only the first reason for their inefficiency. The second reason is the rationale. Their goal is to keep a peace. But no real peace was ever made. The parties have subscribed to a number of agreements, but none of them has held. There is still fighting, and I fear an escalation. The conflict is over territories in Croatia that are populated by Serbs. The key question is whether those territories are in fact part of Croatia. So far Croatia has not been willing to accept the loss of those territories to the Serbs."

The Serb-populated sections of Croatia, the two Krajinas, lie on the southern and western borders of Serb-dominated areas of Bosnia. Part of the struggle has been over territory that would create a link between the two. It would make a contiguous territory consisting of Serb-dominated Croatia and Serb-dominated Bosnia, creating a larger Serbia. "All those territories are now under full Serbian control, but Croatia will not likely accept that for long. At best it means protracted action or, as the American military experts would say, 'low-intensity' conflict, a guerrilla war similar to the Middle East and many other such places."

I was distracted by Ivan's maid, who was scrubbing a rather threadbare oriental rug with a large stiff brush. Ivan noticed me staring and wondered if the noise was disturbing me. "No," I said. "I just wondered why she is scrubbing the rug." He shrugged his shoulders as if to say, Why not? or perhaps that he couldn't be bothered with such mundane matters. Didn't he know that such scrubbing might not be good for his rug, I wondered, but decided to mind my business. Perhaps rug-scrubbing was common in Belgrade. I had seen no modern vacuum cleaner in my hotel room, only an ancient, noisy clunker that my maid rarely used. When she cleaned the rug, she used a broom with a rag tied over it.

"There may be local guerrilla wars in Bosnia as well for many years to come," Ivan continued, "but if I am right that the basic conflict there will soon be over, it will mean renewed warfare in Croatia. I do pray that this will not happen, but I fear that everything so far points to that."

"How do you see the West reacting to this?"

"Already there are signs that the West is less concerned with Yugoslavia. I think this feeling will grow."

"Indifference, you are suggesting?"

"Yes, in public opinion, and in policy to the extent that public opinion shapes it. I do not expect the West to intervene here."

"How do you see this ending?"

"Well, in the long run I think Yugoslavia will be militarily defeated, and should be. Fewer and fewer men are available to fight, and Croatia has been arming itself with the help of the Europeans, especially Germany. Yugoslavia is slowly slipping into full disorganization and is racked by illegal and extralegal structures [both in the economy and in the military] which no government can rely on for very long. Should the Milosevic government dissolve, there will be a period of full, unrestrained chaos within the country. As in the past, that will lead to everyone taking whatever they believe belongs to them, which means Vojvodina, Kosovo, plus border areas with Bulgaria, possibly Hungary as well. They may be under occupation."

"That's a pretty horrible scenario."

"What has already happened is horrible. Could we have predicted three years ago that even some of this would happen? People here were not able to admit there was a war on, even when it was already raging."

I asked Ivan about the persistent use of the word "crazy" to characterize Serbs. "That's meaningless. No nation is crazy or sane. No group other than inmates of a mental institution is crazy. But one can, of course, talk about cultural traits which make groups behave in different ways. In that sense we can look at the Western perception that only the Serbs are guilty in this conflict. In fact all the parties are responsible for what happened, and none of them can be excused. Given that, the two factors that in 1990 aided and promoted the war were the army and the Milosevic government—at that time you would already have to call it a regime. For reasons having to do with their culture, I think, the Serbs were not able to produce any individuals or groups with a nonwar policy, much less make such a policy a viable option." Serbs tended to be more passive than might be good for their welfare.

I referred to Rebecca West's book in which her guide, Constantine, said, "We have no art, no culture, we have something else. We have war."

"That's a very cynical statement," I said, "but it does seem that Serbs do often opt for war."

"Let's look at the man who said it," Ivan replied. "His name was Stanislav Vinaver. He was one of the most brilliant men in Serbian culture. He was a poet, among other things, but is best remembered as a translator. His translations are the best we've ever had. Of course he wrote a lot, published several literary magazines. I remember him from when I was a child. An unbelievably ugly man. He was a Jewish man from a small town in Serbia. He fought in the First World War as a volunteer and wrote a lot about it later. He studied in France mostly, was fluent in several languages. Apart from the war, he had no martial inclinations. You must understand that the First World War was an exceptional one in which most educated people did fight. He spent the Second World War as a reserve officer and as a German prisoner of war. He died in the 1950s. He is himself a major argument against Serbia's tendency toward war. His biography speaks against it.

"But it is also true that wars play an important part in Serbian culture, partly because there were so many of them in the recent past, but partly because there seemed always to be, after both world wars, obstacles to sustained peaceful development. The regimes after both wars were tense with latent violence between ethnic groups that erupted in the 1940s during the war and which has now reappeared. There were always these not-so-latent conflicts between various political factions, so that the peaceful life was perceived as offering few rewards whereas war, especially as remembered, seemed to be rewarding. In addition, there is a very strong martial tradition among the Serbs in the Krajinas, especially the tradition of soldiering as a profession, going back to the Turks. The Austrians established special administrative units among the Serbs to fight the Turks. They were excused from any number of feudal obligations in exchange for protecting the border from the Turks. That is a long tradition to overcome."

I asked Ivan whether he thought Milosevic had been unable to create a new economic policy to replace the old system and thus turned to nationalism to build his power, or whether he was sincerely nationalist in his beliefs. "I can't ascertain his motives, but it would seem that Milosevic's natural choice would be the one he made, if it is the choice between an orderly economy that is structured to develop and grow, and a radical solution of grabbing land and changing boundaries. If you are obsessed by power, as unrestricted as power can be, you cannot convincingly support a viable economy. A viable economy implies an orderly political environment which we most often describe as a parliamentary democracy. Not necessarily parliamentary, but it has to be a stable political order in which property is protected by the government and in which you have unfettered freedom to go into business, do business, make profit, and do pretty much what you want with it. If you have that sort of political order, you have a lot of restraints on your political power."

I told Ivan that Petar had predicted it could take fifty years to restore Yugoslavia to its prewar state. Did he agree? "I'm much more optimistic," he said. "Given the end of the war..."

"In five years, do you think?"

"Maybe. Very soon after the war the republics of the former Yugoslavia will be cooperating easily with one another. There will be a willingness to cooperate. That has happened before. All the atrocities of this war are so terrible that most people have a need to suppress them, to push them beneath the conscious. And they all understand they must cooperate. Then there will be involvement by the West, either in the form of loans or investment or both, so very soon we will have an economy that will give hope. Of course, how long it will take to rebuild every house, who knows? But I repeat, I am more optimistic than Petar—given an end to the war, mind you, and that may take some time. This has already gone on for more than three years. But no war lasts forever, even the Hundred Years War."

Vlada Andjelkovic was not another of those tall, handsome Serb men, though he was well dressed in an elegant tweed sports jacket and slacks. He was small with narrow, sharp features, eyes too close together, but a gentle look, at forty-three almost completely bald, the only bald man under seventy I saw in Belgrade. I was referred to him by his cousin, George Bogdanich, director of the Serbian Media Center in Chicago, the U.S. center for pro-Serb information, who told me that life in Belgrade was dangerous and that Vlada would take care of me. I should call him as soon as I arrived, he said. He would chauffeur me around so that I needn't encounter those dangerous streets. I had no intention of being chaffeured around by anyone, but I had called Vlada first.

In fact it was several days before Vlada returned my phone call. He expressed no concern at all for my safety; anyway, I had learned after only a couple of days in Belgrade that I was in no danger. Apparently a small amount of street crime in the city had frightened people there, and they had told their relatives and friends in the States of their fears. The Serbs in the U.S. assumed from these remarks that Belgrade streets were dangerous. For a Chicagoan, the streets of Belgrade were like a Garden of Eden. I heard of no one raped, robbed, mugged, or even shoved hard. Ljiljana warned me to hold my bag close to me because there were pickpockets out there, but she had not been robbed. In Chicago I'd had my wallet or purse stolen half a dozen times over the last ten years and been mugged once, and many people I knew had had dangerous encounters on the streets or in their homes.

Like so many people in Belgrade, married or unmarried—he was unmarried—Vlada lived with his parents. He was an industrial and advertising filmmaker, but his great devotion was as the only paid employee of an organization of what he called "nonprofessional, not for profit," low-budget filmmakers who used Super 8 mm film or videotapes to make mostly experimental films, "expressing themselves through film." They were amateurs, Vlada admitted, though that word didn't seem to have the same negative charge it had in the U.S. Vlada helped his members produce their films and promoted them wherever he could—on television, in videos, in theatres and clubs, but mostly at festivals, of which there were, pre-embargo, many in Yugoslavia. But, he said, "Our nonprofessional filmmakers are better known abroad than here." He'd been doing this for fifteen years and was dedicated to his membership.

The organization had been founded in 1948 as a government organ, but for the last fifteen years it had been independent. Vlada's salary, about twenty dollars a month, which he supplemented with his own filmmaking, was paid by members' contributions. Members didn't join as individuals but as clubs. There were about a hundred member clubs with three or four hundred individual filmmakers. Most were in Belgrade, but there were "strong" clubs in several other smaller cities. No other such organizations existed anywhere in the world, Vlada said.

A defensive man, he often answered one question with another in his faltering English and husky, dry voice. At the same time he laughed easily, as if to say, "All this is pretty absurd."

We talked over coffee in my hotel dining room late in the afternoon. Vlada opened our conversation by asking, "What do you think is the cause of all this? Your country. . . what are they calculating?" I told him I was coming to the conclusion that the Western powers didn't know what they were doing, that their actions were basically uninformed and unintelligent, not very calculating. The U.S., I said, was acting out of a variety of motives mostly based on domestic needs and misinformation.

"That's the most dangerous thing. So many fools who don't know what they're doing. I wish you could go to some of the villages in Serbia where you would see the people starving." When I said I was limiting my visit to Belgrade intellectuals, Vlada again urged me to get out of Belgrade to see the suffering in the villages. It was a while before I was able to make clear to him that my purposes were only secondarily to describe the suffering that the embargo had inflicted upon Yugoslavia. My main purpose was to try to understand the nature of the conflicts in the former Yugoslavia. I told him of my fantasy of Milosevic hanging from a tree after Belgrade had been bombed.

He laughed and said, "First of all, I don't think Belgrade will be bombed. I think those Western governments are ignorant of the situation here, and that's very bad, but I think they know it would be very bad and dangerous if that should happen."

"Yes indeed, but it could happen. And my fantasy is based on the idea that, if it should happen, the people would string Milosevic up by his heels."

"Milosevic would not be involved in that case. If Belgrade were bombed, it would be the beginning of the Third World War. That's my opinion."

"Who would be fighting whom?"

"I don't know that, but I think it would be another world war."

I explained that I used that extreme image of mine to find out what people were thinking about Milosevic and his role in the events of the last few years.

"Milosevic is the best of all the possibilities we have now. If there is one person who is better than Milosevic, he would be president. It's very simple. There's no theory or mysticism. He is simply the best the parties have to offer. And people know that."

"What role do you give him in the events that have happened in the last three years?" I asked.

"His role in the beginning of the war was not important. Three years ago Slovenia and Croatia were the ones, not Milosevic. He had to protect those Serbs who were living in Croatia. One of the reasons for creating Yugoslavia was for the Serbs. Yes, for the Muslims and others, but mainly for the Serbs. When Tito made those new borders, that was a mistake. But you know, Serbs aren't really interested in politics. They accepted those borders. All they want is to live normally in peace. But for the last few hundred years we are always victims. Our religion is very tolerant, and I think one of the reasons we are always victims is because of that tolerance."

I asked Vlada if he was religious. "Yes, and if your next question is 'Was I in the Communist party?' the answer is no," he said, laughing.

Did he call himself a nationalist? "If you are American, if you like the American way of life, admire American paintings, are you a nationalist? And if you are living in the United States, are you a nationalist?" he tossed back at me.

"The United States is not a good example to use because it is probably the most diverse country in the whole world," I said. "We have millions of every possible nationality living there. It is difficult to be a serious American nationalist."

"Let me tell you something. We have the same situation in Yugoslavia. We haven't millions, but we have some thirty nationalities here, especially in Belgrade. Maria Theresa, the queen of the Austro-Hungarians [in the mid-eighteenth century] tried to make this some kind of melting pot, to bring in all kinds of people, and now we have the results." In fact Maria Theresa, known as Empress, Archduchess of Austria, sent in Germans and Austrians to colonize sections of Yugoslavia outside the control of the Turks, and there had been other such colonizers from other countries over the last few hundred years.

I described the party at Milic od Macva's house and said that I felt this was an expression of pure, powerful nationalism. "No," Vlada said, "it was a reaction to what the world has done to us. He's a very sensitive person. Things happened to him. He had an international reputation and now he is a Serb. Many Serbs have the same opinions now, and that's a normal reaction. It will get worse if things continue. Many Serbs will be like Milic. I think things are going on in the world specifically to make Yugoslavs—Serbs—enemies, and then to fight against them."

I told Vlada of my visit to Belgrade in 1990 when I met a philosophy professor from the university who, when I asked him to explain how Milosevic could so harshly criticize the Croatians while at the same time he was trying to keep Yugoslavia together, answered me, "The Croats are animals."

"Would you call that man a nationalist or was he simply a bigot?" I asked Vlada.

"What do you think?" he asked.

"I don't know."

"Maybe he knew the situation well. At that time, in 1990, the new Croatian constitution said there was no place there for Serbs. When we heard that, we knew what was going on. That was the beginning of everything, if you ask me. Last night I met a famous man who said, 'Croat politics in the last hundred years has been the same as now: pure country, pure Croat country, pure Catholic country.' In the 1850s there were more than 31 percent Serbs in Croatia. In 1921 there were about 20 percent Serbs. In the last statistics, for 1991, it was 12 percent Serbs. Now in Croatia there are about 2 percent Serbs. [The actual percentage is about 5 percent.] There is no reason to talk about Serb-Croatian antagonism. The Croatians made this situation in more or less a hundred years. They either killed Serbs or pushed them out." In fact about two-thirds of the 150,000 Serbs living in Zagreb, which was untouched by the war, had fled to Serbia in the last three years because of their fears of living in the Nazified city and because of discrimination and threats against them.

"In Bosnia the Muslims are really Serbs. Tito made the terrible mistake of recognizing the religion of the Muslims as a nationality. So what are we fighting about? Two nations? It's ridiculous. Bosnia has never been a nation. We are all Serbs. But that idiot Izetbegovic plans to make Bosnia a pure Islamic state with Turkish and Iranian language. You hear those languages now in Sarajevo. If you want to buy something in the stores, you can buy only if you order in Turkish or Iranian." This was the first time I had heard this scarcely believable description of Sarajevo, but there had been a widely reputed upsurge of Muslim religious practice in the last ten years in a country that had been largely secular for fifty years. A great number of new mosques had been built in recent years to satisfy the need for them—or to encourage greater religiosity. This trend had been largely ignored in the West. By contrast I saw no new Orthodox churches in Belgrade. In fact, while there had been some return to religious practice there too, not many churches could be found in the city.

"I traveled to all the countries—not much now, of course," Vlada said. "And I lived in 1991 in Zagreb. Every public place, including toilets, showed the Croatian flag. It was ridiculous. You asked me about nationalism. I can tell you that nationalism started in Croatia. Nationalism in Serbia is a reaction to nationalism in Croatia. It is protection." Vlada either ignored or forgot the great surge of nationalism in the 1980s in Serbia that produced the million-strong rally in Kosovo in 1989.

I asked Vlada whether he felt that the press was free in Yugoslavia. "Is there a free press in the United States?" he wanted to know. "Yes," I said, "we have a free press, but there is a qualification. The government officials and the reporters talk to each other in a very cozy way so that while they are free to say what they want, in fact much of the time the media are in sync with the government. On the other hand the government doesn't control what the media say, and there are times when the media strongly criticize the government and the government can only complain bitterly. But I've been told that much of the Serbian media is under the direct control of the government."

"We have free media. We have Radio B92 and other radio stations."

"But," I said, "B92 doesn't reach beyond Belgrade, and it's having trouble surviving as an independent station."

"It will survive, and there are independent stations in other cities in Yugoslavia. And *Politika* is now independent. And every day there are more papers and magazines going independent," Vlada said. In fact, the four major independent media were all having trouble surviving.

"What makes them independent? Is it whether they are for or against Milosevic?"

"That isn't what makes independence. Milosevic is not so important."

"He is the president."

"Yes," Vlada said, laughing, "but he is not on top of the world."

"So who is?"

"I don't know exactly who."

"Is it Seselj?" Vlada laughed again, saying, "No. I think there are people in the Academy of Sciences who are making policy, and Cosic [the former president whom Milosevic unseated and who now bitterly opposed the government]. But Milosevic is not the only one."

"But someone makes decisions."

"I don't think Milosevic is making the decisions."

"So you wouldn't say, as other people in this city do, that Milosevic is a dictator?"

"Life is more complicated than that," Vlada said, once more laughing.

I asked Vlada about his view of the Parliament. "It isn't a real parliament. It is composed of different groups, arguing with one another. But we haven't had a real parliament for fifty years. If you don't eat for fifty years and someone says, 'Eat,' you have to say, 'How?' It's a question of time before it can work. I think each parliament is better than the last one, but we need a long time before we will have a real parliament. In the media it is a much better situation. We have much more independent media."

"What is going on here in education?" I asked.

"It is a slow process of change. You know, a lot of people considered themselves Yugoslavs. Now they are back thinking of themselves as Serbs. That's very surprising and very difficult."

"And you? What do you call yourself?" Another laugh, and Vlada said, "I call myself a Serbian cosmopolitan. I was a Yugoslav, but now what is Yugoslav? But about that issue and education—the Communist party was Yugoslav and now we have again our religion, we are again Serbian Orthodox, and that creates a tremendous problem for education. Not that the church has much influence, but people are confused. There is no morality now. No Communist morality, no Orthodox morality. In education, in teaching history, we are not explaining what is happening. It is very bad. That's one thing. Another thing is the language problem. We used to have the Serbo-Croatian language. There the Serbs were victims also. Our language was changed by all the Croatian imposed on us by Tito. So, in language, in religion, we were victims. We were weak. Our own traditions were suppressed." The language situation throughout Yugoslavia vaguely resembles the situation of English. The basic language is Serbian, with some minor variants in the other republics and some spread of those variants back into Serbian, but there are not as many differences between Serbia and the other republics as there are between England and the U.S. or Canada. After all, there is an ocean between England and North America and only boundary lines between Serbia and the rest of Yugoslavia. But with the secession of the various republics, the language that for many years was called Serbo-Croatian is now called either Serbian or Croatian, though there are few differences between the two.

"It is a problem today to explain history to the younger generation," Vlada continued. "It was never taught about the Serbs being victims in World War II. And the younger generation is asking, 'Why now?' They ask their parents, 'What are you talking about?' "

"I guess Tito suppressed all that knowledge to keep Yugoslavia united."

"Not united but his slaves. The last Egyptian pharaoh lived here. All Yugoslavia was his home, and we were all his slaves. He was very wise. He allowed us to go everywhere. We voted by foot. All his enemies left, and he was the only one left in power. It wasn't Communist, it was just an excellent life for Tito. He did everything to make his life good, no matter what effect it had on the country. Like making the Muslims a republic. What was that for except to satisfy the Muslims and keep them quiet so he could have his good life? He had no higher aim."

I wondered how the sanctions and the war had affected Vlada's work. "Everything is ruined. You call it sanctions. I call it terror. Real terror. Everything is destroyed. There is nothing to do. Almost everything we did, we depended on things from abroad: film, cameras, and so forth. Now everything is cut off. We smuggle a bit, but it is too expensive. We have a little reserve, but we all see the bottom of it. And what will happen when we reach that? There will be nothing left. And I don't see any end to this terror. The war in Croatia will burst out again, and the West will blame the Serbs. I see a complete plan in the West to destroy Yugoslavia—not only Serbia, all of Yugoslavia—to experiment with us for all kinds of purposes."

"Why would they do that?"

"That's what I asked you. We don't know. We're asking 'Why?' "

"I don't see the history of the West as being so vile," I told Vlada. "They make a lot of stupid mistakes and there is a lot of power playing. But not long-term evil planning like you're describing."

"Well, you're right that they have made many mistakes. And what is now needed is for them to confess their mistakes." It was my turn to laugh. "Countries don't confess mistakes," I said.

"But it's not only mistakes. They knew the truth—that Muslims had bombed their own people, but they put the sanctions on anyway." Vlada was referring to the May 27, 1992, "breadline massacre" bombing in Sarajevo, allegedly by Serbs, that led to the imposition of sanctions. The bombing as reported by the Bosnian government and described in the media was the result of a mortar shell from a Serb attack point. In fact, classified briefings to UN Commander Satish Nabiar, quoted by the London *Independent* in August 1992, stated that the bombing had been carried out by "Bosnian forces loyal to Alija Izetbegovich." The *Independent* quoted the UN report as saying that the bombing was caused by a "command-detonated explosion . . . not necessarily similar nor anywhere near as large as we came to expect with a mortar round landing on a paved surface." According to a United Press account, that UN report was withheld from Security Council members until after the sanctions had been voted.

"I think our problem is that we recognize these crimes by the United Nations," Vlada said. "Not only here, but in the whole Mediterranean. Throughout much of world history, war has started here. I think it is happening again. I am very unhappy to be living under these conditions, but I must do it. And if it happens here it could happen anywhere else the West decides to do their experiments. And here we sit, discussing it calmly."

Just what the nature of the experiments the West was conducting in Yugoslavia, Vlada didn't know. But this was the only explanation he could find for what he viewed as the terrorist treachery of the West. Despite his frequent laughter at what he saw as the absurdity of the situation, he was a man beset with sadness and confusion, unable to accept even the simplest of realities about Serbian responsibility for events, and too oppressed to think the issues through. For this intelligent, even accomplished man, his people were once again— still—caught up in the web of victimhood. It was a strange, almost abstract paranoia that mixed fact and fiction in this part of his thinking, apparently compartmentalized from the rest of his life. I could find no evidence in anything he said about his own life or work that reflected any such delusions. He certainly loved his work. For now, it appeared, he was obsessed with trying to figure out how to work and live under the sanctions, doing what Karl Haupt described so many Serbs as doing: simply wringing their hands.

12 When I arrived at his office that morning, Predrag Simic, director of the Institute for International Politics and Economics, told me in great distress that he and his staff had decided they would soon have to close their offices because they could get no coal to heat their old, drafty, three-story building. They occupied one floor and rented out the rest of the space. Some coal had been available earlier in the summer, but the institute couldn't afford the highly inflated black market prices.

For forty-five years, until two years earlier, the institute had been funded by the government. It functioned, Predrag insisted, as an independent think tank with a staff of about a hundred and the largest library on international relations in the Balkans, with more than 200,000 volumes. While the institute was largely independent, it had a liberal slant. "If you are not liberal, you cannot think," Predrag said. "On the other hand I find that the conservative think tanks, like the Heritage Foundation in the States, are sometimes more realistic. We have had good relations with them and are grateful for their support."

Two years ago the institute's funds were withdrawn by the government "because we were considered traitors," as so many liberals who opposed the government's nationalistic tilt were called traitors. Until the sanctions were imposed, the institute received funds from the European Community and the National Endowment for Democracy, chiefly for conducting courses at the University of Belgrade; but those funds largely ended with the sanctions. Efforts to obtain government funding were prevented by Seselj, Predrag told me, and "Now we are sanctioned from within and abroad, but at the same time we are now 100 percent independent. We do what we want." He had managed to keep a staff of forty together with funds from the EC and other European centers, though, he said, the salaries were so small that "we are essentially volunteering our time." Predrag's salary was three times the wages of the woman who cleaned the institute, or about thirty-five dollars a month. He supported himself with outside consulting and speaking engagements. He also helped keep the institute alive by soliciting money from friends in Belgrade and abroad.

Another tall, slender Serb with a large cowlick in the center of his head of thick brown hair, a small mustache, steel-rimmed glasses, and the sharp features of his countrymen without the good looks of so many of them, thirty-eight-year-old Predrag talked fast and furiously, wanting me to get all his ideas on the problems of what he called "the second Yugo," the phoenix that would arise from the ashes of the ongoing wars—something the West did not seem to look upon favorably. As we sat over Turkish coffee in the conference room of the institute, he was deadly serious, unsmiling, throughout the two hours we spent together, no doubt in part a result of feeling depressed by his decision to close down the building. It might mean the end of the institute, though he and other staff people promised one another that they would work at home to keep it going. Talking with me was an effort he might have preferred not to make that day, but he talked on nevertheless.

When I told him I had decided to limit my research to the Belgrade intelligentsia, Predrag said, "I think the decision not to go outside Belgrade was good. What happens in Yugoslavia happens here first. But to limit yourself to the intelligentsia is not so good, because they are marginalized. I don't think intellectuals here represent any real political power. That comes from the lower strata. Right now we have a change in our social structure in this city because young educated people are leaving by the tens of thousands. As many as 70 percent of my classmates have come to me to lobby for them abroad, to help them get visas. I ask where they want to go. They say, 'Anywhere, out.' If you look at the advertisements in the newspapers, you will see that you can have your choice of flats in central Belgrade that have been inhabited by the same families for several generations.

"And their places are being filled by about 150,000 refugees from

Bosnia, people with less education but very influential. This is important because this nation, like most of the Balkans, is divided by different sets of memories and identities. Serbian Serbs have one set of memories and their own sense of identity. Serbs in Vojvodina have another kind of identity because they lived under the Hapsburg Monarchy for so many years. Bosnian Serbs have their identity. And Krajina has still another. After each of the world wars and now again, we have the same phenomenon—that Belgrade Serbs are losing their identity and their political influence and are being overtaken by immigrants. Those people bring their own hatreds, their own wounds, their own standards of thinking and believing, and they now comprise the core of our political class here because the majority of politicians in Belgrade are not Serbian Serbs. The president himself is a Montenegrin."

When I explained that I was seeking not the raw emotions of the often confused perceptions of the ordinary people, but informed, educated discussions of the roots of the conflicts, Predrag told me that to understand what was going on in Yugoslavia one had to examine the past. "Yes," I said, "my research is based on the theory that only from understanding the past can we understand the present and have a glimpse into the future."

"You have to know that we had here a particular kind of communism, communism funded by American and European money. After Tito's break with Stalin, we had an opening to the West. To add to that, we were the first people in Eastern Europe to get our passports so we could travel wherever we wanted. That made for a very interesting experiment, considering Tito's concept of self-management." The freedom to travel while the rest of the Communist bloc was locked in behind the Iron Curtain for so many years was clearly the greatest gift that Tito gave his people, judging from the value placed on it by almost every person I talked with. All of them had traveled widely; many had worked or studied abroad. Even in times of less freedom within the country, travel rights were rarely withdrawn. Thus the Yugoslavs had a poignant picture of what life was like outside their own country, and aspirations to the freedom and prosperity of the West.

At the same time Tito was clever enough to ensure that Yugoslavia had a relatively prosperous economy, propped up with foreign money, which most people didn't understand. Most people were satisfied. While there were pockets of poverty, people were free to travel to other countries in Europe to work. For many years a large contingent of Yugoslavs worked in Germany and other European nations, sending money home. Tito's experiment was to determine whether free travel could coexist with Communist control. It worked well, especially in the early years when there was a great deal of economic and political freedom. Even when there was repression in the country, most people remained reasonably content. The freedom to travel, and their ability to afford it, were apparently worth any sacrifice.

"This experiment started in the mid-1950s and reached its climax in the mid-1980s," Predrag said. "In 1968 the system of market and liberal reform under Communist rule reached the limits of freedom. It became clear that further liberalization would not be possible within the framework of Communist party rule [as happened in the former Soviet Union in 1990]. So in 1968 we had major demonstrations that echoed Paris and other Western countries. Tito suppressed the demonstrations with guns and tanks.

"Then came Prague Spring that showed Tito how vulnerable he was. He reversed democratic and liberal trends in Yugoslavia and tried to recreate some kind of Communist system. But he couldn't go as far as Stalinism and instead used some utopian, late Marxist mix of ideas. It didn't survive for even a decade, yet all the problems we have now were born in that decade of the 1970s. Communist rule was recreated not on the federal level, only on the republic level. But those republic leaders were unable to build any viable leadership on communism, so they turned to nationalism.

"The first strong nationalist sentiment in the late 1960s and early 1970s was for Yugoslavia as a unified state. It began among the intellectual Serbs. Yugoslavia was the main vehicle for the Serbs [who were spread out in all the republics. It was their protection in the other republics where they might otherwise be swallowed up or be discriminated against as minorities]. We must be Yugoslavs first, and only after that Serbs, they said. In Serbia the leadership was quite liberal and forward-looking. But in 1971 Tito purged all the liberals, all the Western-educated liberals, from business, politics, the university, everywhere, all over the country. That was the end of Yugoslav liberalism. So the anti-Communist struggle, which had been building since the late 1960s, had only one way to go, and that was nationalism. Slowly it became more local and less Yugoslav-oriented. There was no longer room to be a liberal anti-Communist. If you wanted to be anti-Communist, you had to be nationalist. The

Yugoslav system survived only because of Tito, who controlled everything.

"Then, only a year after Tito's death, the system began to come apart when the Albanians in Kosovo decided they wanted to become the seventh national republic. They purged all the Serbs in the government and embarked on a program to get rid of Serbs generally. Here there was a very strong reaction to that among Serbian intellectuals, particularly in the Academy of Sciences, in the writers' organizations, and in the Orthodox church, all of these people having been heavily suppressed in Tito's time.

"Pretty soon, in the mid-1980s, a new generation of Communist party leaders, led by Milosevic, seized the ropes. Milosevic was the first to realize that Tito was dead. He was the first to rock Tito's boat, as people say. That made him popular in the West—a young, daring banker who had spent some time in the U.S. He was quite popular. His people signed a pact with the Academy, the writers, and the church, and replaced the leaderships of Vojvodina, Kosovo, and Montenegro with their own people. This set off alarms in Slovenia and Croatia, where people were always afraid to be dominated by the Serbs [as they had been between the wars], and an anti-Milosevic movement took root in those places. So that was the prelude to what has happened in the last three years."

Then, Predrag continued, came the collapse of communism in Eastern Europe in 1989. "Each political group had to find its own way. The Slovenes realized first that communism was dead, which Milosevic was slow to realize. Milosevic was not a good strategist. First, he didn't realize that communism was dead. If he wanted to play the nationalist card he shouldn't have retained the old structures. In Slovenia they were building a new Western-oriented agenda. And they saw their future not with Yugoslavia but with the West. Slovenia had always been a little foreign to Yugoslavia, closer to Austria and Germany and Italy, and Milosevic thought it was okay for Slovenia to secede. But then they did it in a very selfish way, pushing the rest of Yugoslavia into a civil war. That's the way I see it. They blackmailed Yugoslavia. They said, 'Either Yugoslavia is going to be transformed into a loose confederation or we are out'—without considering what might happen to the rest of the republics, to the country.

"Milosevic, meanwhile, responded very slowly to the anti-Communist movement in Yugoslavia," Predrag went on. "The swan song of what was left of Titoism was occurring at the same time—Prime

Minister Ante Markovic in 1990. He was popular in the West because he introduced good shock-therapy kinds of liberal democratic reforms. We saw very promising trends. Inflation was brought down from 3,000 percent in 1989 to zero in 1990. We saw foreign reserves skyrocket, fifty thousand companies founded in 1990 alone. So it seemed he might prevail."

Then in early 1990 the Slovenians and the Croatians held their elections. "Those elections were won by revanchist forces, especially in Croatia where they were supported by political immigrants from the Second World War. Clearly anti-Yugoslav and heavily influenced by Ustase ideology, very much clerical and right wing," Predrag explained. In late 1990 the other republics held their elections, so now there were two anti-Communist regimes, Slovenia and Croatia; two that could be called post-Communist, Serbia and Montenegro; and two buffer states, Bosnia and Macedonia. In Bosnia the Muslims won, and in Macedonia it was a mix of everything. Very soon, big conflicts emerged. First, no one wanted Markovic. He was not a nationalist. He was a good technocrat but a very bad politician, with no base of support, and so was unable to match the skills of these Machiavellian politicians. Then you had all the machinations that led to the wars."

According to Predrag, the West's view of the Serbian population in Croatia as a tool of Belgrade is a misperception based on ignorance. "The Serbs were surrounded by the revival of the Ustase and, whether real or imagined, feared living under that regime. Every Serb family in Croatia had a brother, father, sister, mother murdered by the Ustase in World War II. They refused to live under that regime and rebelled. There was talk for a year of some kind of solution, with no visible results. Then a small amount of violence occurred, but the Croatian Serbs were reticent to fight. They believed that the only way they could win recognition as an independent state of Krajina was to be victimized by the Croats."

Meanwhile, going back in time a little bit, Ante Markovic had received a clear message from U.S. Secretary of State James Baker that he could use the army to hold Yugoslavia together. "Baker, in June 1991, said on the steps of the Parliament, in the presence of journalists, that he would not recognize Slovenia as an independent state. So Markovic sent tanks into Slovenia, but no infantry, just to scare them. It was very quick. The casualties were nine Slovenians and forty army personnel. How did it happen that the terrible

'Bolshevik' army had forty casualties and the poor, unarmed democratic Slovenians had just nine? But the Slovenians relied on their allies, mainly in Austria, to save the day for them and gain the recognition they wanted. The policy here was so stupid. The army was told to encourage the Slovenians to join them because they were all Yugoslavs. They thought they could stop the secession so easily. But in Belgrade people said of Slovenia, 'Good riddance. If they can sell their washing machines to Germans for five thousand dollars, let them do it. We don't need their washing machines anymore.'

"And then the Croatians had to follow, because they couldn't stay in Yugoslavia without their companions, the Slovenians." But this situation was much more serious because of the Serbian rebellion in the Krajina. Serbs were 12.5 percent of Croatia, and they were demanding autonomy for the Krajina. [Now Serbs are estimated at about 5 percent in Croatia.] While the war in Croatia was conducted mostly by the Yugoslav army, it was not like it had been in Slovenia. The Croats mostly withdrew from the army, and it became mostly Serbian with a few others, including Muslims and Hungarians.

"Interestingly," Predrag said, "the commander of the air force that bombed and destroyed Vukovar was a Croat. Milosevic is still purging the officer corps so that the army will be run by Serbs, mostly from Bosnia.

"After the war ended in Croatia, we had an intermezzo when we could have saved Bosnia. It was different from the other republics because there was no clear national majority. The Muslims were 44 percent, the Serbs 33 percent, and the Croats 17 percent, so there was always a kind of compromise. But Bosnia could be saved only by not recognizing its independence. Or by recognizing it and putting it under UN trusteeship with a strong international force to protect it. But to recognize Bosnia without those conditions was to kill it, and that's exactly what happened. What was the game? Milosevic wanted to preserve a rump Yugoslavia with four nations. So he tried to pressure Izetbegovic to stay. Then he went to Ankara to ask the Turks to pressure Izetbegovic. And Izetbegovic was inclined to go along, but the Bosnian Croats didn't want to stay in any kind of Yugoslavia. And the Muslims decided it would be better to side with the Croats and get rid of the Serbs, and then later get rid of the Croats and establish a Muslim state. This proved to be a mistake."

Meanwhile, the EC held a conference in Lisbon and offered a compromise that would have divided Bosnia into three parts. "Everyone was about to sign," Predrag told me, "and then my good friend Warren Zimmerman, the American ambassador to Belgrade, made the greatest mistake, which he later admitted. He advised Izetbegovic not to sign the agreement and proposed instead that the U.S. recognize Bosnia's independence and force Milosevic to accept it. Then we saw the *New York Times* and the *Washington Post* start a media campaign to get Bosnia recognized. And Izetbegovic came to believe that, if he proclaimed independence, the Serbs wouldn't attack. And if they did, it would just be a matter of weeks before the American cavalry came to save him. It was all a terrible strategic mistake. Your press sent a wrong message to Izetbegovic.

"At the same time Mr. Karadzic, leader of the Bosnian Serbs, had a similarly wrong idea: 'We will take everything we can until the Americans come, and then we will be able to bargain from strength.' The army was made up mostly of Bosnian and Krajina Serbs from poor families, who had no choice but to go into the army. They pulled out of the federal army and made their own Bosnian army with sixteen brigades from the Krajina. This was the whole story of the Bosnian slaughter. Serbs pushed as hard as they could. Croats pushed very hard. And you saw the nightmare. American cavalry never came and never will come, for very selfish reasons—not because you don't want to fight Milosevic, but because you don't want to send half a million of your boys to die for some Bosnians, and Bosnia is much more militarily complicated than Somalia because it is so mountainous." The treacherous mountains of Bosnia resemble the Vietnamese terrain where America lost 58,000 men.

"Do you consider this a civil war?" I asked Predrag. "Yes, of course, but it is not just a civil war. It is also a religious war. These people are killing each other because they hate each other. Historically they are all Serbs. Serbs see Muslims as people who betrayed their ancestral religion to preserve their property and their real estate under the Turks. I don't know how many Croats converted to Islam. But it is all mixed up. For instance, the toughest Serbian nationalist, Vojeslav Seselj, has a Croat background. His great grandfather was a Croat. And he converted from Catholicism to the Orthodox religion because he was working on land owned by the Orthodox church. The father of the former defense minister of Croatia was a Serb. So it's a civil war, a religious war, an ethnic war, a fratricidal war, and, to a certain extent, an aggressive war—but it's very difficult to say who is the aggressor. If you applied present

American standards for aggression to your Civil War, it would be hard to define the aggressors."

As Predrag described the nature of the Bosnian War, I conjured up images of the vicious internecine quarrels over the years between the Ashkenazi and the Sephardic Jews. They never became actual fighting wars, but the antagonism between them has been intense, leading to exclusion and discrimination in Israel that have often threatened the civil peace. Two groups so close together and yet so far removed from each other. It was as if each group, looking at the other, was looking into a mirror and seeing their own most hated traits. Whether the two groups of Jews might have engaged in actual war had they had land and property at stake, as the Muslims, Serbs, and Croatians had, is too far beyond the realm of speculation, given the landlessness of the Jews for so many years. But the comparison is not so farfetched. Like the two groups of Jews, the three groups of Yugoslavs in many respects are more similar than different. The hated traits they see in one another result from a long history of oppression and each group's efforts to live under that oppression. The last fifty years, when these differences were submerged by Tito's emphasis on Yugoslav unity and his hostility to religion, did not succeed in burying these antagonisms. Tito's death meant they were free to surface again as they had in World War II after having been submerged in the interests of a united country under King Aleksander.

"This is also an ideological war," Predrag added, "because of the degree of communism that survived in each place. You have to understand that most people, only about 10 percent, were actually Communists. Even then, communism here was different. Some people were Communists for ideological reasons, but many for pragmatic reasons—to get jobs, for instance. I don't think it mattered very much here. What really mattered was a system of authoritarian rule, a particular kind of social and economic structure. Nationalism overtook the Communist model. You could be a good Communist or a good Serb or a good Croat if you were a member of your class, your nation, or your party. It didn't matter. You were a member of a totalitarian society. That's why communism survived the end of its ideology here. It disguised itself in the clothes of nationalism. Nationalism helps to preserve the totalitarian society. Milosevic and Tudjman were Communists who had no other card to play. They are like Siamese twins. They can't get along without each other.

"Markovic had the right card to play—the anti-Communist card—but Milosevic had to set himself up as different from Markovic in order to win, so Milosevic couldn't play that card, and there didn't seem to be any other beside nationalism. It wasn't clear in the early 1990s which one of them would prevail, but if Markovic had prevailed, I think Yugoslavia would have been transformed into a Western state like any other, or like the Czech model.

"But the process of transformation, as you know, means millions of people are thrown out of their jobs. Nationalism, which led first to much strife and finally to war, prolonged the life of the system. So if you look at who votes for Tudjman and Milosevic, you will see that it is the people who are going to be affected by these market reforms. And that is how the nationalist card is used by these people. All these people who are such romantic nationalists, like Cosic or Milic de Macva, don't understand that. But all the officials throughout the former Yugoslavia know that significant democratic market reforms will mean the end of their rule. And how do you put off those reforms indefinitely? You go to war."

The West, primarily the U.S., encouraged the nationalist process, Predrag said, by failing to support the anti-Communists led by Milan Panic in the 1992 parliamentary elections. "Cosic, who is still a national hero, was supporting Panic after he realized that things had gone very wrong with his nationalistic leadership. If the West had supported Panic, had supplied some oil and some other things badly needed here, Panic might have won the election, and the whole course of events would have been different. The war would have been ended, there would have been market reforms. But I don't think the West trusted Panic. Now they have Milosevic, and he says to them, 'Look, you have no one else who can be the strong man in the Balkans to prevent another Balkan war,' which could start here very easily. And he says, 'If you don't have me, you have Seselj.' Anyone confronted with such a choice would choose Milosevic. And now he is trying to make peace, so they can't say very much."

We concluded our conversation with Predrag's prediction that the wars in Croatia and Bosnia would finally end in a variety of tradeoffs and a realignment of the former Yugoslav republics with their predecessors—the Serbians with the remnants of the Byzantine Empire, the Croatians and Slovenes with the Middle Europeans, and the Muslims with the Muslim world.

Before I left I asked Predrag if, considering the plight of the institute, he was considering leaving the country. "It is easy to leave," he said, "but the excitement is to stay."

13 The local headquarters of the International Red Cross and its branches in Belgrade were located in a group of old three-story houses and office buildings arrayed around a rather ragged-looking courtyard used mostly as a parking lot for the staff. The complex was surrounded by a high iron fence, as if this had once been an elegant group of offices. The street was cramped and slightly hilly, and looked like it was mostly residential, though so many professionals had offices in old houses that one couldn't be sure. This street was wider than many in Belgrade, and boasted more trees and foliage; it might once have been—perhaps still was, despite its by now familiar decay—a street of more sumptuous living.

None of the offices was clearly marked, so I trudged up and down a variety of stairways until I located Snezana Stoskovic, press officer of the Yugoslav Red Cross, to whom I'd been referred by Merijana. She shared a small office with a secretary off a long, wide, high-ceilinged, slightly rundown corridor and reception area on the second floor of a large building hidden away at the end of the courtyard.

As I sat in the reception area waiting to see Snezana, I reflected on all the horror stories I'd heard about the Red Cross, its bureaucracies, and how much money was spent on salaries and staff perks. I'd had no contact with the organization for twenty years, since they came to the rescue and were very efficient and helpful in an apartment house fire across the street from me. It seemed somehow fitting that this next contact was another grim emergency situation—on a nationwide scale—and I wondered how helpful the Red Cross was being this time.

Tired of sitting and waiting, I wandered down the marble-floored corridor decorated with large, mangy-looking floor plants and pictures from the history of the Red Cross. A glass display case contained photos of rescue missions around the world over the years. This introduction to the Yugoslav Red Cross didn't carry the feeling of lavish spending. It all looked down at the heels.

The Yugoslav Red Cross now comprised the Red Cross of Serbia, founded in 1876 shortly before Serbia was recognized as an independent state, and the Red Cross of Montenegro, founded a year earlier when Montenegro, already an independent state, signed the Geneva Convention and agreed to humane treatment of soldiers and civilians in wartime. According to its own statistics on refugees, which now constituted the major work of the organization, as of October 1, 1993, the Red Cross had recorded 512,871 refugees in Yugoslavia —60,670 in Montenegro and the rest in Serbia. This was fewer than the 800,000 figure that had been so loosely quoted to me by several Serbs, but substantial enough to demonstrate that the U.S. view of refugee problems in Bosnia hadn't told the whole story of this monstrous war.

Slightly more than 82 percent of the refugees were Serbs, 7 percent were Muslims, almost 2 percent were Croatians, and slightly more than 9 percent were "others." Children were nearly 43 percent, most of whom were from seven to fourteen years. About twelve hundred children were without parents, the majority from three to seven years old. About ten thousand children had been born "in refuge," which mainly referred to camps outside the city. Of the adults, more than 84 percent were women. About fifty thousand people were elderly and frail, the most poignant picture of the flight of the people from the war-torn areas in Yugoslavia I'd come across. Strange how numbers, which can be so cold and distancing, can sometimes tell the most graphic story.

Unlike her American counterparts in press offices, Snezana looked decidedly unchic for Belgrade. She was the first woman I'd seen dressed all in black—a simple straight skirt, a turtleneck sweater, plain black pumps—an unfashionable outfit in this fashionable city where bright colors ranked high. When I remarked on her outfit, she told me, "I'm not interested in fashion. I don't wear makeup most of the time because I don't enjoy standing in front of a mirror all that time." She wore no jewelry and beige hose, not the more fashionable black ones, a signal to the world that she disdained fashion, unless it reflected the shortage of panty hose in this goods-starved country. She was small and well shaped, with short, no-nonsense dark hair and an open plain face except for big, dark, vibrant eyes. She radiated energy, a quality I had not much noticed in others I'd met, and a down-to-earth, nuts-and-bolts quality often characteristic of journalists. At the same time her somber voice had a familiar chill sound of sadness. This was a saddened city.

Snezana pulled her chair from behind her desk, and we sat at a small end table large enough for an ashtray, the tape recorder, and a couple of cups of coffee. In her heavily accented English, Snezana told me that her Red Cross chapter ran two major fund-raising drives each year in this poverty-stricken country to supplement the funds provided by the International that had been decreasing each year. "There is less and less interest in Yugoslavia, and with the UN sanctions committee making it so difficult to receive aid from abroad, we get less and less," Snezana said. Everyone in the agency had taken a huge cut in salary. Snezana's pay two years ago, before the coming apart of Yugoslavia, when the agency had served the entire former nation, was four thousand dollars a month. It was now sixty-four dollars a month. "And we have much more work to do than we did two years ago. But it is part of becoming poor in the whole society, not only in this agency."

I was amazed that the UN sanctions committee prevented the Red Cross from receiving humanitarian aid.

"Well, it works this way for everyone. If you wish to send humanitarian aid to Yugoslavia, you have to go to your ministry of foreign affairs with a request specifying that you would like to export to Yugoslavia. Then your ministry is supposed to send the request to the sanctions committee. We have information that some of those requests for permission to send us stuff have waited ten months to be granted. Some requests even longer."

"From which countries are your medical supplies coming?" I asked.

"Some of them come from the International, and some we buy from local markets supplied by our own factories, though I should say that the factories have a lot of trouble getting raw materials. So we have a serious shortage. And some of the medicines are so expensive we can't afford to buy them. That is a disaster for our elderly people. Every thirty-six hours a pensioner commits suicide in Serbia. They are so desperate because they can't even afford to buy food. We are looking forward to the opening of more food kitchens. Already we serve about twenty thousand meals a day, but the new kitchens will serve many more. We estimate we have 300,000 needy in Yugoslavia. It is sad that we find ourselves in this condition that we have to install soup kitchens once again in the twentieth century. We had a very nice life until a few years ago."

In addition to giving aid to refugees and the poor, Snezana told me, the agency was trying to continue its traditional activities, mainly in disseminating information about health and safety and the principles of humanitarian work. "In fact we have even intensified this work because it is now so urgent. Of course, we also do a lot of missing-persons tracings, because we have a lot of people who are separated from their families. We have no idea how many missing persons we have. It's impossible to figure while the war is going on. And we have a lot of people in the camps."

"Are you able to bring relief to people in Bosnia?"

"We cannot get into some parts of Bosnia. Just recently we had meetings with the Red Cross of Bosnia, which is operating in Sarajevo, because we couldn't get supplies into Sarajevo. The Red Cross is supposed to be able to cooperate with any humanitarian agency anywhere, but with the war going on, this is not so easy. But we have to try. We are offering as much relief there as we can, but our situation here is so bad that we can't afford to share much with them."

I wondered whether Snezana was referring to the legal market or the black market when she talked about the Red Cross buying medicine on the local market. When people in Belgrade referred to buying something, more often than not it was on the black market. "I was talking about the legal market," she told me. "But we all know that the sanctions are feeding the corruption. Because people who are importing small amounts of medicine have to pay bribes at the borders in order to bring them into the country, they have to add that onto the prices. That's why the prices at the private pharmacies are so high."

"I've been told that the border guards and the police are . . ."

"Yes, and the UN too," Snezana broke in to say. "We have information that they are all taking bribes. Maybe it's not good to talk about it, but when we hear stories that people have to pay three hundred or five hundred deutsche marks to the UN people, then we should talk about it. The United Nations should be aware of the problem. They shouldn't support the corruption. They should find a way to provide free humanitarian relief."

"I've also heard that the border guards are stealing medicines to sell on the black market."

"Those stories are quite common. We cannot talk about it because we are not at the border. But we know that trucks bringing medicines for the Red Cross, that are already cleared by the UN, must wait and depend on the whims of the guards whether they can go through or whether they are forced to stay there for one day, two days, a week. This too adds to the price." Within two or three days prices can rise 10 percent or more with the almost hourly inflation.

"All that is happening here is not only the result of the sanctions. But if we talk just about the sanctions, I would ask for all the children who are dying in our hospitals waiting for medicine, who has the right to do this? Is the United Nations aware of what is happening in these hospitals? Sanctions are usually meant for someone who has done something wrong. What have these children done to anyone? Whose right is it to kill them or let them die, not to provide the medicine and other things they need? During the last three months about ninety babies died at the Institute for Mothers and Children in Belgrade because they were born with cardiological problems, and because of the sanctions there were no spare parts in the surgical units so doctors couldn't operate. I would ask the whole civilization, 'If you had your own baby, would you agree that anyone in the world could punish you this way?' I'm talking about the most basic things. I'm not even talking about information—for instance, letting us know what is going on in the world in science, medicine, culture. We do not talk about that very often, though it is very important to us. We don't even buy and read the newspapers every day because we can't afford them. So you can imagine how we feel. But we survive."

How did she feel about the government? "They are responsible for what has happened to us," she said. "But we—not we, the people—elected that government. All the regulations they have passed—keeping food out of the stores, all that—have made it very hard to live."

"Do you think all of these economic problems would be milder if it weren't for the war? I understand that 75 percent of the national budget goes to the army and to help finance the war in Bosnia."

"Oh no! I can speak on behalf of the Red Cross about the humanitarian problems. But as a citizen of this country I know positively that we are not financing the war, and none of our soldiers are fighting in that war."

"The failure of the economy, then, has nothing to do with the war?"

"No, it has much to do with the sanctions, which are so unjust! Why should this country, which is not supporting the war, be so punished? Anyone can see clearly that the Bosnian Serbs and the Croatian Serbs are fighting their own wars, and we are being punished for them!"

Snezana told me she had traveled abroad extensively, even in the past year. "What are people in the other agencies of the Red Cross feeling about the sanctions?" I asked.

"People are not very well informed, nor are they much interested in our situation. They are concerned with their own needs. They don't much care whether the sanctions are just. My colleagues who come here can appreciate the effects of the sanctions. They realize that all these civilians shouldn't be the ones to suffer so much.

"Maybe I shouldn't say it, but the longer the sanctions last, the stronger the government will become. The system will get more and more support. The Serbian character is that we are very proud and will not sell our dignity for nothing. Maybe we shouldn't talk like that, but that is the truth."

"Do you have the feeling, having spent a good deal of time abroad, that the Serbs are more proud than other people?"

"I wouldn't say so. But we can suffer a lot and refuse to pay."

"Is suffering a national trait?"

"Unfortunately, from our history I would say so."

"Do Serbs suffer from a mentality of the victim?" I asked. Snezana laughed. It was the first light moment in our conversation. She said, "That's a topic for philosophers, psychologists, doctors. You should read Rebecca West." On that note Snezana asked to be excused because she had someone waiting for her, and rushed away. As I walked into the courtyard I found her standing beside a little red Yugoslav. car. She called out to me, with a laugh, "I'm sorry I had to leave you, but I had to get my petrol. You understand." Beside her was a man, obviously a black marketer, siphoning gas from a large can into her tank. I laughed, calling back, "Some things can't wait, I know."

Maja Tomanovic, a young woman in the foreign press office of the Ministry of Information, called me almost every day to find out if she could help. I had called her to ask if she could arrange interviews with a few government officials for me: the president, the district attorney, and the health minister. I also wondered whether she could help me get in to see the patriarch of the Serbian Orthodox church, and supply me with interpreters for any of those people who didn't speak English. Finally, could she be a go-between to arrange an interview with Branimir Scepanovic, the novelist I'd met at the ministry's luncheon who spoke no English?

Maja didn't offer much hope for an interview with Milosevic; he talked with very few reporters. But she might be able to get his wife to meet with me if I would accept that substitution. I had heard that Milosevic's wife, Mira Markovic, was the brains behind the throne, and I agreed, though Maja was never able to arrange an interview. Getting an interview with the patriarch might also be difficult, Maja said, but she would try. He was old and frail and didn't give many interviews. For the others, she was sure it could be arranged. She called on Thursday morning to tell me that Branimir had agreed to an eight o'clock meeting on Friday evening, and she had found an interpreter who was happy to help. He would call me to make arrangements.

Predrag "Draga" Dordevic called on Thursday evening with an offer to pick me up on Friday to take me to the International Press Club to meet Branimir. He would interpret. He didn't mention dinner, so I ate before our meeting, only to discover that Branimir had meant this to be a dinner invitation. We started with coffee. An hour later Branimir and Draga ate Serbian wedding feast dinners, a cabbage concoction that looked delicious, while I sipped on a vodka, much to Branimir's chagrin. This was a special treat on the Press Club menu that night, and he was disappointed that I had failed to understand that an invitation for eight o'clock meant dinner. He couldn't understand why I couldn't eat again. I promised to have dinner with him again if he would invite me. At the end of the meal we all had apple streudel, the largest servings I had ever seen. I laughed. Draga said, "One helping for a Serb is two for the foreigner." When I raved about the streudel, Draga said, "We'll order some more."

Draga was no mere translator. A big, broad-shouldered, curly-haired man of forty-nine with a cherubic, dimpled face, a broad smile, and a slight paunch, he was dressed in a green turtleneck shirt and checked sports jacket. He tried to restrict himself to the translating job but was regularly caught up in the conversation and contributed his own comments, especially after Branimir remarked that this was not the kind of interview he'd ever had before—it was so informal. I told him, in response, that I had wanted not a formal interview but an informal conversation. Draga carried on a running conversation with

Branimir about what he was saying, trying to find the words in English for Branimir's sophisticated language and syntax. Perhaps nothing contributed to my feel for Branimir as much as Draga's regular laughter at his remarks. Though he had difficulty translating the humor, the fact that he was laughing was often contagious. I laughed though I could understand not one word Branimir was saying. His sly humor illuminated his face and gestures. Sometimes it seemed that Draga was laughing at outrageous remarks by Branimir as well as the outrightly funny. But most of his translations, reducing Branimir's obviously complex sentences to simple ones, came through quite straight, because as he admitted, his command of English was not as good as his French.

The Serbs are an emotional, dramatic people. Rebecca West remarked on the differences between Westerners and Slavs, the openness, directness, and flair for the dramatic to be found among the Slavs compared with the dissembling, closed personalities of the West. It seemed to me when I read her that she had obviously not met the American Irish, Italians, Eastern European Jews, and others who appeared to American Anglo-Saxons as the Slavs did to her, though without the same fond reception. For American Anglo-Saxons, the emotional ethnics in their midst were a vulgar embarrassment. Among the emotional, dramatic Slavs, Branimir Scepanovic bowed to none. He regularly roared his responses to me, striking the table with his fist or making other wide gestures, and was delightfully profane. He addressed me, with a flourish, as Miss Flor*ance*, or as "comerade."

When I asked Branimir if he was a member of PEN, the international writers organization that is, among other things, active in anticensorship work, he proudly pulled out his membership card and told me he had been a member for many years. He was also a longtime member of the Yugoslav Writers Union and had served as its vice-president for seven years.

When I had called the International PEN office in New York to ask for the names of some Yugoslav writers, I had been told, "Just call the office there. We don't know anyone." When I talked to Article 19 in London to ask for writers' names, they gave me the number of the PEN office in Belgrade, and said, "PEN isn't much good there." The implication was clear that if a writer wasn't antigovernment, he wasn't worth knowing in Belgrade. I told Branimir this story and he said, "The only criterion they have is if you are against the government. For instance, if Saul Bellow didn't attack Clinton, he would be persona non grata too." Considering Bellow's generally apolitical stance, this was a farfetched example of something not at all true of American PEN but clearly a standard by which Yugoslav writers were judged.

Branimir was clearly not antigovernment. He was one of only a couple of local writers at the government function for foreign writers, though he said nothing throughout the proceedings. He was obviously there simply as an honored guest. He believed in Milosevic, he said, "because he tried to keep Yugoslavia together." He struck me as a bit of a political naif in his support of Milosevic, but political sophistication has never been a mark of writers. But many writers behind the Iron Curtain did develop a certain kind of political sophistication that enabled them to write beyond the censors. It was that or perish. Some perished for it. Branimir told me a story of another writer with far greater practical political sophistication and engagement, Vuk Draskovic, whose big naturalistic historical novel about World War II was widely read in Yugoslavia. "He is a friend," Branimir said. "We play chess together. He asked me to read some of his novel. We sat in a café and he read to me ten, fifteen pages. I said to him, 'In *Crime and Punishment* Dostoevsky killed one old lady and then wrote three hundred pages about it. You killed off thirty thousand people in the first few pages. What else is there to say?' "

Branimir was one of Yugoslavia's best-known writers, having been translated into all the major European tongues, but with only one book translated into English and a screenplay planned for production in Hollywood. One would have thought that International PEN or Article 19 would have known of him. Yugoslavia has had no English-speakers to promote its writers—as, for instance, Philip Roth did for Czechoslovakia's writers—since the death some years ago of Lovett Fielding Edwards, the Englishman who translated Branimir's novel as well as works by the Nobel Prize winner Ivo Andric, Milovan Djilas, and other Yugoslav writers.

Branimir had brought me a copy of his *Mouth Full of Earth,* published in 1974, awarded the October Prize of Belgrade, translated into twelve languages, now in its twelfth edition with eight paperback editions. It was his one novel that had been translated into English, published in the U.S. in 1980. Branimir had published three novels, a novella, and a collection of short stories, and had written for radio, film, the theatre, and television since his first novel thirty years ago.

In recent years two of his plays had been produced in France, the only Yugoslav so honored. Two of his screenplays received Yugoslavia's highest award, the Golden Arena of Pula. But, he said, "I'm not one of those writers who is always running and producing a lot of work. Maybe that's my mistake, but I don't like that. People who publish a book every year write very nice books that say nothing. If a writer writes only two hundred pages in his whole life, but they are for all time, he has done his job." He had three manuscripts on which he'd been working for several years.

The ideas that had preoccupied Branimir for years concerned loneliness and alienation—"the hero against the masses, in which the hero is the victim," a theme popular in the fifties and sixties but long since all but abandoned in American letters. "In that," he said, "I am touching on the absurd and the illusion of being and all the tragic resonance that life brings."

Like all serious Eastern European writers of the last fifty years, Branimir has written against the Communist regime in allegorical terms. He described a novel written thirteen years ago, widely translated, and made into a film, as having "destroyed communism." While much of this literature written in other Iron Curtain countries was published only in the West, especially in the post-Communist era, Branimir's work was published at home along with other modernist, allegorical anti-Communist works. As long as a writer didn't attack Tito directly, he or she could say anything in that "authoritarian" state. Perhaps it was true in Yugoslavia, as in the U.S., that writers' words carried little weight. In Belgrade one does not find the great numbers of bookstores one finds, for instance, in Prague, where there is a bookstore on every other block. People in Yugoslavia clearly did not need to rely on books for entertainment and enjoyment as they did in Prague. They had much more substantial television programming, theatre, music, and, that biggest prize of all, travel.

But Yugoslavs who wanted it also had a serious, modernist literature. Branimir had lived in reasonable comfort, he said, from the sales of what he described as his modernist books and other works, both in Yugoslavia and abroad, though most of his money had come from film rights. He had been published and sold widely. His work had appeared on radio, television, and film, and he had not been censored for his work, not been accused of "decadent bourgeois" writing as happened to modernist writers in the Iron

Curtain countries. I waited eagerly to read *Mouth Full of Earth*.

Though he had occasionally been used by the Milosevic government, Branimir had not been involved in any political struggles over the years. Instead, he said, he was writing. "Thirty years ago I published a novel about the big lie, about the system that was practically destroying human beings, about the mechanics of power of a man who damaged the people just by his appearance. In the book, after the war a man went away, a man whom people thought had been killed in the war. They made him a big hero, built a monument in his honor as a war hero. Then he returned twenty-seven years later, and the people said, 'It is him, he is not dead!' He said, 'I am not your hero.' A lot of people had constructed his reputation on his death. And he said, 'No, it is only me. I am not that person.' So they arrested him, beat him, tortured him, brainwashed him, and then they let him go. So he stands on his monument and makes a speech. He says, 'I am a liar. I was never in the war. By chance, I have the same name as your hero.' He was denying himself! That's metaphysical death! In the end he doesn't know where he's going, what's going to happen to him, because he's no longer himself. I was attacking the system in a time when it was not so simple."

I told Branimir that I had been reading a great variety of novels from Eastern Europe that attacked the system and that had not been published in the writers' own countries during the Communist years. They had been in the drawer during all the years of communism or had been published in Europe. No such censorship existed in Yugoslavia, I assumed.

"Absolutely!" Branimir said. "In our kind of socialism we were like America. My book was published [by a state-owned publisher]. They didn't even attack me. They even printed a second edition." He laughed. "It was always an indulgence." Here was, it seemed to me, another example of the Serbs' fiercely democratic spirit. Despite being able to publish antigovernment works, to say anything they wanted, they nevertheless felt that the Tito regime was devilishly authoritarian and soul-destroying. In Yugoslavia I had yet to hear of any of the harsh measures used in other Communist countries. What accounted for the general view of the Titoist regime, after the 1940s when it was under Stalinist domination, was the control of the economy and the political system by the Communist party. Though that control appears to have been quite benevolent in a variety of ways, with a good deal of small private enterprise and personal freedom, it did feature strict one-party management of the political system and much of industry.

I asked Branimir if his unfinished novels were more strongly against the system or about other things. "It is not good to tell what is in the works. If I want to stay close to my word, I must not talk about it. I think these books will be my best-sellers. They are about everything that is happening today. One novel is about gambling in a way never handled before, like Dostoevsky's *The Gambler*, but it has to be much better. It is not the least bit conventional. It has not been done before, with my kindest regards to all the famous contemporary writers."

I said to Branimir, "I find more modernism, more experiment, more ideas in the Eastern European writers today—with some notable exceptions like Salman Rushdie—than in any other work in the world. It seems to me that when you live under repression you develop ideas and style in a way you don't when there is either complete repression, as in China, or complete democracy, as in the West."

"I agree," Branimir said, "but I would add that when the writer in Eastern Europe or Russia under a totalitarian system finds his freedom of expression limited, he is forced to discover ways to say what he wants without being forbidden or liquidated. He cannot say it the way an American writer can—like Charles Bukowski, for instance, can say President Carter is eating shit for breakfast. If we want to say the same thing about our president, we have to say it in a metaphoric way. Such a literature has much more quality. Such allegories are more complicated, more composed."

"Now the question is," I said, "with the freedom descending on Eastern Europe and the former Soviet Union . . ."

"Yes, now we can do anything you can do in the United States! And you will be surprised by this statement, but there is more freedom of the written word in Serbia today than in the United States. It is impossible to believe how television today is crushing Clinton, telling all the lies they tell. Clinton ought to be able to go into the courts and sue the television networks and force them to pay him—he should be able to sue them, though he may not be able to get big money." He laughed. "Or an actress in Hollywood when they write that her tits fell. It is the same here. Here they can write that she is without tits!" Like most of the people I talked with, it was clear that Branimir watched a lot of CNN.

"So my question is, with all this new freedom," I said, "and no longer the *necessity* to write allegory, what will happen to your literature?"

"Our literature will be weaker, more explicit. Even now it is showing. I don't intend to pay this price for liberation! I am going to write good literature for all time! I have this novel about gambling, and I have a novel about our time, about the hatred, agony, basic cruder instincts—altogether it has become a time of the absurd. All those friends and neighbors who lived together, who had good times together, now in one moment they hate each other and are killing each other. That's real absurdity. And for this, the most culpable is the nice, attractive United States, watching all this.

"Two years ago at this table I gave a three-hour interview with three journalists. At that time Yugoslavia still existed. We were already having trouble in Croatia, but only incidents. I predicted everything that happened. They said, 'You are foolish. What are you talking about?' I told them, 'By logic I came to this conclusion.' Number one, I said, we don't know more than a little bit about the United States' global interests, but we know they will not allow the whole of Europe to be harmonically related and connected with the raw materials in Russia and the cash of Japan. If that happened, America would become the third or fourth power in the world, and America has to be first. America is going to Lebanize Europe! The first area of attention is Yugoslavia.

"Besides, the West has a long, hidden antagonism toward the Balkans, toward Yugoslavia. For a thousand years we have felt such negative energy from the West that no wind could blow it away. They have a monstrous relationship with the Serbian people—because we are Orthodox and because we brought down the Catholic Austro-Hungarian Empire. All that determines what is now happening here.

"On the other hand, what is happening in Bosnia is all foolishness! There are some irrational metaphysical reasons. Politicians blame it on interests and money, but it is not so. It is all foolishness. One Muslim is living in a big house, and fifty meters away is a Serb living in a big house. And their basic instincts of hate come out, and they burn each other's houses down and neither has anything. What is that but foolishness?"

I asked Branimir if he thought this foolishness was related to the mentality of the victim. "Yes," he said, "the victim can forgive the executioner, but the executioner cannot forgive the victim." Golda

Meir said something similar: We forgive you for killing our sons, but we cannot forgive you for making us kill your sons.

Branimir offered a historical example: "In the Second World War the Croatians committed genocide against the Serbian and Jewish people. Even the Nazis weren't as bad. Then came 1945, and the Serbs forgave them. Then came the disintegration of Yugoslavia, and the Croats again threatened the Serbs. They started to take their jobs and their property. The Serbs saw what was happening, especially when Croatia separated and her independence was recognized. At that moment the Serbs understood they were going to be killed again. Then came the war. But for the whole world the fault was the Serbs'. We are chosen to be aggressors and victims at the same time.

"In addition," Branimir continued, striking his hand on the table, "the Serbs have lost the media war in the world! The whole world is on the side of Croatia, on the Catholic side. For instance, you're now here. Let's say a year ago you were here and you saw the killing of a hundred Serbs. You take pictures and, like the honest journalist you are, you send your story to the *New York Times*. And they don't publish it. And then the next day the Croats show the same photo, *the same photo*, saying it shows how the Serbs kill the Croats, and everybody publishes it." There is some evidence among independent photographers that such incidents have indeed occurred. In a film entitled *Truth Is the Victim in Bosnia*, made by American filmmakers, several free-lance American photographers are shown displaying atrocity scenes they claim were Croatian and Muslim atrocities that were ascribed to the Serbs.

Branimir described a speech he had given to a group of about a hundred European journalists assembled by Misa Milosevic, a Serbian publisher in Geneva. "I told them, 'The way Europe is behaving toward the Serbs is disgusting! Europe is all glamorous, with gold and diamonds, and it is beautiful and fascinating. But only on the outside. On the inside it is a prostitute destroying herself with syphilis.' A lot of people didn't want to hear that, maybe because God was having a little nap. Maybe he doesn't hear well. He can't see well. Or perhaps he doesn't remember well. Maybe God is too old. But he should know. In the Second World War 600,000 Serbs were slaughtered. He should remember the screaming. He should at least remember that for eight hundred years in the monasteries of Serbia, every morning and every night, they have rung the bells for God, asking for mercy and justice. Maybe he is deaf or just indifferent to the destiny of the Serbs."

Branimir said he still had many friends among the Croatians and the Muslims. "I never hated anyone, and even now I don't hate them. It is a collective tragedy. I'm not saying the Serbs are angels. When they were threatened again as in World War II, they became awful. Like that American film, *Angels with Dirty Faces.*"

"So let me go back," I said. "Do you think the tragedy of Yugoslavia will prolong allegorical literature, because maybe it's so terrible that it can't be told naturalistically? Just as it's been so difficult to write about the Holocaust in naturalistic forms?"

"Unfortunately, there is no more metaphor. There is no more metaphor."

"That's almost as big a tragedy," I said. "So it's going to be like most of the rest of Western literature?"

"Yes. For instance, I read a book by your Bukowski. Junk! The day of the great Faulkner is dead. Dead! Bloodless!"

Branimir had spoken the last word on literature. He dramatically changed the subject by asking, "Do you know what the new world order is? It is made by the Trilateral Commission, and it is terrible violence. It is a perverse, prostitutical, totalitarian system for the whole world on behalf of freedom, democracy, a new bright future!" Draga added, "That's some perversion." Branimir continued, "I talked with a Greek journalist. I accused the United States in an ironic, humorous sense. I said, Bush cannot sleep worrying about the human rights of the Eskimos, and right opposite the White House the Negro Jim cannot get into one of the fancy Washington restaurants because he has no basic human rights. In Los Angeles, when they had the trouble, Bush sent in the armed forces and it was taken care of right away. But in Kosovo, when the armed forces were sent in because the Albanians also made a riot, it was regarded by the U.S. as Serbian torture. Where is the logic? It is a perversion! The United States can use violence wherever it wants because it is the big power! But all over the planet people will hate the Americans because they make violence everywhere.

"Americans are the most genocidal nation in the world. First, they killed the Indians. Second, they killed thousands of Africans on those slave ships, and today Negroes have no equal rights. Third, it is the only nation in the world that dropped two atomic bombs. Fourth, in Vietnam they threw all this napalm to kill and burn millions of people in the name of freedom and democracy. Maybe I can't prove that America is the most genocidal nation in the world, but this is not a good record from which to call the Serbs genocidal."

In an almost mournful tone, Branimir said, "On a hill overlooking Tel Aviv there is a monument that says, 'To the Serbian people who never persecuted the Jews.' Do you know that the Croats and the Muslims call the Serbians Gypsies because only in Serbia were the Gypsies not persecuted! It makes others nervous. The Serbian people cannot hate anyone. There is a historic figure from the fourteenth century called King Marko, the greatest Turkish hero and the greatest Serbian hero. One story about him is that once in battle, he called for help from a fairy, who came to him and killed his enemy. Then he said to God, 'I'm sorry I have killed the hero who is better than I am.' That is Serbian mythology, the nature of the Serbian people, to recognize that others are better and more clever. After the First World War the Montenegrins [Branimir was from Montenegro] built a monument to the Austrian general they had defeated in a big battle. He was brave, he was a good fighter. And in Belgrade there is a German military cemetery that was never destroyed. Always the Germans have been invaders and occupiers here, but we preserve their dead."

It was time to ask Branimir what he thought of Milosevic. "I think he is very good. He is a patriot. He tried to keep Yugoslavia in one piece. If he had succeeded we would have had no war, no genocide. But the world wanted the disintegration of Yugoslavia. The United States and the world are so upset because the Serbian Serbs are helping the other Serbs in Bosnia and Krajina." His voice rose to a roar. "Why? That's normal! And our opposition is always calling Milosevic a Communist and a fascist. It's a complete lie! Two television stations here are always calling him fascist or Communist, but *they* are the people who are trying to gain power. If Milosevic were to dance to the tune of Helmut Kohl or Clinton, everybody would flatter him. Even if he were killing people they would say he was a democrat. Clinton supports Yeltsin. He killed not one hundred, as they say, but twelve hundred [in the storming of the Parliament in 1993]. But they say that's democracy. It's a disgusting lie! Milosevic does not want war! He wants peace!"

Whether Milosevic actually wanted peace was not clear; he was certainly saying all the right things to establish his claim. But peace would bring the end of the sanctions, most likely, unless the UN then decided that the sanctions would remain until the matter of Kosovo was settled. If the people I'd been talking to were right, the end of the sanctions might mean the end of Milosevic's rule. It was the feeling that he was holding things together in this crisis that was keeping him in power, people were saying. On the other hand, there seemed to be no serious opposition figure on the horizon. And the end of the sanctions might in fact increase Milosevic's power because the country could then begin rebuilding the economy—still another crisis he would be able to exploit.

But I had a hard time figuring out why the opposition (and the Western powers) were calling Milosevic a fascist. I had never been in a city so devoid of uniforms. The army was safely tucked away. There were so few police on the streets that I could never find one to get directions, as one does so easily in other cities. I saw the police in action once, in an evening raid on a group of street vendors selling cigarettes, in which I was almost caught. I commented to my friend David Moss, who was with me at the time, "Is this all the police in this city have to do, crack down on a handful of people trying to make a few bucks selling cigarettes on the street?"

On the other hand, Milosevic had called out the army to put down an antigovernment demonstration in 1991 and might do so again should any strong opposition arise. But such a protest movement was highly unlikely with the absence of the young intelligentsia, so many of whom had fled abroad. Still, economic conditions in the city might lead to social unrest, and one could not easily predict the development of protest movements.

Some suspected that Milosevic was encouraging the larger, Mafia-style black marketing that was taking place, but no one offered me any evidence, either that there was such a Mafia-style black market or that Milosevic was encouraging it. It seemed to me that instead he was simply overlooking all the black marketing that was going on because it was the only way people could get what they needed. Occasionally the police would raid a group of black marketers to display some effort to uphold the law, which was useless at that point. The black market was, in fact, a grey market. Besides the cigarette vendors who were everywhere, men and women on street corners were also selling vegetables, especially potatoes, and all manner of things. And the miles-long line at the border attested to all the people who were buying all kinds of goods in nearby countries to bring back and sell in Belgrade. Some of the stuff made its way into shops and other items were sold on the streets, but the market in Belgrade seemed to be largely a product of smuggling. Most tinned food in grocery stores bore labels from other countries. There wasn't much of that, but there was an even graver shortage of perishables—fruits and vegetables, meat, and milk, though there did seem to be plenty of cheese. And the shops selling other kinds of goods all had foreign labels on their products. I bought a tube of Helena Rubenstein face makeup at a shop in the hotel. It was the only such product the shop had, amidst a small array of other cosmetics and perfumes, all with foreign labels.

Milosevic was also suspected of withholding goods from the market in order to increase the terrible effects of the embargo and thus to arouse support for himself. People were predicting that the shops would be full just before the December election to ensure support for Milosevic's candidates—and then would again be empty afterward. It was all too irrational—people groped for some explanation of their plight, blaming Milosevic for everything, whether it made sense or not. If Milosevic actually was manipulating the market for his own purposes, it was a risky venture that could backfire on him. By all accounts he was a clever man, not likely to take such risks. The fact is that Belgrade depended substantially on imports, not only from the Western countries but from its former national comrades in Slovenia, Croatia, and Macedonia, all of which were participating in the embargo. Vojvodina, a part of Serbia, was the breadbasket of Yugoslavia, but it depended on imported fertilizers, spare parts for farm equipment, and gasoline for trucks to transport products to the city, and all these were scarce.

All of which is not to say that Milosevic was not manipulating the market. Certainly he had miscalculated the Muslim response to his attacks on Bosnia and the response of the UN to his war there. Maybe he was, as the opposition said, so power hungry that he took crazy risks. Maybe, after all, he wasn't so clever.

If the cries of "fascist" leveled at Milosevic resulted from his fomenting of the wars in Bosnia and Croatia, the word seemed badly misused. Rather it seemed that Milosevic was responding to and exploiting a deeply buried nationalist sentiment in his fellow Serbs that took him and the nation much further than anyone intended. As Pogo said, "We have met the enemy, and he is us."

That Milosevic controlled the major television stations and used them to build his power base was certainly a powerful strike against him but still not in the realm of fascism, which would tolerate no independent media to call him a fascist. The opposition was quick to point out that the independent media didn't reach beyond the outskirts of Belgrade, but they failed to say that Belgrade had a population of two million, the biggest voting bloc in Serbia. To put the best face on the opposition was probably to say that the ferocious democratic spirit among them would allow no deviation from full economic and political democracy. This was commendable, of course, but perhaps somewhat unrealistic given the circumstances in all the Eastern European countries following the collapse of communism. While Yugoslavia among the former Communist countries had the best chance to develop a full democracy, it was slow to overcome the apathy that had been created by what everybody described as the good life the Yugoslavs had lived. It made them prey to those who used nationalism to avoid real reform. But it would be difficult to assert that full democracy had come to any of the former Iron Curtain countries. Even the Czech Republic, closest to it, was still groping toward economic democracy.

As for the accusation that Milosevic was a Communist, well, he certainly was part of the party apparatus, and he did avoid the economic reforms called for after 1990. But the transition from communism to a free-market economy has been slow to occur throughout Eastern Europe and the former Soviet Union, not least because of the opposition of Communists who simply changed the names of their parties, as Milosevic did. More likely, the people who said that Milosevic had no real principles, that he was a pure opportunist using whatever he had to in order to build and maintain a power base, were correct. To win the acceptance and recognition of the West, Slovenia and Croatia declared that their separation from Yugoslavia was a flight from Milosevic's communism. But in Croatia there had been less movement to alter political and economic structures than in Yugoslavia. National Socialism seemed more the order of the day. Tudjman seemed more preoccupied with arming the country against what might be another flare-up in the Krajina than with making changes in the economy. And a free press, essential to a democracy, didn't exist in Croatia.

Branimir asked me if I had talked with Milosevic. I told him I was still hoping to get an interview but feeling less and less confident. He seemed to limit his public appearances, including press interviews, to television broadcasts that he could control. Without apologies, Branimir told me I had to have some powerful private connection to get an interview. When I told him I didn't have such a connection, he shook his head.

The conversation shifted to Draga. He told me that his work as a free-lance interpreter had dropped precipitously, that no foreigners were coming to Belgrade, that he had work only once or twice a month. These few jobs were largely at the front in the war. He had recently returned from Bosnia.

Branimir's fortunes had also been affected by the sanctions. A French theatre producer wrote to say he was unable to produce any more of his work. "I replied, 'Go fuck yourself,' " he said, laughing. I asked Draga for the Serbian words for "go fuck yourself." I couldn't go back to the States without a few slang expressions, I told him. "Jebi se" is "go fuck yourself." "Jebem ti majku" is "fuck your mother," and "jebem te u dupe" is "fuck yourself in the ass." Draga told me that the Serbian language is filled with colorful slang.

It was midnight when we finally left the club. We all agreed to have dinner the following week. Draga drove me to the hotel, and as I left we kissed fondly in the traditional Serbian manner—on each cheek once and then a third time on the other cheek—and promised to meet again. Draga promised to take me on a sightseeing tour on Sunday and offered to do any more translating I might need. Through this long evening of struggling to understand and appreciate Branimir, Draga and I had developed a great fondness for each other. I decided that sometime in the next couple of weeks I would use him not as a translator but as a source of information.

14 I had another date to meet with the Social Democratic party president, Cedomir Mirkovic. Same time, same place. I could have found my own way to the Press Club, but Ljiljana insisted on picking me up to take me there. It seemed that she had some interest in sitting in on the interview. Did she want to control what Ceda said? She had certainly made no such indications in the first interview. And he was, after all, the president of their party. Nor did she seem to want to contribute herself. She had said very little the first time. Curiosity? Perhaps. This was a very busy woman whom I regularly had trouble reaching on the phone. Was her curiosity so intense that she would give up a Saturday morning to sit in on this interview that she had arranged? Whatever the reason, she arrived at the hotel in another elegant outfit, and we sped to the club where we met Snezana Popadic who had agreed to interpret for me. Ceda arrived a few minutes later, and we went to the dining room, ordered coffee, and settled in. Throughout the conversation Ljiljana commented softly, mostly in Serbian to Ceda and Snezana, but occasionally to me, as if to amplify, but in fact more as if she were talking to herself.

I told Ceda I had spent the previous evening with Branimir Scepanovic and asked if they were acquainted, since Ceda was a literary critic and I had heard that the literary community in the city was close-knit. He was, he said, a good friend of Branimir's, though they didn't see each other often. I told him that Branimir had said that writers in Belgrade at present had complete freedom, but that I had the feeling that wasn't really true.

No, Ceda said, I was wrong. In the last few decades there had been great freedom for writers to publish and speak out. "There was some global control by the government of the cultural field, but not actual intervention. There always was political danger for the ministries if they intervened in the cultural life. Of course, you were not allowed to criticize Tito or communism, and everyone was aware of that, but you had complete freedom to criticize any of the people around Tito." It turns out that this "complete freedom" was based on a comparison with the Iron Curtain countries, where there was no freedom at all. But Branimir had not said that complete freedom had existed *over the last few decades*. If it had, he and his colleagues most likely wouldn't have been writing political allegories that attacked the regime. Nevertheless, Ceda insisted that "literature offered a place of shelter and refuge because people could act freely there. And in these hard times now, when we can do so little, literature is the best thing we've got, though I may be biased. Of course you are right that *journalists* do not have the same freedom. The situation in television especially is very, very grave."

I asked Ceda about the demonstrations to free television from government control. "On March 9, 1991, there was a huge demonstration, mostly to free television, in which two people were killed. After that the government did relax some of its control. A year later there was another demonstration that marked the first one. At that time I was director of the state-controlled television and did not belong to any political party. I let the opposition broadcast its message. The government gave orders that the broadcast be stopped. And then I lost my job. Even from the government's point of view, I think it was the wrong thing to do. It was very counterproductive. A dialogue between the government and the opposition was inevitable, especially because the war was breaking out at that time.

"But I must be sincere and say that we have a very complex situation here in Belgrade. The situation can justify that act of the government and more like it, but only to a degree. During the fifty years of communism, Belgrade was the capital of Yugoslavia and Serbia, but there was little accord between the two. When Yugoslavia broke up and Belgrade was reduced to being just the capital of Serbia and Montenegro, many people here still subscribed to the policies of big Yugoslavia, which in many cases were viewed here as anti-Serbian. On a lot of the newspaper editorial boards there was confusion between the two groups. The government started purging those boards of anti-Serbian voices even before Yugoslavia fell apart. Later on, after 1990, government repression was applied to others in the media who were not anti-Serbian but who were strongly for the preservation of the former Yugoslavia."

But I understood, I said, that Milosevic wanted to hold the former Yugoslavia together in 1990.

"That was exactly the paradox," Ceda said. "For some time he was saying that, and then it was the opposite, that Serbia was to be paramount. It will remain for historians to figure that out. But I will try to make it simple. In Serbia the people wanted to retain the Yugoslavia they had known. Then all of a sudden it seemed that the old Yugoslavia, big Yugoslavia, was only the love of the Serbians. People felt betrayed, as if they'd been deceived a long time ago. They found they believed in something that didn't really exist. The Slovenians, who had always wanted to run away, now could say they were running away from communism. And then the feeling of the people who wanted Yugoslavian unity disappeared. And the international situation was such that the effort to keep Yugoslavia together could have been construed as aggression, though there was some support for it in the U.S. When the Yugoslav army went into Slovenia with the idea of saving Slovenia from its secessionist leaders, the international community asked a reasonable question, 'Why are you trying to liberate the Slovenians from the Slovenians?' But there was a time when it would have been possible to liberate Yugoslavia without any victims. I believe the international community would have encouraged such a move."

I was trying to get Ceda to talk about the purging of the media and censorship, but he felt strongly that he needed to give me the historical background for all this. It sounded to me as if he were trying to find a path between defending the Milosevic government and attacking it, as if he couldn't make up his mind what he should tell me and so was rambling through recent history to find his way. His own history and present status put him in a difficult position. He had been a loyal government supporter, though in the liberal wing of the party, until he decided to try to be a good journalist and broadcast all opinions. Now he was a founder of a new centrist political party that was supporting Milosevic with reservations, hoping to have some leverage. But while he criticized Milosevic he was also clearly not in the opposition. A tough road to travel in a situation where there were not many grey areas still operating. I didn't envy him.

Trying to get him back on track, I asked Ceda if the people who had been purged from the media were those from other republics, especially Slovenia and Croatia. He replied that it was mostly people from mixed marriages. "That is the great tragedy," he said. "With the breakup of Yugoslavia has come the breakup of many, many marriages. It was the transition from the logic of peace to the logic of war that led to those purges. We can't boast that we had as good journalists as the Western countries did, but we had a pretty high level of journalism. It was controlled by the government, but not in any of the details. When political tensions rose so high and then, when war broke out, those who were more obedient to the government were more valuable to it. The people who were purged were not arrested, but they were forced from their jobs. This is one of the big weaknesses of Mr. Milosevic's policies."

For a year after the war broke out, all events were broadcast throughout the country on all TV stations, Ceda told me. "Then our TV studios began to have great conflicts, and there was no longer overall coverage, only by each republic. I am convinced that no war like this has ever been waged—a media war conducted by all the parties in the conflict, in which conformity and unity have become the most dreadful weapons. This is even worse in Croatia than in Serbia. There even more journalists have been purged, and many were expelled. Today in Belgrade there are a couple of hundred Croatian journalists. Some are Serbs, some are Croatians, and some come from mixed marriages. I am not justifying the government's actions here, but I want you to know that it was worse in Croatia. They have no free press at all. And here we have a little. None of the media is officially owned by the government now, though some are more controlled than others, but the control is often voluntary. Journalists print what the government wants. Milosevic would like to have an objective press that represents his point of view. A little hypocritical. The same is true for all the parties. When we got our new constitution and a multiparty system, I tried to help establish some magazines that we hoped would choke out the ones we inherited from the Communist time, but it didn't happen that way. Instead a lot of amateur journalists took over, and they weren't up to the standards we hoped for. So they are being pulled by one sleeve by the government, and by the other sleeve by the opposition parties, and because the government is more powerful, they bend in that direction.

"*Borba* is supposed to be independent, but its profile is rather vague. Basically it is objective. And *Politika* is also objective. But some magazines, mostly *Vreme*, basically fight for peace. And they are not obstructed. Other magazines are more objective than *Borba* and *Vreme*. TV Politika is more objective. But all of the so-called independent media are too much influenced by the opposition parties, so they are not really objective. On the one hand the government exerts too much control of the media. Then the other part of the media says, 'Okay, we'll balance up and support the opposition.' But those media are much weaker, so there is really no balance, and we have no objectivity. By some estimates about 80 percent of the media's influence comes from the government TV. The circulation of magazines and newspapers is falling drastically because we don't have the raw materials—paper, ink—to print them, and people can't afford to buy them. The situation would be the same if another party were in power. Some of the other parties have already said the policy would be the same. In all the political battles that have been fought, television is the main objective."

I wondered whether Ceda's party managed to get coverage in any of the papers, being neither opposition nor government. "Not much," he said. "Government television excluded us, pretended that we didn't exist. But under new election regulations, they have to give us some time. That was a condition the parties demanded for partici- pation in the elections. *Borba* gives us a little coverage. *Vreme*'s influence is confined to Republic Square [the largest square in Belgrade, a common meeting place, especially for dissidents]."

Did the party get coverage from the independent electronic media?

"Yes, but we are not very satisfied with them either, because they excessively advocate some of the attitudes of the opposition parties. Sometimes Studio B [the independent TV outlet] is like a government glove that has been turned inside out. Maybe it is naive and idealistic, but it would be nice to have something in between. We can't always live with extremes. It tires us out."

I asked Ceda if living at the extremes was a Serbian trait. "There's a lot of truth to that. Among other things, this recession has revealed a quality of inertia within the Serbs that I thought had disappeared a long time ago. We like to think, We can do it tomorrow, the *mañana* attitude of the Latin countries. In certain critical moments I think it's typical of every nation."

It was time to turn to Ceda's specialty, literature. Had there been in Yugoslavia much modernist literature like Branimir's *Mouth Full of Earth,* which I had just read? "As early as the 1950s our literature was strongly influenced by such great names as Kafka and Joyce. Also Albert Camus. Even today Hemingway is influential. You may be interested to know that as soon as any influential writer's work was published, it was immediately translated here. There have always been many literary directions here, not just one. We have realistic novels, lyrical, stream of consciousness—a lot of experimenting. Ever since the Surrealists we have had a strong experimental movement. All this has produced the extraordinary work of Pavic. [The widely acclaimed *Dictionary of the Khazars,* with male and female editions in two volumes, by Milorad Pavic, combines language and history in a mélange of magical realism. It was translated into English by Christina Pribicevic-Zoric and published in the U.S. in 1988. *The Inner Side of the Wind,* another highly imaginative work, was published in the U.S. in 1993.] It is widely felt that Pavic today is what Faulkner was in his day. Generally speaking, Serbian literature is powerful. We have been cut off from the rest of the world because our language is not an important one, but it is now being translated into English and French, and some of our writers are becoming known worldwide. But now we are cut off because of the sanctions. It is not an exaggeration to say that our literature is brilliant. If we cease to exist as a nation, we shall leave a very rich heritage."

I told Ceda that the audience in the States for experimental literature was tiny. Was the same true in Serbia? "I can't give you any numbers, but the influence of the experimental writers is tremendous. It was a great surprise to American writers who visited here to find out how well known our writers are among our people. By tradition, writers are public persons. And it's interesting that now, despite the recession, more people are buying books and attending the theatre and concerts."

Were books and theatre tickets cheap? "Everything is expensive for us these days, but people are buying so many books that you will find our bookshops almost empty. And concert halls and theatres are overcrowded." Snezana commented, "It's a paradox."

"Perhaps not," I said, "perhaps it's an escape."

Ceda said, "There may be something else involved. It is an attempt to find more permanent values in this situation. Until recently we were able to afford practically anything. And people became euphoric. We had become a consumer society. Now that we can't do that, we are looking for answers to some universal questions. Especially this is true of the intellectuals."

I asked Ceda what role he took as a critic. "I am interested in the different generations and the different genres. We have some specialized critics, but my major concern is to interpret those works that offer new intellectual ideas, philosophical ideas, sociological ideas, political ideas."

Ceda had written, in addition to his several books of criticism, a volume of short stories and a novel with a modern setting based on the psychology of the *pogorelci*, people who were proud to have been the victims of widespread fire in World War II. "Their houses were burned to the ground, and they were living on the margins. They had been defeated, but they were proud of their fate."

"So is the book really about the psychology of the victim?"

"The psychology of the loser," Ceda said. I wondered if he knew the book by the Polish writer George Konrad, called *The Loser.* Yes, he said, he knew that work, but his was completely different. "Konrad's is another kind of loser."

Proud in their loser fate? Their victim status? "Do you feel that the mentality of the victim is a Serb characteristic?" I wanted to know.

"In our tradition, in our mythology, you can find the story that glorifies the victim. The myth of the celestial victory and the earthly loss. But as you are probably aware, in the last two centuries the Serbian people have been on the other side. They have been winners. They have contributed a lot to freedom in Yugoslavia. They fought on the side of the Allies in World War II, with a very small number of quislings and an enormous number of people who were killed. So we can't say that our mentality is that of losers, but we have a certain amount of inertia. It takes us a long time to wake up."

"The old song, 'Wake up, Serbia'?" I asked. Snezana smiled and gave me the Serbian name of the song. I went on, "It seems to me that in the last few years there has been a revival or reawakening of that earlier mentality."

"I agree," Ceda said. "The crisis has brought out that mentality and people's worst features."

I wondered whether the huge demonstration in Kosovo in 1989, marking the fall of Tsar Lazar, signaled a return to that victim mentality. And whether the whole story of the war in Yugoslavia was not associated with that demonstration that Milosevic called for his own purposes.

"You are right. Milosevic's rise is associated with that demonstration. It was really a celebration. He promised protection to those Serbs who were in an inferior position in Kosovo, and that protection has become his powerful tool."

"Many of the problems that have developed since then—were they sparked by that celebration?" I asked Ceda.

"No, you couldn't say that. Some people accused Milosevic of taking part in that big event and then forgetting about it. The true beginning of the problem was eight years earlier, when there was an armed uprising in Kosovo. That was used in two ways. The Serbian nationalists said, 'Look what the Albanians have been doing to us.' Milosevic responded with a wave of repression against the Albanians. "And the Communist politicians in Slovenia and Croatia found that a very convenient tool to use against Serbia. That led to a real clash between Slovenia and Croatia and Yugoslavia. The trouble was always there. It was there during World War II. And then it built to the conflict we now have. But the celebration, or as you call it, the demonstration, was not a turning point. It was just a big show."

"I thought it was the turning point because the fierce nationalism expressed there would have struck terror in the hearts of the other republics that they might be taken over by the Serbs."

"The demonstration, as you call it, was too loud, but it had no other implications. Do you know that all the other Yugoslav leaders joined Milosevic at the celebration? It was only an outward show of unity, covering up serious problems. Each Yugoslav nation began to be afraid of the others. Rumors went around that the Slovenians took all the money. The Croatians were accused of conducting subversive activities. And the Serbs were accused of wanting to swallow the rest. It's like a badly organized family. No one believes anyone. The fact is, it's too complex a problem to be able to explain it simply."

"But unless I can understand it myself, I can't explain it to others," I said.

"You should understand the attitude of the Serbians toward the Americans. It's possibly inertia, but whatever Americans do or don't do, we unreservedly believe that Americans are our friends. It is deeply rooted in the mentality of our people. When our people hear that America supports some opposite party in the conflict, we believe it is the result of confusion or that they are merely pretending. It could not be the truth. This has some historical grounds. In World War II, when we were fighting on the same side, Serbia was bombed by the Allies with President Roosevelt's approval. Nevertheless, Serbia's orientation is to the West, even though its geographical position suggests something else."

I told Ceda about the anti-Americanism at the Milic de Macva party. "Milic and his friends are special people. He is a gifted painter, but he shouldn't be taken seriously as a political speaker." I told Ceda I had been amazed and amused that after hours of anti-American ravings, the crowd then applauded David Moss's defense of the Americans. Ceda said this only confirmed what he had said, that "We can't believe that the Americans are not supporting us. We can't accept it. We can't conceive it. People like Milic believe they can pull the American people's ears if they don't like them." We all laughed loudly at this proposition and then said our goodbyes.

Leaving the Press Club, I said I would walk back to the hotel. No, no, no, Ljiljana insisted, she would drive me. Walking, which appeared to be a favorite sport in Belgrade, seemed anathema to Ljiljana. How could I think of walking when she had her car? But first she had a small errand to run nearby. It would take only a moment and then we would be on our way. I told her that I had an appointment back at the hotel. She assured me that we would have plenty of time. I found myself unable to resist this strong woman, though I would have preferred to walk.

We went back to the car, where she took from the back seat a package that she said she needed to take to her dressmaker. We then walked to a decrepit-looking building down a side street and took the creaky elevator to the fifth floor, where the dressmaker kept an apartment. It looked like those I'd seen in public housing projects in Chicago—a small living room with an adjoining kitchen, a matching velour sofa and chairs, a coffee table with a crocheted doily, and a huge television set blasting away.

The dressmaker was out. Her thirteen-year-old granddaughter, tall and sweet-faced with long blond hair, invited us to wait and offered coffee. While we waited about an hour, Ljiljana told me about the terrible problems facing doctors treating cancer patients after I asked about the incidence of lung cancer in this country where almost everybody smoked. "It's high," she told me, "but there were not so many deaths until we could no longer get surgical tools, parts for x-ray equipment, and chemotherapy drugs. We can no longer do mammograms because we can't get the film and all the things we need for the diagnosis. We do not even have cotton for surgery, let alone the anesthetics." She then repeated the story that Snezana Stoskovic had told me earlier about ninety babies dying from lack of cardiac surgery. "It is criminal what the UN sanctions committee is doing. We were contacted by a Jewish food wholesaler in New York who wanted to send us some supplies, but he could not get the permit."

Finally I had run out of time. I had an appointment at the hotel in the next few minutes. Ljiljana decided she could simply leave the fabric she had brought and talk with the dressmaker by phone. Meanwhile I would be late for my appointment. Somehow this little piece of tragicomedy, the telling of these awful stories while we waited for a dressmaker, as the television played American cartoons, in a building that was falling apart, in the midst of a city under siege where people couldn't afford to buy a newspaper for a penny, struck me as poignantly ludicrous. No matter what, Ljiljana would go on with her life. I had not yet seen her in the same outfit twice; clothes were clearly one of her obsessions. I was determined not to feel shabby wearing one of the three outfits I had brought to Belgrade, despite Ljiljana's teasing me about wearing sandals all the time even as the weather was turning crisp. "They are comfortable, I'm sure," she said by way of condescension.

While she still made regular trips to the dressmaker and the hairdresser, Ljiljana did not escape some consequences of the collapsed economy. Her hospital salary had been reduced to practically nothing, and she and her husband had been forced to take in her daughter, Sonja, and Sonja's husband, to live with them. They had lived in another apartment in the building that Ljiljana had inherited from her once-wealthy family. The two families had decided to share Ljiljana's apartment in order to gain the income from renting the daughter's apartment. Sonja and her husband owned a pharmacy on the ground floor of the building, but medicines were so difficult to get and so many bribes had to be paid that the business didn't produce much income, and Ljiljana's husband, Branka, was receiving his tiny retirement pension. Among all of them, they had not even a hundred dollars a month income, a drastic fall from their generous incomes of a couple of years before. Still, life must go on, and so Ljiljana made her trips to the dressmaker.

The literature of Eastern Europe and the Soviet Union of the last thirty years is richer with political novels than perhaps at any time in literary history. I'm not talking here of the crass Socialist Realist novels that poured from the pens of Soviet and Eastern European writers for fifty years, but of the modernist, Kafkaesque novels that went largely unpublished in their homelands, except in Yugoslavia, until after the Iron Curtain fell. Such writers as the Russian Yuz Aleshkovsky, the Czech Bohumil Hrabel, and the Albanian Ismail Kadare are only a few of the many whose works have now been published at home and have been widely translated and published abroad in recent years. The tradition of the political novel in Yugoslavia is well established. Branimir Scepanovic's *Mouth Full of Earth,* published in 1974, can be read as a political allegory, though it is much more than that, just as Kafka's *The Trial* or *The Castle*, from which it derives, were more than extraordinarily prescient political novels.

In *Mouth Full of Earth* a man finds that he has cancer and decides to kill himself. He then decides to return to his village to die. On his way there the train stops at an isolated station and, for reasons he doesn't understand, the man leaves the train and begins to walk across the fields. He arouses the attention of a couple of men who pursue him to discover who he is and where he is going. The two men are joined by others, until soon there is a crowd madly pursuing the man, as if he is a dangerous criminal. The man is desperately fleeing ahead of them, dropping his clothes as he goes to lighten his weight. At the end of the day he finds a place to hide and dies there.

The two original pursuers, alone after the crowd has at last dispersed, find him naked on a rock, dead. Guilty about their mindless pursuit of this innocent man, they are nevertheless unable to fathom the whole event.

The story is told alternately from the victim's point of view and that of one of the pursuers. It operates at several levels: the personal story of a man pursued by his own devils, on one hand, and on the other, of the pursuers who are driven by what they know not; another story of man's inability to live his life, to make his own decisions, without the censure and pressure of society, any society, and the irrational nature of that censure and pressure; and a third story, a political allegory of the specific destructiveness of Communist society on the individual. It is, in Branimir's terms, a story of loneliness and alienation, whether because of one's inner devils, because of the demands of the outer society for conformity, or because of communism's soul-destroying effects, or all three.

One passage will give the reader a feel for the intensity of this eighty-page novel that left me gasping at the end. The italics are the author's. All the passages about the victim are in italics. In this passage the victim has temporarily found a place to hide and is resting from his flight:

"He raised himself on his elbows and tried to discern from the glistening sun-flecked shadows how long he had been lying under the leafy gold crown which screened the sky from him. But, though he at once convinced himself that not a shadow had moved even by a fraction of an inch, he could not rid himself of the impression that he had long remained in that cool, shadowy place. He could hear the chaotic calling of birds and could feel quite clearly the whole forest breathing deeply and peacefully. His body responded with fresh strength and his awareness, til recently sunk in lethargy and emptiness, began to pulsate more and more rapidly, roused to wonder by the undeniable fact that a single moment, in which nothing had happened, seemed to him as long and immeasurable as if it were endless. He smiled. He knew that the impression originated in the illusory feeling towards time which always mirrors the human condition. He also knew that a moment of pain always lasts longer than a moment of joy. For all that, he asked himself if, should he reconsider and decide to live as long as it were fated for him to live, that strange law of nature would apply to him too; if enough time were left to him, would every moment of suffering really seem longer

or, on the contrary, melt more and more quickly and grow smaller as
a piece of ice held in a warm hand? Would this be the final illusion?"

There was still another dimension to this tightly packed novel: the psychology of the victim, what I'd come to view as a particularly Serbian view of the world. The hero as victim, or the victim as hero, the man pursued by forces unknown to him, condemned to death by natural forces (cancer) but actually killed by malevolent human forces, by forces that will not let him rest until he has exhausted all his human energy, that will let him rest only in death, naked, on a rock, exposed to the elements. His pursuer says at the end, "Perhaps I might have felt a certain compassion for his great suffering, or at least that he died alone, without any of his kin, on that rock where no one would ever find him, had not some strange pity in his smile, maybe addressed to us only, prevailed. That, at least suddenly occurred to me. To confirm that last impression, I turned to Jacov. He, however, was weeping silently and looked at me as if he no longer recognized me. Night was beginning to fall; the whole landscape, the whole universe, suddenly vanished in the gloom, save that solitary hollow rock on which we two—separated by the mysterious naked man who smiled at us even in death—sank into troubled silence." In the end, the pursued and the pursuers are equally victims of terrible unseen forces. Only Kafka's victims are so hapless. Branimir's victim from another novel, whom he described to me earlier, suffers a similar fate, though he lives. He is hounded and persecuted by the crowd and the state apparatus until his identity is lost. Is this merely a literary convention in which Branimir has found his métier, or is he expressing the deep Serbian victim psychology that afflicts his countrymen? I suggest it is the latter.

15 Kovinka, my favorite and most regular waitress (*kelnerica*) in the hotel, was thirty-eight, very tall, slightly overweight, red-haired (from a bottle), with tired eyes but a constantly cheerful demeanor. She worked nine hours a day, seven days a week, to help keep her family afloat. She had an eighteen-year-old daughter and a fifteen-year-old son, both in school. She told me, with poignant gestures, bending over and holding her back, how tired she was. It was a hard (*tvrd*) life, she told me in her few words of English. Yet every morning, when I rang room service and whoever picked up the phone and recognized my voice passed the phone to her because she knew a few words of English, she was charming and helpful, immediately bringing me my bread and cheese, juice, and a double Turkish coffee. On this morning, Sunday, she was handling the dining room herself, willing to work when no one else would, to help her family keep alive the memory of the days before the economic collapse. I longed to talk politics with Kovinka, but we didn't have enough language between us. I imagined that her hard life and goodwill toward this American customer meant that she had neither the time nor the energy to watch the television broadcasts that made villains of Americans.

Ah, a day off on which to be a mere tourist in a strange city. Draga Derdovic would give me a tour of the city's historic places. It was a perfect day for the excursion, the air crisp but warm, the sun bright. Our first stop on the Avenue of the Rulers was the rough-hewn stone building with a small tower—the officers' club where a plot had been hatched in 1903 to assassinate the despised King Aleksander Obronevic and his wife. A few blocks away was the site of the palace where the brutal killings took place, the palace now destroyed. This was one of the killings that are cited to show the primitive brutality of the Serbs, yet the number of assassinations in Serbian history does not at all outnumber those in English history or even in the short history of the U.S.

As we continued on our tour, Draga pointed out the Ethnographic Museum that I would visit later, and the National Museum of Art that I had seen on my previous visit, with its huge collection of ancient frescoes and a lame representation of nineteenth- and twentieth-century art. We were heading for the famous Kalemegdan Park. Parking on the street across from the park, we walked along a wide path that took us up a hill to the small zoo. Kalemegdan Park was one of the largest in the world, a 580-acre site that included a small "luna" or amusement park, the zoo, endless paths over small hills, and the ruins of Roman and Turkish battlements. The stone parapets, some as high as twenty feet, were strategically placed on hills overlooking the convergence of two rivers, the Sava and the Danube, with the Turkish walls often built on top of the Roman.

On these historic stone walls there was a great deal of graffiti, as was true of all of Belgrade. Not protest graffiti. The wall of a building across from my hotel had scrawled on it in huge letters a sentiment that in translation read, "My life is beautiful." Or was this sarcasm? The amount of graffiti in the city led me to believe that it was tolerated by the government. There had clearly been no effort to erase it. Much of it was worn away by the elements. The voice of the city's youth, no doubt.

The view from the top of the hill overlooking the meeting of the two rivers was magnificent. Surrounded on land by the great stone walls and paths and great expanses of meadow, one looked out on the Danube gently flowing from the northwest and the Sava from the southwest, and across the water at the towers of Novi Belgrade (New Belgrade), a new town of high buildings being constructed on what had been farmlands. On the south side of this spectacular view was the entrance to the Balkans, on the north to southeast Europe, which might account for Belgrade's slightly schizy personality, its remarkable pride and resistance to defeat, and, on the other hand, its victim mentality.

From the park we drove across the Danube to Novi Belgrade and then to the community of Dorcol to see the monument the Serbians had erected in 1990 to the memory "of all Jews victims of Nazi genocide in Belgrade and Serbia 41–45. Erected by the people of Serbia, City of Belgrade, and the Jewish Community." The inscription is written in Serbian, slightly battered English, and Hebrew. Nandur Glid, the artist who sculpted the monument, a huge bronze abstract version of a menorah, was a concentration camp survivor. The statue sits on the edge of the Danube, in front of a new ten-or-so-story housing development of white stucco with brown trim and well-maintained landscaping.

We then drove to Zemun, the old city dating from Roman times that is slowly being restored. The tiny houses sitting up against each other abut narrow cobblestone streets. Zemun survived World War II intact because it was then part of Croatia and thus was not bombed either by the Nazis or the Allies. Nearby was the former site of a Nazi extermination camp. Driving through the town, we passed an ancient church that I insisted on stopping to see. It was now functioning as a coffee house—a very rundown coffee house at that. I was once again struck by the scarcity of churches in Belgrade. Though Tito never outlawed the church and it continued to function, the actual church structure clearly did not play a large role in people's lives. Here was a lovely old church that had been abandoned.

In Zemun, Draga took me to the ancient family home of Theodor Herzl, the founder of Zionism, who was himself born in Budapest. According to Draga, the family had lived in this small house since 1739.

Not having asked for a tour of the Jewish historic sites, I was obviously getting one. Draga had apparently decided that I would appreciate such a tour and next took me to the Jewish cemetery to show me yet another monument, inscribed "To the heroes fallen for justice and unification for the memory and glory of the Serbian Jews," with a poem by the national heroic poet, Njegos, in Serbian and Hebrew:

Generation created for the poetry!
During the century the fairies
will rush to make for them a decent wreath.
Your example will teach the poets
how to communicate with immortality.

The Jewish cemetery—to be specific, the Ashkenazi Jewish cemetery, for there was a Sephardic one across the road—looked like all the other cemeteries in a row on the outskirts of Belgrade, graves close together but with enough room for shrubbery and grass, so unlike the old Jewish cemetery in Prague, confined to a small plot of land in the ghetto, where there was hardly an inch between tombstones. There was no ghetto in Belgrade.

From the cemetery we drove back to the city to Karadjordje (Karageorge) Park, where there was a statue of the first Karadjordje, Djordje Petrovic, who led the first great revolt against the Turks in 1804 and who founded a dynasty that came and went with the tides of Serbian fortunes. Another Karadjordje, Aleksander, ruled between the two world wars and was assassinated in 1934 in Marseilles by a Croatian. His son, Peter, was too young to assume the throne, so the country was ruled by a regency until he became king in 1941. He was deposed by the Partisans in 1945. But that wasn't the end of the Karadjordjevic dynasty. A current pretender to the throne, Crown Prince Aleksander, lived in London and had the support of some Serbians, especially the surviving Cetniks and some of their heirs.

On the grounds of the park were a new, modern building of the University of Belgrade and the Byzantine-style Saint Sava Church, the largest Serbian Orthodox church in the world. Its construction had begun before World War II, was abandoned under Tito, was then taken up again in 1985, but it was still not finished in 1993. The Serbian church clearly was not a powerful force in Belgrade.

Saint Sava is the patron saint of Serbia, having founded the Serbian Orthodox church in 1219, won the independence of the church from the Greeks in 1222, and melded a strong church-state federation. He established the first educational and health-care systems, and wrote a book of instructions about how to rule the state. He died in Bulgaria, and his body was taken to a monastery in Serbia. During the Turkish reign his remains were taken to Belgrade and burned. The church was built on the grounds of the pyre.

Draga then drove me around the city showing me statuary commemorating the heroes of Serbia, including a huge statue of Nikola Tesla, an engineer who migrated to the U.S. in the nineteenth century and made important contributions to the science of electricity.

"Well," Draga said as we drove up to my hotel, "you have seen the historic sites. Not a lot. There wasn't much left after the bombings in World War II." Perhaps, in the long run, the Serbs would have been better off capitulating to the Nazis first, as most of the rest of Europe did, instead of waiting until they were on their knees with no choice left. But don't tell that to a Serb.

"It's All So Unbelievable!
I'm Fed Up!"

16 When I called to ask for an appointment with Vuk Draskovic, the leading oppositionist in Belgrade who in the spring of 1993 was arrested and beaten by the police in a demonstration at the Parliament in which a policeman was killed, I was told he was too busy to see me. I didn't believe he couldn't find an hour at some time to speak with me. Apparently American journalists didn't rank high on the lists of the Serbian Renewal Movement. Draskovic's spokesman, Ivan Kolocovic, offered himself instead. Did I have a choice?

When I arrived at the Movement office after a long ride to the outskirts of Belgrade, I was told I'd have to wait fifteen or twenty minutes. Ivan was in a meeting. Half an hour later, I was told that Ivan couldn't see me because he had to accompany Vuk to a hospital where he would give gifts to wounded soldiers. I suggested I go along. It was agreed. It wouldn't be an interview, but I would see in action this writer-turned-politician who was described as a highly dramatic, bearded-prophet type.

Sitting beside me in the secretary's office was a young TV journalist from Germany. She had an appointment with Vuk and was doing a profile of him. She too decided to go to the hospital.

As I waited, I talked with another Serbian Renewal official about whether the party would participate in the December elections. They were still trying to decide, he told me, and gave me a report by the media monitoring unit of the European Institute for the Media detailing the media coverage in the 1992 election, in which Milosevic received most of the attention. The report stated that in the areas of Belgrade where the independent TV Studio B and Radio B92 had the strongest signals, the vote for the opposition parties was the heaviest. Serbian Renewal's decision would be based partly on the agreement that was being drawn up between the opposition parties and the government about access to television.

At one point while I was reading the report, I noticed that the German TV reporter was no longer in the room. It made me nervous, so I walked out of the office and into the corridor where the other offices were located. All the rooms were empty. I went back to the secretary. "I take it," I said, "that the party has left for the hospital."

"A few minutes ago," she told me.

"They didn't inform me."

"Oh, I guess they forgot you were supposed to go," she said apologetically.

"Yes, I guess they did."

"Would you like to follow them in a cab?" she asked.

"No, thank you. I've seen enough of Vuk Draskovic and the Serbian Renewal Movement," I told her. "Please call me cab."

Ileana Cosic had been the translator for the Ministry of Information's writers' conference. Unlike most of the people I had met, she was not an attractive woman, displaying an arrogance that I had rarely seen in Belgrade, except by implication in Vuk Draskovic. She was the only person I met who asked to be addressed as Doctor, having earned a Ph.D. in drama. During the conference she had cozied up to a variety of government officials, sitting on the arms of their chairs and chatting with them during the proceedings in conspiratorial tones when she was not called upon to interpret. Her physical appearance matched her personality—brilliant strawberry blond hair heavily sprayed, brightly rouged cheeks, and mascaraed eyes on a thin, bony face that cried for subtlety. Close to sixty, she was obviously hating the aging process.

Ileana called to tell me that she needed to talk with me to make sure I got some facts straight that I might not get from others. I hesitated but decided to hear her out. Perhaps, indeed, she had facts that none of my other sources had. She came to the hotel to meet me, and we talked over coffee in the dining room. Now she was using her conspiratorial tones with *me*. As she warmed to her subject, her drama school training emerged loud and clear. But then the Serbs do tend to be dramatic speakers.

"If you want to understand the Kosovo problem better," Ileana began, "you must know that during the Second World War part of Serbia—Kosovo—was occupied by the Italians because they created the so-called Great Albania. Among their plans was to resettle about 100,000 Albanian families in Kosovo in order to disturb the ethnic balance." Was that their motive, I wondered privately, or were they merely trying to acquire more land in the usual way of conquerors? "And they expelled all the Serbs," Ileana continued, "and the Albanians became the overwhelming ethnic majority. After the war the Communists pursued absolutely the same anti-Serb policy there. They kept all the Albanians settled there during the war, in defiance of all international agreements which do not recognize forced resettlement, and they prohibited the return of the Serbs. At the same time they passed a law saying that the property of anyone who didn't return in three months would be confiscated. So a small paradox: you are prohibited from returning, but if you don't return you lose your property! Meanwhile, after 1948 more Albanians came to Kosovo under the pretext that they were escaping Stalinism in Albania.

"The whole policy was engineered by the Vatican, you see...."

But, I interrupted, "the Albanians are Muslims. Why do you think this was engineered by the Vatican?"

"Because it was anti-Orthodox policy. The Vatican considers the Orthodox to be more dangerous than the Muslims. They are harder to convert. The pope paid one of his recent visits to Albania because they are trying to convert them to Catholicism. They are easier to convert because they are attracted by the money." The pope never visited Albania, but he did visit Hungary, a Catholic country.

"Now wait a moment," I protested. "You are talking about Communist policy in Kosovo at the same time you are saying that the policy was determined by the Vatican. How can this be?"

"Because we are sure that Tito was the extended hand of the Vatican. Everything he did here about the Serbs was absolutely in line with Vatican strategy, centuries old. During the war, Italy wanted to have the two gateways to the Adriatic. Italy is on one side and Albania on the other. The Vatican, of course, during the war, was with Italy, although not openly. But everywhere in the world where you have the Orthodox, you have the Vatican. They consider this part of the world as *terra mozione* [earthquake]. Now you have the same problem in Montenegrin churches and in Macedonia. They want to split us up and make them Unitarian churches first and then gradually Catholic." Ileana seemed to have forgotten that Tito defeated the Ustase that was supported by the Vatican.

I listened, fascinated. Ileana was right—I probably wouldn't get these "facts" from anyone else. Was this woman paranoid, altogether delusional? Was there any sense to be made from what sounded like ravings? On the other hand the Vatican had played an ugly role in Croatia in World War II, fully cooperating with the Ustase and forcing thousands of Serbs and Muslims to convert or be killed. If this theory of Ileana's was mostly mad, which is seemed to me to be, it wasn't entirely surprising that a Serb could concoct such a theory remembering World War II. I hadn't yet met anyone who so clearly believed the Serbs to be victims of the world's villainies. This, however, sounded closer to Anthony Di Iorio's description of the Serbs as paranoid.

"So," Ileana went on, "it was a matter of totalitarian regimes. First it was the fascists and then the Communists. That's why Dobrica Cosic said, 'Kosovo is a democratic problem.' Once they understand that they are citizens with equal civic rights and not Albanians who have the right to secede and take away our territory, there will be no problems. Like in Florida where you have all those Cubans. As long as they consider themselves American citizens, then privately they can be whatever they like. Despite the fact that America took Cuba away from the Spanish, and Kosovo was ours taken away by the Albanians." Ileana laughed as she made that comparison.

She now switched to Bosnia, which she described as a hell, as "utter darkness because it has always been a battlefield of diverging interests." Well, so far so good. No one would quarrel with that statement. Bosnia had indeed been a bloody battlefield of conquest, including Serb conquest, since the Middle Ages. On the other hand, most Serbs spoke of modern Bosnia as the heart of Yugoslavia, a prototype with all the ethnic and national groups living peacefully together—until the war broke out.

"In the Second World War, Germany was very interested in attracting the Muslims, considered them good fighters, good soldiers.

They created the Croatian Handzar SS division, including many Muslims [that was to fight alongside the Germans]. But they were a great disappointment to each other. [The Handzar was the Turkish curved dagger.] The whole idea was born in the head of the Haj Amin, the mufti of Jerusalem, who is Yasir Arafat's uncle." At that point Ileana took out a book printed in Cyrillic that told the story of the Nazification of the Bosnian Muslims. She insisted that I survey the pictures of the Muslims saluting the German generals and of Muslim atrocities against Serbs, many of them committed by the Handzar unit that returned to Bosnia after German training. Allegedly their goal was to protect Muslims from the attacks of the Croatians. Whether the Handzar SS division was "born in the head of the mufti" is not known, but that he went to Sarajevo to support it is certainly true, and that he lived part of World War II in Berlin is also true. The division, it turned out, had no interest in fighting beside the Nazis; it had its own fish to fry in Bosnia.

Ileana returned to the Vatican, this time with reference to the church hiding Nazis and helping them to escape. She offered to photocopy for me her copy of *Ratlines*, a book by two Englishmen that documented the Vatican's role in the postwar escape of Croatian Nazis. "There is a statement in that book that ten thousand war criminals from the official lists entered the United States after the war, and that is why you have now that [pro-Croatian] policy in the United States. It is their children who are promoting it."

Now Ileana changed directions again. With almost no prompting, she was giving me her version of the causes behind Yugoslavia's troubles. Current world policy on Serbia, she said, was a continuation of the policies of the Austro-Hungarian Empire. "After we fought the Germans, the slogan was 'Serbs must die.' But since Hitler didn't exterminate us then, the sanctions now are meant to produce the same effect, to destroy the national being of the Serbs. During the war it was one hundred Serbs for one killed German. They were killing children then, and now we have children dying in our hospitals. It is the same idea."

Now we were back to the Vatican. "You know, you from the Western world cannot understand Catholicism the way it is here. It is very different. In the United States it's just another religion. Here it's a very aggressive force that wants to rule. I have a young woman friend, a Serb, married to a Belgian diplomat. They wanted to buy a house at the seaside [in Croatia], but the Catholic priest who was managing the property for the owners who were in the United States refused to sell because the wife was an Orthodox Serb. The husband was appalled. That could never happen in Belgium. But here that kind of thing happens. They want to convert all of us to Catholicism now in the twentieth and twenty-first century when religion is no longer important. And the fundamentalist Muslims are also dangerous, which you in the West may not recognize."

"We recognize the spread of Islam," I told Ileana, "but the belief in the U.S. is that this is not a threat in Bosnia, that Izetbegovic has given up his fundamentalism."

"Absolutely not, unfortunately. I know a lady, a Serbian doctor who lived in Sarajevo before the rise of nationalism became so strong. Then, it made no difference who you were—you were colleagues, doctors who were emancipated. The Muslim lady doctors were well known for their love of clothes, especially jewelry. All of a sudden they lengthened their skirts, started using much less makeup, and wore only one chain around their necks and no bracelets. And very modest clothes. All of a sudden even the intellectuals, willy-nilly, who knows whether it was their choice or whether they were under pressure, but they changed their life-style. Many women are wearing the chador. But I think the majority of people do not want this. They remember their Serbian roots, and they know they can't get along without Yugoslavia. I think Izetbegovic has influence in Sarajevo only. He thought he could win this war much faster with the mojahedin who were committing all these atrocities. And he thought that money would start flowing in from the East. But it didn't work that way, and now they are suffering. They all thought those petrol dollars would come flowing in if they put on chadors and went to the mosque five times a day, but they are finding out it isn't happening, and now the modernists are trying to make the peace. They can't accept that way of life anymore." There was some truth in Ileana's report on the rise of Islam in Bosnia.

"In the 1970s, when Tito granted the Muslims nationhood, it was a great blow to the Serbs. You see, the overwhelming majority of Muslims are Serbs. What Tito wanted was for Bosnians to have to declare their national identity as Muslim. Then Bosnia would not be overwhelmingly Serbian. You know that Bosnia during the Middle Ages was one of the Serbian states."

This piece of history is believed by all Serbs and most others, and may in fact be true. But in a 1994 book, *Bosnia: A Short History*, the

English writer Noel Malcolm makes a case, based on archaeological evidence, that Bosnia was a separate nation for nearly three generations in the Middle Ages, loosely allied to the Catholic church, until it was overrun by the Turks in 1463. Like all history texts, Malcolm's is open to interpretation and subject to revision, and some Balkan experts immediately questioned Malcolm's premise, pointing out errors and obfuscations. The fact that Serbian or Serbo-Croatian, as it was called until the war, has long been the language of the Bosnians, along with the Cyrillic alphabet, seems to offer strong contradictory evidence. Language, spoken and written, has always been one of the key tools used to identify early civilizations and one of the factors that bind people together. One of the reasons it was so easy for the Serbs to bid Slovenia goodbye was that the Slovenians had always had their own language, clearly marking them off from the rest of the former Yugoslavia.

Continuing her story about the history of Bosnia, Ileana described how, in the nineteenth century, after a revolt against the Turks by the Bosnians, supported by the Serbs, the Turks were forced out of Bosnia. At the Congress of Berlin in 1878, Bosnia was handed over by the European powers to the Hapsburg Monarchy to be governed as a separate nation. No question about these commonly known facts. In 1908 the Austrians annexed Bosnia, much to the anger of the Serbs who felt that Bosnia was a sister state, part of their natural territory.

"The reason there are so many Croats in Bosnia today is because the Austrians brought them in to govern because they could speak German and were Catholics," Ileana added. This was news to me but made sense.

"The church, which was in league with the Austrians, was very influential. Bosnia was very poor, and the church would buy their souls. They would give them food if they would convert to Catholicism." In all of this Ileana had her facts straight, according to most historians writing on the subject. Why did she every once in a while career into left field? Had the Vatican continued to play the destructive role in Yugoslavia that it played in World War II? Was Germany playing out a role begun a century ago? Or was this an extreme case of the Serbs' victim mentality?

Still talking about Bosnia, Ileana reminded me that many Muslims "smeared their arms up to their neck in Serbian blood. They joined the Ustase and were told they would be paid for shedding Serb blood. And then, when the Serb Cetniks in Bosnia retaliated and massacred the Muslims, the Muslims started rethinking that policy and they stopped. My father was a judge, and he was sitting with another judge at the Serbian Academy of Sciences and talking about this. The Communists never told about the Muslim slaughters of the Serbs, only about the retaliation [the Communists despised the Cetniks]. My father's friend said, 'It was such a crime what the Cetniks did.' And my father, who had been a prisoner of war in Germany, said, 'It was retaliation. Without it, the crimes against the Serbs would have been much worse.'

"At the end of the war you had the Muslims and the Serbs together being killed by the Ustase. Like in this war now, the Croats are killing Muslims and Serbs. A famous professor from Sarajevo said not long ago, 'No matter what happens, after all these atrocities the only choice for the Muslims is to go with the Serbs. It's their natural side. It's their own people.'" It would seem that the Muslims disagreed, having made a compact with the Croatians in early 1994, at the urging of the U.S. How long this agreement can hold is to be seen. In World War II the Muslims were also thrown together with the Croatians, by Germany, but that agreement came apart after only a couple of years.

"In Western Herzegovina you have a lot of Ustase who were generations back Serbs who converted to Catholicism, and whose souls were poisoned to hate Serbs. They had to prove they were good Catholics by hating the Serbs. That is what you cannot understand in the United States. There you don't have to prove that you are a good citizen by hating another citizen. Basically, these wars we are having are religious wars."

Ileana returned to her favorite subject, the Vatican. "When you read *Ratlines* you will be appalled, just appalled. The man who was in charge of evacuating all the Ustase was a well-known priest. He left too, but after twenty years he came back and is living peacefully in Bosnia. Some people said the Ustase bought him. You don't buy Catholic priests. He was on a mission."

I had to cut Ileana short for another appointment. It was time for me to go to Mira's office to settle my weekly bills and get some money from Meme. She brought me 1.6 million dinars for my fifteen dollars. The previous week she had given me 840,000. That money would buy me taxicabs, cigarettes, and an occasional meal for less than a week. Whole families lived on the same amount for a month.

At Mira's office I met a young man who, in protest against the station's policies, had quit his job in the news department of TV Belgrade eight months earlier. He was supporting his family on an unemployment compensation check of $3.75 a month, plus his wife's $15 a month salary. I asked him if he would make an appointment to talk with me further. He told me he was afraid to say anything more. "I have enough trouble already," he said.

After again asking my impressions of the city, Mira launched into an angry tirade. "What is happening here is not only because of the sanctions. It is Milosevic! Iron face! But the Serbs are crazy. They will once more vote him into office. We have five hundred years under the Turks and fifty under Tito, and now we'll have fifty years under Milosevic because the people sit around and wring their hands but don't do anything. It's all so unbelievable! I'm fed up! Serbs are always the helpless victims. At least under Tito we lived well."

But, I told Mira, "you only lived so well because of the billions of dollars the West pumped into the economy because it was a buffer against the Soviet Union."

"Yes, and we didn't pay our bills, but we didn't know about that. They didn't tell us that part of the story. We only knew that the U.S. was our very good friend. And now we can hardly believe what the U.S. is doing to us. But do we put the blame where we should, on Milosevic, for his crazy nationalism, for stirring up all this trouble? No, we sit around and suffer and say, 'It will be okay.' It won't! We will go farther and farther down. Now, before the elections, Milosevic promises fuel oil for everyone. And the stores will fill up with goods. Until after the elections! Then, watch to see what happens. It will go down, down, down! Unless he should lose the election, which I don't think he will. He makes sure of that. There are no honest elections. And there is no real competition. Those politicians! Milosevic is smart, but the rest of them? They are fools!"

Mira then launched into a description of how the wars were the consequence of German manipulation. As the major power in Europe, Germany's economic purposes were best served by destabilizing Yugoslavia, an argument I had heard before from several others. The argument that Mira made was as garbled as all the other efforts to explain this. If there was any truth to this argument, which Germany's great haste to recognize Slovenia, Croatia, and Bosnia as independent nations, and its pressure on the U.S. and the international community to follow suit seemed to indicate, it didn't look like I would find any clear analysis among my Belgrade intellectuals. Perhaps it was true that a unified Europe no longer served Germany's economic purposes, nor those of the U.S., as Mira and others maintained. But it seemed to me that their anger at Germany for pushing for recognition of the separate republics and thus tearing Yugoslavia apart, leaving the Serbs exposed to the dangers of living in what they viewed, somewhat realistically, as hostile territories, was so great that they had created an economic rationale for Germany's actions that just didn't add up. It had the feel of a paranoid vision of the world by people who viewed themselves as victims of the world's malevolence.

I had not seen even one pregnant woman on the streets of Belgrade. An occasional woman pushing a stroller with a toddler in it, but not one bulging belly. It was like the Great Depression years in the U.S. when birthrates fell dramatically. Normally, Serbs had the lowest birthrates in Yugoslavia, but this was exceptional. Were people deciding not to have babies in the midst of the economic crisis that enfolded them, with no clear vision of the future ahead? This was one of the questions I would discuss with the minister of health.

17 Walking up the dozen steps to the American Embassy, an ugly, formerly white but now grey stone structure that, like so many buildings along this embassy row, spelled power and influence, I was suitably impressed by this imposing but nondescript building. In the barren lobby was the only "no smoking" sign I saw in the city.

It took me a few minutes to convince the guard that I had a bona fide appointment, because I had forgotten to bring my American passport. He called the press attaché with whom I was scheduled to meet, then invited me to sit down and wait.

Michael Siedenstreiker had served fourteen years with the United States Information Agency, three of them in Sarajevo—1982–1985 —and the last three months in Belgrade. He spoke fluent Serb and seemed already to know his way around the town. He was a studious-looking man of about forty who worked in his shirt-sleeves— probably unique in Belgrade, considering the shortage of heating oil and coal. Everyone else I had talked with in the last couple of days, since the weather had turned cool, was bundled up. The government announced that it would provide enough heat to raise the temperature in its buildings to fifty-five degrees. In privately owned residences or offices, or in places that were not centrally heated, oil and coal were available only in small quantities on the black market. Some people, like Ljiljana, who had converted to electric heat a few years ago, were warm but were threatened by brownouts when the weather turned icy and people began using space heaters. The American Embassy obviously had no problem getting fuel; it could afford black market prices.

Michael and I chatted, mostly about my own observations. He said, "The fellows in the State Department would appreciate hearing from you." I asked why he didn't tell them himself about the effects of the sanctions that we both knew about. He smiled and said, "It would come better from you." He agreed that the department prob- ably hadn't a clue that the sanctions were counterproductive to their aims. "They believed that political democracy would be strengthened by the sanctions, but it's pretty clear it's been seriously weakened, especially by the constraints on the independent media that result from the sanctions," he said. He had subscriptions to the major U.S. magazines sent over in diplomatic pouch and was distributing them to the independent media. Pushed, he said it was only a handful of journalists who had gotten this scarce resource that Petar Lukovic complained so bitterly about not having. "We are trying to help out with equipment for the media, but I admit it's very little," he said. "Practically none?" I asked. "Yes," he admitted.

When I asked him about the failure of the UN committee on sanctions to sign off on permits for medicines, as reported to me by Snezana Stoskovic at the Red Cross and others, Michael at first blamed Milosevic's government. Finally he admitted that the com- mittee was holding out on the permissions, but he had no idea why.

We talked a little about the long history of sanctions imposed by governments on others, and the fact that the first use of such comprehensive sanctions by an international organization was in the case of Iraq after the Persian Gulf War, when Iraq refused to let the UN inspect its weapons systems. The United Nations' all-inclusive embargo on Serbia and Montenegro was only the second such case. Both, I said, were instigated by the U.S., both with the misguided aim of bringing down the leaders of those countries. Both had proved to be totally counterproductive but were nevertheless still in place.

Michael protested that the sanctions had been imposed by the UN, with the U.S. as only one of the parties involved. I laughed and said I found it hard to believe that the U.S. was ever just one party involved in UN policy. In this case especially, it was the U.S. that first adopted the formal position that Serbian aggression in Bosnia Herzegovina was the cause of the war there, and only then were sanctions imposed. Michael smiled weakly.

I asked what he thought about the claim made by the Milosevic government that it was not involved in the war in Bosnia. "Someone is supplying the Serbs with weapons," he said. "They are still shelling Sarajevo. Besides, you can't just forget about what happened there." Pressed, he admitted that there were plenty of atrocities to go around among all the parties involved. "But what about Vukovar, the destruction of an entire city?" he asked. Were the Allies branded war criminals when they firebombed Dresden, a German city completely uninvolved in World War II except that it was a historic German city, I wondered. And how about the Allies bombing Belgrade and other Serbian towns occupied by the Germans? "Well," Michael said, "you have a point."

Knowing what he knew of the situation, did Michael see Milosevic as a war criminal? "There is a UN tribunal investigating that issue right now. They will decide. For myself, I can't say," Michael said, smiling broadly. We sparred a little longer, then I said my farewells, feeling as if I'd done my duty by making my presence known to the embassy, having expected to get even less information than I got.

18 It was a long walk up, five high flights, to the offices of the International Orthodox Church Charities. The old building had obviously once housed upper-middle-class families—big spacious rooms, lots of big windows, a wide elegant staircase, fronting on a courtyard with the wild remnants of what had been a garden, across from a couple of other buildings that were of similar vintage and looked to be similarly spacious, one with generous balconies. Now it was all terribly run-down and seedy looking, like so much of central Belgrade.

The Charities offices looked like they were run by a group of volunteers who had never worked in an office before. Any semblance of organization was not apparent to a visitor's eye. The large front office, with a big bay of windows at one end, had some old rugs scattered on the floor and several odd desks and chairs arranged haphazardly around the room. Constantine "Dean" Triantifilou, who was in charge of this office, sat across a table from me in the middle of the room. As "country representative" of the organization, he was in charge of all aspects of humanitarian aid to all peoples of Serbia and Montenegro and in the former Yugoslavia. He had come to Belgrade in early 1993 from his home in Texas, first to supervise the handling and transport of commodities to targeted areas, and six months later to take over the top job. But he still went about twice a month to Bosnia with a delivery of food, medicine, and other goods.

The Charities had been founded in the U.S. in 1991 to provide aid to Orthodox Christian people around the world, but it didn't limit its aid to the Orthodox; in Bosnia all the factions that could be reached were served. "The church people in the United States wanted an aid organization similar to other churches, but to concentrate in countries where Orthodox people are involved," Dean explained. The organization had offices in Russia and other Balkan states as well as in Belgrade. The Belgrade office had opened in December 1992 with two people; a year later thirteen local people worked in the office.

Dean was of medium height but an oversized man with huge biceps, longish curly black hair, and dark olive skin—a true Greek, a twenty-nine-year-old product of Texas A & M University and the devout son of an Orthodox priest in Austin, Texas. He had spent a year and a half in Africa as an aid administrator and missionary for the church, went home and enrolled in law school, but quit in the spring of 1993 to take this job. "It is more my kind of thing," he told me. When I asked him if the other workers in IOCC were all church-connected, he said, "I can't speak for anyone else. I grew up in the church and it's a strong part of my life. That may make me unique in this aid business. I represent an aid organization. At the same time I'm Orthodox, I'm working in an Orthodox country so that I can help, on a personal level, the Orthodox church. I can't let my job and my religion mix, though. I can only help by being professional. It's a double-edged sword for me. But of course we came here to help the church build an aid organization, so we've done most of our work with the cooperation of the church. They were already working for a year and a half before we came."

Talking about bringing aid to the Muslims of Bosnia, Dean said, "It's a difficult situation working from this side. We go into hospitals, schools, wherever we can get in, but the Orthodox church is not necessarily welcome in the Muslim sections, even with aid. As an American, I can go where the church may not be able to. Like last month I went into Tuzla, a UN-protected area, and we have food going into Sarajevo Saturday. And now we have made an arrangement between the UN High Commission on Refugees and the church to go into the protected zones with aid. That way the church can show the true Christian humanitarian principles that thousands of years of Orthodoxy represent, which is good for our reputation. At the same time we can reach Serbs that we couldn't reach otherwise, because there are Serbs in those protected zones as well as Muslims.

"We are now working directly with the UNHCR. We've carved out our own niche. The UN has tons of flour. We're not going to just dump more flour on the pile. We're going in to give specific aid to specific groups of people. We're a small organization. We can't compete with the big guys. And let's face it, we're trying to raise money among the Serbs, and for them it's 'Who cares about Bosnia?' But we want to make a real impact. We're also working directly with the World Health Organization to target medical supplies."

IOCC had spent about $3 million in Yugoslavia in its first nine months, but Dean couldn't talk about an annual budget. "I'm going for funding for specific projects, like one I've got for $200,000 for three months of supplementing food and medical supplies in only two protected zones. I was told my goals are too small, but I want to see some projects get funded first before we go after the really big bucks. I just want to be able to show that the church can do this. A pharmacologist here has helped us analyze medical needs, and she developed a kit that will supply the needs of one hospital with 250 beds for six months for $30,000, so that's another project we will do. We have a monitor going out to the ob-gyn clinics in Serbia, and another guy will go out to Montenegro. We hope to visit all the institutions here and find out what the true needs are and find the little corners where we can help. It's impossible to help everybody. You've got all these premature kids. One of our guys is monitoring the heroin clinic. And another guy is doing the AIDS clinic. The whole place is falling apart. And it isn't easy to raise money. We go to the international organizations or we go to the organizations in the States and say 'Serbs' and everyone turns his back."

I asked Dean about the patriarch of the Orthodox church whom I would talk with in a few days and who was viewed as a saint. "He *is* a saint. A friend met him last week, and when we came out he said, 'He seemed to have a different accent.' I said, 'It's the voice of God.' You see that holy spirit, the glow in the eyes, the voice. I'm 250 pounds and he is 100, but I feel like a leaf next to him. I was under a lot of pressure last week, and I realized the only one I could turn to was the patriarch. He is like the word of all wisdom. He represents all Orthodoxy. And he's surrounded by people who have that same glow. This is a time when attention is being focused on the church, and it is a time when the church can show what it is. Orthodoxy is two thousand years old. It's not going away even though some people say it's under attack. It's been under attack for two thousand years."

Dean and I spent another hour talking about the nature of the Orthodox church. He told me that one of his tasks was to help reintroduce the church to people who had been estranged from it under the Communist regime. "One of the things my background at home showed me was that, while the American Orthodox church has moved into the twentieth century, the one here hasn't yet. But we're going to start having cocktail parties and such things to teach people about modern Orthodoxy. The Catholic church has long since passed us up in spreading the word. The Orthodox church here has just not grown up. It has taken a war with everything falling apart to put the Orthodox church on the map a little bit."

Dean worked twelve weeks with a week off to go home to Texas to escape the pain and stress of his job. Though he had been in the

UN-protected zones in Bosnia and in the Serb sectors of Sarajevo, he had not yet crossed the battle lines there. He was awaiting a bulletproof vest he was having made in the States for his oversized body. Of all the church workers I had met in my life (a considerable number), Dean was the first body-builder I had run into. I couldn't stop staring at this big, bronze, 250-pound man, trying to imagine him as a missionary in Africa. Or as an aid-giver in Bosnia or in the refugee camps in Serbia. I had trouble reconciling his compassionate view of the world, his view of himself as a person destined to do good, to help his church, with his physical image. It was a refreshing jolt to my stereotypes.

Draga met me in the hotel dining room with a question. What did I want to talk about? He was always interested in talking with me, but why would I want to interview him? He was only a translator, a modest man. His only accomplishment was his skill with languages. Yes, he had read a lot and had taken a special interest in knowing his city inside and out. He had traveled quite a bit, but so had most people in Belgrade.

For starters I said, "Give me your opinion of Milosevic."

"Well, for now," Draga said, "he is the best we have. He is the only one who can deal with everyone—with the West, with the UN, with the Bosnians, with the other republics."

"But how can he deal with the other republics when he stirred up so much nationalistic hatred of them?" I asked.

"That was merely a device to bring people together. It's not important in the long run. What's important in the long run is what will be the definition of the new world order. Everybody now is playing poker—Germany, the United States, Japan. We are in the middle of all this. Pretty soon the situation in the Far East is going to change. Right now everything there is up for grabs with China, Taiwan, North and South Korea. The whole trading situation is in turmoil with the fight for raw materials. Do you know two years ago they found in Serbia the largest deposits of a precious metal that is used in space technology? How it will be developed, who will develop it, who knows? But you know the United States is interested."

"So you don't think the war in Croatia and Bosnia was made in Yugoslavia?" I asked.

"No, the people were manipulated from outside. Like maybe you have a hidden desire to be a writer of big best-selling novels, even though you are a writer of little literary short stories. And someone tells you that you can do it. You find that your psychological base, your desire, has some support, even if it is all illusion. So then you have this idea that when you write the book you are going to be rich and famous. Like the West told Russia it could be a big capitalist country. And like Germany told Croatia and the others they could have these wonderful independent states. And Macedonia. You heard what happened in Macedonia yesterday?"

I hadn't heard any news. I had to rely on people to tell me the news, being unable to read the newspapers or listen to the television or radio. *Politika* had a weekly English-language section, but it was so brief that I got very little news from it. "In Western Macedonia the police arrested eight Albanians they had been watching for a long time," Draga said. "They had been organizing a paramilitary force of twenty thousand men to stage an uprising to make an independent state of Western Macedonia, which is 85 percent Albanian. Two of the men were very high officials. One of them was deputy minister for national defense."

"So there's going to be another war there?"

"Most likely. The Albanians are obsessed. All this is happening because of the internationalization of these problems. Why do you think the Americans are in Macedonia? [The UN had a thousand peacekeepers in Macedonia including five hundred Americans.] To understand all that has happened here in the last two years, you have to use your imagination, your instincts, not on one level but on many. You have to guess based on what you see, what you feel."

"I'm trying," I told Draga.

"And when you talk of nationalism here, you have to ask yourself what displays of it you have seen. Is it like in Croatia where they have big nationalistic festivals every few weeks, in all the big towns, and always blasting nationalistic music in the squares and on the streets, and all the flags and symbols from the Ustase? And the proclamations—'Croatia is for the Croatians.' I haven't been to Croatia since the war started, but I have friends who have been there and reported to me what they saw and heard. They are singing 'Danke, Deutches'—Thank you, Deutschland. Here you see none of that. You haven't heard Milosevic say, 'Serbia for the Serbs only.' Television did a lot of nationalist stuff for awhile—the 'Greater

Serbia,' but that was all. The people never did it, except for maybe a few private parties. But even when Milosevic talks his nationalist talk, it is never to exclude anyone. It is to take back the control that Serbs once had. Even that was only talk, a device for him to get the people behind him, and the people knew it."

I had to admit that in Belgrade I had seen very few signs of the nationalism that Draga and others had described in Croatia. No flags or national symbols were displayed anywhere. As for music blasting away, I had looked in on a couple of weekend parties held in my hotel, where traditional music was being played by young musicians whom I suspected normally played the rock music that was so popular in Belgrade, and people were dancing traditional dances, which I was told was new in Serbia. I had also heard traditional music on taxi radios. But there was certainly no great nationalist presence visible in Belgrade.

I changed the subject to ask Draga if he knew of the antiwar activists. "Yes," he said, "they are like Latin lovers. 'I want to make love because I want to get off.' They are just antiwar. They have no discussion to explain their ideas. They're just attacking, but they're not doing anything. But they are just a small group. You have talked to this woman, Sonja?" I told him I had. "If she had a job, and the job paid the value of three hundred dollars, she would not be doing that."

I disagreed with Draga and told him I thought Sonja was completely dedicated to her cause. "Well, maybe. There are always people who want to be in the opposition, who are masochistic. There is a group of intellectuals who meet every Sunday to discuss their opposition, the so-called Belgrade Circle. Once I went to a meeting. They are philosophers who speak on a very idealistic plane but have no practical applications for any of their ideas. They are, like, meditating."

As if from one of those deeper layers of his mind, Draga said, "You know they blew up the four-hundred-year-old bridge in Mostar." It was not known in Belgrade whether the Croats or the Muslims blew up that historic bridge in the battle for Mostar. In the battle to split Bosnia into Serbian and Croatian fiefdoms, Croatia had proclaimed the beautiful old city in western Bosnia as its capital in Bosnia, and it was desperately defended by the Muslims, with the result that the city was destroyed. Draga's face was masked, drawn, with his eyes closed, as if that bridge signified to him all the terror of the last two years. "We have all this destruction in Sarajevo by the Serbs that is condemned by the world. We have to ask where is the condemnation of the Croats, who were most likely the ones who destroyed that great historic monument and killed I don't know how many people? Or maybe it was the Muslims, who have done their good share of atrocities, including shooting their own people and blaming the Serbs in order to incite the West against the Serbs. But all that is ignored, and only the Serbs are the bloodthirsty aggressors killing off the innocent Muslims and Croats. For this only the deepest imagination can help understand. Not newspapers and television. They tell you nothing to help you understand. What are the facts? Does anyone really know them? Maybe in a hundred years someone will make sense from all this."

It was time for Draga to go. We said au revoir. We would see each other again tomorrow evening when we would have dinner with Branimir.

19 When I returned to my room last night, I was greeted by cold blasts of air and the stench of burning wires. The weather had started turning cold a few days ago. My room had been cool but not uncomfortable. But this day was much colder. I had turned on the heater earlier. The repairman who came up to check my heater said it had burned out, that I would have to change rooms. After I turned down a couple of uncomfortable rooms on the same floor, the room clerk moved me up three flights to the room above the one I'd had. A better view of the city from the seventh floor. The clerk explained that because of the shortage of fuel there would be heat only for two hours in the morning and two hours in the evening. I was glad I had brought a big wooly sweater and a warm robe that I bundled into in the morning to read and write a bit, unable to face the city right away.

I knew that all over the city people were bundling up to keep warm. For just a little while I didn't want to hear their stories of being without heat or hot water. And I didn't want to see the empty shops and restaurants, the hundreds of people crowding into the trams. Everyone who traveled by tram in Belgrade was late. It was expected. I didn't want to see any more crumbling old buildings,

buildings not a hundred years old that looked like they were three hundred years old. One sees old crumbling buildings all over Europe, but they are ancient, centuries-old structures. I didn't want to get into any more elevators that sank with my modest weight, or didn't work. I didn't want to use the phone that so often buzzed with static and made it so hard to get through to the person I was calling. I didn't want to face the filth of the streets that resulted from so many refugees living on them, despite the fact they were washed down every night. (On my visit three years earlier, one could have eaten off the streets.) And the broken sidewalks and curbs that required that you keep your head down all the time for fear of tripping. And I hated seeing all the parked cars on all the sidewalks covered either with a thick coat of dust or canvas covers because their owners couldn't get the gasoline to drive them. I couldn't face all the people standing behind their cardboard boxes selling stuff to earn enough to buy bread, or people standing on every street corner shuffling dinars to indicate they would change deutsche marks or francs or dollars into dinars or vice versa at better rates than the banks. I didn't want to hear of any more little shopkeepers like Ljiljana's daughter, who went out on the street every couple of hours to change her money because of the inflation. I didn't want to think of what that process did to people. Did they become inured? Or did they suffer terrible emotional stress from such a forced habit? I couldn't face buying a few pears or a bunch of flowers and knowing that most people in the city could no longer afford such simple luxuries. I couldn't face watching the breadline outside my hotel dining room window every morning—all those well-dressed people queuing up for the means to exist. I didn't want to see any more angry, sullen faces on people wearing ill-fitting country clothes, resenting the well-dressed Belgradians and the fact that they were here in this city instead of on their farms or in their towns in Bosnia or Croatia, angry at what they couldn't understand. I didn't want to hear about how Germany had engineered the disintegration of Yugoslavia or the extreme opposite view that Slobodan Milosevic had caused these wars himself. I didn't want to hear about how everyone had lived before the wars, how they traveled everywhere, bought their clothes in Italy and France, bought all the electronic equipment they could want, never realizing that they lived largely on Western loans that came due when Yugoslavia was no longer needed as a buffer against the Soviet Union. Now their economic problems were chiefly due to the tens of billions of dollars in foreign debt that had been called in. I was tired of the extremes I was hearing, the people who scoffed at the notion that Serbian nationalism was at least part of the cause of the wars, but who were themselves fiercely loyal to the idea of a strong Serbia; and the others who blamed nationalism and who scoffed at any role the West might have played. In other words, after all this time in this economically war-torn, bewildered city, I was feeling bedraggled, perplexed, and depressed like everyone else, needing to crawl back into bed and read a good mystery.

For those few moments all the excitement and exhilaration of my days in Belgrade were blotted out by a great sense of fatigue. Standing at my windows and gazing over the rooftops of the city, I had an early morning picture of Belgrade that made me despair. Missing were all the moments of delight I'd experienced, the exuberance, warmth, and congeniality in all the people I'd talked with, even more so the strong feelings I'd had of a group of intelligent adults trying to think their way through the dilemma that confronted them, trying to carry on with their lives despite enormous hardships, with the courage and determination to stay while so many of the younger generation had fled, and the resolve of so many to help their fellow citizens however they could. I had walked away from most of my interviews feeling that I had added a small dimension to myself, and here I was wailing about the pain of it all.

I had also forgotten for the moment all those walks through the city when, despite all the decay and rot, all the deprivation, and despite getting lost all the time, I had felt wonderfully at home in those little streets and wide boulevards, feeling somehow sheltered, even tranquil, as I had felt on so many afternoons of my youth wandering aimlessly around in Greenwich Village, as if the old and slightly rotten was somehow comforting and homely. The scale was just right, neither too big nor too suburban, a real urban place built to human dimensions, people living close to one another but not piled up too high or in spaces that crowded out their privacy, with little shops everywhere selling everything anyone could want, and lots of trees everywhere to remind city dwellers that a natural life contributed to their welfare, providing shade in the summer and proof that summer would come again in the depths of winter. Even the occasional supermarkets were small enough to be human. No ugly malls. All the cars were small, but large enough to accommodate the long legs of all those tall Serbs. And the parks at regular intervals were little oases that made urban life sweeter. Even the dim old incandescent street-lights contributed to my feeling of comfort in those streets. They gave the city at night the feel of a daguerrotype, shadows and shapes, enough light to find one's way but not enough to change night to day. I had the feeling of safety in the shadow of those dim lights, as if the city had never had to light up the night in order to protect people from criminals. Coming from Chicago, it took me a little while to walk those dim streets without feeling frightened. But within a few days the warm glow of those dim lights actually became comforting and aesthetically pleasing. I had thought often in the last couple of weeks that I looked forward to coming back to Belgrade when the siege ended, though that looked like it might be years.

Draga and Branimir picked me up at the hotel for dinner at eight. I suggested a restaurant not far away that had been praised highly for its game. Draga said he doubted they had any game. The wars had interfered even with game hunting, he suspected, but we would go there and he would ask. He was right. They had a lot of veal on the menu. "Very ordinary," he said. Branimir suggested his favorite restaurant, Vuk Serbian Restaurant, and Draga eagerly agreed. An old-fashioned restaurant just off Knez Mihailo, Vuk was apparently a very popular place, now almost empty. Branimir ordered the plum brandy that the Serbs drink both before and after meals and any time between when they feel like having a drink. I ordered vodka. Branimir asked the waiter what kind of vodka he had. Baltic, he was told. "No, you mustn't drink that. It's awful stuff. Order something else," he insisted. I ordered scotch, though I had come rather to like the Baltic vodka that was served regularly in Belgrade. The men ordered sausages and veal steak with the salad that seemed the most popular in Belgrade, tomatoes with crumbled cheese. I ordered the *kupus salada*, Serbian cole slaw, that had become my favorite vegetable among the few choices available. I ate it almost every day. Draga suggested I order, as an entree, a specialty of the house, *rumaki*, chicken livers wrapped in bacon. And for dessert I had what was advertised as strudel but in fact was a cherry tart, rich and heavy, far too much after a huge order of rumaki.

While the food was good, a delightful change from all the grilled veal I'd been eating, the dinner was slow and unhappy. Branimir announced that he had to leave at ten to see someone off on the bus.

He was subdued, tired, impatient, alternating with short moments of his usual enthusiasm and openness. His face was periodically a map of exhaustion and pain. For a little while after dinner he lightened up when we talked about *Mouth Full of Earth*, which I reported I had read and loved and would quote from in my book. I told him that if he had been trying to bring the book into my own realm of knowledge by describing it as resembling a lynching, he must have only slight knowledge of lynchings in America. There was, I admitted, a group hysteria in a lynch mob, but it was socially sanctioned and most often successful. A lynch mob rarely had the confusion of the mob in Branimir's book. Everybody knew exactly what they were doing. They weren't stalking an unknown quarry for reasons they didn't understand. And not many victims of a lynch mob died exhausted on a rock. Most hung by the neck. He insisted the analogy was of the roughest sort.

Branimir had originally lent me the book, but now he said he would inscribe it and give it to me. He and Draga worked together to translate his inscription. Draga's written translation was in the same broken English he spoke:

To respected colleague,
to Mrs Florance Levinsohn
this book about human aloneness without the world's mercy to remember sometimes your pursuit of the knowledge of Serbia, which still loves America—

> Cordially
> Branimir Scepanovic

I wondered privately whether Branimir's emotional state sprang from something that had happened in recent days as a consequence of the embargo. I had one of those moments many Americans feel while abroad—of being the ugly American. Yet he had told me he loved America. What did he love about America, I asked him. The products we make, he and Draga both said. What a thing to be loved for! The great aesthetic romance of Europe was slowly being swallowed up by America's romance with materialism.

Then Branimir's face turned fierce. "We are the Indians of your Old West, being slaughtered the same way." I told him I felt like the anthropologist Franz Boas, who went west to record Indian life before it disappeared. "Yes, it's a good thing to do," he said, "but maybe we'll survive better than your Indians did. We have survived for a long time." With that he grew silent, trying occasionally to talk but unable to say much. Draga and I chatted loosely but were made too uneasy by Branimir's dense mood to pursue anything for long. Then Branimir announced he must leave. He urged us to stay, but we insisted that Draga would drive him to the bus stop.

When we had dropped Branimir off at a corner where he would meet his friend, Draga and I talked about his bad mood. Draga suggested it might have been caused by the loss of a friend. Perhaps the friend he was seeing off was emigrating, as people were doing every day. Of course, I agreed, that must have been it. The sadness in the voices of so many people who had told me of the emigration of their friends and families echoed in my head.

20 No other day on this voyage of discovery could equal the pathos of this afternoon's visit to the Sanski Venac Polklinska, a diagnostic and treatment clinic where Ljiljana headed the physical therapy program. It was a huge five-story brick structure across the street from an inpatient hospital, with every kind of medical and dental facility, including a large pediatric wing. Ljiljana met me at the back door of the clinic that opened directly to her department. We went first to the staff lounge, a small room with chairs against the walls and a coffee table in the center. Two doctors, a man and a woman, and two physical therapists were sitting in their white coats over coffee and cigarettes. Ljiljana introduced me and then took me to her spacious, comfortable office where we left my jacket and briefcase. She then took me on a tour of her department, a dozen diagnostic and treatment cubicles providing one or another kind of electronic treatment, all screened by yellow curtains that looked as if they hadn't been laundered in months. They had, it turned out, but the hospital didn't have enough detergent to get them clean. The sheets on the tables looked the same. There was also a gym and a water therapy room.

One patient was receiving heat treatment. Another was getting water therapy for his arm. His wife sat with him. The towel wrapped around his arm, Ljiljana told me, was the patient's own. The clinic did not have enough detergent to wash a supply of towels for the patients. Only one patient was receiving electronic therapy instead of a dozen, as had always been true in the department, because the service lacked the materials required for treatment or because the machines were down for lack of spare parts. She pointed out that the jars that normally held the various solutions needed for treatment were empty. There was no alcohol. Even the jars that had once held cotton balls were empty.

In the gym a patient who had been severely injured by a bomb that went off in a restaurant was lying on a table receiving manual manipulation. He had considerably recovered, the therapist told me. He could speak a little, could move his limbs a little, but it would take a lot longer to restore him to normalcy. I suddenly realized that the room was quite cold and mentioned it to Ljiljana. "Yes," she said, "we have practically no heat. It is hard to do manipulation in a cold room. It will take that man much longer to recover because of that."

The physical therapy department was almost a ghost town, but it was not nearly as deserted as the other departments that depended much more on medications and complex equipment. I saw only one other patient in the whole clinic, in the pediatric wing, a great hall of a room with little red chairs lining three walls. There a mother and her baby stood waiting at the reception desk. The baby's whimpers seemed to echo in the huge empty room.

In the ophthalmology department, the doctor hugged a machine and told me, "This is my baby. I fear for its life all the time. If one part breaks down, I'm done for." But this doctor had no patients because, while he could examine eyes and could prescribe glasses, the glasses cost as much as a year's wages. He used to be able to prescribe glasses and send his patients downstairs to the optician on the first floor where the glasses were free. Now the clinic optician had no materials to make glasses. They could be bought only from private opticians, and few could afford them. If a patient had a disease of the eyes, the doctor could write a prescription for medicine that the patient could buy from a private pharmacy at outrageously high prices; or the patient could travel to Budapest or Timisoara to get it cheaper. If a patient needed surgery, he had to bring his own anesthetic. The hospitals had none.

From the ophthalmology department, Ljiljana took me to dentistry, where the dentists and their assistants were also having coffee. They lacked the most basic materials to do any work.

Even for the simple examinations given babies and small children,

Ljiljana explained, "Parents aren't coming in because they can't get here. They can't take small children and babies on those trams. You've seen them. How could you take a baby on them? They can't drive their cars because they have no petrol, and they have no money for taxis. And the same is true for many other people. If you don't feel well, you don't want to take the tram. People are neglecting their health. They think, Why go to the doctor, even if it's free, if I can't afford to buy medicine? So they wait until they are very sick, and then they go to the hospital and they find they can't do much for them there. It's all so hideous. Two years ago we always had more patients than we could handle. Now we sit and drink coffee." Pausing a moment, Ljiljana stopped in the middle of the corridor and said, "And we have to help the refugees from all over the former republics, and also we have to send help to the Serbs who stayed in their homes. We have to feed them and everything. So what to do? We can die!"

In the ob-gyn department three doctors were sitting over coffee. They could no longer do pap smears or mammograms. The laboratory lacked needles to take blood tests and the materials to analyze the smears and the film for mammography. The techniques used in the laboratory had now reverted to those used two centuries earlier by the French chemist Lavoisier.

The gynecologists told me that, contrary to my impression, the rate of pregnancy hadn't changed much, though natives of Belgrade did seem to have fewer pregnancies. This was offset by the refugees who became pregnant more often and because of a general lack of birth-control devices. I wondered about this statement because by far the greatest number of refugees were women—or did this reflect my lack of imagination? But, the doctors said, most women didn't carry to term. They had voluntary or spontaneous abortions, or they miscarried due to stress, anemia, or malnutrition, or they had premature births owing to malnutrition. The babies born early died because the hospitals hadn't enough working neonatal equipment to accommodate the numbers. For babies who were carried to term, malnourished mothers had no breast milk, and no baby formula was available because of the sanctions. The cow's milk that mothers were forced to feed their babies caused anemia and diarrhea.

Even when functioning, this clinic was not the most modern by American standards. The x-ray equipment looked to be twenty-five years old. There were only five CAT scanners in the city; this huge clinic had none. But medicine is not all technology, as some in the

U.S. are beginning to learn. Everyone I talked with spoke of their kind, caring, competent doctors. The illness that now surrounded everyone in Belgrade distressed people more than the other consequences of the sanctions. They weren't used to much illness, they said. "People here have always been healthy, and when they do get sick, they get very good care—or used to. Now they are dying all around us because there is no medicine except for the rich," Gordana Logar had told me.

As we walked downstairs to return to her office, I asked Ljiljana how she managed to keep her sanity in the midst of all this madness. "How do you stay cheerful?" I asked her. "I don't," she said. "I get very depressed. But most of the time I stay in my office and pretend it's all not happening. And I try to live a normal life. You just survive because you have to."

The previously well-paid doctors and nurses who spent their time smoking and drinking coffee in their offices while waiting for the rare patient were working for tiny salaries, about fifteen dollars a month, like so many other employees who worked for government-run institutions and businesses. The system was, in effect, a massive dole. "The whole nation," Ljiljana said, as we sat talking in her office, "is one big ghetto."

Ljiljana described the male-female divisions among physicians. Though there were exceptions, for the most part women specialized in pediatrics, internal medicine, ophthalmology, nose and throat, and physical therapy, while men did ob-gyn, surgery, neurology, and psychiatry. Men and women were found equally in cardiology. (Such a spread is only now beginning to emerge in the U.S.) Men and women were paid equally, but auto mechanics earned more than physicians, she said, a fact that had been true in all the Communist countries and something Americans found hard to understand, given physicians' incomes there. Only in the U.S. and South Africa is medicine still a private enterprise in which doctors are the most highly paid members of the society because they can charge what they like. Everywhere else in the world, medicine is subsidized by the government, and doctors are, in effect, civil servants, earning civil servant's wages—though it is only in the formerly Communist countries that they receive less than auto mechanics.

I wondered about Ljiljana's background. David Moss had described her as "somewhat of a social butterfly," and surely she was what my mother used to call a "clotheshorse." Yet she was not only a doctor but head of a large department in a large clinic; she was also a founding member of a new political party; she loved and understood classical music; she read a good deal; and she seemed to know everyone in the intellectual world of the city. She had arranged for five of my interviews, all with well-known members of the intellectual elite. Where had she come from?

Her grandfather was a minister in King Aleksander's government between the two world wars. Her father, who had volunteered for the army in World War I at fourteen, became a successful and wealthy lawyer who was a prominent official in the Democratic party before World War II. With the triumph of communism, the many properties owned by the family were nationalized, and the family was left with the building in which they lived, the same one in which Ljiljana and her family currently lived. During the civil war and after Tito came to power, her father strongly opposed the Communists. The extraordinary stress under which he lived caused a cerebral hemorrhage in 1951 when he was in his early fifties. He survived but was an invalid for many years after. The family cared for him at home. Because of his opposition he was denied a pension. The family had lots of possessions but no money. They lived in stringently reduced circumstances for years, selling their possessions for whatever they could in order to live. Relatives helped as they were able. Though Ljiljana suffered in her early years as the child of her despised father, she was permitted to go to medical school. Her sister had earlier married an Italian and moved to Rome. She sent Ljiljana a little money to get through school. Despite her powerful heritage, she was for the most part self-made.

I told Ljiljana that I was having a good deal of trouble understanding the West's animosity toward the Serbs. As guilty as they were of atrocities, the blame attributed to them in the wars far exceeded reality. It seemed to me that a fierce enmity existed especially in the ranks of the U.S. government. What was the Serb explanation for this animosity?

"Well," she said, "the Serbs have always been more independent than the rest of Eastern Europe. While the Poles killed Jews and while the Bulgarians and the Hungarians and the Albanians and the Romanians were all allied with the fascists, we were fighting them. And we have never followed the West's lead. So we have to be punished, brought to our knees. I heard a program from Croatia on television in which a man from your State Department was being interviewed and talking about the punishment of Serbia. The reporter asked him if the forces of Serbia and Milosevic would be defeated, and he said, 'Don't worry. We are doing our best with the sanctions. Now they are pushed back twenty or thirty years from where they were.' My God! I thought, Is he normal? It's not only that you are getting paid to do this, but it is so immoral to say that.

"You know, the West knows nothing about our country. Mr. Cosic, who is our good friend and who was president last year, went to many international conferences with just the people who are now responsible for our condition, and he would come back and tell us how amazed he was that the Western leaders had not even the slightest knowledge of our history."

Walking through Belgrade on a rainy night is a humbling experience. One seems to lose all control. One is at the mercy of the elements and of a city not designed to aid pedestrians under these conditions. When I was ready to leave the clinic, I asked Ljiljana if someone would call a taxi for me. I was going only a few blocks to meet Snezana Popadic at the Hotel Slavija, but I wasn't sure I could find my way, and it was pouring. Ljiljana said she doubted they could get a cab for me, but she sent her assistant with me to the front desk to make the effort. The receptionist said it was very hard to get a taxi to come to the clinic; she made two calls and gave up. The doctor assured me that the Slavija was only three blocks away and gave me directions.

Naturally I lost my way. I walked about a mile before I found the hotel. I discovered I had circled it three times. The torrential rain and the darkness had disoriented me. I was drenched to the skin when I arrived. My feet were soaked through because the sidewalks were so full of holes that they filled up with water, and in the dim light I didn't see the holes. What's more, gutters on the buildings ran down to the ground where they emptied onto the sidewalks, so I was constantly walking into those floods. And because there were few sewers for water runoff, stepping down from the curb meant stepping into a huge puddle.

Snezana hadn't arrived yet, so I went into the bar of the hotel, ordered a double vodka to warm myself after my drenching, and used a table napkin to dry my hair. When I returned to the lobby to find Snezana, I was distressed to see that she had one small umbrella. We had three more blocks to walk to her house. Oh hell, I thought, I'm already so wet it doesn't matter. We walked the three blocks trying to share the umbrella, with little success.

At Snezana's apartment she hung my dripping jacket over a chair and put my shoes next to the space heater. She brought out a hair dryer, made some coffee, and opened a bottle of slivovitz she had gotten for me in a little town outside of Belgrade where she said they made the best plum brandy in Yugoslavia. We had plenty of time, she reassured me. The judge with whom she had arranged an interview for me would no doubt be late—he was taking the tram. It would be a test of my journalistic skills to conduct this interview after a double vodka and two glasses of truly tasty slivovitz, but I no longer felt like a victim of a Mississippi River floodtide.

The judge was indeed late, about an hour. Meanwhile Snezana told me of the little town where she had gone to get the slivovitz, where she had a small shack that served as her dacha. Everyone in Belgrade had some kind of country place, she told me, many on the Adriatic coast that were now lost in the war. The Croatians had confiscated all the country houses of the Serbs along the Adriatic. I remembered that Mira had told me that she and her husband had lost their seaside property. Snezana hadn't been able to afford such a luxurious setting. She merely had a shack with no electricity and no indoor plumbing in a little town on a lake a few miles outside Belgrade. But it was her castle, she said, where she and her neighbors had a wonderful time.

When the judge arrived he seemed immune to the rain. His hair was wet, like his raincoat, but it was just another shower to this obviously stoical man. Very tall and gangly, he looked younger than his forty-some years with unruly black hair and a boyish, almost roguishly handsome face with a jutting chin. I imagined Snezana being quite taken with this student of hers. His manner was all charm. It was a terrible shock to the adamantly anti-Communist Snezana to discover that this man whom she believed was learned and sophisticated, a criminal courts judge, was in fact a diehard Stalinist who would, over the next three hours, defend every attack not only against his fellow Communists in Yugoslavia but those in the Soviet Union as well. I hadn't imagined myself asking the kinds of basic questions about Communist rule I ended up asking this man, the kinds of questions I had put to American Communists twenty years earlier but that had long ceased to be an issue. I didn't think anyone in 1993 was still defending communism and attacking the U.S. in such ignorant ways. My naiveté. Snezana's too. She was much more shocked than I, since she had been teaching this man English for several months and had recommended him to me as someone who could speak intelligently about the conflicts in the former Yugoslavia.

Both of us were also surprised that the judge, having agreed to the interview and traveled a long way to get there, at first refused to be taped. He acceded only when I explained that his voice, speaking in Serbian, need not be taped, that we would record only Snezana's translations. Needless to say, he refused to allow his name to be used. When I asked him what could happen to him if he permitted me to use his name, he shrugged and said, "You never know." Whom was he afraid of? Everyone, it seemed, but particularly those in the government who were responsible for his appointment as a judge. It was the old Communist's fear of talking with someone from the West, a fear that apparently hadn't been present in Yugoslavia for thirty years. When he actually began to speak, however, he recited the Milosevic nationalistic party line almost verbatim, though denying at the same time that he could speak knowledgeably about the Yugoslav conflicts. Only someone highly placed in the government, he said, could give the correct answers to my questions.

When our conversation began to deal first with the merits of the Yugoslav judicial system and then the merits of communism, my anonymous informant finally opened up. He warmed to his subjects, becoming dramatic and adamant about the defects of the American judicial system and the merits of communism. The American system, he insisted, was based entirely on precedent. A judge could rule only within the limits set by precedent. No new law could be made. In the Yugoslav system the judge had no such limitations. His judgments were based solely on the case at hand. And while trial by jury might have some merit, on the whole it seemed a grossly unfair way to judge a person's guilt or innocence. The accused deserved to have a trained, experienced judge to hear his case. I thought of all those judges in the Communist countries who had sent so many people to prison and in the Soviet Union to the gulag.

But his most dramatic remarks were directed toward the merits of communism, not only the judicial and prison system but the economic system—the fairness of the system and how well it worked for everyone. I got sucked in. Was he aware of the turmoil and failure of the Communist systems in the last few years in the Soviet Union and Eastern Europe, I wanted to know. It was all Western propaganda, he replied. The discussion became heated, mostly because I was constantly amazed by his comments, which ignored the history of the past seventy years and were bound to an ideology without any underpinning of reality. More important, he seemed oblivious of the events of the last few years. He reminded me of an old Communist I knew in Chicago who had also ignored all the history of the Soviet Union and was distraught over its collapse. But my acquaintance was American, far from the realities of communism, reading what he chose, and in his eighties. It didn't pay to argue with him. This man was a Yugoslav of not much more than forty. He knew of Tito's break with Stalin, and surely he knew of the obscenities of Soviet rule. This man was a judge in the criminal courts who regularly decided, by himself or in concert with two other judges, the fate of the people accused of crimes who came before him.

When he was finally on his way, three hours later, he thanked me profusely for such a stimulating conversation, though he fervently wished that it wouldn't be printed. He offered me an invitation to return when the Communist party was again in power in Yugoslavia. When he was out the door, Snezana apologized for putting me through this exchange and brought out some of her wonderful treats—sardine paste on homemade bread, a sumptuous repast, so welcome after three hours of sparring with this unreconstructed, unapologetic Communist who insisted that whatever repressive measures taken under communism were necessary for the good of the state, and so on, ad infinitum. People with such attitudes could still be found in the Soviet Union, I knew, but to encounter one in Belgrade was shocking.

Snezana and I sat together over a late-night Turkish coffee and one final slivovitz, shaking our heads. I wondered privately how she would handle her next lesson with this man who had so profoundly disappointed her. She was, after all, the daughter of a Cetnik and still held to his anti-Communist views. She was proud never to have had to join the party in order to ease her way in the world. She still vividly remembered with bitterness the Stalinist era in Yugoslavia when people were arrested, imprisoned, and tortured for opposing the regime. On the other hand she had told me, with great sadness in her voice, how comfortable the Yugoslavs had been before the wars. After all, she had been able to go to Italy every year to buy her clothes.

I went back to the hotel with my head whirling, furious at Snezana for having gotten me into this debate and angry with myself for having been sucked into it. It had been clear almost from the judge's opening remarks what I was dealing with. I should have made it short. I had no time or energy to argue with a diehard Communist. But I hadn't been able to resist it. My fault, not Snezana's. I'd been fascinated to find such a dinosaur in Belgrade. On the other hand, it was interesting that this dinosaur spouted the nationalist line, contradicting the strict Communist line that had decried all nationalism. All over the world, nationalism had become the rallying cry for demagogues and the excuse by millions for wanton killing and brutality. Some of my informants had told me that in Yugoslavia nationalism had substituted for opposition to communism. Here was a man who, comfortably it seemed, included both in his intellectual baggage.

21 I'd been thrilled the day before when Maja, at the Ministry of Information, called to say that she'd been able to arrange an interview for me with Patriarch Pavle. Draga agreed to interpret. He arrived to pick me up wearing a snazzy Italian topcoat and a suit and tie. "You in a suit? And an elegant topcoat?" I asked, laughing. I'd never seen him in anything but a turtleneck, slacks, and a jacket. "For the patriarch, one dresses," he explained as he straightened the tie that he was so unused to wearing.

Since 1346, with some exceptions, the Serbian Orthodox church has been an independent entity over which the patriarch reigns, though the church has no such policy as papal infallibility and none of the rules that govern daily living that characterize the Catholic church. Administratively, it more closely resembles the Protestant churches. The present patriarch was elected in 1990. He appears to be a spiritual rather than a temporal leader, with no real authority over the wider church. The American Serbian Orthodox churches seem to play a much greater role in their parishioner's lives than do the Serbian churches, and the patriarch seems to have no authority over the American churches that have large congregations, imposing church structures, and plenty of money, unlike the bare-bones Serbian churches.

The building that housed the residence and offices of the patriarchate was a drab, unadorned, square red brick building, one of the
rare brick buildings in Belgrade. It had been built in 1935 across
from the cathedral, an 1848 edifice equally drab-looking except for a
baroque cupola topped with the double cross of the church. The
interior of the patriarchate, except for some religious paintings on the
dingy walls, was as bare as the exterior. The meeting room where we
met the patriarch was a large spare room with ornate high-backed
upholstered chairs and a few small round mahogany side tables—to
hold the Turkish coffee that accompanied every gathering—ranged
around three walls, the fourth wall being a sliding door. At the head
of the room was a slightly larger rectangular table obviously desig-
nated as the speaker's table. On the walls hung a few undistinguished
icons. This was not the property of a rich church. Fifty years under
communism, though the church was never suppressed, obviously
hadn't enriched its coffers. And the sparsity of churches in Belgrade
attested to a population not much interested in the church, though
most people insisted they were religious. All Serbs apparently had
big celebrations for their *slavas* or saint's day, but that seemed to be
the extent of their religiosity. On the other hand, there appeared to be
much veneration for the patriarch, and all Serbs attached a religious
devotion to the ancient monasteries that would be lost to them were
Kosovo to be recognized as an independent state.

The church had not always been such a small player in Serbian
life. It had been instrumental in the development of the national state
and was once a powerful landowner and leader of the people,
exerting strong influence and playing a sometimes venal role in their
daily lives, just as the Roman church did in earlier history. That the
Vatican was more successful than the Orthodox church proves that
nothing succeeds like success. By sword and by might, the Catholic
church conquered much of the world, succeeding quite early in
gaining the status of a separate state. Despite its early powerful role
in the state, the Orthodox church became, first under Turkish rule and
then under Catholic Austro-Hungarian rule, mainly a spiritual home for
its people, hence declining in the increasingly irreligious last century.

The patriarch was led into the room by one of his black-robed
entourage. Draga kissed his hand. I shook hands with this tiny,
frail-looking man with searching blue eyes looking out over a flowing
white beard and a sharp pointed nose. Though only in his early
eighties, he had the look of an ancient scholar. He wore the Orthodox

priest's simple long black clerical garb with a black mitre on his head, and on his chest a large cross decorated with what seemed to be semiprecious stones. In all, he looked no different from any other Orthodox priest. His hand felt like a child's in mine. He looked so frail that a gentle wind might blow him down. Draga had translated for him before and told me that he tired so easily that he never gave an interview of more than half an hour. When we finished I was nonplussed to discover that an hour had passed. Draga smiled appreciatively at me when he too looked at his watch.

We sat down at the head table, and Draga explained who I was and what I was doing. The patriarch listened patiently, smiling sweetly at me several times. He interjected a few questions in a small but strong voice. Then I told him that I had heard it said in Belgrade that the Vatican's efforts to destroy the Orthodox church had led, in the West, to animosity toward the Serbs.

"I don't see it quite like that," the patriarch said, smiling. "But the Vatican is a state. They are concerned not only with religion but with the other things states do. The premature recognition of Slovenia and Croatia was done because they are Catholic lands. And in Bosnia, even though it has Muslims and Orthodox living there in addition to Catholics, the Vatican was among the first to recognize it. As I see it, that's political. There is a little religion there, but mostly politics."

"You said you don't think the Vatican is trying to destroy your church. But you imply that the Vatican in its state functions may be doing just that," I said.

"No, I was just trying to explain the difference between our churches. Our church has no political functions. It is only the work of our church to maintain the traditions of history."

But, I said, "I do sense that you suspect some ulterior motive of the Vatican."

"Yes. As I said about the recognition of the republics, especially Bosnia Herzegovina, without wishing to be obscure, that's what I meant."

That his church took no political role was a statement that would have been laughed at by the dissidents in Belgrade and others who pointed to the role the church had played in raising nationalist consciousness over the preceding ten years. I asked the patriarch what role the church had played in the rise of nationalism.

"Our mission is always to serve the people, to serve the nation, not to serve one side, like the Vatican. Before we had Christianity here, there were peasants with a primitive culture, but they didn't have a written history. When they became Christian they entered history with their own alphabet that was enriched by Christianity. And they developed a culture like the other European nations. There developed the sense of a nation, and the church contributed to that attitude of one nation, speaking with the same language as the people. But this nationalism has passed the limits of healthy nationalism. And that's bad for the nation and the church too."

The patriarch then told me a story of the mother of King Stepan Dusan who, in the fourteenth century, welded together the Serbian empire. The story went that the scribe for the king attempted to lead astray his courtiers with lies. Dusan's mother told him, "Better you should lose your head than bring that sin upon your soul." That, the patriarch said, "is the soul of the Serbian nation." And, he went on, "the lesson of Kosovo is not to take the territory of others, not to usurp the freedom of others. King Lazar only wanted to protect his own liberty and his own land, and he was saying, 'I will rather have my own religion in heaven.' At this time the church has no interest, no family interest, no personal interest, no national interest, no God's interest that can be answered with the crimes. Yes, to defend freedom of the person. But if someone is making a crime, one doesn't answer it with another crime.

"The Duke of Montenegro [the poet Njegos] in the last century formulated that principle with two phrases. He wrote a book, a masterpiece, entitled *Humanity and Heroism*. In it he said, 'Heroism means to defend myself from the enemy, and humanity means to defend the enemy from myself. Even in the fight against the enemy, I cannot treat him inhumanly.' That wasn't his invention, but he formulated it for us. But not everybody abides by this principle. Unfortunately, in this war there is the crime committed by one side and also from the other side. Only God's scale can measure on which side there is more crime."

I asked the patriarch if he had tried to mediate in the wars. "I'm always speaking about that, and I'm praying for everybody to be human. God sees everything, and his mind knows our thoughts and his judgment awaits everybody. No one can escape his judgment. With lies, with injustice, with crime. With love, truth, and justice we are serving God, and one day love, truth, and justice will be victorious." I could see in this man, as he spoke, his clear little eyes shining brightly, what Dean Triantifilou had described, a true holy man.

Feeling very unholy, however, I pushed a little. Had the patriarch sat down with any parties to the dispute to discuss the issues? "Of course," he said, "because I view these men as human."

I could see I would get nothing more concrete. I wanted to be cynical and think he was evading my question, but there was about him something so blessedly innocent—though he was not at all naive—that I couldn't sustain my feeling, despite stories I had heard of his meetings with Milosevic and others. But perhaps his role was limited to appealing for peace in the name of God and the church. One bit of evidence of his political dealing I *was* able to see was a letter sent to Pope John Paul II on January 17, 1992, four days after the Vatican had recognized the independence of Croatia. The patriarch wrote, ". . . We do not deny Your right as a Statesman to act in the interests of your State, but nonetheless, we request that You perceive the use of the authority of the Church in political aims in the light of the Theophany (which is celebrated by both our Churches these days) and in the light of the Epiphany of the One Who, as man, had nowhere to lay his head. In the same way, we do not contest the right of the Croat and Slovene People to have their own States outside of Yugoslavia and outside of a common State with us Serbians; but we are astonished that Your Holiness does not recognize such a right for the Serbians as well, who are an autochthonous People and in the majority in the Serbian Krajinas, and who never were citizens of the Croatian state until 1941 and the creation of the Nazi satellite state, the Independent State of Croatia. . . .

"You, the first Slav Pope in history and Sovereign of the Vatican State, have shown Yourself, Your Holiness, of being able—for a goal you considered significant—to even bless and consecrate the means which were used by the bearers of the young Croat democracy, recent followers of the Croatian Communist Josip Broz Tito and the historical heirs of the Nazi criminal Pavelic, in which many clergy of the Roman Catholic Church in Croatia also took part. We believe, however, that a tree is recognized by its fruit, and goals are judged by the means employed. We are informed that many Roman-Catholic priests, monks, theologians, and God-loving faithful in Croatia, in Slovenia and in the whole Roman-Catholic world, by their statements and concrete behavior, refused to take responsibility for everything that was done yesterday and is being done today in Croatia; not only against the Serbians but also against the Croatians who are not utterly obedient to the 'democratic' order of Tito's former General, who declares himself pleased because his wife is neither Serbian nor Jewish. Therefore, this appeal is addressed first of all to them, and then to You. Nonetheless, we have in these troubled days come to the conviction that neither the politics of the Vatican State nor the diplomacy of its Curia nor the bitter fruits of an ethics which is also demonstrated in the world by Your activity towards the recognition of the Croat State, have not been able to destroy the spirit of that original Church which, in the first millennium of Christian history, was 'presiding in love' amongst the Churches and adorned Heaven with a multitude of martyrs, saintly bishops and ascetics of piety."

The patriarch ended this letter with a call for "a true ecumenical dialogue between our two sister Churches." On paper at least, it seemed to me, the patriarch was a good match for the pope.

I wondered then how the patriarch believed the differences between the Orthodox and the Catholic churches affected the peoples of the nations who had for so long been faithful to those churches.

"There are definite differences. For instance, in Bosnia there are three main religions there. For the Muslims, their Koran teaches the *jihad*. The religion is furthered by the holy war. In the gospels there is no such thing. There is no permission in the gospels to spread Christianity by violence. To get freedom, yes, but to spread the religion by violence, no. One of the great bishops of Constantinople, in the fourth century, said, 'God did not give us a sword. The sword he gave us was the word to bring to people the truth of the gospels if they want to accept it.' It is not our duty to convince people, but only to expose them to the truth. Our duty is to convince ourselves. No one can convince anyone else if they don't want to be convinced. Of course, it is very difficult to sustain this principle, and in Islam and in the Roman church they do not believe this. And that approach is part of the troubles we now have.

"As God is my witness, I don't wish to present the Serbian people as better than they are, but no worse than they are. If I tried to present them better than they are, I know that God is seeing and we can't cheat him. Just like I can't cheat the people. Please, I'm begging you, in this role you have, that you see the truth everywhere. Not like the Serbs try to present the truth. Not like the Croats or the Muslims. You have to look everywhere to see everything. I understand this is very difficult. I myself cannot understand how something so inhuman could happen. It is difficult for everyone to understand. The guilt is not on one but on all. And also guilty are Europe and

America. Before the war started in Bosnia, they had a meeting in Portugal of the representatives of all the parties. And they agreed that Bosnia would be three ethnic cantons, like Switzerland. But then Europe and America recognized a unified Bosnia, and Alija Izetbegovic withdrew his signature from the agreement. Who was responsible for that? The American ambassador to Yugoslavia, Warren Zimmerman, was the one who led that. Which is to say, we are guilty, but many others are guilty too." He rose, and the assistant who had brought him in arrived to take him out. As we shook hands, he said, "Many thanks to you, madam. I spoke to you in the interest of the truth and serving God in which I believe."

I asked whether I might take a photo of him. He agreed quickly. As I looked about the room for a good setting, the assistant suggested the adjoining room. He opened the sliding door to reveal the throne room, more elaborate only in the large unadorned wood throne and in an imposing religious painting on the wall opposite the throne. I took a photo with the patriarch standing before the painting.

Draga and I left the patriarchate and went across the street to the cathedral that sits on a square block of land with a high iron fence around it, facing east as all Orthodox churches must. In the yard in front of the church a group of children with a few adults and a couple of priests were engaged in a service. Draga explained that this was a celebration of the birthday of Vuk Karadzic, the "father of the Serbian language," for whom the children's school was named and who was buried in a tomb in the cathedral's outer wall. The ceremony, which took place in front of the tomb, mainly consisted of the group chanting prayers led by the priests swinging their incense censers. Other tombs were placed in the walls both inside and out, with those of the early great kings on the inside.

Just inside the entrance to the cathedral was a wall of burning candles, the upper half expressing wishes for living people and the lower for the dead. Across the corridor was a small shop that sold candles and other religious objects. Beside it was a large Christ on the cross, carved from wood and painted rather garishly. From the outer corridor one walked through a set of swinging doors into a huge nave dimly lit by one massive crystal chandelier. There were no pews. The Orthodox pray standing. For the sick and elderly there were sculptured wooden seats against the walls. Way up on the massively high, dingy walls were primitive icons in bad shape, covered with a thick coat of dust. Some had been removed for restoration. The cathedral had been damaged in World War II bombings and was only now slowly being restored. There was in this church no pulpit, no choir loft, and no adornments of any kind except the icons. The altar behind the west wall had an opening in it through which the priest could be heard. Tradition required that the priest not be seen during the liturgy. A dozen or so people were in the church, which was never locked, unlike most churches in the U.S. People were lighting candles and moving about in the nave.

This church had been built surreptitiously, Draga told me, under the noses of the Turks, who either didn't know what was going on or ignored it. Directly across the street was the Shepherds Inn where the workers drank and travelers stayed. Hoping for some reflected glory from the cathedral, the owner renamed it the Cathedral Inn. The church fathers frowned on this den of iniquity being named for it. The owner, not wanting to give up his association with the church, but unable to use the name, simply named it "?," which it remains today, like the No Name tavern in Greenwich Village.

As we drove back to my hotel, Draga thanked me for giving him this opportunity to see the patriarch again. I asked him if he was religious. "Sure," he said. "Do you go to church?" I asked. Very rarely, he said. "But that doesn't mean I'm not religious. It is in your heart. All Serbs are religious. It is just our faith, our heritage. We don't need to go to church to feel it. Everything the patriarch said, I believe. You can't separate the Serbs from their religion, even if it costs them their lives."

Suddenly I felt the full impact of what I'd been hearing and reading for months—the sense of the Serbs as a proud historical people deeply attached to their idea of their church as a symbolic, if not very active, institution in their lives. It was suddenly clear to me how enmeshed the church was with the history of the Serbs and why so many of them had died in Croatia in World War II rather than submit to forced conversion by the Catholics.

Milan Bulajic was a large, somewhat florid-looking man in his sixties with a great head of greying hair and grey-framed glasses, wearing a grey pinstriped suit. He had the Victorian gentlemanly manner of the European lawyer and diplomat he had been for ten years in Washington and New York, Indonesia, and intermittently in Belgrade. Having retired from the foreign service, Milan joined the Serbian Academy of Science and headed the committee appointed by the government to reply to the charges of war crimes addressed against Milosevic and other officials. He told me that he no longer held that position because of "differences with the government." By other statements he made clear that he had refused to deny atrocities committed by Serbs against Muslims and Croatians, though he also believed there were atrocities on all sides and that the Serbs should not be singled out for their crimes. Milan also headed the Serbian Genocide Museum that documented the horrors committed by the Croatians and Muslims against the Serbs in World War II. He described it as being like Vad Yashem, the Holocaust museum in Jerusalem.

Milan picked me up at my hotel to take me to his apartment a block away. His family owned it, and his son's family had lived there until he emigrated to the U.S. a year earlier. He and his wife hoped that their two sons, who were born in the U.S. and who were there now, would return when the troubles were over, but they were not expectant. The apartment now stood empty except for occasional foreign guests visiting Belgrade.

Milan's apartment was in a relatively new, well-maintained building. The elevator didn't creak loudly when we stepped inside. The apartment had the look of an elaborate, expensive hotel suite designed by someone with ongepotchket taste—fake French provincial living room pieces, fake Oriental rugs, psuedomodern dining room furniture, and art for the worst of the nouveau riche—odd-shaped abstract canvases decorated with pieces of mirror. Slavka, Milan's wife, had even bought a new queen-sized bed for their guests. She bemoaned the fact that they hadn't known me earlier so that I might have used the apartment for my stay. I was only half sorry I hadn't had the advantage.

Slavka Bulajic was a classic Serb diplomat's wife—large-boned, nearly six feet, with a carefully coiffed head of black hair, large dark eyes, a smooth youthful complexion, and a full mouth—a stunning woman of about fifty-five clad in a black suit, white blouse, and gold earrings. She hovered over us with Turkish coffee and straight-from-the-oven cherry turnovers. Having served these treats, she made ready to leave, not wanting "to be in the way." Her husband insisted that she stay, and she sat down at the dining table with us, inserting remarks periodically, mostly about how she was "divided all the time with half myself in the States with my children and half here in Belgrade." Their children regularly urged them to come to America, but, Milan said, in his slightly accented English, "I can't go. I must stay here to help my country."

Milan spoke slowly and carefully, at first in almost a monotone, though his speech gradually became more forceful. About the war crimes commission he said, "I was documenting war crimes in World War II, and I never thought I would be doing it again. But the idea of an international court for war crimes, especially for Yugoslavia, I think and believe, professionally, is not going to be a court of law but a political instrument, because this is the first time in international law that the so-called international court was established for only one country. You had Vietnam, Iraq, Somalia, with military interventions, but no international court. This is the first.

"Secondly, this court is time limited from the beginning of 1991, but the basic principle of international law, when we speak of war crimes and the crimes of genocide, has no statute of limitations. So who can limit it to 1991? Maybe there is some explanation for that. But if you take it as prescribed by international law, then many other crimes might be involved.

"But the basic question is, Why only Yugoslavia? After the Nuremberg Trials, the idea was to have a general international criminal court. In 1957 they had already dropped that idea and couldn't get any agreement on it. Now this court has been established by the United Nations Security Council. In my opinion, the Security Council is not empowered to establish such a court. According to the charter it is a subsidiary body, so then what kind of a court is this that is supposed to be above, created by a lower body?

"We ask why Yugoslavia? I was in New York in February, and I went to the United Nations where I have spent many days over the years, and there I found documents showing that the initiative for the court came from the Bosnians, from the minister of foreign affairs of Muslim Bosnia and their leader, Alija Izetbegovic, helped and supported by the United States. The basic premise of the United States, according to these documents, was to determine individual responsibility, that is, who killed whom. That's important, because if anyone killed an innocent man, woman, not to mention child, which is the worst crime you can commit, he should be punished. But in my opinion, if you speak about this great tragedy in Yugoslavia, the starting point should be why and who is responsible for creating such a situation, such an environment that these crimes have been made possible. Who made this Yugoslavia that existed for seventy years, and who wanted it to be broken up? It is here that I see the basis of all the war crimes and genocide.

"If we had saved Yugoslavia, I deeply believe there would have been great problems, but this, as it's happening, would never have happened. And I think the best proof is if I ask you, not Lord Owen or Lord Carrington, what can we do to give everyone a little of what they want? We would have found a way to do it. You know, we have enriched the English vocabulary with the word 'Balkanization.' Mixed religions, mixed nationalities, mixed ethnic origins, and so on, in one state." Milan did not understand the English meaning of the word Balkanization. He put a positive spin on a word that has a definite negative meaning, namely, to do just what has happened in Yugoslavia, to divide nations into small antagonistic ethnic enclaves.

"If the European Community and the United States had wanted to save this country, the best way was to force it, with a little money, into the European Community. Day by day, the importance of borders would have diminished. By establishing borders that never existed, these problems were created. Take the little place where I was born, on the border between Montenegro and Herzegovina. I was born on one side of the border. My mother was born on the other side. And my grandma was born on a third side. Then there were no real borders. Now when I go to my town, I find they are building customs offices at this new border. It is crazy. If you proclaim these boundary lines never established by the will of the people, you cut into the live tissue of the people, and blood will flow.

"Everybody is claiming the right of self-determination, and on this basis Yugoslavia is being broken up. But let me tell you, my Ph.D. thesis forty years ago was on the right of self-determination. It does not mean the right to secession. It's the right to be united, the right of people to really determine their own lives within a state. In the United States Constitution, in Germany, none of the states has the right to secede. In France there is Corsica. In Spain there are the Basques. None of these states has the right to secede. Now I heard that Mr. Yeltsin is deleting from his constitution the right of self-determination to secede. And that's all right with Mr. Clinton. It's all right with everybody. Why was it not all right for Yugoslavia? I wrote an open letter to President Clinton asking him if he remembered the fight over secession in his country in the last century. It was a bloody war, and everybody says it was right. If it was right, why was the right of secession in Yugoslavia supported by the world community?

"You know, the year 1991, when this war broke open, marked 110 years of continuous diplomatic relations between Serbia and the United States. With how many countries did the United States have such continuous relations? It is a beautiful history. We were on the same side in the First World War and in the Second World War. The U.S. was the first country to recognize the first Yugoslav state in 1919. In World War II Mr. Roosevelt was the strongest defender of the integrity of the Yugoslav state against the Nazis. After the war there was great understanding of all the power relations. I remember all that. Now, all of sudden, I cannot understand. Mr. Bush was signing a decree proclaiming Serbia and my little Montenegro as an enemy country. Why?"

"Do you understand why?" I asked Milan.

"It is difficult. I have some ideas. You see, after the breakup of the Soviet Union, the United States found itself the only superpower in the world. The United States has an ambition to dominate the world, but in the present circumstances, particularly having in mind the economic conditions in the United States, it had to create something called the 'new world order.' Exactly what that meant we never learned, but it had to do with the United States' power in the rest of the world. And in Europe they believed they could not surpass Germany. Germany united is the greatest European power, and the United States has to accommodate it. And Germany, from the First World War and the Second, wanted to destroy Yugoslavia because any big country, especially one with a strategic position with pathways to the Middle East and to Africa, is in its way and represents competition for Germany. It is said that Serbs have built their house on the road to the world. It has to be broken up into little states so that you can play with them as you want.

"Plus the Vatican. It was against the first Yugoslav state. After the breakup of Austro-Hungary, which was really the basis of the Vatican, they lost that basis in the Balkans and Middle Europe. Then they wanted at least the little Catholic states of Croatia and Slovenia, and they were doing every possible thing to get them, such as supporting the Nazi regime in Croatia under Pavelic. Not only recognizing but participating in crimes against the schismatic Orthodox church. It is difficult to understand why they were more opposed to a Christian church with the same Bible than they were to the Muslims and Islam. So that's the first stage. Germany and the Vatican were the first states to recognize the independence of Croatia and Slovenia, leading to the dissolution of Yugoslavia. And then there was the direct economic pressure of Germany and the moral pressure of the Vatican on the rest of Europe and the United States to follow them. But in 1919, after the whole world had recognized the Kingdom of Serbs, Croats, and Slovenians, only then did the Vatican recognize it. The last to do so. And now they are the first. This, it seems to me, is very clear evidence of their responsibility."

Milan pointed out that the pope received Franjo Tudjman in a private audience in 1991, just as Pope Pius II had received Ante Pavelic in 1941. And after the audience Tudjman visited the acting papal secretary, just as Pavelic had. The visit to the secretary was highly unusual because he normally received only those visitors who had made an official state visit to the pope. Neither the Ustase state in 1941 nor Croatia in early 1991 had international recognition, so they could not have made official state visits. Following his visit to the Vatican, Tudjman went to the papal Croatian Saint Jerome Institute in Rome, just as Pavelic had done in 1941. There the head of the institute, Monsignor Ratko Peric, assured Tudjman that "throughout its history, the Institute has always devotedly and tirelessly strived to preserve the identity of the Croatian nation and worked in favor of its territorial integrity."

In gratitude to the pope, Tudjman said, "If, in a specific way the efforts of the Catholic church and program of the Croatian Democratic Union hadn't fully coincided, everything that we have achieved in establishing democracy, that spiritual unity and rebirth of the Croatian nation, and which is in a way a miracle, wouldn't have been possible."

"In the next stage," Milan continued, "the oil states, the Muslim states, wanted to have their own state in Europe. The U.S., having its own sins with Iraq, with Libya, with Lebanon, wanted to accommodate the Muslim countries. They said, 'We are with you.' Of course, it was not only idealistic. They needed oil, they needed their money. So what I think the United States is doing—at least I wish to believe that—is not rationally against the Serbs, because I think the Serbs are the natural allies of the United States, much more than the Croats, who declared war against the United States in World War II. I think the United States will come to realize that. This is the only interpretation I can offer."

Milan had given me copies of two of his several books, *Ustashe Crime of Genocide, Tudjman's 'Jasenovac Myth,'* a reply to Franjo Tudjman's claims that the crimes against the Serbs by the Croatians in World War II were a myth concocted by the Serbs; and an abridged edition of his two-volume work, *The Role of the Vatican in the Break-up of the Yugoslav State*, from which I quoted above. He was finishing work on another book, *The Break-up of the Yugoslav State, the Crime against Peace; Germany and the Vatican*. About the writing of *The Role of the Vatican*, he said, "I went to the Vatican in 1990 on the eve of this tragedy not as a political partisan but as a man whose religion is the truth, really. I wanted to see documents from World War II and more recently. They wouldn't show me anything. Since I was heading a committee in our Serbian Academy of Science, the president wrote to our minister of foreign affairs, who was my colleague and friend, asking for an official letter to the Vatican saying that I was a bona fide researcher. Then I went back and checked whether I was accredited as a researcher, and it was all done correctly, and when I met the head of the archives he was very nice, very kind. I told him I had brought my manuscript and I wanted him to read it and tell me if it was accurate. But at the same time I wanted to ask for certain documents that I knew of but had not been able to see for myself. Imagine my shock when he answered, 'We'll be happy to give you everything up to 1922'—before I was born. After that, nothing! I told him, 'You have published twelve volumes from the Second World War. From them I found connections with documents I had that were not included in those volumes.' He tried to convince me of some principle that not even the pope could change. He said a cardinal wanted one of the documents and even he couldn't get it. Well, being a diplomat, I said, 'Well, you can't give me these documents that you do not want to disclose, but can we talk? Can I ask you about what's in those documents, what I'd heard, whether it was true.' No. 'Well, can we do anything?' I asked him. No. So I told him, 'Monsignor, the only thing left for me to do is write a chapter that I didn't have in mind, which will be the first chapter: My fight for the truth and what you told me today.' "

One of the documents that Milan did find in his research was a public letter written by three Croatian Catholic priests in Paris in 1991 in reply to a proposal by a Serb printed in the Paris *Le Monde*, asking for a reconciliation of the Serbs and the Croatians. The priests' letter said, "From the beginning of the century up to the present day, the Serbs have constantly been carrying out a genocide against the Albanians (Kosovo) and the Muslims in Serbia and Bosnia; Serbian authorities have been conducting the same policy throughout the century toward the Montenegrins as well; in World War II, the Serbs carried out a genocide against the Jews; the Serbian policy of repression and violence against human rights has also been felt against the Hungarian and Croatian minorities in Vojvodina; in the postwar period the Serbs destroyed the German minority; the oppressive Serb policy is unprecedented in regard to the Macedonian nation." Furthermore, "The three Catholic priests," Milan wrote, "claim that everything the Ustase had really done (and what is ascribed to them or what is fabricated) was just the consequence of a desperate reaction to Serbian terrorism." The document continues, "When the Serbs realize what we and the Pope know very well, and when they beg for forgiveness from neighboring nations because of the wave of injustice and crimes against them (which would be 'a real miracle'), then everyone, the Pope and the Patriarch and the representatives of the Muslims and all those whom this concerns, could lay the first cornerstone for the temple of reconciliation."

There is simply no evidence for any such Serbian terrorism described by these three Croatian Catholic priests. On the other hand, Croatian terrorism against the Serbs is well documented. "So there is this real problem, to document the truth of what happened," Milan said. "Before we have the answer to these questions, there will be no solution to these problems. How long it will take I don't know. I don't know the truth, but in researching this book I'm learning a lot I didn't know. Even as secretary of the State Commission on War Crimes and Genocide, I didn't learn enough. Next week I go as a private citizen to the Hague to see my colleagues at the University of Amsterdam to check my ideas with them, because I am not one of those who believes in his own theory exclusively.

"In April I went to an international meeting in Cairo. I wanted to talk with people to check my ideas, but it didn't look like I would get a chance. Then they set up a workshop on the dissolution of states and the new economic order. It was supposed to be about the Soviet Union, but my Russian colleagues didn't come. The conference leaders didn't know what to do. Then they asked me if I would talk about Yugoslavia. I couldn't believe it. Just what I had gone there for. Well, I explained my ideas, just as I have to you, and they supported my views, especially the Indians. Just think what it would mean if the precedent of Yugoslavia was used if the Indian states started to secede. The whole world would be up to their knees in blood."

I asked Milan to tell me more about the war crimes commission. "I understand charges have been brought against Milosevic and Karadzic and others by the World Court," I said.

"No, no charges have actually been brought. Only political charges have been made by my friend of many years, Larry Eagleburger. That makes my point. Let them bring real charges. Against Milosevic. But then what about Hans-Dietrich Genscher? Then the foreign minister of Austria? And His Holiness? Let's start from the very roots of the problem. And let's look at the proof they have been able to collect. The UN secretary-general has established a special war crimes commission. I talked with the head of the commission and I asked him, 'What kind of a court is this? Where are the rules of evidence? What kind of evidence is admissible for you? You have invited everybody in the world to submit whatever they have without any criteria. How can you make a judgment of what is true from maybe four, five thousand documents?'"

Milan's account of the World Court's action is quite accurate. No actual charges had been filed as of spring 1994, but the government of Bosnia did file suit against Yugoslavia in the court in 1993, charging it with genocide, so broad a complaint that it could only have had political significance. The court responded with a warning to Yugoslavia to stop committing or sponsoring acts of genocide. In the complaint the Bosnian government also asked the court to rule that the UN arms embargo on Bosnia was illegal, and that any partition of Bosnia would be illegal. The court refused to rule on these issues. According to a September 14, 1993, dispatch in the *Chicago Tribune*, "Francis Boyle, an American law professor and advisor to Bosnia [who filed the suit], called the decision 'a great victory for Bosnia-Herzegovina. He said . . . Alija Izetbegovic would use it to strengthen his case at peace talks at Geneva.' "

Anthony D'Amato, professor of international law at Northwestern University who has closely studied the Yugoslavian situation, told me, "The suit certainly served an important political purpose, as many lawsuits do, but the suit was within the jurisdiction of the court under the Genocide Convention that Yugoslavia signed in 1954 and that Bosnia signed as a separate nation when it was admitted to the UN."

"When I was at the United Nations last year," Milan continued, "I saw a document establishing a fact-finding mission for areas where international peace and security are jeopardized, especially where local authorities are not functioning. That certainly applies to Yugoslavia, but so far no mission has been sent. This just proves what I said earlier, that this is not going to be a court of law but only a political court. Otherwise they would not be mentioning all these names all the time, because everybody is considered innocent until proven guilty. You are accusing people whom you have no real evidence against. I wrote to Boutros-Ghali, whom I knew from when he was a visiting professor in Belgrade, to ask him about these missions. And we are doing our own investigations."

"Are you looking at the crimes of all the parties?" I asked Milan. "My position from the beginning," he said, "was that a crime is a crime regardless of who has committed it. When I had evidence of crimes against Muslims, that had to be told. When somebody destroyed the mosques, that was a crime. On the other hand, if someone was shooting from the tower of the mosque, then it was a crime on both sides. But if you destroy a mosque just because it is a mosque, that is a crime."

I wondered whether Milan could summarize the findings of his committee. "What's happening in the crisis of Yugoslavia now is that it is not really a civil war. It is a religious war, an ethnic war. In this kind of war all sides have crimes and responsibilities. If someone is killing my father or my brother, I don't know what my reaction would be. I might be killing someone, but never an innocent person. I might be burning something. But I never would justify myself. I might try to explain but never try to justify. So for this reason we need to ask, who killed who? But first we need to ask, who created this situation in Yugoslavia after seventy years of happy living together in this country? We had so many possibilities for a very high standard of living. Our country is not overpopulated. In the whole of Yugoslavia we had only about 23 million people, and we can accommodate 50 million. And now we have a repetition of what happened in World War II.

"As a friend of the United States, where I lived for ten years, I really tried in the fall of 1991 to avoid these troubles. I went to Washington and succeeded in reaching the seventh floor of the State Department to talk with Mr. Eagleburger. I suggested in that year, on the 110th anniversary of Serbian-American relations, why didn't we have an unofficial summit? We would have people of integrity, people who had proven their friendship between the two countries, to see what the United States wanted from Belgrade and what were the interests of the Yugoslavs and Montenegrins and others in the Balkans. If we couldn't resolve the problems, at least we would have a clear picture of the differences. I was nicely received. They probably thought this Bulajic is a nice guy, but why should we bother? Instead they suggested I set up an institute here in Belgrade for contemporary Yugoslav history. Nonsense. My idea was to have Kissinger, David Rockefeller, and others—all of them I know, and they know Yugoslavia. It's illogical! It's absurd, this decree signed by President Bush that Serbia and Montenegro are enemy countries."

We talked for a few minutes about the effects of the sanctions. "Did you hear yesterday that the UN sanctions committee permitted the importation of five thousand tons of cigarettes, of poison? Just what we need for babies and the elderly! That's a crime. One of the doctors here wrote to Boutros-Ghali, 'I have now three hundred children who need surgery. I have resources to do only thirty operations. Would you please choose the thirty who are not supposed to die?' Who has the right? I really hate the face of Warren Christopher. I heard from his own mouth when he said, 'Serbia is going to be a pariah nation.' Who has that right? You know, you can punish a government. You can punish a state. But you cannot punish the people, the babies, in behalf of so-called human rights."

Had Milan any thoughts about the Serbian sense of their own victimization. "Well, it goes back a long time, to Kosovo. So much suffering for so long. So there are facts behind it. But there is something that seems to be in the genes, in the mentality of the people that they see themselves as victims by destiny, that they are the chosen people, like the Jews. They have chosen the heavenly kingdom symbolized by Kosovo. They are not always completely rational. They don't always do what they should do. For instance, facing this international court, I told them, 'Instead of worrying about this heavenly court, first think about this earthly court.' " We laughed together, put on our coats, and walked back to the hotel where I thanked Milan and his wife and promised Milan I would read his books before I began to write.

It had been a long day. I wasn't sure I was up for an evening with Ljiljana, her husband Branka, and a couple of other guests she had invited for me to meet. I called to ask whether we could postpone until the following evening. Couldn't be done, Ljiljana said. So I rested for an hour and made my way the few blocks to the Dimitrijevic home that turned out to be a spacious and luxurious seven-room apartment, tastefully furnished with a blend of modern and antique furniture, with lots of fresh flowers and rather ordinary but pleasant paintings. A little jarring in the rather plush living room was a huge television set sitting prominently at one end of the room. The apartment was warm and cozy, and I settled in to enjoy what I hoped would be a relaxed evening. It wasn't to be. The evening was more intense than many of my interviews had been. I wondered if, under present conditions, Serbs ever relaxed.

Ljiljana had offered me this occasion to meet a well-known musician. Only after we started to talk did I discover that he was also a member of Parliament and of the executive board of Milosevic's party, and was more interested in talking politics with me than music. Our long evening was punctuated with lots of Turkish coffee and grappa, an Italian brandy that was much more palatable than the Yugoslav plum brandy preferred by most Serbs.

Aleksander Pavlovic was a smaller man than most Serbs, though not small by Western standards. With thinning grey hair, in his late fifties, he had a bright smile and the liveliest blue eyes I had seen among all these lively, blue-eyed Serbs. His manner, relaxed and friendly, matched his casual grey sweater and corduroy pants. He was a violinist, a professor of music at the university, and conductor of the twenty-year-old, seventeen-piece, world-renowned Belgrade Strings, which played the whole repertoire of Western music plus modern works by young Yugoslav composers. The group regularly toured the West, and Aleksander served as artistic director for the Aberdeen, Scotland, summer music festival. All that ended with the embargo. All the concerts scheduled for 1992, including fifty-seven in the U.S., were canceled because of the sanctions.

"It is a crime," he said. "Culture has no borders. The worst effect is on the players. They can no longer believe in democracy. What has their music to do with politics?" Gordana Logar had told me that sports figures had been exempted from the embargo. Sports figures and not musicians?

Aleksander's wife, Ljiljana, called Ljila, sat quietly through the first two hours of the evening until her husband proudly told me that she was also a journalist. She had covered cultural events for the

Sunday magazine of *Politika* for twenty-three years and was now its editor, though she still wrote for the cultural section every week. A dark, handsome woman with a longish, casual hairdo topped by a stylish black hat with a turned-up brim that she wore all evening with a tartan plaid suit and knee-high brown boots, she looked every inch the busy editor, even on this relaxed Saturday evening. Having sat silently in a large wing chair until her husband gave her the opening to speak, she quickly became almost shrill in her conversation, often jumping up to make her pronouncements in the center of the room.

Having settled down with a cup of coffee in one corner of the room beside Aleksander, I took out my tape recorder ready to tape whatever might be said, not expecting to do a formal interview. Pointing to the machine, he said, "For that we should go into another room. But first I think you would like to see a video I brought along that will help you understand what's going on here." The video, called *Ratlines*, had been made in England by Mark Aarons and John Loftus, two British writers, and was based on their book by the same name. It was a documentary consisting mostly of newsreel film and talking heads portraying, in part one, the collaboration with Hitler of Ante Pavelic, the Croatian dictator during World War II; Pavelic's henchman in the church; and the pope in the treatment of Serbs, Jews, and Gypsies from 1941 to 1945. Part two described the career of Pavelic before the war, his rescue after the war by the church, and the complicity of the British government in that rescue.

There were news clips of forced conversions to Catholicism of thousands of Serbs, of the Jasenovac death camp in Croatia and the vicious slaughter of thousands. Pavelic's policy for the Serbs was described: one-third to be forcibly converted, one-third to be expelled, and for the other third, Pavelic is quoted as saying, "We have three million bullets." The scenes of murder in this film were more horrifying than those from the Nazi repertoire, the kind that make you put your head between your legs.

In part two some original footage was combined with newsreel clips to depict places where it was assumed Pavelic had fled, pretending to be a simple refugee in a displaced persons' camp. There he was rescued by Catholic clergy and secreted away, first in local monasteries and then in the Vatican, from whence, with forged papers, he was sent to Argentina. Much of this was speculative, but there appeared to be sufficient evidence to indicate the complicity of the Vatican in the rescue of one of World War II's worst criminals and in the genocide against Serbs, Jews, and Gypsies.

When we had recovered from the film, Ljiljana led Aleksander and me to a study where I could interview him privately. In heavily accented English and a soft, melodious voice, he told me that his orchestra was financed by the city, just like the symphony orchestra. The only foreign concert the orchestra had given since the embargo was in Russia. "As an example, last year we were scheduled to appear in a festival in Cardiff, Wales. About ten days before we were scheduled to leave, we got a letter that the town council had forbidden our appearance there. Politics once again got the upper hand. That was a great hurt to us, to our sponsors, to everyone involved, but the greatest damage was to the belief in democracy for the members of the orchestra.

"The sanctions have had catastrophic consequences for our culture. We are cut off from the world. We do maintain our own culture, and there are a few artists who still come, but there is a definite ban by the big orchestras and the ensembles. For instance, one of my former students is now the conductor of the Munich Philharmonic Orchestra. He came here every year, but now he can come only if he is playing for some humanitarian cause. Otherwise he would lose his job. I can only compare this with the worst time of anti-Semitism. For instance, for the hundredth anniversary of our prize-winning novelist, Ivo Andric, twenty-three different institutions—linguistic and English departments all over the world—had planned a special academy here devoted to his work. It was forbidden by their countries to attend.

"You know, this country is in the process of democratization. You don't change from one system to another in one year. Changing the system is a techtonic process, a catastrophe to any country. We should be left to make those changes as we can. The embargo doesn't help. It is the most massive embargo in human history, but it is counterproductive. I don't see the reason. If you read Konrad Lorenz on the behavior of animals, you see that even the most nonaggressive animal once cornered will become aggressive. So in this country you have the extremists on both sides raising their heads. If the embargo would stop the war and help democratization of the country, it would be okay even for all of our suffering, but it has just the opposite effect.

"We were not like the other Eastern countries. Here democratization would have been much easier and faster, but now... Everybody now is admitting that all the sides in the war are almost equally guilty, but only one side is punished. Even medical books and journals and scientific books are embargoed. But as you have seen in

this movie, what we see in politics is only the tip of the iceberg, so
how can we judge?"

Then Aleksander said, "I don't want to mislead you. For the past
three years I've been a member of Parliament and of the executive
board of the Socialist party. I've never been in any party before. I
was never in the Communist party, for which I'm a little bit thankful
because then you had to be a little bit better to succeed. I didn't have
that protection, that help. In the last few years I thought that anyone
who has any kind of name, a reputation, a member of the spiritual
elite, so to speak, has a social responsibility, and when I had a choice
between different parties, I joined the Socialist party. I am responsible
for the council for culture in the party." Smiling, Aleksander said, "I
was so naive I didn't realize that the Socialist party was Milosevic's
party. I actually thought we would lose the election as many left
parties had lost in the other Eastern countries, and I thought a good
social democratic opposition was very much needed in this time of
transition. If I had known the party was going to win, I wouldn't have
joined, because I don't like to join the winners.

"I was very much afraid that in the transition the state would give
up its responsibility for culture and education. Although I was never
a Communist, I always believed that the state has this responsibility,
to maintain a certain level of support. It should not be left to
sponsors, not to the commercial sector. That's very good for entertainment, but not for culture. I was talking to someone in England who
was justifying Margaret Thatcher's theory that people who want to go
to concerts and plays should pay the full price. And I said, 'I agree, if
you will agree to leave the financing of the army to the free will of
people. For me, culture and education are as important for the safety
and independence of a country as the army. So I am there trying to
prevent what I call 'early capitalism,' so-called primary acquisition
which we are witnessing here in which families are profiting by
stealing, smuggling, and so on. A good example is the Hado Castle
in Aberdeen, where I spent my summers for ten years until the
embargo. It was a huge, fantastic castle where musicians came every
summer to write and compose and perform. The owner of that castle
once told me, 'You know how we got this castle? In the fourteenth
century we were the best cattle thieves. The money we got bought us
titles and all this. Now we are very fine respectable people.' So it was
all right in the fourteenth and fifteenth centuries and even in the
nineteenth century, but now, on the brink of the twenty-first century,

going back is disastrous. And this embargo has made it much worse. You can see how successful it is now. You see a whole subculture. Some of the smugglers are even doing a good job. But it doesn't help culture. It doesn't help democratization.

"I thought I had done what I had for my musical career, and I'm still doing it, but I felt very selfish doing only that and decided I had to help my country. Our Socialist party is now more democratic than the Social Democratic party in Germany or the Socialist party in France, and so on. But there is no real role here for a social democratic party. There is no philosophy behind any party now. The first time in history. I'm not calling it the end, but there is a vacuum. For the first time in history we have only the ideology of profit, and fast profit, all over the world. And I'm very much afraid for culture, not only here but everywhere. The natural law of the jungle is operating. Since men began to think, the aim was to neutralize this merciless law of the jungle. If we let ourselves give in to this lower level of the jungle without trying to be a slight corrective to it, we are animals ourselves. So the role of socialist parties today should be to act as the human corrective."

I told Aleksander of a visit I had had with a Czech Communist member of Parliament who referred to the slogan of the Prague Spring, "Communism with a human face." I asked him, "And now what you want is capitalism with a human face?" Aleksander smiled and agreed. "You must admit that communism had one benefit for the Western world. It helped the working class everywhere organize and get their rights to the point where they no longer had to look to communism to defend their rights. And that is when communism stopped spreading. But now that balance is no longer there. Very luckily it is not there, but I'm wondering whether the human greed of those who have will endanger those who don't. Everywhere now you are beginning to have extremely rich people and extremely poor people. The middle class is disappearing. And if we are not careful about that, we may see some catastrophic consequences."

I asked Aleksander if he was an atypical member of his party. "I would be an atypical member of any party," he said, laughing. "But we did a survey and found that 68 percent of our members had never belonged to any party, which is about the average of all the parties now."

"There were never a lot of members of the Communist party?" I asked. "Oh, it was huge. It was a sort of a Rotary Club for all those opportunists. If you were a member, things were easier. I don't think they had many convinced Communists, but a large membership. Now, in our party most of the members joined because they were social democrats. But in every party, the left and the right and the liberals, about 20 percent were Communists and the leadership is all ex-Communist—Milosevic, Seselj, Draskovic, they were all Communists. But the people have changed. I think the leadership of our party is going back to the original sources of socialism, Christian utopianism. We believe in a mixed economy, that all property should have the same equal treatment. We believe in free schooling from the beginning to the end, which means that everybody has the same access. We believe in the state sponsoring culture so people can go to anything they want inexpensively. If they want to bring Pavarotti here, which would be extremely expensive, they could find sponsors, but an ordinary man who loves opera should be able to go. We believe in equal access to everything. Eight years of education, but then strict selection according to ability, so the top studies are for the most able. It should not be only the rich and those who have position who can rise to the top. The difference between us and the other parties is that they think the first eight years should be free, and then only those who can pay should be able to continue."

I changed the subject to ask about Serbian military assistance to the Bosnian Serbs. "About 17 percent of our federal budget goes to help the Bosnian Serbs—food, medicine, and money." Of that 17 percent, what percentage was used for arms? "I don't think any," Aleksander said. "It is needed to buy oil, for tents, and such things. But most of it is for food and medicine. We would be living much better if we were not giving them that help. One of the parties says that all that help should be stopped. But I don't agree, as no one would who has a feeling of national identity—I don't mean nationalism. I think you would help your Jewish community somewhere if they were living in such conditions. And there are definite difficulties from the other side, the UN and others, so that we could not send arms. Probably there is some smuggling, but you must know that a very big part of the Yugoslav army stayed there—all the Bosnians, with Bosnian officers, with the arms from the army. The same thing is true of the Muslims and the Croatians who were in the Yugoslav army before the breakup and then stayed in their own armies. Some parties here think we should have the Yugoslav army in there, but we don't think we should do that. We would agree to any kind of peace agreement in

Bosnia and Croatia, and we have made great peace efforts because we need it badly in this country to get rid of the sanctions. But I think the only thing we could do to satisfy the international community would be for us to send our army to fight the Serbs there. Nobody can ask us to do that. It is too much. A lot of Serbian people have a lot of bad conscience because we are not helping more. We are standing here and saying, 'Fight your own fight.' And now, if we lose the election, it will be because we didn't help enough.' So we are really suppressing the will of the people not to help more."

I said to Aleksander, "There were claims made that the last election was stolen."

"If it was, we are very bad thieves. It's an absolutely stupid claim. How could the election be stolen with all those observers? Every party was represented in the vote counting. But if we were in a position to steal, we did a very bad job, we should have won the majority. We won 101 places out of 250. We needed another 25 to have a majority. Any decent thieves would not have been such idiots not to steal another 25 seats. Those who are in Parliament believe they were elected democratically. They don't think their elections were stolen. Those who were not elected thought it was undemocratic. Those in the opposition who were elected, they also thought it was democratic."

"Why is Milosevic calling a new election?" I asked.

"Because the Parliament cannot function anymore. Because we have a minority government. We have passed only twenty-two laws in the last nine months. The problem in this country is that you need a lot of new laws. The old laws don't work anymore, and we have to make a whole new system, which the Radicals opposed. Then, a little while ago, Seselj and the Radicals called for a vote of confidence, but the opposition could not agree to make a coalition government. Now we cannot pass any laws at all. We thought of making a coalition with a small democratic party that is very influential with the cultural elite but not a populist party, but they had only seven members. It was not enough, so Milosevic said, 'Let's go to elections. Let the people judge again and try to make a stable government with a majority party or two parties that can make a coalition. Instead of us sitting there and discussing and fighting, we will try to make a government that can work.' "

In fact the Parliament was a good show for the public but little else. In the December elections that took place after I left Belgrade,

Milosevic again failed to get a majority, but was only three seats short. Six members of the New Democracy party joined him, so he had the coalition he needed.

Aleksander expected that Seselj would lose popularity now that Milosevic had denounced him. In the 1990 election Seselj won only one seat. In 1992, when the slogan of the Radical party was "We support Milosevic," they won seventy-three votes. "A lot of people thought we were in a coalition with Seselj, but we had nothing to do with him. He ran a very clever campaign, implying that there was a coalition when there was none. Once, when Milosevic was asked about it, he said, 'He's very good because he doesn't change his principles,' but he didn't say his principles are good." But Milosevic also didn't say that Seselj's extreme nationalism and warmongering were bad, either. "In time it became clear that he is extremely radical, chauvinist, he's not for the Serbian nation. We have a very great national pride, but we don't hate other people. I don't call it nationalism. I separate nationalism from national identity. Defending your national identity doesn't mean that you hate other people. Maybe it's all idealistic, but I don't think so." In the end, Milosevic was forced to denounce Seselj, though he had clearly used him when it seemed politically expedient. In the December election, Aleksander's prediction proved to be correct. Seselj's party won only thirty-eight seats.

"What is very much neglected, not taken into account," Aleksander said, "is the mentality of the Serbian people."

"Oh yes, indeed," I said, happy that he had brought up this subject himself.

"It is strange. The Serbs will do anything for spite. There is a famous professor teaching ethnology who tells his students that the Serbian people will do anything for spite if they are crossed. That's another reason the embargo is not working. We have to persevere or else we are lost. It's similar to the problem the Jews had. This is our Jerusalem. We'd rather defend it as it is rather than just have one Wailing Wall. It is an old culture. We have about fifty monasteries in Kosovo. They are not only churches, they are the monuments of our culture." Aleksander then launched into a discussion of the problems in Kosovo. "If the Albanians were content to live in this country, they would have twenty seats in Parliament and they could live equally, democratically, any place in this country. Instead they want independence, schools in their own language, and an undemocratic regime. But Kosovo is a place of Serbian national identity that we cannot give away, just as Israel can't give away Jerusalem. This is something the people outside, especially in the United States, don't understand. This is a very old culture, not like the United States."

With that we ended our conversation and returned to the living room where Ljiljana brought a plate of homemade biscuits and the bottle of grappa. I had planned to leave within an hour or so, but the conversation stretched on until one o'clock, ranging over such subjects as freedom of the press in Belgrade, including Ljila's contempt for *Vreme*, which she said was a joke, without influence, and well supported by Western interests. She claimed the staff at *Vreme* earned big salaries paid by Europeans and Americans. I knew that the deputy editor there was making the same wages she was earning, about twenty-seven dollars a month.

We also talked about the devastation Tito had worked on Serbia's economy in an effort to reduce its influence in Yugoslavia. Ljila drew a map to show me how Tito had closed the major Serbian port, Bar, on the Adriatic Sea in Montenegro, and diverted the shipping of goods to and from Serbia to a circuitous route through Croatia. "Our self-sufficient economy was dismantled by Tito," Ljila said. In fact, Tito built a railroad from Bar to Belgrade, realizing a long-held Serbian dream. "That is why we are in this position today. Before World War II we had, for instance, an airplane industry here in Serbia. Tito moved that industry to Slovenia."

Once again the subject of the affinity of Serbs and Jews arose. Aleksander told a story of going to Odessa to play a recital with the local orchestra. "I played Debussy, which was banned as decadent music in Russia, and I played the Bal Shem Suite by Ernst Bloch. [The name of the suite refers to the leader of the Jewish Hasidic movement.] It was during the Passover, and the conductor of the orchestra, who was Jewish, asked me, 'Mr. Pavlovic, are you Jewish?' and I said, 'Who is not?' The hall was full, two thousand people, not for me as the violinist but because of that piece. Everyone wanted to hear it. Jews and Serbs have such a similar history. At the beginning of the war my father told a Jewish friend of his, 'Let me take your two sons to the village and hide them.' And the man said, 'No, they will be all right.' And then came the bombardment, and the Nazis came and they all disappeared. Like lambs they went. And in Croatia in the war, some Serbs were called to the village square, and they went and were slaughtered. They went, like the Jews, into the concentration camps, like lambs. There were at least twenty churches in Croatia where the people were put into churches and the doors were locked and the churches were burned down. That was only fifty years ago. And now, without the protection of the federal state, the Serbs in Croatia were again at the mercy of the people there. The same symbols from the Ustashe are now in the streets. You cannot find one Serb family that did not have lots of victims. So you see the Serbs feel close to the Jews."

"But," I said, "there is one strong difference between the Serbs and the Jews historically. For centuries the Jews' only resistance was to retreat into their identity. Since the Masada they have never fought back against all the people who were persecuting and killing them— until Israel. The Serbs have regularly fought back through the ages."

"Yes, that's true, but at the same time they have also regularly gone like lambs. This resistance that you talk about is what happened in 1991. The memories were too fresh. They did not want any more. Imagine somebody coming, even in Germany, to a Jewish community with the swastika and the Iron Cross. The Jewish community that I have seen all around the world has taught me a lot. If we don't, here in Serbia, behave as the Jews did *after* the Holocaust, which we had as well . . . this was the only country that had a resistance movement against the Nazis where a hundred Serbs were killed for every German killed. Ljila's mother was a professor in the gymnasium [upper school] when a whole class of children and the professor were killed. Until that is known to the world, it will never understand. Often the world accuses us of relying too much on our history. My answer is that only those who are ashamed of their history tend to forget it. We don't have anything to forget in our history."

Ljila interjected that the Croatians' hatred of the Serbs predated the Nazis by hundreds of years. "It is deep dyed in their beings to hate the Orthodox," she said.

"Not to differ with my wife, with whom I differ as much as anyone in marriage," Aleksander said, "but an agreement was attempted between Serbs and Croats. They had a secret meeting in Oslo. Then a German official went to Zagreb and told Tudjman, 'We can't support you if you make this agreement with the Serbs,' and a telefax was sent to Oslo to stop the talks."

When Ljila asked for my impressions, I said I thought I was witnessing a tragedy that had been in the making for some time, that the sanctions had simply been the last straw for a declining economy.

My remarks set off in Ljila and Aleksander a subtly angry response in defense of their people. This finally emerged strongly when Aleksander began talking about the press.

"The whole press is in the hands of the opposition, which I don't mind. A few days ago I saw on the Third Channel, which goes all over Serbia, the whole evening, three hours, devoted to a Yugoslav film director who is called Dusan Makavia, who has signed an appeal to bomb Belgrade. This is shown on state television! He was a member of the Communist party, he was A Number One when I was a second-class citizen. Then there is another man, Slobodan Selenic, a writer, whose every book is promoted in Great Britain as the work of the Serbian Rushdie, who is opposition like Rushdie to the Muslims, I guess, but still, all his dramas are performed in every, *every* theatre in Belgrade."

I stopped Aleksander to say that all this defensive talk wasn't necessary. "Yes, it is necessary," he said. "Just by chance you met me. It is the first time you are meeting someone from the Socialist party, which is called the governing party even though it is not governing. No, it is not governing. You have met only people from the opposition before."

"Oh no," I protested. "I have met all kinds of people."

"Okay, but you have not met anybody from the Socialist party. Why didn't you try?"

I explained that I had wanted to meet the intellectuals, not the politicians. "You met Cedomir Mirkovic, but nobody from the Socialist party," he said.

"I met Cedomir because Ljiljana introduced me. She wanted me to talk to him. Should I have refused because he is a politician in addition to everything else he does?"

"But why did you want to meet so-called intellectuals? What is an intellectual? Isn't an intellectual someone who, as part of his job, is concerned with society?"

And, Ljiljana added, "The truth."

"Yes," Aleksander said, "you are looking for the truth."

"What I wanted was people who were not affiliated with the government but who were thinking about all the issues involved."

"Don't you think the governing parties are thinking that way?"

"But the governing party has a role to play and a job to do, and that's not what I wanted. I wanted people who were thoughtful, who could think through the issues, but who had no stake in the government. My goal was not to meet politicians, though I'm very glad I met you. But you are the exceptional politician. Most politicians are not artists or intellectuals. I wanted to talk with you as an artist, and I got that and a lot more, which is fine."

"That's nice. One thing I forgot to tell you about was the democratic elections in 1992. You asked me if the election was stolen, and I told you that if it was, we were very bad thieves."

I told Aleksander that I had asked the question mainly because Milan Panic, the American Serb multimillionaire who went to Yugoslavia and ran for president against Milosevic in 1992, was appearing regularly on American radio and television claiming that Milosevic had stolen the election. Some people I had met here had also made that charge.

"Panic is simply a clown, nothing else. But I want to say that during Bill Clinton's campaign he sent a very sharp letter to Yitzhak Rabin asking him to stop supporting George Bush and to remain neutral, as foreign governments should not interfere with the domestic politics of another nation. Then, during our last election, not only in private encounters but also publicly the United States was giving enormous support to Panic and nobody else. I was invited to the American embassy to participate in a satellite broadcast with David Wilhelm, the head of your Democratic party, during our election, and I asked why Clinton wrote that way to Rabin. He said it was absolutely inconceivable that any foreign country should be involved in the election of another country, and Yitzhak Rabin had been sending very strong signals to the Jewish community in the United States, which was a very important community. And they had to stop it. And I said, 'Well, that's a very good answer. But let me ask you, what should you advise us to do with such open support of your government for Panic? What should we do?' Wilhelm said, 'You should protest very strongly about this.' " Everyone laughed loudly. "So if the election was undemocratic, it was undemocratic against us, against the Socialist party."

"Panic is saying in the States that he would have won the election if Clinton had given him more support," I said. Another round of laughter. "He is the laughingstock here. No opposition party would want him to come and run under their banner," Aleksander said. Everyone agreed.

I wondered how it could happen that this American billionaire could come back to Belgrade after thirty-five years and be made a prime minister by the Socialist party. "I thought," I told them, "what kind of crazy people are these Serbs?"

"Not many people welcomed him," Ljiljana said.

"But he was made prime minister," I protested.

"It was a game. He bought his way in. And then he tried to buy the election," Aleksander said, "but he failed." He then proceeded to talk about America. He had lived in the States for two years as a visiting professor at Stanford University. "There is no hospitality like American. I stayed in people's houses and was treated like one of the family. I stayed with Roy Harris, a great composer. I played his sonata. I felt like it was my own home. You wouldn't find that even in Serbia, which is very hospitable. I liked it there very much. I enjoyed the people very much. I had an offer to stay and I was tempted, but you know, you have your roots. So I am not anti-American. But when I hear nowadays, 'If we want to preserve our leading role in the world, we must do that and that and that.' You know, this great democratic society that the United States claims to be, who has elected them to be the leaders of the world? Who made that election?" Everyone laughed.

We then turned to Milosevic and the peculiar Serb mentality. Aleksander said that the sanctions had worked for Milosevic. "With the whole world against him, the Serbs would all vote for him." I wondered whether, in fact, that was not a normal reaction that would be found in any nation. "If the whole world were against Clinton, all Americans would vote for him. We call it circling the wagon against the enemy. It's a natural human reaction."

It was 1 a.m. We were all very tired. Everybody had had a long day even before the evening began at 7:30. Aleksander and Ljila drove me back to the hotel where we parted as good friends.

"An Intellectual Has to Be Independent"

22 A day off to read, write, and relax. As I wrote at my little desk in mid-morning, Slegana, the maid, cleaned around me, chattering "great," her one word of English, and *dobra* (good) after she finished each task. When something went wrong she exclaimed *picku materuni*; this I had learned from Mira meant "shit" or "fuck," more literally "mother's cunt," and functioned in Serbian in all the ways "fuck" functions in English, as a noun, a verb, an adjective, an adverb, expressing dismay, disgust, anger, joy, or anything else. I fucking well enjoyed Slegana, who every day dusted everything in sight, wiped the bathroom floor on her knees, cleaned the rug with a rag wrapped around a broom, washed the mirror, made up the bed in such a way that I remade it when I went to bed, and laughed loudly at the two large pillows I requested for reading in bed. She laughed too at the Ballantine's scotch bottle on the side table that I finally convinced her contained slivovitz that Snezana had brought me. I did this by giving her a taste, at which she again laughed loudly, exclaimed *dobra*, and patted my arm. That day the floor around my desk was covered with petals from the roses I had let wilt too long. I asked Slegana, by gesture, to vacuum. When she finally understood, she said, "Bzzz *postra*," and gestured that she would do it later even as she reassured me in Serbian, expecting me to understand. We carried on a brisk conversation with only *dobra* and *picku materuni* as our shared language, a tribute to expletives.

Like so many other Serbian women, Slegana's hair was dyed; she was a bright yellow blond. Obviously, hair dye was a hot item on the black market. She regularly wore curlers in her hair, large costume earrings, and heavy makeup—to clean hotel rooms. She had the blue leather work shoes worn by many women workers who were on their feet a lot—flat-heeled, open toe and heel shoes that laced up over the ankles. She was practical, but she had her pride. She was surviving on a tiny salary and was probably standing in line to get her "Bush packages," but she was always cheerful, laughing easily and hugging me regularly when I gave her a pack of cigarettes.

If Slegana had spoken English or I Serbian, she would probably have talked politics with me, not high-level politics but complaints about the government and the United States that Serbs feel has betrayed them. She was probably as consumed with politics as everybody else in this country seemed to be, including people who had never taken any interest before. After all, life was good. Mira had told me that even hotel maids earned good wages. Why worry about politics? There was little one could do except oppose the regime, and that was almost a fruitless endeavor. And why bother anyway? The regime kept everybody content. Now no one except the black marketers were content. It was time to worry about politics.

Watching Slegana work in my room, I wondered how aware she was of what Aleksander Pavlovic had insisted on calling loyalty to one's national identity instead of nationalism. I regretted not asking him how he distinguished the two, how he defined nationalism. He clearly disapproved of nationalism while heartily endorsing the concept of national identity. Part of his negative reaction to nationalism was framed by the fierce hatreds of extremist Serbian nationalists like Seselj and Arkan, who saw the Croatians and Muslims as potential objects of extermination. Pavlovic's voice told me that he recoiled from the violence that nationalism had come to represent. Another part of this opposition was likely the traditional liberal argument that nationalism is essentially a feudal sentiment incompatible with the modern democratic nation-state. Yet he emphasized his respect for and loyalty to national identity, to the history and traditions of the Serbian people, which is not very consistent with the modern concept of citizenship, though it is more and more taking hold of people's imaginations all over the world.

If national identity, as described by Aleksander, is to be the core of the nation-state, as he implied, it cannot easily coexist with other national identities in a modern multinational state such as Yugoslavia was before its breakup. Each national identity within such a state would be striving for dominance and, in the end, for its own state, as occurred in 1991 when Slovenia and Croatia and later the Bosnian Muslims and the Macedonians all opted for their own national identities as nation-states, and with the Albanians in Kosovo who wanted recognition as an independent state.

Those attributes that contribute to the national identity in Yugoslavia have always favored the Serbs. They have the longest history of a single locale, language, religion, and traditions of all the people in Yugoslavia; all the other ethnic groups in the area reflect those traits of their conquerors or their original homelands more than any separate, individual national traits. Slovenia and Croatia are largely the products of the Austro-Hungarian Empire, while the Muslims and Albanians are creatures of the Ottoman Empire, with the Macedonians being originally Bulgarians. The Serbs' greater numbers in Yugoslavia and their stronger and uniquely local culture and religion made for a formidable, dominating presence among the country's other nationalities, hence a natural resistance to their influence among the lesser national groups. This resistance was most strongly reflected in the Ustase state of Croatia in World War II and, finally, in the nineties, in wars of independence.

Declarations of independence by the several Yugoslav republics left the Serbs in an untenable position. Serbs were scattered among the states that sued for their independence. They had lived there for hundreds of years with their culture and religion intact, despite the occupation of the Turks, the Austro-Hungarians, and the Nazis. Suddenly they were faced once again with foreign occupation, that of the Muslims and the Croatian Catholics. This time natural resistance to dominance by a stronger national identity was a Serb motif—the decision to fight to the last man, what Aleksander described as the reaction of "spite."

Whether the struggle of the Serbs with the Croatians, the Muslims, and perhaps, in the future, the Albanians should be described as nationalist struggles or struggles to maintain national identity seems to be a matter of semantics, obviously important to Aleksander

Pavlovic but not necessarily important to history. While Aleksander insisted on distinguishing the struggle for national identity as one distinct from what he viewed as the hatred for other peoples implied in nationalism, the effect seems to have been the same.

What is astonishing to people in the democratic liberal states is the ferocity with which people—in many other regions as well as Yugoslavia—will fight to defend their national identities. It seems to be a primitive reaction, almost as if people were defending their own families, like the blood feuds that characterized some sections of the Balkans, described so beautifully in the Albanian Ismail Kadare's novel *Broken April*. But to call it primitive is to deny its modern reality, its ongoing historical significance. Obviously national identity has deep roots that will not be disgorged by any supposedly democratic liberal tradition. Though it may be tempered by history, it will rise again to reassert itself at such propitious moments as occurred in the 1970s and 1980s in Africa, at the end of the European occupations and brutal dictatorships that followed, and in the late 1980s in Eastern Europe and the former Soviet Union, with the end of communism and its suppression of nationalist strivings. With few exceptions it seems that people around the globe will offer their loyalties to a larger, purely civic, multiethnic union only for relatively brief periods, despite the apparent benefits of such unions. Michael Ignatieff, in his book *Blood and Belonging*, argues that the liberal civic polity as it has prevailed through most of the last two centuries in the Western world "runs deeply against the human grain and is only achieved and sustained by the most unremitting struggle against human nature."

It will not work to say that greater education will undo these ethnic ties. Many of the fiercest nationalists have been well educated, including the leaders of the Yugoslavian nationalist movements. Radovan Karadzic, the leader of the Bosnian Serbs, is a psychiatrist. Vojeslav Seselj, the most extreme nationalist in Serbia, and Franjo Tudjman in Croatia were both articulate leaders in the Communist party. Milosevic was a banker.

And it will not do to say that nationalism is the invention of a few demagogues who twist the will of the people. Demagogues can only convince people who are ready to be convinced. Clearly, the call to nationalism by those who may be viewed as demagogic leaders has fallen on ripe ground all over the world in recent years, whether as a result of new civic freedom or as struggles to throw off tyranny.

There can be no question that South Africa's Mangosuthu Buthelezi was a first-class demagogue, but his nationalist leadership of the Zulus found an all too ready following. On the other hand, it is a tribute to the leadership of Nelson Mandela and others in the African National Congress that they have been able to weld, in most of South Africa, an almost all-African unity among the many disparate tribes of blacks. Whether that civic unity will be sustained with the passing of the elderly Mandela, whether there will not arise tribal national-isms with the new civic freedom, in the absence of its most ardent and beloved advocate, is still to be seen.

I called Ljila to ask if I might visit her office. She told me she would have to get permission from the Ministry of Culture. *Politika* was still owned by the state and, though its journalists were now free to say what they wanted, strictures were still exercised. I told her not to bother. It wasn't that important.

I read quickly through Milan's books, though it was hard going because they had been locally translated into English very badly and published by the Ministry of Information with all kinds of errors. Both books were scholarly efforts by a man who was essentially a partisan diplomat and lawyer. Both books did indeed document the Ustase crimes. As for the role of the Vatican in the breakup of Yugoslavia, much of the argument centered on the role of the local clergy in Croatia in World War II, who were assumed to be acting on the advice and instruction of the Vatican; but there was precious little evidence of direct Vatican intervention. The fact that Milan was unable to get into the archives of the Vatican may explain this. Or it may be that the Croatian clergy acted on its own. That the Vatican did recognize the independent state of Croatia during the war and received its leader with open arms, and then later received Tudjman as the head of a state that had not yet received international recogni-tion, does point to the Vatican's approval of this Catholic breakaway state. Beyond expressing its early approval, what role the Vatican played in the breaks is still not known.

23 Time again to go to Mira's office to settle my hotel account and exchange money. Mira invited me to lunch at one of the open-air restaurants in Skadarlija. It was a warm though overcast day, one of the last when the restaurant could serve out of doors. We were the only customers. I excused myself to go to the washroom. Mira reminded me to ask the waiter for a napkin—there was no toilet paper in any public washroom. Prague, when I was there in 1990, also had a shortage of toilet paper. One paid an attendant for it. No such thing in Belgrade. Waiters provided paper napkins.

I asked Mira to order for me. I should have learned my lesson by this time. She ordered a plate of grilled veal sausages, the specialty of the house, she said. Very tasty, but still veal. I swore that when I left Serbia I would never again eat veal.

Thank God for Mira. She was the only person in Belgrade with whom I was able to relax completely. No longer playing Belgrade's unofficial hostess, she now treated me as a warm friend. We talked about men and women, comparing notes. Serbian women had achieved a good deal of equality in the arts, in the professions, and in business, but when they went home at night they found no equality. Mira complained about Serbian men: "Arrogant! Patriarchal, as if we couldn't think for ourselves, as if they are the only ones who can think. Why do you think we have such high divorce rates in Serbia? When they are courting they are chivalrous and talk all the time about equality. After marriage they forget all that." I had a hard time seeing Mira or any of the other women I'd met in such marriages. On the other hand, Gordana was divorced, and Sonja had never been married. Ljiljana clearly did not have such a marriage. I also had a hard time seeing all these men I'd been talking with, who treated me so respectfully and chivalrously, as marital tyrants; but I had a certain amount of faith in Mira's words. She was a sophisticated woman. American men wore their hearts on their sleeves. One could often guess how they treated their wives from the way they treated strange women. Mira insisted that was not true in Serbia. Men were universally polite and chivalrous to women outside the home and quite the opposite at home. Nevertheless, she had been married to her present husband for a long time.

We also talked about local customs, food, clothes, the town, our children, and, of course, politics. Having stopped being an ambassador for Belgrade, Mira had emerged as a cynic, cursing the government and the former regime. *Picku materuni* came to her lips often. Mira was furious at the government for the outrageous inflation. She had gone to the grocery to find something to eat and found a ham for ten million dinars. She refused to pay but the next morning changed her mind. At least it was something to eat. She went back to the store at 7:30 the next morning. The ham was now fifteen million dinars, about twenty dollars. "*Picku materuni!*" she exclaimed. "It is criminal that they let them get away with that. But you'll see, they'll reelect Milosevic anyhow. It is the Serbs' need to suffer and prove they can survive."

After getting lost again in the evening dark, I found my way to the offices of the Serbian-Jewish Friendship Society where I was scheduled to interview Petar Zdazdic, the former editor-in-chief of Prosveta, Yugoslavia's largest publishing house. State-run like all publishing houses had been, it had put out a book a day before the nation's disintegration, publishing such writers as Ivo Andric and Milorad Pavic. Once again Ljiljana sat by listening silently, having arranged this interview for me. Petar was a rotund, white-haired man in his seventies, casually but elegantly dressed in slacks, a turtleneck, and a sports jacket, and carrying a handsome leather shoulder bag, as did many men in Belgrade. Throughout our interview he was more relaxed than most of those I had talked with, stretching out in his armchair and speaking easily and comfortably, his eyes focusing sharply on me, though his every word had to be translated by Snezana Popodic. He was the only person with whom I talked who didn't seem to give a damn whether or not he convinced me of his views.

Petar had been a Communist, had to be in order to rise to such a position. He told me that he had joined the party to "fight Stalinism, which one could only do inside the party, especially in the cultural field." By conviction he was, he said, a "Western-style social democrat." Now he had no ties to any party. "An intellectual has to be independent," he said, without even a smile.

I had wanted to talk to Petar because Ljiljana had told me that he had a theory about what I was calling the Serbs' "victim mentality." When I confronted him with a question about this, he told me that rather than calling it a victim mentality, he would call it "history that repeats itself, not only in this region but all over the world. Don't forget Russia. Don't forget 1917 in Russia, and now that has repeated itself with the storming of the White Palace. The West either knows little about it or doesn't want to learn about it. The same thing has happened here in the defense of their own territory by the Serbs. It has been interpreted in the West as Serbian aggression."

"Yes, I understand there has been the actual history, but I think there is in the Serbian mentality some sentiment like, 'We are destined to suffer,' " I told Petar.

"If you take into account that the Serbs were under Turkish occupation for five hundred years and have been exposed to merciless treatment, we can talk about it. Something in the collective philosophy of the Serbian people gives ground to believe in something like a victim mentality. It is the so-called 'Kosovo determination,' associated with the famous battle of Kosovo in 1389 when the Serbian Empire fell. The epic poetry that is so highly regarded by the Serbian people, and has to a certain extent formed their mentality, created a myth of Prince Lazar who decided to choose the heavenly empire. In a way, that could be interpreted as the acceptance of collective suicide. No people in Europe are so intensely exposed to the radiation of their epic poetry as the Serbs. They believe in this poetry as pure truth, even though it is only the product of the poets' imagination. They have followed those ideas, and their heroes today are the same as those who decided to die for Kosovo. It is a nationalist subconscious. History supplied the models for the heroes of today. And this poetry is not only the poetry of the intellectuals. The peasants of Montenegro know enormous amounts of this poetry by heart, especially those poems associated with the battle of Kosovo."

I wondered whether the wars now taking place in the former Yugoslavia weren't an expression of this victim mentality, the feeling that death and destruction were near and that life had to be defended at all cost.

"Our Nobel prize–winning writer, Ivo Andric, spoke about Njegos, a famous poet from Montenegro, as a poet of Kosovo determination. It was also Mr. Andric's idea—and he was also a brilliant ethno-psychologist—that the Kosovo poetry influenced the formation of our psychology. But I believe this would require a more meticulous investigation. I have to say that the willingness of the Serbs to fight to the last man could be the result of such a mental state. But you are forgetting all the wars that preceded this one, even the Hundred Years War, and your Civil War."

"Well, yes," I said, "but I sense a strong feeling of victimization emanating from the Serbs in Croatia."

"Yes. The Serbs living in Krajina are virtually ready to die. The same young men who are now waging such fierce battles saw their fathers and their grandfathers slain by the Ustase, and now the Ustase are back again, which is why the Serbs are so ready to fight and die. In addition to the historical background, there is another factor. Those people can endure a lot of hell. They have a lot of tenaciousness."

"That's precisely what I was referring to in this discussion of the victim mentality. It seems to me that that very tenaciousness has to do with the assumed destiny to suffer."

"A certain parallel could be drawn between the Serbian and the Jewish people. Both have this feeling of their destiny to suffer. Though there are different reasons for their suffering, with the Jews suffering at Christian hands and the Serbs suffering because they were located at such a strategic political position, it is certainly true that both peoples are predestined to suffer."

Once more I brought up the objection to the analogy of the Jews and the Serbs—that the Jews did not fight back against their oppressors until their battles in modern Palestine, whereas the Serbs regularly fought back fiercely over the centuries.

"One very important element is missing," Petar said. "The Jews have changed their mentality. At least in the last half of this century, they have taken command of their destiny. They have been fighting just as the Serbs fought historically."

"Would you say that the five hundred years of the Turkish occupation was a foreshortened period comparable to the two thousand years of Jewish persecution, and that something happened in the minds of the Serbs at the end of it just as something happened in the minds of the Jews at the end of the Holocaust?"

"Well, it is true that the Serbian people were the only people that liberated themselves from the Turks. There was some self-contained power among the Serbs to enable them to do that. There were a number of causes."

"So it was a gradual buildup of anger? There were a number of insults?" Snezana balked at the word "insults." We finally agreed on the word "tortures."

"Yes, there were many tortures, but there was one in particular. A high tower was built entirely of the skulls of Serbs at Nis in 1809." The tower was a reprisal for the 1804 uprising of the Serbs. According to Paul Pavlovich, a Canadian Serb writing in his 1988 book *The Serbians*, during the Russo-Turkish War the Turks "left a physical reminder of that Serb defeat: the Pasha of Nis ordered that the heads of the Serb warriors be used as decorative pieces and that a pyramid of skulls be put up."

"One may say that the uprising was not unlike the war the Serbs are waging in Bosnia against the Muslims, who are the same Turks whose forefathers did all the terrible atrocities to the Serbs," Petar said. "Not only did they take away their property, but they humiliated them in every possible way. For example, a Turk would come into a Serb's house and take his wife. It was a tradition that he would send the husband to walk around the house with his shoes in his hands. [Serb peasants traditionally wore a cloth shoe with elongated turned-up toes.] It was like walking the dog. All the while the Turk was making love to the wife."

I stared at Snezana and said, "Not making love, that was rape."

"I was just trying to be polite," she said.

"Having been bisexual," Petar went on, "the Turks would also seduce the sons of the Serbs."

"That sounds apocryphal," I said.

"But it could be true," Petar said.

I had not advanced much further in my search among the intellectuals for someone who had thought through the Serbian mentality. I felt there was more to be said than I had heard. Perhaps the present circumstances had so blatantly aroused the feelings of victimization among the intellectuals, as well as all others, that it would take another generation to probe this national trait. On the other hand, who among us is able objectively to see ourselves? I wished that Ivo Andric were alive. His novel *Bridge on the Drina* reveals, for the years of the Turkish and then the Austro-Hungarian occupations in Bosnia, a people mostly supine under the treacherous rule of the conquerors, living in a friendly truce with the converted Muslims that ended only with the assassination of the Austrian archduke by a Serb nationalist. Having the distance and the imagination of a novelist, he would likely be able to spin a tale about the Serbian mentality.

24 Tmusic Miodrag was a roly-poly bear of a man in his sixties, with a big paunch and a great head of kinky grey hair around an almost cherubic face despite steel-rimmed glasses. He had an impish grin. His laugh was infectious and, though Draga had trouble translating them, I got enough sense of some of his many jokes and anecdotes to laugh. Like his answer to my question, "Why do you think the Communist countries have had so little crime?"

"One of Beria's deputies [the head of the NKVD, the secret police in the Soviet Union under Stalin] explained it very well. He said, 'We have one informer for every four criminals,' [only a slight exaggeration]. A person only commits a crime if he thinks he won't be discovered. But under socialism he knew he'd be discovered, so he didn't try. As we get more democratic, we're going to catch up with you. We don't exactly understand all that, but when you study criminology, you realize that the criminals are always ahead of the science."

Tmusic had been the Belgrade district attorney for thirty-two years. In order to get his job he had to be a lawyer and pass a judge's exam. He also had to be a Communist. "Now I am a Communist like I am a Christian. I don't belong to any party. They all disgust me."

I asked Tmusic if his salary, like everyone else's, had gone down. "No," he said wryly, "it's going up. Numerically. Lots more dinars."

His spacious office, comfortably set out with handsome modern furniture, paintings, and sculpture, with a lovely view of the city, was in one of the international-style high rises built for government offices in the last thirty years. We sat around a conference table and drank Turkish coffee and mineral water as Tmusic reeled off statistics that the Ministry of Information had asked him to prepare for me. Were they accurate? Or were they figures conjured for the benefit of an American journalist? Tmusic's devil-may-care attitude said, on the one hand, "What do I care what they think of our crime rates here?" and on the other, "Why not give them the kind of figures that make us look good?" For a city of two million, the crime figures were so low that I was astonished. Chicago suffered more murders in one month than Belgrade had in a year. In 1992 Belgrade had 71 murders while Chicago had 941 with a population not much greater than Belgrade's. Tmusic explained that until 1992 Belgrade was a very safe city, with practically no crime. I knew that crimes against property and persons had always been low in the Communist countries, whether because "there was one informer for every four criminals" or because there was so much more equality and so much less contrast between the rich and the poor than in the Western countries.

CRIME STATISTICS AS REPORTED BY THE BELGRADE DISTRICT ATTORNEY

	1990	1991	1992	1993 (first 10 mos.)
Murder	31	53	71	51
Manslaughter	2	72	70	49
Suicide	115	115	115	115
Armed Robbery	57	113	216	357
Assault	22	13	20	9
Burglary	13	110	75	83
Rape	46	24	65	34
Including a number of other categories of minor crimes, the total number of crimes was:	1130	1100	1778	1423

The only figures in Tmusic's statistics that I had to protest were those for suicide. That they had been the same every year, and that even for the first ten months of 1993, the numbers so drastically contrasted with those I'd heard from Snezana Stoskovic at the Red Cross, made me suspicious. "Wait a minute," I said to him. "I heard at the Red Cross . . ." He anticipated me and interrupted: "They want to make a lot of publicity out of that. Some retired people who have nothing to eat or are sick."

"So there are two kinds of suicide?"

"If people die from not enough food or they die from sickness, it's hard to prove it's suicide. You have to consider your source, the Red Cross. We couldn't figure out whether those people killed themselves. And then so many times the reason is hidden. We don't know why people kill themselves."

"So what do you think is the basis of the Red Cross's estimate that every thirty-six hours an elderly person kills himself?"

"If you want to know my personal opinion, it is because of this electoral campaign coming up. They are blowing up these facts to damage the government. I can't say they're not correct, but we don't know anything about it because such suicides would not come to us."

"So you want me to believe that every year since 1990 except 1993 there were exactly 115 suicides and that for the first ten months of 1993 there were exactly 115 suicides, not more or less than 115."

"That's the figure I have. What can I say? But I can say that not only here but universally, fewer people commit suicide in hard times than in good times." That sounded like a generalization that confounded common sense, though social science often confounds common sense. Tmusic explained that people are less concerned with their emotional problems, which cause most suicides, in times of economic crisis. The fact that the suicide rate among blacks in the United States is lower than among whites, given their higher unemployment and generally more depressed economic conditions, might offer some validity to Tmusic's argument. The fact that American blacks tend toward greater violence against others in times of crisis, however, raises a question about that thesis, especially if one views black-on-black violence as a form of suicide.

About the elderly in Belgrade who I'd heard were committing suicide because they could no longer tolerate the economic crisis, Tmusic had nothing more to say. If it was true, he said, it contradicted the facts as he knew them, but he was inclined to doubt the figures the Red Cross was claiming.

I didn't doubt those figures, and it seemed to me that the nature of the crisis for the elderly might exceed previous economic crises. Several people had told me that conditions in Belgrade were worse than those under the Nazi occupation.

The rise in armed robbery and burglary over the last two years Tmusic attributed directly to economic conditions, but he insisted that most of it was done not by natives of Belgrade but by immigrants who had nothing and felt forced to rob. I asked him whether his burglary category included both businesses and homes. He laughed. "What is to steal in the businesses? The shelves are empty. And the banks are safe. I doubt if they have any money."

I told Tmusic that some of my Serbian friends in America had warned me before I came to Belgrade that the streets were dangerous. He laughed. "Well, maybe some Gypsy boy might steal a chain from your neck, or maybe steal your purse, but not enough for anyone to be scared about. Even with all the evil we have now, Belgrade is still much safer than most cities in Europe. But people here are sad because of even this street crime, because we never had that before. Anyone could go out at any time of the day or night and not worry. Now people worry, but it is not bad at all. It's like the priest who asked a man how his ailing wife was, and the man said, 'She's dying,' and the priest said, 'Oh, everybody's dying.' "

Such street crime was included in Tmusic's total figures, he said, along with drunkenness, domestic violence, forgery, and other crimes. "But we don't have much drunkenness, for instance. We are not Sweden," he said, laughing. But he added that though far fewer cars were being driven, the number of auto accidents was about the same as in previous years. "Maybe people are driving faster, or are more careless, or maybe there are more drunk drivers. We don't know. We have to do research."

One crime that had been increasing, Tmusic said, was auto theft, but he had no figures because this thievery was handled by local governing units—like boroughs or wards—of which there were sixteen in Belgrade. With so many cars permanently parked on the streets because of the shortage of gasoline, auto theft was much easier. On the other hand, with gas so hard to come by, it was surprising that auto theft had increased. In addition to local auto theft, Tmusic said, there were a lot of illegal cars in Belgrade, cars stolen in Bosnia and Croatia and brought to the city with forged papers.

I was impressed that there was so little assault, often the result of stress causing anger between people. I told Tmusic I was amazed that the hard conditions under which people were living had clearly not resulted in they're being more short-tempered and violent. "Yes," he said. "The only clear result of the conditions is the dramatic rise in armed robbery and burglary. That is because men come from the war with guns, and they are desperate. And we expect, after the war calms down, even more will be coming, especially the criminals who went to fight on their own. And others who weren't necessarily criminals but who, when they come back, will be overwrought, and they will get into trouble until they can calm down and live normal lives again. After a war you always get that. There are a lot of psychopathic personalities coming out of a war. And then too, Belgrade criminals who left here are coming back because we have this terrible black market. They think they can get rich with it."

I asked him whether his crime figures included economic crimes, arrests of black marketers. He said, soberly, "We don't arrest them. It is too much. It is everywhere. It is the economy. How could we arrest them?" I was reminded of Sonja Beserko and Gordana Logar's charges against the government that it was encouraging the black market. Was this reinforcement for their argument? On the other hand, there was no doubting Tmusic's comments. The black market was so pervasive in Belgrade that it would probably be impossible to make more than a small dent in it by arresting a few, just as it became impossible to control the black market in liquor during Prohibition in the U.S. and it is now impossible to control drug trafficking despite billions of dollars spent on it.

Any American reader living in any big city will be as astonished by the Belgrade crime figures as I was. The only thing that made them plausible to me was the fact that the district attorney's office had only thirty-five attorneys for a city of two million. By contrast, for the more than five million people in Cook County, of which Chicago accounts for a large part, in 1993 the state's attorney's office had more than nine hundred attorneys to prosecute the thousands of accused persons passing through the criminal justice system.

While Tmusic was out of the office attending to an emergency, I looked over his wall of bookshelves. It was lined with art books, all kinds, Western as well as Yugoslav, modern as well as classical. I said to him when he returned, "With so few crimes in your city, you have plenty of time to read your art books."

"Oh," he said softly, "that's my hobby, music and painting." I wondered how many district attorneys in the U.S. one could find who would share Tmusic's interests. I tended to think such interests would make him more humane in a job that he says is universally hated and feared. But I was reminded of Nazi officials who played Beethoven and Brahms in their concentration camp quarters.

The process of putting a person through the criminal justice system is essentially the same in Belgrade as in the U.S. and most Western countries. Tmusic suggested that "Sometimes we are accused of being less democratic than Western countries, but I can prove that we are more democratic in our criminal law. For instance, here not only police evidence is counted in the trial. A special investigative judge must make his own separate investigation of all the evidence. And the evidence must be very hard. In the U.S. police evidence is taken as proof. That is not very safe or fair to the accused person."

Though the 1990 constitution abolished the death penalty, Tmusic said, "that didn't work out, and we still have it, but it is rarely used." More often, the sentence for first-degree murder, the stiffest sentence on the books, is fifteen to twenty years. Sentences are based not only on the category of crime but also on the way the crime was committed. It is up to the judge. A particularly horrendous murder could get the death sentence.

I asked Tmusic how many people were now in prison. He didn't know but said the number had increased in the past year since Parliament had passed a law requiring that anyone carrying a gun illegally went direct to prison. And, he added, laughing heartily, "We don't have any political prisoners."

"No political prisoners," I said, "but you must have some categories of political crime."

"Political crime? Like what?" he wanted to know.

"Like what happened to Vuk Draskovic last spring."

"We treated him like any other hooligan," he said. "He damaged windows in the Federal Assembly Building. He damaged cars. He was a politician, it was supposed to be political [a demonstration], but he acted like a hooligan. In that melee a policeman was killed. That's some politics. But the opposition tried to tell the people and the Western press that he was roughed up because he was in the opposition. It was not because of his politics. It was what he did, the worst kind of hooliganism. And then what happened? You know, in medieval times, the ruler or the monarch had the right to pardon the person. Now we have the president who has that right. He said, 'We're not going to prosecute that man.' It was good politics."

"Was anyone accused of the murder of the policeman?"

"We couldn't find the person who did it. Vuk could have been accused as the leader, but he was pardoned."

"I presume you have a crime of treason."

"We still have such laws from the Tito regime. We have a law that says that a person can be prosecuted for trying to destroy the order of the state or giving aid to the enemy."

As Draga and I got up to leave, Tmusic said, "I want to send a message to my colleagues in the United States. I hope they will take more interest in the socialist countries, not only to help us but perhaps to give them more understanding. Americans think theirs is the only way. And lots of people here want to copy America, and Americans agree they should. Theirs is the best way. First we had the Russians who wanted us to copy them. Now we have the Americans."

From Tmusic's office, Draga and I drove a short distance to the Serbian Ministry of Health, located in a three-story stucco prewar building, where I was to interview Zojan Vlahovic, the deputy minister of health. In his dreary, dingy office, we met Zojan, a man of about forty, small, skinny, with bad teeth, glasses, a bad haircut, an ill-fitting suit, and an intense, unsmiling face. His salary had fallen from seventeen hundred dollars a month to thirty-two dollars. He was distraught over the statistics he had received from his staff to satisfy the questions I had posed to the Ministry of Information. He hadn't known how bad things were. "All our health statistics until last year were the same as in the developed countries. Now it is very different," he said.

In the first eight months of 1993, cases of contagious diseases such as tuberculosis and AIDS had increased 5 percent over 1992. In 1992, 68,770 people were afflicted with a contagious disease. In the first eight months of 1993, the number was already 72,210. In 1992, 49 people died of contagious diseases. For the first eight months of 1993 that figure was 154. There was a 22 percent increase in epidemics such as flu or food poisoning in the same time. Death rates had risen from 9.5 out of 100 in 1990 to 10.4 in the first eight months of 1993. "Our health services can no longer deal with the problems," Zojan said.

Infant mortality rates in Serbia had fallen dramatically in the eighties but were rising drastically again in 1993, a result of malnutrition and a shortage of equipment to handle premature babies and those born with defects. At the same time fewer babies were born in 1992 and 1993. Births had declined about 5 percent. Abortions declined as well. While abortion rates had been falling all over the developed world since the mid-eighties, there was a dramatic drop in Serbia in 1993, when there were 7.3 percent fewer abortions than the previous year. I commented to Zojan that I had not seen a single pregnant woman since I'd been in Belgrade.

"Yes, we recognize that. Fewer births, fewer abortions, no better contraception, maybe not even as good. It is not as easy to get pills or condoms or what you want. What does it mean? We have been talking about that with some experts and have decided that one of the consequences of these hard times is that people are not interested in sex. They have so much to do just to survive, and they have so much worry for themselves and for their children. They have no energy for it," Zojan said grimly.

"It is ironic. For years we fought to teach people contraception to cut down on the number of abortions. Now we have 'natural' protection. Less contraception, less sex, less abortion. The sanctions are achieving our aim. We would rather not have gotten our results this way."

Interestingly, Zojan said that the IUD contraceptive device, all but discredited in the States, was widely used in Belgrade. All contraceptive devices had been available, however, and cost nothing. "Before the sanctions we had plenty of them, whatever anyone wanted. But now we have none. If a woman can find it in a private pharmacy, she has to pay a lot of money," Zojan said.

"Since we have democracy, our health programs are much narrower. Before we had every kind of health care socialized. It was accessible to everybody and covered everything. The World Health Organization used us as a model because we had such good health coverage. Now our health care is a skeleton of what it was. People go to the doctor only when they are very sick. They put their health problems on a lower level after their existential problems. And we don't have equipment or medicines when people come to the doctor. And we know that people are suffering from all kinds of problems. The water supply is not as good. There is not enough food, or money to buy what there is. There is not enough heat. People suffer from great stress. With the first wave of cold weather, we had a great strain on the psychiatric hospital. Ten people died in that hospital because they had no heat. We are not publishing all these figures because they would be too upsetting to people."

Zojan, in a strained voice, then launched into a discussion of the sanctions. "They have nothing to do with politics, with the government. They are a direct attack on our people to reduce us to animals so that we can no longer function in the civilized world," he said.

On that harsh note we said our goodbyes, and Draga and I went to the Ministry of Information to see Maja, the foreign press officer, who had asked me to come by. We had been talking on the phone almost every day but hadn't met. She was a short, slender, dark, and attractive woman in her late twenties, with long flowing hair. She wore a miniskirt, a silk shirt, and high heels. Ushering me into the office, she brought some coffee and proceeded to ask for my impressions. Though I appreciated all her help, I was reluctant to talk with this foreign press officer for the government. I made some polite remarks, telling her I had enjoyed my stay and hoped to write about it when I got home. When she apologized for not having been able to arrange for an interview with Milosevic, I assured her that it was all right, that I hadn't really expected to get in to see him, having heard that he granted few interviews to the press.

Maja then brought out a pile of printed government materials that might help me better understand the situation in which Yugoslavia now found itself. I thanked her and we left.

I had to stop in at Mira's office to collect the money she had gotten from Meme for me. I tried to convince her to join Draga and me for dinner but she refused, saying she had too much work. Draga had agreed to let me take him to dinner. He had refused to take any compensation for what he had done for me, refusing even to let me pay for some of the petrol he had used to drive me all over the city. I knew he hadn't worked in many weeks, and I had offered him money as delicately as I could, not wanting to insult what had developed into a fond relationship. We went to a favorite restaurant of his, a huge lower-level place off Skardarlija. There were only two other customers. He ordered a bean dish for me that he said was one of the house specialties. A big bowl of beans and sausage, wonderfully flavored but oh so heavy. I promised myself that on my first night home I would go to my favorite Japanese restaurant.

25 It was the long way around to *Vreme*'s office. The street was easy to find, just off the Avenue of the Rulers, only a few blocks from my hotel. I have to pause here for a moment of wild speculation on that name, Avenue of the Serbian Rulers—Ulica Srpskih Vladara—renamed in the frenzy of anti-Tito feeling, from Marsala Tito (Marshal Tito Boulevard). This is the main street through central Belgrade, a long, wide boulevard lined with cafés, some of them with outdoor patios, restaurants, nightclubs, large and small shops, office buildings, historical sites, the beautiful nineteenth-century Moskva Hotel, and parks. On it is the tallest building in Belgrade—twenty-nine stories. Down its center run the old trams that are now the major means of transportation in the city. It is always crowded with people window shopping or busily on their way somewhere, black market peddlers and their customers, and little groups of people just standing and talking or eating a delicacy from one of the food stands. Clearly the name had to be changed, just as Leningrad had to be changed and statues of the hated Communist leaders had to be torn down and street names changed throughout the Soviet Union and Eastern Europe. But Avenue of the Serbian Rulers?

Without having talked to those who were responsible for the name, it seemed to me to signify that there were all too few rulers of Serbia who were unequivocally beloved: Stepan Dusan, going back to the fourteenth century, who gave the country its law, or Karadjordje, who staged the first revolt against the Turks in 1804. But since then the chaos that for so long characterized Serbian life under foreign occupation, with only brief periods of independence, meant that battles over the governing of the country have been long and terrible, with a long and continuing rivalry between the Karadjordjevic and the Obrenovic dynasties. The Serbs could have gone back to the early sainted leaders to name their main street, but instead they settled on a tribute to all the rulers in a completely political gesture by whatever committee was responsible for this renaming. Decision by committee! No insult intended to anyone, they said in effect, but this is the best we can do given our rather bitter history. So we came up with this slightly foolish name, like the pretentious Avenue of the Americas in New York City, instead of the plain old Sixth Avenue it was for so many years.

Walking down Naradnog Fronta (People's Front), which runs on a diagonal from Srpskih Vladara, I looked for the offices of *Vreme* at 45. I walked the length of the street on one side, then back the length of the street on the other side, about five blocks each way, looking for the number on one of the old houses in the street until I discovered that the building that housed *Vreme* was just beyond the corner where I had started. The street numbering in Belgrade leaves something to be desired, as it does in so many ancient cities in Europe. And I had expected that the magazine would be housed in an old building, nothing like what I found, a newer building that also housed a nightclub and a theatre. After I found someone in a tobacco shop on the ground floor who spoke English, it was easy to find the offices on the third floor.

No drama here, just a busy and drab editorial office. The offices didn't look like the magazine was being well financed by the Western powers, as Ljila Pavlovic had claimed. They were small, crowded, and barren-looking, with old used furniture. The computers were not particularly new or high-tech, just little old computers like the one on my desk at home, or like I'd seen in the offices of the journalists in Prague, who were also operating on a shoestring. On the floor just inside the door were packages of returns, issues that hadn't been sold. I counted about two hundred—normal returns, not the thousands I expected from Ljila's remarks that *Vreme* didn't sell many copies.

Petar had said he would introduce me to his staff and spend more time with me. I had a few questions for him. But the editor was away, and Petar was in charge and very busy. He took me into his office, sat me down across the desk, and riffled through papers while we talked. I told him of Ljila's assertion about *Vreme*'s funding sources. "My God," he said, "we're barely surviving. We got help with newsprint a couple of times from Soros. That's all."

I asked Petar to clarify the status of the media in the country. I hadn't been able to figure out exactly what was owned by the state and what was independent. Petar told me, "The Socialist party does not actually involve itself in the management of the papers, but they exert control through their people there who are very supportive of the party. There is no official censorship, but you can read the political comments and figure out on what side they are."

"Just like everywhere else in the world," I said.

"Yes, the editor is in charge. He sets the policy. Like any newspaper in the world! But the government gives to the papers that support it tax breaks that the rest of us don't get."

"I had the impression that *Politika* was actually owned by the state. Am I wrong?"

"It's not clear, really. The question of property in this country is not clear. The most famous scientist couldn't figure out what belongs to whom. For about forty years nothing belonged to anybody. It doesn't belong to the workers, not to anyone. We were calling it society's property, the people's property. In the transformation now, it's all very unclear. So the question of *Politika* is also very unclear. Some people believe it belongs to the workers. Some people believe it belongs to the state because the government gives it money in the form of not having to pay taxes. *Borba* and *Vreme* have to pay the taxes, so we are completely independent."

That no one, in fact, owned any property accounted for so much crumbling real estate and infrastructure in the city. No one was in charge of repairing and maintaining it.

I asked Petar whether Serbia had made the same effort as did the Czech Republic and Hungary to sell stock in state property. "Three years ago, when Ante Markovic was prime minister, he started that kind of privatization system, but the Milosevic government realized that if they let all the big industries go on the open market in stocks, they would lose control, so they stopped it. They let it go on only for small factories, small enterprises. But the big systems, the post office, the electric company, are state owned." The public utilities in many countries are state owned, I pointed out. "Yes, but now everything is in limbo. The government says that with the sanctions it's not a good time. There is no economy anyway, so how can we talk about transformation to private enterprise?"

I told Petar I had been with Mira the night before while she drove around the city in search of cigarettes. She refused to buy on the black market, so she kept going into stores that she knew sometimes had them. She found none. She finally exclaimed, "How can he [Milosevic] do this to us?" I asked Petar whether he thought there was anything Milosevic could do about the economic situation.

"Does she think he doesn't know what's going on?" he angrily shouted. "Of course he does! He is doing exactly what he wants to do. Whatever is happening here is the result of his policies. This regime is completely criminal. From the top to the bottom. He dictates what we have."

"Do you think the shortages are phony?"

"No, they are real. You can buy some things, but at what prices? My father's pension last month was one deutsche mark, a half a dollar."

"What is Milosevic's motive? What can he gain by bringing down this state?"

"I don't think he wants to bring down the state. You have to go back to the beginning. He wanted to be a big hero in Serbian history. He wanted to put all the Serbs in one state, make a big, big state. He used everything he could. He used communism, then he used nationalism, then he used the war. He accused the international community of making the war. He used peacemaking. He used inflation. Now he's using the economic situation to put pressure on us so that he can be in charge. He is simply an egomaniac. A sick mind. And a lot of people don't know who Milosevic is. He is very intelligent, very sharp. He never tells what he really thinks. He changes his mind every day. A political chameleon. I wouldn't be surprised if one day he would say, 'I've always been for peace. I never wanted the war.' Just anything. He enjoys power. And that is very dangerous. But he doesn't want to privatize the economy. Because the market economy makes people too liberal, too independent. So he is keeping the socialized economy going, with millions of workers receiving much bigger salaries than mine for doing nothing. And they are being paid to support the regime. They can say, 'Okay, he's bad, but we support him because he keeps us going.' So everything here is being destroyed."

I was torn. I was perfectly willing to accept Petar's judgment that Milosevic was an egomaniac, a sick mind who would use any means to maintain his power. But another part of me was saying that Milosevic had simply gotten in over his head and didn't know what to do. Was he the brilliant man that some people insisted he was, or was he simply a muddling fool who was bringing his society down around him?

"I keep saying to myself that the people are going to wake up and realize what is going on," I said to Petar.

"Never! Not as long as he is paying them some money. They are sitting and waiting for the cataclysm."

Petar had to go just at the moment when I was about to ask him why he thought the Serbs would sit and wait for the cataclysm. He insisted that his hypothetical worker knew that Milosevic was "bad" but was unwilling to withdraw his support because he was earning enough money to get by. But no one in this society was earning more than subsistence after years of being very comfortable. It didn't make sense unless the people nourished within them the concept that their destiny was to suffer. On the other hand, it did make sense that Milosevic had convinced the people that not he but the international community was responsible for their plight. And to some extent that was true. Certainly the international community was punishing Milosevic—read Serbia and Montenegro—excessively for crimes that were shared by Bosnia Herzegovina and Croatia, though much of the initial inspiration for those crimes could be laid at Milosevic's door. But it was far too simplistic to say that all the blame for the crisis enveloping Yugoslavia could be attributed to one man, regardless of his lust for power, any more than one can lay the blame for Germany's crimes purely on Hitler. His lust for power was shared by many of his countrymen, and his ravings fell on extraordinarily fertile soil. Milosevic's lust for power was met equally by Franjo Tudjman's and Alija Izetbegovic's, and their combined nationalist ravings fell on fertile soil.

Petar's view of Milosevic as the devil incarnate might be accurate, but it seemed more rational to believe that Milosevic's efforts to manipulate the society for his own power purposes had gotten out of hand, that the main reason he wasn't talking to the press was because he didn't know what to say, that he was overwhelmed. He had indeed used communism, nationalism, and a war, and he had been overcome by the consequences. But all this was, just as Petar's comments were, mere speculation. His detractors called him a crazy egomaniac, and his supporters said he was the victim of the international community's hatred of Yugoslavia. Only future historians would figure it out.

In the weeks after I'd talked to the dissidents in Belgrade—Petar, Gordana Logar, Sonja Biserko, Slobodan Nakarada—I had been so inundated by the stories of others that I had almost forgotten the intensity of the feelings of those dissidents. Listening to Petar's angry comments refreshed my memories. As I thought about them, it seemed to me that in a sense they represented the archetype of the victim mentality, a concept the dissidents dismissed as foolishness.

Their rage at the government grew out of their idealism, out of their hopes for a post-Communist society, a liberal democracy that would take its place in the Western community and in which they would participate as patriots of their country but also as citizens of the world. Instead of liberal democracy, their country had been plunged into war and into disgrace in the eyes of the international community they had aspired to join. I sensed that their world-weariness combined with a harsh fury had replaced a vibrant energy fueled by hope.

These dissidents had not shared their countrymen's belief in their destiny to suffer. They had rejected the mystique of victimhood, the legends of Kosovo. But here they were, a few short years later, seeing their country as the victim of an evil ruler and their fellow citizens as victims of stupidity and inertia, unable to see the complexity of the situation and unable to analyze it in any objective way, caught up in their disappointment and consequent rage.

American society has always had a sizable critical element. In both world wars men went to jail rather than fight what they considered immoral wars. Newspapers and little magazines were always around to criticize the government. Independent, dissident candidates regularly stood for election. And there was a long tradition of antigovernment actions of all kinds, some of which were bloody.

By contrast, for fifty years there had been only the faintest stirrings of criticism of the regime in Yugoslavia, only an occasional dissident who was easily quashed. Only quiet hope was nourished in the breasts of many, along with the feeling that it was their destiny to suffer. When at last they were free to criticize the government, it was with a vengeance that knew no bounds. They hadn't planned it that way. They hadn't imagined it that way. They had imagined a society in which their right to criticize would be respected, and in which they would, from time to time, question the government's policies. To be so engrossed in attacking the government was not part of their plans. But the government had disappointed them, as had their fellow citizens who supported the government, who had willingly gone to fight in an immoral, unnecessary war brought on by their leaders' lust for power. So these dissidents were perhaps the truest victims, in the psychological sense, of the unholy conflagration that had gripped their country.

Perhaps the idealists in the Communist countries suffered more than others when the dreams they cherished for so many years, encouraged by the Western world, proved to be scarcely more than dreams, when they were confronted with massive disorganization and unemployment, fierce nationalist struggles, war, and finally, in some places, the reinstallation of their former enemies, the Communists, now calling themselves reformed socialists.

One of those idealists who continued to plow along, seemingly undismayed by real events, was the portly Ljuba Tadic, now in his seventies, with a great head of white hair and a ruddy, kindly, smiling face. When we talked he was wearing an old crumpled pair of slacks and a cardigan sweater over an old shirt. Ljuba hadn't had a steady job since 1975 when he was expelled with others on the faculty of the

University of Belgrade, where he'd been professor of political philosophy, because of his political activities.

Ljuba's political activities were chiefly concerned with the publication of *Praxis*, the organ of a small group of dissidents called the Praxis Group, founded in 1964. *Praxis* was a widely read international intellectual journal with contributors from around the world, expounding left-liberal ideas for the economic and social democratization of the Communist countries as well as for the Western countries. While it was anti-Stalinist, it supported democratic socialism. In 1968, stimulated by the Praxis Group, other ferment in the society, and the rebellion of the young throughout the Western world, a large student demonstration in Belgrade matched those in the European capitals, the U.S., and the Prague Spring. In Zagreb the movement took an unfortunate turn and developed into a nationalist movement for which the Croatian members of the Praxis Group were purged from government jobs and the university. In Belgrade, meanwhile, demonstrators were jailed for the crime of "free thinking," Ljuba said, and many students were later expelled from the university. Some served as many as three years in jail. Eight faculty who had been involved with Praxis were fired. "Our authoritarian Communist rulers, though nominally anti-Stalinist, did not like our movement at all," Ljuba told me. "They used to call us Western agents and such names."

Praxis came to an end in 1975 when, after more than ten years of happily printing the journal, the printers issued a statement that as a self-managed company they had decided they no longer wished to print it, no doubt on orders from Tito. The movement continued, but the possibility of its supporters being jailed increased, frightening people away. Passports were seized and there was general harassment. Only the intervention of Western intellectuals, including Herbert Marcuse, Jurgen Habermas, Heinrich Böll, and others, including students, prevented the imprisonment of Ljuba and other Praxis leaders.

In reaction to the government's harassment, the group established a Board for the Defense of Thinking and Expression, with Dobrica Cosic, one of Yugoslavia's best-known writers as its nominal chairman. "Our task," Ljuba explained, "was to spite the regime and to fight for freedom of expression. We wrote petitions. We protested when Alija Izetbegovic was arrested [for publishing his Islamic tract], when Croat or Albanian nationalists were arrested on the grounds of what the government called 'delinquency of thinking.' "

While dissidents in the early and mid-seventies had suffered considerable harassment and even imprisonment, their influence on the regime was inestimable. Following the student demonstrations and the influence of the Praxis Group, Yugoslavia became a much more democratic state with far greater freedom of the press and of speech—as long as one didn't criticize Tito or communism—many more international cultural and scientific exchanges, and the introduction of limited private enterprise.

Out of the Praxis Group emerged the Serbian-Jewish Friendship Society, where we were meeting that day, under the quiet eye once again of Ljiljana and with Ileana Cosic translating. Ljuba was the current president of the society. He was not Jewish, but many of his colleagues in Praxis were. Most of the Praxis Group were now members of the society.

After he was fired from the university, Ljuba had regularly done research at the Institute for Philosophy, part of the university, and was currently at work on a project called "Language and Rationality," for which he was in charge of one section concerned with the relationship between rhetoric and philosophy. The project would eventuate in a series of books. He had also spent a number of years teaching abroad, in Prague, in France, and in Germany, and had published several books in political philosophy.

I asked Ljuba whether he had a theory to explain the rise of nationalism around the world in recent years, after almost a century in which nationalism had been virtually absent from the world. Ljuba said, "Nationalism here is just a continuation of what occurred in the Second World War. I think your perception is peculiarly American. Actually, there has always been in Europe a great deal of nationalism, but it is not open, it is not discussed. For instance, the English turn a blind eye to what's going on in Ulster. Instead they point to nationalism in Serbia. In Corsica, in France, in Spain, the Basques are considered mere hysterics. But the U.S. throws all the blame on us for nationalism, which is very easy for them because they are the masters of the world."

I suggested that perhaps the growth of nationalism resulted from the decline of religion and the rise of a materialism that did not satisfy people's spiritual needs. Perhaps people had turned to nationalism as a substitute for religion or, as in the case of the Muslims, a return to religion that included nationalism.

"This turn was at first good," Ljuba said, "because it satisfied people's basic needs, but now we have reached a regressive stage of all this progress. Now it is destructive of everything—the environment, people's inner lives, everything."

Ljuba was still a dissident, a member of the Democratic party that criticized Milosevic, but he had little sympathy for the current crop of younger dissidents who held Milosevic responsible for all of Serbia's troubles, who saw Milosevic as evil incarnate. "He is a politician who does not hold democracy very close to his heart." Ljuba said. "We, however, don't support the opinion in the West that he is an assassin. We consider him a product of the general Yugoslav process of the last twenty years. He is from the same political environment as Mr. Tudjman and Mr. Izetbegovic. In the Western world, particularly in the United States, Milosevic is satanized, but Tudjman and Izetbegovic are viewed as democrats. That is preposterous. Mr. Tudjman is an intimate enemy of all kinds of democracy. He is an extreme chauvinist and anti-Semite. He has shown that in his book. Mr. Izetbegovic is an Islamic fundamentalist. I am very familiar with his ideas. I have read very carefully everything he has written. I personally defended his right to speak, but he is certainly no democrat.

"I don't see how Milosevic could be beaten by anyone else. He is so unjustly attacked by the West that our people support him. This is an indirect effect of the sanctions. Now, what I am about to say is fully rational and not emotional at all: we feel that these sanctions are not just at all, and the Western powers do not want to admit they were wrong when they accused the Serbs of being aggressors. What we have going on is a civil war, but still the West continues to accuse the Serbs of being the aggressors. Look at the city of Mostar now! You have a war there between the Muslims and the Croatians, a savage fight, and no reactions from the Western world. What are we to think of that?"

26 Ljubomir Madzar was also a dissident with a more benign view of the world than the younger upstarts. He was a free-trade economist on the faculty of the university who had served in Milan Panic's government and had little use for Milosevic and his government. A beanpole of a man in his sixties, with sparse, greying hair, Ljubomir put off meeting me as long as possible to enable him to work on his book while the weather was still warm. He feared his hands would not allow him to write well when the cold weather arrived and his home and office were without heat. Finally, only a few days before I was to leave, he agreed to meet me. The temperature had fallen into the upper thirties, unseasonably cold for Yugoslavs who enjoy a temperate climate. Ljubomir suggested the Press Club, but, classic academic that he was, slightly abstracted, it didn't occur to him that the dining room, where he expected we would talk, was limited to members and their guests. He wasn't a member. He was at a loss. I finally found us a place to sit in front of a computer in the press room. Every other available space was busy. We were asked to move a couple of times as reporters came in to use the computer.

I asked Ljubomir about the economy as it had been for the past fifty years and still was essentially. For instance, I wondered whether agriculture had been collectivized as it had been in the Soviet Union. "It was at the very beginning. In 1946 there was a large move toward nationalizing the land, but by the end of about 1951 it was quite clear that it wasn't going to work, that it was going to be a disaster. The government gave up and more or less gave the land back to the peasants," he told me in his precise English.

"Did this happen because of greater resistance by the peasants here, or because Tito wasn't willing to use the tactics that Stalin used?"

"It didn't work anywhere, that was clear, and Yugoslav politicians were more pragmatic than the Soviets. By that time they were already quarreling with the Soviet Union, so they were inspired to make big breaks with the Soviet regime. They found this was a very nice way of departing from the Soviets without really jeopardizing their own power."

"So the market economy in agriculture has always prevailed here."

"Yes, except for a few distortions. For instance, the government had a monopoly on purchasing staple farm products, so it was basically a market economy without certain segments of the market such as private wholesalers. Also missing was a capital market, which is necessary to agriculture but absolutely unacceptable from a Marxist point of view."

"When American money began to pour into this country... when was that exactly?"

"In the early fifties. The break with the Soviet Union came in 1948, and it took about two years for Yugoslavia to readjust and for the United States to realize that something had happened in Yugoslavia that apparently should be supported."

"What did that aid consist of?"

"It was versatile. Much of it came in goods. Wheat was one of the basic products given to Yugoslavia. But then also a lot of armaments, heavy artillery, and trucks. And also currency. Between 1952 and 1960 that aid amounted to about 7 percent of our GNP, an awful lot."

"I don't understand why the U.S. had to give the country wheat. Vojvodina is a huge breadbasket, isn't it?"

"Yes, but in those years we had severe droughts. In those years every other year was very bad for agriculture. But also, agriculture was not yet mechanized, it was mostly a very backward activity that couldn't supply enough food for the country. Most important, because the peasants were not in harmony with the regime, the agricultural policies adopted by the regime were inimical to production. First, the government paid very low prices, so that the peasants earned less than half what nonagricultural workers were earning. Second, they limited the amount of land a peasant could own, only about twenty-five acres, which limited production because on such a small piece of land you couldn't use the best productive methods.

"Later the policy loosened up and became more amicable toward the peasants in an effort to improve agricultural output. At the same time the peasants proved to be very efficient despite the negative policies. They worked hard, they saved a lot, and they bought a lot of equipment, so that by 1980 Yugoslav agriculture had become one of the most mechanized agricultures in Europe. Because the constraint on the amount of land they could own remained until 1989, we had a lot of small peasants, each of whom wanted his own tractor and other machinery. As a consequence, from a strictly economic point of view we had much more machinery than we needed."

"Now we come to the nineties." I said. "I have the impression that Yugoslavia is not producing enough food for itself."

"I think that's not true. This smaller Yugoslavia is definitely producing more food than it needs. Remember, we still have the Fertile Plain in northern Vojvodina, which by itself can produce more food than all the old Yugoslavia needed. Even this year, with a severe drought, we produced more than we needed. But there is a problem. The peasants, in order to supply food for the cities, must get something in exchange—like fertilizers, other commodities. The problem is that in nonagricultural sectors production went down drastically, and we are unable to exchange with the peasants. The peasants will not give their products for free to us who don't produce."

"I heard that the government is buying from the peasants at very low prices."

"That's true, and the peasants are not happy, but they are not forced to sell. They can deposit their wheat, for instance, in big silos, and it can be kept for them there without any obligation to sell it. So, many peasants have just refused to sell. I don't know what future developments will be. There may be even greater problems as the nonagriculture sector grows worse. If the state takes the wheat by force, that will have disastrous consequences for future production, because then nobody will be willing to produce."

I wondered how much actual private enterprise there was in Yugoslavia by comparison with 1980. "Since 1980 we have much more private enterprise in the nonagriculture sector. About 14 percent of the assets are now privately owned. The rest is still under social ownership."

What about the process of selling stock in industry in order to achieve private ownership? "In the beginning it was very successful. In 1990 and the first half of 1991, before the war, there was very good momentum. Then the war interrupted. It is still going on, but much slower. I suppose that the Czech Republic and Hungary have surpassed us now because of the difficulties we face with the war and the sanctions. But before that we were ahead of them."

"The problem in the Czech Republic, with which I have some intimate knowledge," I said, "is that so much of the industry is so obsolete that what is being sold isn't worth very much. Is that also a problem here?"

"Well, one has to distinguish between the quality and work of the enterprises and the rate at which they are being sold. You can sell anything if the price is right. So Czechs have adopted a system of privatizing by giving away for free. They have this voucher system. I don't know their latest figures, but I hear reports they have done very well. And they have also been able to attract a little bit of foreign capital, which helps a lot. That goes for the Hungarians as well. Which is not true of Yugoslavia. Because of the war and the uncertainty, nobody is willing to put any money here."

"But you don't have a voucher system, do you?"

"No, we have a very peculiar system based on shares of companies purchased by the workers. Because we had social ownership and self-management, and not state ownership, the state was not allowed to sell social property. Those assets belonged to everybody and nobody at the same time. The sole authority to sell came from the self-management organs—factories and businesses and so on. That put a severe constraint on the privatization process. It had to be designed so that the self-management organs were willing to sell. If they don't, there is no privatization. So the way it was done was to see that the workers received real benefits. What was done was to offer huge discounts on shares of stock. For instance, if a worker bought a hundred shares and put his money in, he would get up to seventy more shares free. The discount was 30 percent plus one percentage point for each year of employment."

I asked Ljubomir if industry in Yugoslavia was fairly modern or as obsolete as it was in the Czech Republic and other former Iron Curtain countries. "Yugoslavia had one of the highest rates of economic investment in the world. A lot of modern equipment has been purchased. I wouldn't say we were always able to get the most modern technology, but it was far above the economies of East European countries, somewhat behind the Western countries, somewhere in between, but closer to the West than the East."

I told Ljubomir of visiting in Prague the typesetting shop of the biggest newspaper there and being shocked to discover equipment I hadn't seen in the U.S. since the early sixties—hot-metal linotype machines. In Belgrade I had called the typesetting shop of *Politika* to ask how they set type and was told it was all computerized. "Yes," Ljubomir said, "it is all advanced technology. The graphics industry has also been modernizing its technology. As a matter of fact, we have a lot of small print shops that have the most advanced technology and can save a lot of money."

"How much of all this modernization has been financed by Western capital?" I asked.

"Well, I have to explain, we had several sources of income. A lot of Yugoslav workers went to Europe, mostly to West Germany, to work and sent back money. Remittances in some years amounted to $3.5 or $4 billion dollars, a huge amount by Yugoslav standards. That was one source. Another one was loans—petrol dollars made it easy to get credit in the West. The World Bank and the International

Monetary Fund were also active and gave us a series of loans."

"It is my impression that those loans kept being refinanced and were not paid back."

"That was true to some extent, but by 1989, the last normal year, they were being serviced pretty well. There was a lot of pressure from the IMF, and domestic policy after about 1985 was based on servicing those loans, not only those by the IMF and the World Bank but also those of commercial banks."

"So the problems of the economy in the late 1980s were partly the result of having to pay off those loans?"

"Partly yes. There were several layers of causative factors. We had a tremendous drain on our resources to service those loans. But it was mostly the consequence of an irrational economic system that was not based on markets and property, so I think we share this malaise with Eastern Europe for not having a proper private enterprise system with proper incentives. This is the basic reason. Also, much in our development policy was opportunistic in the sense of having high rates of growth for a limited time while simultaneously preparing a slowdown in the growth process for some future period. You have a high rate of growth in the short run, but then you exhaust the resources. You incur more foreign debt than you can properly service. The government wanted to achieve good results in the short run, to look good, but then they had to pay later. They invested in consumer goods that were not capital intensive, for instance, and neglected infrastructure. You can go for a couple of years by neglecting your infrastructure, but sooner or later, it catches up with you."

"So what you're saying is that while in theory the self-management system is good . . ."

"No, it is a very bad system."

"Why?"

"Well, take the example of how, under capitalism, a company, in response to a rise in the price of its product, would increase production. Under self-management the contrary happens. When the price increases, it's assumed that sales will decline, so production is decreased. Again, under capitalism, when there is uncertainty in the market, a normal firm reduces production. Under self-management, uncertainty results in increasing employment and output." To avoid uncertainty and scarcity, the least employable people are given jobs.

"One of the Serbian-American economists I read said that the theory of self-management was good, but it was corrupted by party control, that it never got a chance to function properly."

"To be honest, there are quite a few people who believe that. I can only tell you my personal opinion. Let me amend my statement to say that our system worked better than the systems of the East European countries because it was a decentralized system with much more freedom and autonomy for the firms. Many people will agree that efficiency depends on the amount of freedom that is built into the system. So from that point of view, this was a superior system to those in Eastern Europe, and I believe it would be easy to demonstrate that it performed better than those systems."

"To change the subject," I said, "at this point, when 75 percent of the budget is devoted to the army and the war . . ."

"That is a misunderstanding. The actual fact is that 75 percent of the *federal* budget—which is just one budget and is not the biggest one—goes for the army, and that amounts to about 8 percent of our GNP. The war is something else. The war is being fought in Bosnia Herzegovina and in Croatia, and not here. This is just for the maintenance of the army."

"But the armies of the Bosnian Serbs and the Serbs in the Krajina are probably being financed from here."

"That's a tricky question. No figures are available. I can't confirm that. But I wouldn't refute it, either. Remember, I was a member of Panic's government, but I still didn't know. These are decisions made very high up and not shared. To be honest, the way I see it, and as far as I can see it, it is hard for me to imagine that the Bosnian Serbs and the Serbs in Krajina could go on fighting the war with financing only from their own resources. But I don't know the facts. I am certain, though, that the federal budget to maintain the army is used only for that purpose—to pay salaries and feed and house the soldiers and maintain equipment. But there might be other money being used for the war that I don't know about. if there is money being used for that purpose, it is above the 75 percent for the army."

I returned to history. "I've been told by several people that the reason the embargo has been so fatal is because Tito moved the manufacturing facilities that were in Serbia before World War II—those that were not destroyed—to Slovenia and Croatia, in order to build those republics and deemphasize Serbian influence. Is that true?"

"It is not."

"It's not? It didn't make a lot of sense to me. It didn't seem reasonable to move factories for that purpose, but some people are convinced that happened. Normally you would move factories to save money, as in the U.S. they move factories to the southern part of the country or abroad because labor is cheaper. But this was a socialized economy, and motives might have been different."

"A number of factories *were* actually moved, but they were not moved only out of Serbia into Slovenia or Croatia. That kind of nonsense nobody would do. There has been a big research project on that, and the research concluded that there was no systematic movement of factories at the expense of any republic. So this is just Serbian nationalist propaganda. They want to prove that Serbia was oppressed and exploited like that, but it's not true."

What about the effects of the embargo on the economy, I wondered. "It's my impression that the economy was in bad enough shape that the disaster might have happened anyhow."

"That is correct," Ljubomir said. "I share your opinion, because the unfavorable downward trends began in the early 1980s. There was almost ten years of unfavorable economic performance before the war broke out. The irrational, ineffective economic system was demonstrating its weaknesses before this new turmoil happened. The next factor was the falling apart of Yugoslavia, which was a great economic shock to the system with the severing of economic ties between different parts of the country. Many factories were cooperating with each other across boundaries, supplying each other with all kinds of components and all that. Severing these ties caused immeasurable damage quite independent of the sanctions. And the war itself caused a lot of trouble not only in Bosnia and Croatia but also in Serbia and Montenegro. There are many refugees who must be accommodated. Our resources are being stretched to the limit, and on top of that we have the embargo. It is just one factor, but it is biting now very unpleasantly, and I don't know how it will end. It is very bad indeed."

"Do you see this society putting itself back together again? Do you see the possibility that a free-enterprise system can emerge and function within the next twenty-five years?"

"Oh yes. It is inevitable. I don't see any alternative in the long run. Certainly there will be a free enterprise system because these are the planetary trends and nobody will be able to escape those trends, fortunately."

"What I meant was, do you think the economy, with all its poor billionaires walking around, will be able to rebuild, or will it be another third world country?"

"Well, there are many third world countries that have become developed and prosperous. Yes, I believe that in the long run this country will be able to organize itself and develop, but before that there will be very trying times, very difficult times, and these will have to be overcome. I don't know how long it will take, perhaps only a couple of years. But this political situation will have to be settled, and once we are stabilized politically, I think the economy will be able to make a start. There will probably be some kind of international assistance and support, because I believe it is in the world's interest to have a stable and prosperous state here. If we are poor, we will be restless and there will be trouble."

"You were in Panic's government, so I assume you are opposed to Milosevic's policies."

"Yes, I am in the opposition."

"Do you belong to a party?"

"I was vice-president of the Reformist party, which was initiated by Ante Markovic, the former prime minister. I was active for about a year, and I decided I had spent enough time in politics with no results, and I don't like being busy with activities that have no results. In the meantime, some friends with whom I worked went abroad, so I was more alone. But the main reason I withdrew was because I did not go into politics for good. I never intended to stay there. I simply wanted to jump in during this transitory period and help the new democratic system if I could, and then I would come back to my professorial work. So that was my plan, but I concluded there was little hope to make any breakthrough, so I left."

"Do you believe Milosevic is encouraging the black market?"

"No, I don't believe he even thinks about it. Indirectly he is helping it by printing a lot of money and by allowing his government to control prices severely. Inadvertently he might be developing the situation that is favorable for a black market, but I don't think he is doing it deliberately."

"Could he take any measures that would make the situation better?"

"If I were to advise the creators of our economic policies, I would first of all tell the government not to interfere with the economy, because by doing so it makes it still worse. Second, I would liberalize the private financial sector. In short, I would introduce the same program that Yeltsin introduced in Russia—free trade for everything and anything. That would help a lot. But the main thing—and that has tremendous political implications—is a drastic cut in public expenditures."

"Pensions and so on, you mean?"

"I mean a lot of money that goes to the army and to maintaining unprofitable public enterprises. I mean the money that is being paid to workers who don't do anything, who don't produce anything—huge outlays that are absolutely destructive from the point of view of the economy. They would have to be cut in order to stop printing such huge quantities of money. We have to curb inflation, because with this inflation we're going to perish."

"But if you stop paying the wages of all the people who are out of jobs because of the sanctions, it would be like Poland, with millions and millions of unemployed. The result of that was that they voted the Communists back into power."

"Among those people who are being paid by the state are many who shouldn't be. Much of that money is being given whether one asks for it or not. So I would stop that and say, those who are unable to help themselves—and I would underline *unable*—let them ask and we will see how much we can give them. This is one thing. Another way the government is subsidizing the population is by having these ridiculously low prices for staple foods. This is crazy. Why should the government subsidize me? There are those who are even poorer than me. Why should I pay for bread at a price which is about a third of the cost of production? Let prices rise to cover the cost of production, which would then mean that the government would not have to cover the losses of bakeries and other firms. Those who could not afford to pay normal prices would go to the government for help. And I would see to it that all those who receive state money know—and their communities know—that they are social cases, that they are unable to provide for themselves. So everyone who asks the government for money should feel uneasy. The general slogan should be the American one," Ljubomir said, laughing, " 'Don't ask what the government can do for you, but what you can do for the government.' "

"And you don't think the government should do anything about the black market?"

"The only reasonable thing to do is liberalize it and say, 'You are free to do what you have been doing anyway.' "

"So you consider it free enterprise when someone goes to Budapest and buys five hundred dollars' worth of goods and comes back and sells them?"

"I consider it a patriotic act. This is a way of alleviating the situation. If it were not for all those people who went to Romania and Hungary and brought in those commodities, we would have died."

Finally, I asked, "What were unemployment figures before the embargo?"

"About 12 percent. There were tremendous regional variations. In Kosovo it was 35 percent. In Slovenia it was below 8 percent. As a matter of fact, for many years Slovenia had the lowest unemployment rates in Europe."

After hearing so many stories and reading so many accounts of the Yugoslav economy, I finally had a factual account I felt I could trust. This was partly because Ljubomir inadvertently verified my impressions that while Tito's self-management economy had had severe defects, it had been not much more defective than the capitalist economies. With some changes in the system, it might have been a more humane and efficient system than the capitalist system. Ljubomir also confirmed my impression that the free-trade economists in Eastern Europe, among whom he was one of the more eminent, were taking their lessons not from the liberal humanists in the West but from those Western economists whose interests favored the rich at the expense of people who were unable to compete in the complex global economy that had developed in the last thirty years.

27 At seventy-two, paunchy, with a thick head of white hair and crossed eyes that seemed to wander in a daze, Dobrica Cosic was a highly complex man who should not have had any label attached to him. But his was one of the strongest voices against the government. When Ljiljana told me she could arrange an interview with him, I was thrilled. He was called "the spiritual father of the Serbs" because his novels and other works had ignited the reawakening of Serbian nationalism. At one time he had gloried in that title. On the strength of his national reputation as a writer and his works on Serbian history, he had been elected to Parliament and then elected president by the Yugoslav Parliament in

1992 after the secessions of the various republics. But less than a year later he was deposed when Milosevic engineered a vote of no confidence after Cosic had shown his marked disfavor of Milosevic's policies. Milosevic no longer wanted Cosic representing Yugoslavia in the halls of Geneva. He was too conciliatory. And Milosevic could not take Cosic's outspoken criticism. Now, Dobrica told me emphatically, "I am not the spiritual father of the Serbs. All I was asking for was equality of treatment—democratic equality, not war. I am an opponent of the government and of the opposition too."

It was Dobrica Cosic who was the main source of "enlightenment" to the Serbs about what he described as the discrimination practiced against them by Tito. It was Dobrica who reminded the Serbs of their long history of oppression. And he spoke with great authority. He was among the most popular writers in the country and had fought with Tito against the Germans and then turned against him. He was enough of an opponent of Tito's for twenty-five years that two of his books were banned, the first in 1971. *Power and Apprehension* was called "hostile to the Tito regime." In 1984 *The Real and the Possible* was banned as nationalist and antisocialist. Still, Dobrica lived a long, comfortable life under Tito, publishing his popular historical novels, two of which had appeared in English, and other essayistic books, all of which had been widely translated, and occupying a spacious, comfortable office in the Academy of Sciences. While he was not a member of the Praxis Group, Dobrica was always a friend. He nominally headed its Board for the Freedom of Thinking and Expression in the 1970s, and later was one of the founders of the Serbian-Jewish Friendship Society.

As much as anyone in Serbia, Dobrica Cosic suffered from the sense that it was the Serbs' destiny to suffer. Yet he was also the foremost leader of those who believed it was time to end that suffering. But, he told me, Milosevic had twisted his purposes to barbaric ends.

The work that became the source of much controversy, that Milosevic misused so badly, according to Dobrica, was a paper written by him and several members of the Academy that called for, in his words, "democratic equality" for the Serbs. As we sat around a coffee table in his lovely book-lined office at the Academy, Dobrica, sipping on slivovitz, explained his views. Ljiljana sat listening while Ileana Cosic (no relation) translated. (I finally figured out that Ljiljana was sitting in on all these interviews merely because she liked to be at the heart of things. And at this point, this American journalist making her way among the Belgrade intelligentsia, so many of whom were Ljiljana's friends, was at the heart of things.)

I asked Dobrica to tell me about his literary work. "I will leave the evaluation of my work to the literary critics," he said. Dobrica's twenty books had been translated into thirty languages. "The French and the German critics usually compare me to Solzhenitsyn and Grossman [Vasily Grossman, a Russian writer, whose *Life and Fate*, a massive historical novel, was smuggled out of the Soviet Union and first published abroad in the 1980s]. Well, I don't think I should be compared to Solzhenitsyn because I differ from him in my poetics and my philosophy. When I was young, Faulkner was one of my favorite writers. Also Camus. And we can talk about that eternal man, Tolstoy. In the fifties and sixties I was one of the protagonists of modernism in Yugoslavia. Now, in the era of so-called postmodernism, I really don't know what I am." Talking to Balkan scholars in the United States, I discovered that Dobrica's work is comparable to Solzhenitsyn in its scope and seriousness, though it is, as Dobrica says, very different in its worldview and is better written. His novels are part of a long tradition of serious historical novels in Europe; we have no such tradition in the U.S.

I said, "Will you tell me about your political views?"

"My political view is that radical changes should take place both with regard to the policy and the system. We need a radical separation from Titoist policy and this way of thinking. I support a free democratic market society."

"I am particularly interested in your views on nationalism since I have heard several times that you have, in your writings, built the best case for Serbian nationalism," I told him.

"Whoever speaks of my building a case for Serbian nationalism is wrong. It is a deceit. I've been fighting for a democratic, civilized society in Serbia for thirty years at least. I only pleaded for equality for the Serbian people within the Yugoslav federation, and nothing more. I only requested the same rights enjoyed by other people and ethnic minorities. Nothing less, nothing more. For me, the Serbian question has always been a democratic question only and nothing else."

I asked Dobrica for his view of Tito's persecution of the Serbs. "I have described at great length the background of my view in a book entitled *The Disintegration of Yugoslavia*, which will soon be published in Serbian, English, French, and Italian. So you must understand that it's very difficult to summarize these ideas in just a few sentences. But I am willing to make an effort. First, you should know that until 1935 the Communist party was anti-Serb and against the existence of Yugoslavia. It wanted to disintegrate Yugoslavia. In 1924 the Comintern [the Communist International organization founded in 1919] became aware that class struggle is not predominant and cannot mobilize national and civic energy. That is why the Comintern decided to take advantage of various national dissatisfactions and turn that energy into breaking up the existing multinational states. That is why in 1924 the Comintern declared the national issue as one of the top issues. And the Serbs, being the most numerous people in the Balkans, were considered by the Comintern to be hegemonic, having united with the Croats and the Slovenes. For that reason the Communist party wanted to turn the energies of all the other people against the Serbs."

"The idea was to channel nationalist feelings against the Serbs in order to build support for the Communist party?"

"Yes, it was to instigate nationalist feelings against the Serbs. I have good evidence that the Communists were, by definition, anti-Serb. The Serbs are well known as freedom-loving people, as free thinkers, and as some kind of rebellious people. That is why, on March 27, 1941, we broke the pact with Hitler and aligned ourselves with the Western Allies. We were severely punished for that by Hitler. The occupation was particularly painful. Only the Jews had a more painful destiny under Hitler than the Serbs. We were the first to rebel against Hitler in Europe. We had two antifascist movements, the nationalist and the Communist. But it was our great misfortune, a national tragedy, that along with our fight against fascism and Hitler, we were also engaged in a civil war between the nationalists and the Communists.

"From the beginning of the Second World War, the Croats and the Muslims committed ferocious genocide against the Serbs. Those who survived joined the more militant movement, then the Cetniks. The Communists understood and started fighting more militantly and unsparingly, and attracted those unhappy Serbs.

"For the sake of the survival of Yugoslavia after the war, the country pardoned that atrocious genocide by the Muslims and the Croats. It pardoned them believing that in the new Yugoslavia everybody would be absolutely equal and free. Unfortunately the

Serbs were deceived. The deceit, of course, had its evolution. Already in the early 1950s the process of assimilation had started and the Serbs began losing their national identity. In the mid-sixties the coalition between the Croats and the Muslims also relegated the Serbs to a subjugated position. Under the pressure of that Croat-Muslim coalition, 200,000 to 300,000 Serbs fled to Serbia. Toward the end of the sixties there was a systematic expulsion of the Serbs, close to genocide, from Kosovo. More than 200,000 Serbs were expelled from Kosovo.

"Then, in 1974, a new constitution broke Serbia into three entities, with Kosovo and Vojvodina called autonomous provinces of Serbia. But they were actually granted statehood and had all the properties of a state. Serbia, on the other hand, was put under some kind of tutorship. The provinces were absolutely free in adopting laws, but when Serbia wanted to adopt a law, it had to be approved by these two provinces. So you see, the Serbs, the most numerous people in this state, enjoyed fewer rights than the national minorities in Kosovo and Vojvodina. And at the same time in Croatia, the 700,000 Serbs living there had fewer rights than the 26,000 Italians who lived there. We are talking about political and civil rights, not to speak of the economy, investments, the development of non-Serb regions at the expense of development in Serb regions and Serbia itself. For instance, the government's per capita investment in Serbia was less than one-third of what it was for Slovenia and less than half what it was for Croatia. Now you understand how, in Tito's Yugoslavia, the Serbs were always pushed aside and consequently dissatisfied. That is why, after Tito's death, dissatisfied with their position and their status in Yugoslavia, they rebelled. Woke up, so to say. And that very justifiable dissatisfaction was well understood by Slobodan Milosevic. He took advantage of it to place himself in the lead. He was the first to start fighting for the equality of the Serbs *within* Yugoslavia. Later on he did not remain faithful to these initial ideas, and he turned out to be like Tito, a dictator.

"The Serbian intelligentsia, including myself, fully supported Milosevic while he was struggling for equality for the Serbs—and I emphasize equality, not supremacy. It was on the basis of that struggle that he won our support. But later, when he betrayed these ideas, when he stopped fighting for democratic principles, and when he established the party state, he lost my support and the confidence of the Serbian intelligentsia."

Several people had told me that Milosevic was the only politician who could keep the country going. "When I asked them if there was no one else on the political scene who could govern, they said there was no one. Do you agree?"

"It is the tragedy of our people. Milosevic is not serving for the good of our people. On the other hand, I am not satisfied with our opposition. That's why I also oppose them. That's our national tragedy." Dobrica dropped his head in his hands, as if in despair. I waited briefly until he raised his head and ran his hand through his hair. Then I asked, "Do you see any way out of this dilemma? I must tell you that I will go home in a few days very depressed for you. I can't see any way out."

"From the intellectual point of view, we can find the way out. To give you the answer, I will have to quote Hegel. In history there are situations that Hegel calls 'natural situations.' On the historical, political, and economic scene, you have powers that are beyond individual control. We are now in the midst of a great seismic tragedy of a tempest, a hurricane that has struck us, so it will take some time for these natural calamities to abate, and then we shall be able, after the natural flow of things, to reach a solution. If we were able to decide on our destiny in Belgrade, I could give you the formula right away. But our destiny is in the hands of Washington, London, Paris, and Bonn. So we have to bear their policy until they get tired or until they understand they should change it. American policy is catastrophic with regard to the Serbian people. But you ask a difficult question, and to answer it you must get a plethora of information and you must have a very good background of knowledge.

"I have believed for twenty years that Serbia as a country was simply untenable. After the constitution of 1974, Yugoslavia ceased to exist. It was kept together only by the authoritarian hand of Tito. If Tito were alive, Yugoslavia would not have been able to survive the economic crisis and the disintegration of the Soviet Union because of the constitution he wrote. He ruled in very propitious times for his ability to play one bloc against another, because it was a bipolar world. Once that situation was gone, Tito couldn't have survived. Tito, on the one hand, held Yugoslavia together, and on the other hand was its grave digger."

When I said goodbye and thank you to Dobrica Cosic, I felt I was saying goodbye and thank you to Belgrade. I was glad I had left my interview with him till the end. It was a fitting farewell.

End Note

In my last interview, with Dobrica Cosic, I heard the majority view of Belgrade's intelligentsia succinctly summed up by a veteran writer whose subject for most of his life had been Serbia, and who was a mentor to many Belgrade intellectuals. How much reality there is in this picture of themselves as a persecuted people, and how much is a consequence of the victim mentality that bedevils their senses, I will leave for another book, for a historian, for another time when the tragedy of Yugoslavia has somehow found an end. That the Serbs are not bloodthirsty monsters intent on the destruction of their former fellow countrymen I hope is clear from these pages. That they are, in fact, a colorful, highly intelligent, and humane people I also hope to have made clear. And that they are willing to accept their share of guilt for this monstrous war—but no more than that—I hope is apparent.

The future of Serbia and Montenegro is dim. While the war with Bosnia continued, the problem of Serbia's relationship with Kosovo festered. What will happen when that problem begins to boil up again, as it has in the past, is an unknown, but Kosovo is certain to be a grievous trouble spot. It was the one question that I put to people for which they had no answer. For most Serbs, Kosovo is sacred land. They can't think beyond that.

To rebuild the Yugoslav economy will require large injections of foreign aid and investment. While the memory of massive U.S. aid to rebuild Germany after it was destroyed in World War II is still clear in my mind, the memory of the refusal to help Vietnam after wholesale destruction of that country is even clearer. And the general reluctance to go to the aid of the former Communist countries is living evidence that Yugoslavia can expect very little, if any, help from the U.S.—for that matter, from any of the Western nations. Furthermore, unless American policy changes quite drastically, whatever aid is given to rebuild the former Yugoslavia will no doubt go first to Bosnia Herzegovina and Croatia. Whether it will take, as Ljubomir Madzar predicted, a couple of years or the fifty years predicted by Petar Lukovic will depend on so many factors that it is impossible to predict.

I left Belgrade at 10 p.m. in a van filled with people on their way out of the country, some for the long haul and others for brief visits abroad. On our way to the Budapest airport I was filled with feelings of relief to be escaping from the tragedy that had engulfed me. At the same time I regretted leaving what could only be described as a war zone, a war between the West and tiny Serbia, a place where the action was—war action without guns. What better place for a journalist to be? I would miss being in the middle of the action and, despite the terrible sadness there, I would miss the many hours of pure enjoyment and marvelous stimulation I had found among the Serbs.

As we drove through a snowstorm on a two-lane unplowed highway at twenty miles an hour for seven hours in the middle of the night, in a van that had no headrests, no reading lights, few shock absorbers, and little heat, some people slept sitting up. I kept myself happy with visions of sashimi and steamed spinach in sesame sauce, a long hot bath, a cup of strong American coffee and a weak American cigarette, a stable five-dollar bill, hearing English spoken all around me, and my warm, cozy apartment.

I chatted part of the time with Slobodanka Ast, who turned out to be the correspondent for *Vreme* in America. Her husband was teaching at Purdue University. She was returning from a visit to her family. She didn't know when she and her husband and daughter would return home, but they had no plans to stay permanently in the U.S.

It was clear to me that Slobodanka, who shared the attitudes of her friends at *Vreme*, had little faith in my being able to make sense of what was going on in Yugoslavia. An American simply couldn't understand the Serbs, she seemed to say. It would take years of living among them to comprehend the peculiar patterns of thinking, the peculiar worldview of the Serbs. In essence she shared the contempt for her people voiced by her fellow dissidents while at the same time missing home, family, and those peculiarities to which she was accustomed. I wondered how much I could capture of the peculiarities I had observed among the Serbs in Belgrade, but I hoped that this book, that lets so many of them speak for themselves, would convey some little bit of what Slobodanka was so ambivalent about and what I had been so amused, awed, annoyed, and delighted by. Of one thing I was certain: I would return.

Epilogue

Perhaps never before were images of a wartime conflict so discordant as those of the 1990s in the former Yugoslavia. Western governments and media painted the participants of the wars in Bosnia and Croatia as primitive peoples, particularly the allegedly reckless, barbaric Serbs who, it would appear, had just emerged from the Middle Ages to use primitive tactics while at the same time they were heavily armed with modern weapons. No swords and spears for these primitives. Serbs, it was said, raped fifty thousand Muslim women, in part to terrorize and subdue the population, in part to spread their seed to Serbianize the Muslim people. Like warriors of the Middle Ages, the Serbs allegedly burned down whole villages, plundered them, and raped, tortured, and killed the inhabitants. While the Muslims in Bosnia and the Croatians certainly tried to fight back, they were, so the story went, hopelessly outnumbered and outgunned by the relentless, brutal Serbs who would settle for nothing less than total control of the land. Primitive people that they were, they could not be counted on to abide by any civilized agreements. And while the Serbs were the most barbaric, all of Yugoslavia was painted as backward and unsophisticated by Western governments and the media.

At the same time it was widely recognized that the main instrument used by the Serb leaders to arouse enthusiasm for war was the modern electronic medium of television, skillfully manipulated by the warmongers. That the same techniques were used by Croatian and Muslim leaders, that the wars were carried out on television as well as on the battlefield in all the former republics, was largely ignored. While radio had earlier played a role in the propagation of war, it is a flimsy weapon beside the inflammatory images created by television. It was television in America that finally brought the horrors of the Vietnam War before the American people, turned the tide of opinion against the war, and brought down the president who was largely responsible for it. So too, the Yugoslavs, Bosnians, and Croatians were convinced by what they saw on television, resulting in a fierce war.

So we have a strong contradiction. These supposedly primitive peoples were fighting a war with the most modern methods of mass communication and armaments. In addition, these supposedly backward peoples had used a modern Western public relations agency to tell their stories abroad. Of course most governments have successfully used propaganda as a tool to help win wars. Most of us who are old enough have clear memories of U.S. victory stories coming out of Vietnam, most particularly the body counts that were later proven to be fabricated by the government. And of course governments all over the world have used public relations consultants, particularly in elections.

But the use in war of paid professional propagandists whose loyalties are bought with large fees—thirty thousand dollars a month in the case of the former Yugoslav republics, except Serbia and Montenegro, who could not avail themselves of these services—is an especially new tactic, not one that might be expected from an unsophisticated, backward nation. The use of an American public relations firm by the former republics of Yugoslavia reflected great sophistication—the recognition that paid agents from the West could do a better job than the governments themselves in influencing world opinion. Bosnia, Croatia, and Kosovo hired the American firm of Ruder Finn to take their story to the American and European publics and to the United Nations because they believed their struggles would be won in the hearts and minds of the Western public and its representatives in government and the UN. Only with intervention, especially American intervention, against the Serbs, could Bosnia and Croatia (and Kosovo) hope to win. To gain that intervention, it was crucially required that the Serbs be demonized, that the West sympathize with the plight of the former republics in their heroic struggle against the barbarians.

And so these allegedly backward people took a step never taken before. They hired foreign propagandists to help them win their wars. The propagandists of their own governments had neither the credibility nor the skills necessary to carry out this mission. The American media and government are well used to dealing with public relations firms, and they would be much more likely to accept information as reliable coming from fellow Americans than from the government of the obscure and unknown Bosnia, for example.

The former Yugoslavs had the notorious example of Kuwait, at the end of the Iraqi War, using the American public relations firm of Hill and Knowlton to create, especially in the U.S., sympathy for the Kuwaitis and anger at the Iraqis. Governments have often made similar efforts. Certainly, early in World War II, before American entry into the war, British propagandists tried to influence Americans to join the conflict. But these efforts were largely made through diplomatic channels. With a few notable exceptions, efforts directly to influence the minds of foreign citizens were still mostly a dream until more recent times. The successes of paid propagandists may have far exceeded government efforts. While Hill and Knowlton's dramatic staging of a young Kuwaiti woman testifying before Congress about thousands of rapes and the slaughter of babies by the Iraqis was later exposed as a fraud, it was at the time highly successful in arousing the American people and government against Iraq.

In the early stages of the Yugoslav wars a steady stream of press releases flowed to American and European media and to the UN from Ruder Finn. Mirjana Kameretzy of the *New York Times* describes receiving releases from Ruder Finn every day. The content of those releases was material fed to Ruder Finn by the former Yugoslav republics. While some public relations agencies check the facts they receive from their clients, this is a journalistic obligation "more honored in the breach than in the observance" by PR people. Instead, most PR people see their jobs as publicizing their clients' claims in the most dramatic way possible, in order to make the claims credible and print-worthy to the media. The claim, for instance (not unlike the Kuwaiti woman's charges against the Iraqis), that Serbian men were raping Muslim women in order to spread their seed among the Muslims needed to be made credible. On the face of it, it sounded mighty weird. But if one already believed that the Serbs were a primitive and barbaric people, such a satanic idea could be made credible, just as Hill and Knowlton's staged denunciation of the Iraqis was made credible after President George Bush had repeatedly referred to Saddam Hussein as the new Hitler. The campaign to paint the Serbs as barbarians was already well under way when the rape claim was released. It both helped the propaganda campaign and was itself helped by previous efforts.

The "Serbianizing" of the Bosnian Muslims followed reports by the Muslims of massive rape by the Serbs, an alleged 50,000 by late 1992. As of July 1994 the UN reported that it had 800 documented rapes committed by Serbs, Croatians, and Bosnian Muslims—800 in all. Not 50,000 or 5,000, all committed by the Serbs, but 800 rapes committed altogether by Serbs, Croatians, and Bosnian Muslims, and witnessed by 1,700 people. Even given the fact that many women may not have chosen to come forth publicly, and that the UN had missed some cases, the gap is substantial. Where did the 50,000 figure come from? From the heads of the Bosnian Muslim leaders. How did it miraculously reach us in the United States and Europe? Through the good offices of Ruder Finn, which made no effort to check out such improbable numbers.

Ruder Finn dropped the Bosnia account in the summer of 1993 because that country was ninety thousand dollars in arrears. The loyalty of paid propagandists depends on their getting paid. Later the agency also dropped Croatia. By that time the Bosnians and the Croatians had learned some valuable lessons, but their credibility did not match Ruder Finn's. For example, the famous breadline massacre in Sarajevo on May 27, 1992, while Ruder Finn was still on board, was widely attributed to the Serbs despite a UN investigation that clearly linked the tragedy to "Bosnian forces loyal to Alija Izetbegovich." UN investigators reported that the explosion, which killed twenty-two, was caused by a "command-detonated" explosion under Muslim control, not by a mortar shell from a Serb position above the town, as the Bosnians had claimed. Craters in the street indicated, the UN report said, that "The impact . . . is not necessarily similar nor anywhere near as large as we came to expect with a mortar round landing on a paved surface." But the carefully orchestrated media campaign that charged the Serbs with this tragic shelling over-whelmed the UN's report. How could it be possible that the Muslims had bombed their own people? The consequence was world outrage and the imposition of a draconian economic embargo of Yugoslavia.

This incident reads like a terrible nightmare. It was one of the events of which Sylvia Poggioli, a widely respected reporter for National Public Radio, wrote in the fall 1993 issue of *Nieman Reports*: "There have been innumerable instances where those of us who have covered these conflicts have fallen into the disinformation trap." And, she wrote, "Policy in Western capitals—or lack of it—has increasingly been based on news reports. . . ." Poggioli suggested that one reason the Serbs were demonized in the West was because "little or no effort has been made by the Belgrade government to try to win over the hearts and minds of the West through its media." She failed to mention that because of the embargo, the Belgrade leaders had no access to such firms as Ruder Finn, though, of course, earlier they might have taken such measures had they not had what Poggioli described as "the deep-rooted conviction that throughout history they have been the victims of foreign powers" that "put them at a disadvantage in the propaganda war."

Ruder Finn was no longer on the scene for the February 5, 1994, attack on the Markale Market in Sarajevo. Once again the Muslims blamed the Serbs, and the Serbs denied responsibility, insisting that the Muslims had bombed their own people, killing sixty-six. Once again the UN investigated and issued a report that contradicted the Muslims. That report said officials hadn't determined who was responsible; it could have been either side. This time, without the help of Ruder Finn, the Bosnian Muslims could not so easily overwhelm even that equivocal UN report. The media dutifully reported the doubt, but were quick to forget it. The disinformation trap laid by Ruder Finn for its clients was still in place, if a little shaky. In fact, the agency's representatives were still unofficially advising the Bosnian Muslims.

But with Ruder Finn no longer on hand to keep the hinges oiled, some enterprising journalists began to take a second look. For instance, there was the matter of a classified UN report that unequivocally blamed the Muslims for the Markale massacre. The report was first denied by a spokesman for UN Secretary General Boutros-Ghali, then simply dismissed with a "no comment." But in the U.S., Israel, England, Italy, Greece, and France, reporters were examining the evidence and insisting that the attack could not have been carried out by the Serbs. An article by Paul Beaver in *Jane's Defense Weekly*, a British publication widely referred to on military matters, quoted in the February 9, 1994, issue of the London *Independent*, said, "I find it difficult to contemplate that a 120 mm mortar shell could cause this

number of casualties even in a confined space like the Market. . . .
I'm not aware of such a high number ever having been killed by a
single shell." In France a television reporter, Bernard Volker, who
claimed to have seen the UN report, broadcast that the UN privately
held the Muslims responsible for the explosion but was refusing to
make this information public. Why would the UN withhold this
information? Was it too tangled in the disinformation trap to be able
to confront such a monstrosity?

For the most part, the media and Western governments were still
under the spell of the bitter and often cruel anti-Serb campaign waged
by the Muslim government and its paid propagandists. But there were
now small breaks in the armor. Despite President Clinton's remark
that he found it "highly likely" and Warren Christopher's "gut
feeling" that the Serbs were responsible for the Markale Market
massacre, the February 21, 1994, issue of *U.S. News and World
Report* reported that Pentagon officials who had been monitoring the
area for a year said that "the Muslims . . . fired on their own people to
provoke Western air strikes." While this and other similar reports
were largely ignored, the fact is that the UN continued to waffle on
bombing the Serbs. All through the war, military reports that questioned Serb responsibility for attacks had been ignored in the rush of
Muslim propaganda. But even as it demonized the Serbs, the UN, led
by the U.S., failed to act on its threats to bomb them. Officials
argued that attempting to bomb Serbian positions would present a
strategic nightmare given the Bosnian terrain, and that there was not
enough public support for such a move. Perhaps there was another
reason, to be found in recurrent reports that the Serbs were not quite
the devils they were described to be by the Muslims.

Fast forward to Gorazde, Bosnia. Now it is April 1994. While a
cease-fire seems to be holding in Sarajevo, where some of the fiercest
fighting in the Bosnian War has occurred, the Serbs suddenly attack a
Muslim "safe haven" established by the UN in eastern Bosnia. The
Serbs claim that the Muslims attacked first; they were only defending
themselves. These claims are ignored and, after two years of vacillat-
ing over intervention, NATO, led by the U.S., bombs Serbian
military positions. Warren Christopher tells a Senate subcommittee,
"We are getting into Bosnia" to vindicate U.S. leadership and to
deter the Serbs from expanding the war in the Balkans. "We just
cannot turn our back on the situation," Christopher says.

The Serbs are enraged at what they believe is unjustified bombing and retaliate by striking again at Gorazde. For three weeks, reports of heavy shelling, huge casualties, and widespread damage emanate from the Muslims in Gorazde. The UN threatens to bomb again but holds back, allegedly to avoid threatening the fragile cease-fire in Sarajevo and ongoing peace negotiations. But it seems there is some doubt about the Muslim claims. Perhaps the European Union (formerly the European Community) and the U.S. are listening with half an ear to the claim made by Bosnian Serb leader Radovan Karadzic, who says that the Muslims are using Goradze and the five other UN-declared "safe havens" as "strongholds from where they're launching very heavy offensives. Muslims have been killing Serb civilians from Gorazde even though safe havens aren't supposed to have a single soldier except UN peacekeepers."

Some UN officials are beginning to wonder whether, after all, the Serbs aren't telling the truth about Muslim attacks. An anonymous UN official is widely quoted as saying that reports of the damage in Goradze were highly exaggerated. He says, "Reports on Gorazde were deliberately exaggerated in order to shame the world into doing something. The attacks were not of the dimensions suggested. A false impression was given to the international community to help stir a vision of the Bosnian Serbs as the enemy and, unfortunately, all this very nearly went out of control." He adds that the reports came from UN military observers who were of a "low standard," from "overly emotional" relief workers, and from "untrustworthy" Muslim ham radio operators who had, incidentally, been reporting on alleged Serb atrocities throughout the war. "A big problem," the UN official says, "is that the Muslims believe they can bring the Americans into this war. A dangerous overreaction was stirred up in international capitals. The talk of wider use of NATO air power, hitting ammunition dumps and infrastructure went well across the line that would have turned the UN forces here into combatants," ardently wished for by the Bosnian Muslims.

The spell was broken. The media reported thereafter that UN officials, some of whom were later silenced by Boutros-Ghali, were questioning Muslim intentions and integrity. The hold of the disinformation trap was clearly loosened, creating an opening to a measure of clarity and truth in the former Yugoslavia.

None of this recounting is intended to whitewash or in any way excuse or forgive the atrocities committed by the Serbs in Bosnia.

But with the loosening of the disinformation trap, the myth of a barbarous and primitive Serbian people attacking innocent people, albeit also primitive, and all the contradictions that have seemed to characterize these wars, may in time be replaced by a more enlightened picture. Perhaps the view of the Muslims and the Croatians as helpless victims of these wars will be replaced with a more realistic picture of three peoples fighting each other on fairly equal terms, all of them ethnically similar but with cultural and religious differences. Their legitimate fears of domination were exploited by power-hungry leaders who led them into a war they thought would end swiftly. Instead it became a nightmare beyond their worst expectations in which all sides committed barbarities.

With some changes in attitude may come a recognition that the UN embargo on Serbia and Montenegro was a tragic mistake; that the modest help offered by these two republics to the Serbs in Bosnia and Croatia did not exceed that given to the Muslims and the Croatians by sympathetic nations and supporters—may even have been less, since Serbia and Montenegro are much poorer than Germany, Austria, and the Arab nations; and that the Serb paramilitaries aiding the Bosnian Serbs may not have outnumbered the mojahedin from Afghanistan, Iran, and Saudi Arabia who went to Bosnia to help their fellow Muslims and the ex-patriot Croatians who returned to fight beside their fellows.

Most likely, though, in the nature of history, these wars will be long forgotten soon after they end by all but historians and the participants who will be existing uneasily side by side in an arrangement that satisfies none of them. Most likely Serbia and Kosovo will continue to coexist in an intolerable balance because they cannot risk war. Serbs in Croatia will live nervously among their hosts after another flare-up of war there that the Croatians will win. The former republics will trade with one another and again travel across borders. Families will be reunited. Love affairs and marriages will blossom across the borders. Economies will be restored, and historic allegiances to other nations and parts of the world will be strengthened. Germany will have its long-desired path to the Adriatic. The Muslim world will have a tiny enclave in Europe. And the U.S. will renew its longtime relationship with Serbia. The former Yugoslavs will have a tenuous peace and legitimate places in the world of nations. Until some new spark reignites the bitter historical hatreds.

This scenario is years into the future and may be all too rosy, just as peaceful democracies in the former Soviet Union and in the rest of Eastern Europe will come, if they do, only in the far distant future. The destruction wrought by Communist dictatorships in Eastern Europe and the Soviet Union—even Tito's relatively benign one in Yugoslavia—will take more than a generation to undo. It will be years before the nature of the economies emerges in the post-Communist countries, but it is unlikely that the highly conservative Chicago School of economics will win its way there, considering the reemergence of the Communists in various governments. More likely, some forms of mixed economy will emerge.

In Belgrade in January 1994, Slobodan Milosevic's government performed what appeared to be a small miracle of partial economic recovery. Inflation was eliminated, the stores filled with goods, and government payments to the unemployed and the pensioners were raised enough to enable people to buy the necessities of life. My friends in Belgrade, with whom I talked by phone, were as amazed as I was by this turn of events only a couple of months after everyone was predicting further economic chaos. I called Ljubomir Madzar, the economist I'd interviewed in Belgrade, to ask how this supposed miracle had been accomplished and whether he believed it could last.

Ljubomir explained that the government, under a program devised by economist Dragoslav Avramovic, a former World Bank employee, had introduced a new "super" dinar pegged one-to-one to the deutsche mark and based on foreign reserves. It had stopped printing the worthless money that had driven inflation up to 25,000 percent. To get the new dinars, people had to trade in their deutsche marks, providing the treasury with real money in foreign currency to add to its 300 million deutsche mark reserves. For many people, this meant digging into their savings. On the other hand, the inflation had been growing so fast that people had been using their savings to live.

To further reduce inflation the government had cut expenses, though what was actually cut was known only in the recesses of the federal building. "We never got an accounting of how money was being spent, and now we haven't been given an accounting of how expenditures have been cut, only that they have been cut," Ljubomir told me. He did not know whether military expenses, which were 8 percent of the federal budget, had been cut, or whether relief help to Bosnian and Croatian Serbs, which had never been admitted, had been cut. At the same time, monthly pensions that had fallen to less than a dollar were raised to about fifty dollars. Taxes and utility rates were also raised.

As a consequence of a stable dinar and stabilizing prices, manufacturers who had stopped producing because inflation had in effect destroyed the market, once again started producing. This, in combination with the black market that continued to thrive, put an end to grave shortages. Even the pharmacies were full, Ljubomir said. And the expense of government unemployment compensation was greatly reduced with many workers back at jobs, though there remained a high rate of unemployment that had begun long before the wars.

Indeed it seemed a miracle! I wondered why such measures had not been taken earlier, and remembered those who insisted that Milosevic was deliberately manipulating the economy to enhance his power. At the same time I recalled my own estimate that Milosevic had not a clue about how to manage the economy, how in fact he had turned to nationalism and war because he could see no way out of the declining economy that faced the nation but was determined to find a way to sustain and enhance his own power. Now at last, when the bankrupt economy threatened his power, he had found a way to solve the problems.

But journalist Petar Lukovic had a jaundiced view of the future. "Already [four months after the program was initiated] people are having trouble exchanging their dinars, and the only reason people aren't hurting for money is because they still have their foreign currency. This was a political decision to shore up Milosevic and soon we will see everything go back to the same. No new factories are opening. There is still not enough production. It can't last."

Ljubomir was also not sanguine about the long-range success of the program. He didn't trust Milosevic. "Now, four months after it was introduced, it is working, but whether it can continue to work depends on a lot of factors which are unknown. It will depend on political decisions, and we never know what they will be or how they are made. The government is not dependable to make the right decisions, but we just don't know. It is hard to see it permanently succeeding."

Whatever Milosevic might have done, it was hard to see how this short-range program could succeed without normal trade, without normal buying and selling across borders with states that had been so economically interdependent—that is, with the sanctions remaining.

That it gave people some breathing space from the tortures of the previous two years, however, was certain, and that it strengthened Milosevic's position was abundantly clear. That a reasonably stable economy in Serbia and Montenegro might also have strengthened the position of the Bosnian and Croatian Serbs could also have been true. Bosnian Serb leader Radovan Karadzic was quoted in the *Chicago Tribune* in May 1994, four months into the recovery, as saying, "We will sign nothing before the sanctions are lifted." Under the earlier economic conditions in Yugoslavia, he might have been less likely to take such a strong stand.

As I brought this book to its end, the future of Yugoslavia was unknown. From the words and actions of the leaders of the community I talked with in Belgrade, it was clear that Yugoslavia had the capacity and the will, the spite, the courage to survive regardless of what the rest of the world did. Even those who rejected the idea of the "Kosovo determination" as historical bunk shared the pride and love of their country and the anger that comes with feeling victimized, whether that victimization was seen as the work of traitorous leaders or the outside world. Such anger is the stuff of wars but also the stuff of rejuvenation. There was plenty of anger to be found in 1993 in Belgrade where the rejuvenation would have to be initiated and nurtured; it was unlikely to dissipate until real peace and security could again be found there. One could only hope that the Serbs might put aside a feeling that it was their destiny to suffer in order to rebuild their lives.

Chronology of Events in Yugoslavia, 1987–1993

Mid-1986	Serbian Academy of Science, led by Dobrica Cosic, circulates memorandum attacking Yugoslavia's 1974 constitution and calling for unification of all Serbs in one nation.
April 1987	Slobodan Milosevic gives ringing nationalist speech in Kosovo at six hundredth anniversary of major Serb military defeat.
May 1987	Milosevic wins control of Serbia's League of Communists.
January 1989	Ante Markovic becomes Yugoslav federal prime minister on program of economic reform and political democratization.
February 1989	With his authority as head of the Communist party, Milosevic imposes a state of emergency in Kosovo and ends Albanian political autonomy.
November 1989	Fall of Berlin Wall; end of cold war.
January 1990	Emergency Congress of League of Yugoslav Communists collapses over democratization and use of federal troops in Kosovo, resulting in disintegration of League and secession of members.
April 1990	Slovenia and Croatia hold first multiparty elections; Slovenia elects Milan Kucan, former Communist leader; Croatia also elects former Communist, fierce nationalist Franjo Tudjman; anti-Serb campaign begins in Croatia.
July 1990	Kosovo's Albanians declare independence; Serbia terminates autonomy as decreed by Tito in 1974 of its two former dependencies, Vojvodina and Kosovo; Milosevic forms Socialist Party of Serbia from merger of Serbia's League of Communists and Socialist Youth Alliance.
August 1990	Outbreak of armed conflict between Croatian government and Krajina Serbs who proclaim Serb Autonomous Region of Krajina.
October 1990	Slovenia and Croatia propose transformation of Yugoslav federation into loose confederation; Serbia refuses.

November 1990	Bosnia Herzegovina elects Muslim fundamentalist Alija Izetbegovic and Muslim League of Democratic Action to head government.
December 1990	Milosevic wins Serbia's first multiparty election.
March 1991	War between Serbs and Croatians heats up.
May 1991	U.S. suspends economic aid to Yugoslavia because of human rights violations in Kosovo; parliamentary crisis follows Serb representatives' refusal to allow Stepan Mesic, a Croatian, to take office as federal president in Belgrade.
June 1991	U.S. Secretary of State James Baker visits Belgrade and warns Slovenia and Croatia against secession; Slovenia and Croatia declare independence; Yugoslav army attacks Slovenia but quickly withdraws; war begins between Yugoslavia and Croatia.
August 1991	Pope John Paul II visits Hungary and gives blessing to Croatian independence.
September 1991	Macedonia declares independence; UN Security Council imposes arms embargo on all Yugoslav republics.
December 1991	Germany recognizes independence of Slovenia and Croatia; Ante Markovic resigns as federal prime minister in objection to military spending.
January 1992	Led by Radovan Karadzic, Bosnian Serbs declare Serb Republic of Bosnia Herzegovina; European Community (EC) recognizes Slovenian and Croatian independence and brokers a cease-fire in Croatia.
March 1992	Bosnia Herzegovina declares independence; outbreak of war between Serbs, Croats, and Muslims in Bosnia.
April 1992	EC and U.S. recognize Bosnia Herzegovina independence; Bosnian Serbs begin siege of Sarajevo, and fighting breaks out elsewhere in the area; Serbia and Montenegro form Yugoslav federation.
May 1992	U.S. and EC recall ambassadors from Belgrade; European Conference on Security and Cooperation excludes rump Yugoslavia; UN admits Slovenia, Croatia, and Bosnia but refuses to recognize new Yugoslavia; Sarajevo breadline massacre blamed on Serbs resulting in UN economic embargo against Yugoslavia.
June 1992	Dobrica Cosic elected president of Yugoslavia.
July 1992	Bosnian Croatians declare Croatian state of Herceg-Bosna with Mostar as capital; American multimillionaire Milan Panic named Yugoslav prime minister.

October 1992	UN Security Council establishes "no-fly" zone over Bosnia Herzegovina.
November 1992	UN Security Council tightens economic embargo on Yugoslavia.
December 1992	Milosevic defeats Panic in Serbian elections.
April 1993	Outbreak of fierce fighting between Bosnian Croatians and Muslims in western Bosnia Herzegovina; UN again tightens sanctions against Yugoslavia.
May 1993	UN Security Council establishes international war crimes tribunal in The Hague to investigate crimes in former Yugoslavia.
June 1993	Milosevic succeeds Cosic as federal president; Krajina Serbs vote for union with Bosnian Serb Republic.
	U.S. deploys 325 troops in Macedonia as part of UN peace-keeping force.
July 1993	NATO deploys combat aircraft in Italy and Adriatic to carry out UN's threatened air strikes against Serbs.
December 1993	Milosevic wins another Serbian parliamentary election.

Glossary of Significant Names

ARKAN. Real name Zeljko Raznatovic, a criminal wanted on charges of murder and extortion in several European capitals. Organized the Arkanovici (Arkan's men) to fight in Croatia and Bosnia. With the Cetniks they were known as the bloodiest, most brutal fighters. In 1992 he won a seat in Parliament. He ran again in 1993 but lost heavily.

HANS-DIETRICH GENSCHER. Lawyer and West German politician, foreign minister from 1974 to 1992. He was the foremost supporter of Croatian and Slovenian independence as Germany's natural allies by dint of long cultural ties and as an extension of the rights of East European countries to leave the Soviet bloc, though Yugoslavia had not been part of the Soviet bloc.

ALIJA IZETBEGOVIC. President of Bosnia Herzegovina, elected in first multiparty election in 1990. A lawyer long active in Bosnian politics for the Muslim cause, he was jailed twice in the early 1970s for circulating a tract advocating that Bosnia become a Muslim state. He reprinted it for wider distribution in 1990. He declared independence for Bosnia Herzegovina on April 5, 1992.

RADOVAN KARADZIC. President of Bosnian Serbian Democratic party, a psychiatrist who formerly worked for Sarajevo's football team. He established the rump Serbian Republic of Bosnia Herzegovina with himself as president and acknowledged spokesman for the Bosnian Serbs.

ANTE MARKOVIC. Founder of the League of Reform Forces in 1990 while he was federal prime minister. In his tenure, 1989–1991, he attempted to introduce "shock therapy" economic measures that made him popular in the West but feared and hated by many Yugoslavs. He is viewed by many as "the last Yugoslav" since he favored a unitary, democratic, pluralistic Yugoslavia.

SLOBODAN MILOSEVIC. President of newly wrought Yugoslavia, a longtime lowly Communist party functionary who served on the boards of a major utility and the state bank. In a masterful political stroke in 1987 he took over the party and was elected president of Serbia in 1989. Under intense public pressure after the fall of communism, he called the first multiparty election in 1990 but used the party apparatus to all but prevent other parties from reaching the public. With just 48 percent of the vote, his renamed Socialist Party of Serbia won the election in the English-style electoral system he had written into a new constitution. He was elected president by the Serbian Parliament, and then of the Yugoslav Parliament after the breakup of the republics in 1991, a position he held until June 1992 when Dobrica Cosic was elected president. After a vote of no confidence, Cosic was deposed and Milosevic was again elected president. In successive elections in 1992 and 1993 the party also won and he retained the presidency.

MILAN PANIC. Serbian-born American multimillionaire, a chemist who made his money in pharmaceuticals and health products with large sales in Yugoslavia. He returned to Belgrade in mid-1992 with the implicit approval of the U.S. State Department and his money to assume the position of prime minister, advocating an end to the war and free-market reforms. But the U.S. gave him no support and instead kept raising the stakes against Yugoslavia. Seen by most Serbs as a stooge for the U.S., he was deposed later that year when he opposed Milosevic for president with the backing of several opposition parties. He returned to the U.S. claiming that the election had been stolen.

VOJESLAV SESELJ. President of the Serbian Radical party, the most nationalistic party in Yugoslavia, he came from eastern Herzegovina. He led the royalist Cetniks who in 1991 called for the extension of the boundaries of Serbia far beyond its present borders and boasted of their atrocities against the Croatians. He was the sole member of his party elected to Parliament in 1991, but after making an unofficial alliance with Milosevic, his party took seventy-three seats in 1992. He then proceeded to obstruct the work of the Parliament and called for Milosevic's resignation. After Milosevic denounced him, he lost influence and won only thirty-eight seats in the 1993 elections.

JOSIP BROZ TITO (1892–1980). Ruler of Yugoslavia from 1945 to 1980. He had a long allegiance to the Yugoslav Communist party and to the Soviet Union until 1948 when he broke with Stalin and began a course of reform in Yugoslavia later known as Titoism, involving revision of Stalinist doctrine and National Communism. He led the Partisan fight against the Nazis and then, as Communist party leader, fought the Cetniks and others for control of the country. While the early years of his reign were marked by harsh Stalinist measures, he was a brilliant compromiser who made many concessions to keep the peace and in his later years was quite benign. For the West, Tito represented an opponent of the Soviet Union in the midst of the Iron Curtain countries and was rewarded with huge sums of money in loans, grants, and aid that helped make Yugoslavia a relatively tranquil, prosperous country.

FRANJO TUDJMAN. President of Croatia, elected in 1990 in the first multiparty elections on a strongly nationalist program. He was the youngest general in the Partisan army in World War II. After the war he became a military historian and in 1989 published *Wastelands of Historical Reality*, a revisionist history of the genocidal aspects of World War II. Always loyal to Tito, though jailed in the 1970s as a dissident, his reign was viewed as highly dictatorial. After his election he wrote a constitution that all but eliminated the large Serb minority from citizenship. He declared Croatian independence in June 1991.

WARREN ZIMMERMAN. Longtime U.S. State Department official who served in a variety of positions including political officer in Belgrade from 1968 to 1970. He was named ambassador to Yugoslavia in 1989 and participated in the various negotiations between the republics. He was famous for encouraging the Bosnian Muslims to declare their independence and supporting recognition by the U.S. despite warnings of war. He was recalled from Belgrade when the U.S. broke off diplomatic relations and imposed sanctions on Yugoslavia in 1992.

Index

For the past fifteen years Florence Hamlish Levinsohn has been an independent journalist specializing in politics and urban affairs. Before that she was a punch press operator, a waitress, a nursery school teacher, a social science researcher, a reporter, a radio script writer, an editor, and a writer of self-help books. She has published poetry and short stories in literary magazines and has had two plays produced by little theatres. She has edited six books, among them *School Desegregation: Shadow and Substance* and *Financing the Learning Society*, and is the author of *Harold Washington: A Political Biography*. Ms. Levinsohn is the mother of two daughters and lives in Chicago.